Anglo Republic

Anglo Republic

Inside the bank that broke Ireland

SIMON CARSWELL

PENGUIN

IRELAND

PENGUIN IRELAND

Published by the Penguin Group
Penguin Ireland, 25 St Stephen's Green, Dublin 2, Ireland (a division of Penguin Books Ltd)
Penguin Books Ltd, 80 Strand, London WC2R ORL, England
Penguin Group (USA) Inc., 375 Hudson Street, New York, New York 10014, USA
Penguin Group (Australia), 250 Camberwell Road, Camberwell, Victoria 3124, Australia
(a division of Pearson Australia Group Pty Ltd)
Penguin Group (Canada), 90 Eglinton Avenue East, Suite 700, Toronto, Ontario,
Canada M4P 2Y3 (a division of Pearson Penguin Canada Inc.)
Penguin Books India Pvt Ltd, 11 Community Centre, Panchsheel Park, New Delhi – 110 017, India
Penguin Group (NZ), 67 Apollo Drive, Rosedale, Auckland 0632, New Zealand
(a division of Pearson New Zealand Ltd)
Penguin Books (South Africa) (Pty) Ltd, 24 Sturdee Avenue, Rosebank, Johannesburg 2196, South Africa

Penguin Books Ltd, Registered Offices: 80 Strand, London WC2R ORL, England

www.penguin.com

First published 2011
1

Copyright © Simon Carswell, 2011

The Photo Credits on p. 330 constitute an extension of this copyright page

The moral right of the author has been asserted

Set in 11.5/14.25 pt Bembo Book MT Std
Typeset by Jouve (UK), Milton Keynes
Printed in Great Britain by Clays Ltd, St Ives plc

A CIP catalogue record for this book is available from the British Library

ISBN: 978–1–844–88270–0

www.greenpenguin.co.uk

For Vanessa and Amy Rose

Contents

Prologue

Close to midnight on Friday, 8 June 2007, the Georgian terraces and modern office blocks that house the many large professional firms south of the Liffey had long since shut up shop for the weekend – with one exception. The single biggest Irish business deal of the Celtic Tiger era was on the verge of being completed at the offices of William Fry Solicitors at Wilton Place near the Grand Canal.

The financial and legal teams gathered by the vendor, Crownway Investments, and by the bidders had been negotiating for many hours. John Gallagher, the head of Crownway, led the negotiations. This was the culmination of months of work for him and the other shareholders in the Jurys Doyle Hotel Group – the Gallagher, Monahan and Roche families – whom he represented in the negotiations to sell the group's budget hotel chain Jurys Inns.

Gallagher and the families he represented – all related to the legendary hotelier P. V. Doyle, who had built the Jurys Doyle group – had been through a great deal of drama over the previous two years. In two separate deals in July and November 2005, the most sought-after properties in the group – Jurys Hotel in Ballsbridge and the adjacent five-star Berkeley Court – were sold to the property developer Sean Dunne for a combined total of €379 million. At that stage, the Jurys Doyle group was still listed on the stock market, and Dunne and other developers had made moves towards a possible takeover of the company. The Gallaghers, Monahans and Roches had been reluctant to see the Ballsbridge hotels sold, and wanted a greater say in what happened to the other key properties in the group. To this end, they borrowed €1.6 billion from Allied Irish Banks (AIB) to take the business off the stock market and into their own hands.

The sale of the Ballsbridge hotels – at €54 million an acre – had set a new price record for land purchased in Ireland, but the frenzy was not over yet. Property was changing hands in Dublin at higher prices than in London's upmarket Chelsea. The families thought it was time to sell up and reduce their exposure to Irish property, which they felt was unlikely to rise much further in value, and in March 2007 the Burlington Hotel was sold for €288 million to the developer Bernard McNamara.

The families wanted to hold on to the Westbury, just off Grafton Street in the centre of Dublin, and their hotels in the US and the UK, but they had no emotional ties to Jurys Inns. There were twenty hotels in the chain, fourteen in the UK and six in Ireland, with 4,835 bedrooms in all.

By the summer of 2007 it was the group's last big asset on the block, and the proceeds of its sale could be used to pay down most of the outstanding AIB loan that had funded their purchase of the wider group. The families were risk-averse and uncomfortable holding such large levels of debt. 'Forget about the upside,' John Gallagher would often warn; 'protect the downside and the upside will take care of itself.'

By 8 June 2007, three players were in the running for Jurys Inns: Quinlan Private; Lydian Capital, the investment company owned by horseracing tycoons J. P. McManus and John Magnier; and the European private equity fund Orion Capital. From the perspective of the families – operating for the purposes of this deal as Crownway – the key to securing the highest price possible was to keep each bidder in the race until the very end.

Based on the earnings of €60 million a year at Jurys Inns and the potential to expand the business, the chain was worth at best €700 million, according to industry estimates. But in a frenzied market, the price could rocket upwards if the sellers could get the right bidders into the mix and the right bidding process in place. Credit was cheap and plentiful, and the Irish property market had created huge fortunes, so any number of potential Irish buyers could afford to pay over the odds for the hotel chain. The continued involvement of both Quinlan Private and Lydian Capital could result in a very high sale price indeed.

Crownway was particularly keen to keep Quinlan involved. He was an aggressive bidder when it came to big-ticket deals. His investment firm had outbid Alwaleed Bin Talal, a cash-rich Arab prince who was the world's fourth wealthiest man, to buy the five-star Savoy Hotel Group in London for £750 million (€1.1 billion).

Quinlan's strategy was always to be holding the biggest cheque in the room – it was all about scaring off other bidders. A deal junkie, Quinlan lived for the kind of atmosphere that Crownway, together with their investment bankers from Merrill Lynch and their legal team, had created in William Fry's office that Friday night. Perhaps most importantly, he had the backing of Anglo Irish Bank, Ireland's most aggressive property lender.

Quinlan, with his usual pre-auction posturing, had been putting it about that Jurys Inns was going to be an Irish deal; but it was also believed that Quinlan was only willing to bid a little more than €1 billion and was insistent that he would go no higher. If Quinlan's price was to be pushed up, other bidders had to be kept involved.

All the due diligence – the research that needed to be done and the paperwork that had to be drafted for the sale of such a large business – had been completed. A detailed buyer's pack had been drawn up. Each of the bidders had sight of everything they required. The key was to keep everyone – Quinlan, Lydian and Orion – in the race.

The sellers organized an unorthodox auction. The bidders were all in the William Fry building, each on a different floor. The investment bankers ran between the floors with details of the latest offer. Quinlan Private had completed many deals during the boom but had rarely, if ever, found itself in this position.

Despite Quinlan's presence, the outcome was not a foregone conclusion. Lydian had not just the backing of two of Ireland's wealthiest businessmen in McManus and Magnier; it also had the legendary dealmaker Denis Brosnan, the former chief executive of food business Kerry Group, leading their negotiations.

Buoyed by Anglo's lending firepower and with senior executives at the bank, waiting at the end of a telephone, ready to back the bid, Quinlan made his final offer: a staggering €1.165 billion. Crownway, however, had concerns about Quinlan's capacity to conclude the deal and were leaning towards Lydian, even though they had submitted a bid that was below Quinlan's. Quinlan Private knew that Lydian had bid lower, but not by much.

For a transaction of this scale Quinlan would need something like €400 million in equity ready to fund the deal, with a loan from Anglo to cover the rest. Crownway wanted the deal concluded that night. It was put to Quinlan's team that if they wanted to win the bid, they had to show a commitment from Anglo to bankroll the transaction before anyone left the building.

In the meantime, Lydian's negotiator Brosnan had run out of patience with the Merrill Lynch bankers who were running up and down the stairs with the latest updates. At one point, according to people close to the bidders, he put down his papers and walked out of the building with his team. Crownway put legal staff on the stairs as sentries to prevent Quinlan and his advisers discovering that the Lydian team had gone home.

Not long after midnight, Quinlan signed the contract.

'He was like a coiled spring,' said one party close to the negotiations. 'At that moment Derek would have signed anything. He was so coiled that he was going to compete. This was high-octane stuff – there were lots of lawyers and there was lots of pressure to agree a deal.'

The signature did not conclude matters, however. Crownway were still insisting that Quinlan Private show it had the money to complete the purchase. At around 2 a.m. a senior lender from Anglo arrived at William Fry with a bank draft for €1.165 billion. The deal was done. The auction had been a high-wire act, and Anglo had carried Quinlan to the other side.

In keeping with the standard Quinlan Private model, Derek Quinlan wasn't acting as a personal investor: he would be selling the deal on to the many customers of his firm. Anglo financed the full purchase amount in the expectation that Quinlan would later raise about €400 million from private investors. Based on the percentage fees Quinlan commanded, he and his firm stood to make upwards of €20 million.

The bank's backing – and its willingness and ability to produce a draft for over €1 billion at two in the morning – had given Quinlan the muscle to close the deal. Anglo had bankrolled the single biggest transaction of the entire Irish property boom and had produced a cheque covering the largest price agreed for an Irish business during the Celtic Tiger years.

The deal was typical of the bank Anglo had become. As of June 2007, Anglo was by almost any measure the most successful bank in Ireland. It had achieved that status through aggressive deal-making and close-quarters client-care of the sort that secured the Jurys Inns deal for Quinlan Private, and through a willingness to commit a huge proportion of its loan book to a single business sector: property.

But the Jurys Inns transaction was one of Anglo's last hurrahs. The conditions that had made the bank's rise possible began to change by the time that summer of 2007 was over. By September 2008 the bank required an extraordinary intervention by the Irish government to prevent it from going out of business. By January 2009 it was in state ownership. And by November 2010 the Irish state itself, facing losses in the tens of billions on Anglo, required a potentially crippling bailout from the European Union and the International Monetary Fund.

This is the story of how a small Dublin bank became too big to fail and too rotten to save – and how it dragged an entire country to the brink of bankruptcy.

1.   The Birth of a Bank

1964 – Anglo's value: €127,000

On 10 August 1964 the Beatles were at number one with 'A Hard Day's Night', the price of a pint of Guinness was two shillings (10p) and the average house cost about £3,100. That same day Henry Fottrell, a Dublin solicitor, laid the foundation for a new financial institution, Anglo Irish Bank.

Fottrell was acting on behalf of the London banker Lionel Essex and his business partner, accountant Henry Prevezer. The name of the bank reflected the bank's connections in London and Dublin.

Joining the two Londoners on the board was well-known Dublin businessman Gerry Wheeler. As a director of numerous companies and a former tax partner of Stokes Kennedy Crowley, one of Ireland's biggest accountancy firms, Wheeler could make important introductions for the English bankers. He started as company secretary of Anglo and went on to become its chairman.

The conservatism of Irish banking at the time was reflected in the balance sheets of the banks: collectively, they had loans of £260 million, which were more than covered by £436 million in deposits. But the banking industry was on the brink of major changes. International businessmen were looking to tap the economic growth that had been spurred on by the economic and industrial reforms of the Fianna Fáil government led by Sean Lemass. It was a ripe time to set up a new bank in Ireland.

Anglo began trading from a building at 50 Merrion Square in Dublin city centre, close to the offices of many of the firms whose business it hoped to attract. (The first home of what became the country's most prolific lender to builders and property developers ironically now houses the Irish Council of Social Housing.) The bank began by offering a range of financial services – personal loans, car finance and some mortgages to help businesses to buy their own premises.

To help attract business, Anglo recruited a key ally: Liam McGonagle, a Dublin solicitor and friend of Fianna Fáil politician Charlie Haughey. Both would later end up among the many depositors at Ansbacher, the secret bank set up by Haughey's bagman Des Traynor to evade tax through the 1970s and 1980s; Haughey would go on to become Taoiseach.

The founders of Anglo Irish Bank were not alone in seeking to exploit the potential of the emerging Irish economy. Between 1967 and 1970 the number of banks outside the big three – AIB, Bank of Ireland and Ulster Bank – grew to thirty-three. Beyond those, seventeen new industrial banks and hire-purchase companies were set up. They helped households and businesses buy everything from hoovers and fridges to bar counters and machinery.

But the Central Bank was uncomfortable with the vast number of banks being set up. The 1971 Central Bank Act was introduced to enable regulators to reform the sector.

It had been easy to set up a bank until then. A bank licence could be bought off the shelf for £1 from the Revenue Commissioners. The aim of the legislation was to combine the smaller, weaker institutions to form bigger, stronger banks. The Central Bank Act stipulated that no more than 20 per cent of a bank could be owned by one individual or one company that was not already involved in banking. It also limited foreign ownership by requiring that a significant shareholding had to be held by Irish investors. The enforcement of the Central Bank Act helped to reshape the sector.

One purpose of the new law was to force out some of the more colourful players who were taking deposits from customers and using the money to invest in their own personal projects, many of which were speculative and risky in nature. They were treating these deposit-taking institutions as their own personal piggy banks.

Anglo had become one such bank. By 1971 it had been taken over by Co. Wicklow-based businessman Colm Dunne, who had an 85 per cent stake. Wheeler was retained as the bank's chairman.

The Central Bank was uncomfortable that Dunne held such a large shareholding in Anglo. It didn't want the control of a bank resting in the hands of a single individual. The Central Bank was also worried that Dunne was using depositors' money to fund his own risky property deals.

A brand-new institution about which the Central Bank quickly came to have similar concerns was Irish Trust Bank, which had close ties to Anglo; Gerry Wheeler was the chairman of both. Irish Trust Bank was set up in 1971 by London businessman Ken Bates, who would later become famous in the world of English football for selling Chelsea football club to Russian billionaire Roman Abramovich before going on to take over Leeds United.

Bates saw that the Central Bank was giving Anglo's owner Colm Dunne a hard time and he suggested to Dunne in 1973 that they merge their two banks. Such a move would leave Bates and Dunne with a smaller share of the new merged entity than each had in his own bank, and Bates thought this might appease the Central Bank.

I interviewed Bates at his home in Monte Carlo in 2005. He said that he had wanted to call the merged institution Anglo Irish Trust Bank, but the Central Bank blocked the deal. His only regret looking back was that he had not turned Irish Trust Bank into the sort of bank that Anglo Irish had become at the time of our interview, though I imagine his opinion might have changed since then.

Bates became embroiled in a legal dispute with the Central Bank, and in 1976 Irish Trust went bust. Wheeler stood down as chairman of Irish Trust but remained on at Anglo. Dunne, meanwhile, succumbed to pressure from the Central Bank and reduced his personal stake in Anglo to less than 20 per cent. The Central Bank was still unhappy. Anglo had a deficit of about £90,000 if it continued to trade, £150,000 if it was shut down. The Central Bank eventually forced Dunne to sell his stake entirely as it lined up new investors for Anglo.

Although his troubled banking career at Anglo ended in 1973, Dunne would later be involved in colourful scrapes involving the personal use of depositors' savings by investment managers. These episodes confirmed that the Central Bank's concerns were well founded.

In 1973 the Central Bank asked Limerick accountant Tom Duffy if he would be willing to source more cash for Anglo. He agreed to invest heavily in the bank personally and through his company, Duffy Enterprises. He also enlisted two wealthy Irish builders living in Manchester, Joe and John Kennedy, who were originally from Mayo. Duffy knew the Kennedy brothers well. He audited the books of their Lakeside Hotel in Killaloe, Co. Clare, and he knew that they had surplus cash. Duffy and the Kennedy brothers became the main shareholders in the bank, though they later brought on board other investors in both Ireland and England. The Kennedy brothers had close ties with Manchester United football club. They were friends of Sir Matt Busby, the club's legendary manager in the 1950s and 1960s, and Sir Matt is listed on Anglo's share register in 1975 and 1976 with a holding of 5,000 shares.

(John Kennedy became better known in Ireland as one of the businessmen who contributed £1,000 in cash to the £8,000 'dig-out' for Bertie Ahern, then Minister for Finance, at a dinner in Manchester in 1994. Kennedy explained the payment to the Mahon Tribunal in December 2007, saying: 'He was Minister for Finance and he had just parted from his wife and it was a terrible thing that the Minister for Finance for the Irish nation didn't have a bob in his pocket.')

Anglo was tiny when Duffy joined. It employed just five people: Pat Casey, the financial controller and a former Irish rugby international; Eamonn Dundon, who had left Irish Trust to join Anglo as general manager; two secretaries; and a former Bank of Ireland official who helped out from time to time. The bank's biggest loan was about £25,000.

Between 1972 and 1976 Anglo racked up losses of £300,000, and held £2 million of depositors' cash. In 1977 the Central Bank, still not confident in the stability of Anglo, demanded changes at the top and ordered an increase in the bank's capital reserves to protect depositors. In an act of appeasement, Anglo appointed a number of high-profile names to the board to help manage the bank, including the well-known accountant Dermot Shortall, Philip O'Donoghue, previously with Trinity Bank (now Investec Bank Ireland) and John Donovan, a former president of the Confederation of Irish Industries. Also at the behest of the Central Bank, Senator Alexis FitzGerald, a Fine Gael politician, was appointed trustee over Tom Duffy's 110,000 shares, about 25 per cent of the total. The appointment of a trustee reassured the Central Bank that someone reliable was controlling a big chunk of Anglo's shares.

Even so, the appointments did not fully allay the Central Bank's worries. In early 1978 Timothy O'Grady Walshe, a senior official at the Central Bank, asked the larger and longer-established City of Dublin Bank to look at taking over Anglo. City of Dublin Bank, which had been floated on the Dublin Stock Exchange in 1971, had a staff of about sixty at the time. O'Grady Walshe thought its chief executive, Gerry Murphy, was a capable and forthright guy, and a safe pair of hands for the smaller bank. Murphy recalls that the Central Bank was very unhappy about two builders and an accountant from Limerick owning an Irish bank: 'This was not the formation that they wanted,' he says.

City of Dublin Bank agreed to take over Anglo, and the Central Bank covered any losses that it incurred in the takeover.

City of Dublin Bank itself had an interesting history. It had started as a hire-purchase company called Irish Buyway in 1964, set up by businessman Howard Robinson. The hire-purchase business was big at the time, as most people couldn't afford to buy basic household appliances such as fridges, washing machines and televisions outright. Irish Buyway grew and grew, and eventually applied for a licence to take deposits, becoming a fully fledged bank in the mid-1960s. Howard Robinson's portrait hung for many years on the wall by the spiral staircase in Anglo's head office on St Stephen's Green. He retired in the mid-1980s. (Mary Robinson, Howard's daughter-in-law and former Irish President, was keen to stress the significant difference between City of Dublin Bank in her father-in-law's time and what Anglo Irish Bank later became: 'It was a very small concern, cautiously managed, and perhaps the size of a small branch of AIB or Bank of Ireland, with a capital value I gather of less than €10 million,' she said.)

In 1974, at the encouragement of O'Grady Walshe, City of Dublin Bank had come to own another bank, the Irish Bank of Commerce. One member of staff there was a young accountant from Bray, Co. Wicklow named Sean FitzPatrick.

The son of a farmer and a civil servant, Sean FitzPatrick attended secondary school at Presentation College in Bray before obtaining a commerce degree at University College Dublin. He wasn't the brightest student – but he was at least bright enough to know that, he later said. He got only one honour in his Leaving Certificate (in French), but secured a place in university on the strength of five passes in the Matriculation exam, which offered another way into UCD at the time. 'I have always been keenly aware of my own limitations,' he told *The Investor* magazine in March 2008.

FitzPatrick qualified as a chartered accountant in 1972 with Reynolds, McCarron & O'Connor, which, following a string of mergers, would later become part of Ernst & Young, the firm that later audited Anglo Irish Bank's books. His ambition was to become a partner in Reynolds, McCarron & O'Connor, but his plans were set back when he was the only trainee in his intake who was not offered a position. Undaunted, he joined Atkins Chirnside & Co., which soon merged with Craig Gardner. After two years there – where one of his contemporaries was Charlie McCreevy, a future Minister for Finance – FitzPatrick applied successfully for a job at Irish Bank of Commerce. The job paid £3,750 a year. As part of his signing-on agreement he was given a loan of £7,200 to buy a £6,800 house in Greystones and play the gilt market with the remainder, investing in government bonds. He later said that he didn't even know what the gilt market was at the time. '[I] had no idea what banking was,' he said. 'I had no idea I was going to make a career in banking. I just wanted a loan. Really.'

FitzPatrick recalled his first day at the bank in an interview with Ivor Kenny for his 2005 book *Achievers: Visionary Irish Leaders Who Achieved Their Dream*: 'I shook hands with all my new colleagues and was led to my office where there was an *Irish Times* and an *Irish Independent*. I picked up the phone and rang my mother and told her, "I've got this huge office and *two* newspapers and I've got a carpet with such a deep pile you can't hear anything." I left the office at ten o'clock that night and every night for the next number of weeks. At Easter, I worked Good Friday and Easter Saturday – in fact I worked Good Friday and Easter Saturday for the next six years of my life.'

FitzPatrick's first task in his new job was to prepare Irish Bank of Commerce's accounts for the year ending March 1974. Irish Bank of Commerce was a lender to businesses, offering much larger loans than City of Dublin Bank. A loan of £100,000 was big business at the time in Ireland. The accounts showed a loss. The problem wasn't Irish Bank of Commerce; it was its majority owner, Jessels Securities.

'It wasn't that the bank was trading badly – in fact we had turned the corner to profitability,' he told Kenny. 'It was simply that our largest shareholder had gone into liquidation and people were naturally worried: would there be a run on the bank by the depositors? We had to arrange standby lines from Bank of Ireland, which were supported by the Central Bank of Ireland.' Thirty-four years later, FitzPatrick would find himself in a similar situation as chairman of Anglo, except that the numbers would be exponentially bigger.

FitzPatrick's recollection to Ivor Kenny of his ascent to the top job at Anglo in 1980, just six years into his banking career, reveals much about the character of the man who would become a dominant figure in Irish banking for decades to come. He recalls being told by Irish Bank of Commerce finance director Gerry Watson to have recruitment company Hay MSL 'draw up a list of suitable candidates for the role of chief executive for Anglo Irish Bank', the previous chief executive, Pat Casey, having departed to insurance brokers Sedgwick Dineen. 'Before I went down to Hay MSL, it struck me that I could do that job,' said FitzPatrick. 'Even though I was now financial controller in a senior influential position, it was unlikely that I would become general manager in Irish Bank of Commerce in the foreseeable future. On the other hand, while Anglo Irish Bank had gross assets of less than £500,000, I would be the CEO, I would hire new talent, and, over time, together we would grow Anglo into a serious bank.'

Watson was initially reluctant, telling FitzPatrick that he didn't know enough about banking. But the decision rested with Gerry Murphy, the chief executive of City of Dublin Bank, and Murphy felt that Anglo needed a new manager: 'We decided that the best thing was to take Sean FitzPatrick out of Irish Bank of Commerce and put him in as managing director of "Little Anglo",' he recalls. 'The bank had all sorts of business – loans of between £30,000 and £40,000. They didn't have big loans but loans here and there, mainly on property, and loans given to a fellow with a piece of land.'

FitzPatrick's actual title was general manager, which, he told Kenny, 'was a very exalted title for such a small bank. We employed four people. But I jumped at the opportunity of running my own ship although it was probably closer to a canoe.'

Anglo was doing little new lending when FitzPatrick took the helm, but its fortunes quickly improved. On 11 December 1980 City of Dublin Bank reported that Anglo had increased its profits to £100,000 from £60,000 for the year ending the previous September.

In 1981 City of Dublin Bank, whose own profits were declining, sold a 40 per cent stake in Irish Bank of Commerce to the Crédit Commercial de France; the French bank's stake rose to 80 per cent three years later. Anglo was not part of that deal and remained a subsidiary of City of Dublin Bank.

Anglo at this point occupied a banking space somewhere between City of Dublin Bank, which continued to specialize in domestic hire-purchase loans, and Irish Bank of Commerce, which lent to businesses. Operating from an office on the ground floor of Huguenot House at 35 St Stephen's Green (where Sony now has a store), FitzPatrick tried to carve out a niche for Anglo, developing a new type of lending not being offered by the other banks: 'bridging' loans to professionals who had been offered long-term mortgages but who often had to wait months for Ireland's notoriously sluggish banks and building societies to advance the funds. To bridge the gap, FitzPatrick gave them a loan for a few months, charged a big fee and was then repaid quickly. This wasn't big business, and it didn't tend to repeat, but the bank earned its way and bridging loans filled much of Anglo's loan book between 1978 and 1982.

A former senior executive of the bank recalls that Anglo had very limited resources of capital and deposits at the time: 'It needed to get the money back as quickly as possible to re-lend it again. This small-bank mentality remained with Anglo until the late 1990s.'

From the early 1980s Anglo had branched out into lending to small builders, publicans and, most significantly, to professionals looking to buy their own property – solicitors and accountants seeking loans to buy offices, or dentists and doctors buying their own surgeries. Anglo also offered those professionals the financing to buy additional properties to rent out as an investment.

In April 1982 FitzPatrick hired Peter Killen, a senior lender from the country's biggest bank, AIB, where he had worked for fifteen years. No other appointment to Anglo would shape the bank in its formative years as significantly as that of Killen. He was a prudent lender with a forensic mind for loan-risk assessment and was a cautious foil to FitzPatrick's gung-ho attitude.

Years later, in an interview with the *Irish Times*, FitzPatrick recalled the work he and Killen did at Anglo in the early 1980s deciding whether to approve certain loans: 'We had red ledgers that we used to look at on a daily basis. Every Monday, myself and Peter Killen would look at them and shout across to each other whether we would do this loan or another. We were talking about loans of about £5,000 and £10,000. Progress was when we got two ledgers, one from A to M and another for N to Z, then three, and then we moved to computers.'

The two worked closely and often well into the evenings, driving out together on occasion to visit the homes of defaulting customers.

Under FitzPatrick, Anglo became more enterprising in its approach to winning new business. It brought in Terry Wogan to record a series of radio ads promoting the bank. The slogan on one of the Wogan ads went: 'We are legends in our lunchtime because the bank is open over lunchtime.'

Anglo played up the fact that it was a small but plucky bank willing to take business from the bigger players in the market. An old Japanese proverb – 'A little bait catches a large fish' – was prominent on one of its front-page newspaper ads.

In February 1983 Anglo moved to new offices in St Stephen's Court, the building at 18–21 St Stephen's Green formerly occupied by the Irish subsidiary of the US bank Chase Manhattan. It occupied the ground-floor lobby and the first floor. As the bank grew, it would take over the third floor as well.

FitzPatrick used the relocation as an opportunity to promote the bank's deposit rates and lending business. St Stephen's Court was 'smack between Dawson Street and Kildare Street', its latest advertisement said, referring to the two busy arteries that connect with the north side of the Green. 'You can do all your business banking and feed the ducks' was another of the bank's enticements in an ad campaign in February 1983. Anglo targeted the upper end of the market in its push for business customers, sponsoring events such as the Irish Seniors Tennis Open. FitzPatrick also sponsored golf events at his local club in Greystones.

By then the bank had a branch at The Crescent in Limerick and planned to open another in the centre of Galway. Anglo also started a safety-deposit service, with 400 boxes in the old vault in the St Stephen's Court basement. The strongroom was officially opened with some fanfare by Fine Gael Minister for Foreign Affairs Peter Barry. Although the safety-deposit boxes never became popular (lenders remember going down to the dank vault to retrieve dusty copies of property deeds in later years), the bank used the opening of the vault to announce publicly that it had increased its deposits twelve-fold and its loans seven-fold since FitzPatrick had taken over.

In the mid-1980s Anglo's core lending was business mortgages. Customers appreciated Anglo's personal touch and its ability to make quick decisions on loan applications. FitzPatrick and his senior lenders made themselves available at short notice, and loans were often agreed within days of the initial inquiry.

The average Anglo customer had two banking relationships – one for their day-to-day 'transactional' banking needs on a current account or overdraft, usually with a bigger bank such as AIB or Bank of Ireland, and the other with Anglo to finance the properties from which they operated.

FitzPatrick described mainstream banking and its offerings of overdrafts and personal loans as 'commodity lending'. This was a dog-eat-dog business and Anglo avoided it because it couldn't compete. 'If you did any of the commodity-type lending, the big guys put the lights on you and you were dead. They would reduce the rate and kill you,' he told the *Sunday Tribune* in 2005. 'The trick, which we didn't cop onto for a long time, was not to go forward as an alternative to AIB and Bank of Ireland, but as an addition to them. That was the breakthrough. We could offer customers a diversification of their lending. It allowed us to talk to people, to build a relationship.'

FitzPatrick had spotted a gap in the market. 'The retail banking customers were well served,' he said. 'The finance houses looked after the cars and the JCBs, anything in the region of £10,000 to £12,000, and then the merchant banks looked after anything over £100,000. The gap was between the finance houses and the merchant banks.'

Anglo didn't want the narrow-profit-margin business of handling cash transactions or current accounts – that would require a much larger operation with branches across the country and many multiples of the staff it employed. 'We were after the other end of the market, the cream,' Fitz-Patrick told Ivor Kenny. 'We only wanted to play at the sexy end.'

FitzPatrick called this 'low-maintenance' banking: 'If we approved a loan to an owner-manager, we wouldn't see him again until his annual review. We weren't ringing him every day wondering about this cheque or that.' It meant that Anglo could keep its cost-to-income ratio – a key measure of how heavily staffed a bank is – at 30 per cent, among the lowest in Irish banking. This fell to 17 per cent in 2008 – less than one third of the industry average. FitzPatrick wanted to create a 'bottom line' culture, pushing the profits of the bank by keeping lean, moving quickly and staying close to borrowers. In all of these respects, Anglo was a very different beast from its much bigger rivals AIB, Bank of Ireland and Ulster Bank.

A ruthless networker, FitzPatrick pressed his small but dedicated team to build up business by banging on doors. They were more salesmen than bankers and they relied heavily on word of mouth for new customers. 'It was 24/7 selling, taking every opportunity, with friends, casual acquaintances, old university pals, at dinners, the rugby club, the golf course. It was non-stop,' he said.

FitzPatrick's people skills were responsible for generating much of Anglo's new business. 'Sean could work a room better than any politician,' says a former long-standing colleague. 'He had a great ability to find the right comment. He was very charming and amusing.'

FitzPatrick played competitive rugby for Bective Rangers well into his forties, and the club rugby scene was a good hunting ground for new customers. Outside the office FitzPatrick grew to be known simply as 'Seanie', a gregarious banker who could talk a good game and win over your business. Inside the bank, FitzPatrick was known as 'Fitzie', but never to his face.

Anglo was starting to do good business. By December 1984 City of Dublin Bank chairman Thomas Kenny described Anglo as 'the jewel' in its group, telling shareholders with pride that the bank 'earns good money and the return on capital employed is well above the sector average'. In 1985, after comparing Anglo's profits with those of its parent bank, Fitz-Patrick picked up the phone to Gerry Murphy. He wanted a place on the board of City of Dublin Bank.

FitzPatrick recalled his exchange with Murphy to Ivor Kenny: ' "How could the group make only £175,000 when we made £600,000?" He said, "Well, we have a lot of bad debts and so on." I then said: "Gerry, can I go on the group board?" Gerry said, "Yeah, I will support you but Tom Kenny will need persuading." '

That was no problem to FitzPatrick. With help from Murphy, by November 1985 he had argued his way onto the board of City of Dublin Bank.

During that same year FitzPatrick hired two bankers who would go on to play an influential role at Anglo over the following two decades: Tiarnan O'Mahoney, the new head of treasury, and John Rowan, who went on to run the bank's business in the UK from 1988 until 2005. Killen, meanwhile, was rewarded for his part in Anglo's success, becoming an executive director in October 1985. Former Anglo insiders say that the key to the good working relationship between Killen and FitzPatrick was that Killen had no desire ever to be chief executive. As a result, FitzPatrick never saw him as a threat and they built a mutual respect and friendship.

'Peter was Sean's right-hand man,' says a former Anglo executive. 'He was the only guy who stood up to him. Peter was God in terms of dealing with Sean because he could say no and that was it.'

As Anglo started to develop its business in the mid-1980s FitzPatrick wanted to put some new names on the board to enhance the bank's credibility. The treasurer of Trinity College Dublin, Franz Winkelmann, was appointed a director, as was Michael Walsh, a professor of banking at FitzPatrick's *alma mater* University College Dublin, though he resigned after just eight months. Walsh would later become chairman of Irish Nationwide Building Society, and play a critical role in Anglo's fruitless attempts to secure government support for a merger with the building society as the bank was facing collapse in September 2008.

FitzPatrick saw an opportunity in the continuing decline of City of Dublin Bank. In the summer of 1986 he met Gerry Murphy and suggested that Anglo and City of Dublin Bank should be merged and renamed Anglo Irish Bank Corporation. Murphy agreed. The child had outgrown its parent.

FitzPatrick recalled thinking that 'Anglo Irish Bank' had 'a beautiful ring' to it when recounting the details of his proposal to Murphy in one of a series of interviews with the journalist Tom Lyons for *The FitzPatrick Tapes*, the book Lyons and Brian Carey would publish in 2011. 'City of Dublin Bank was far too local,' he said. 'Because, do you know what? We are going to be huge in Ireland, huge in the UK, and we will probably have to change it to Anglo Irish Bank Europe later on because we will go out there too.'

The plan to push Anglo to the top of this small banking pyramid was announced to shareholders and the public in October 1986. FitzPatrick would become chief executive of Anglo Irish Bank Corporation and Murphy deputy chairman and later chairman. Killen was appointed head of retail banking. The following month the bank said that it would raise £3.9

million from shareholders to fund the merger. Shareholders were happy to pony up – 'little Anglo' had made a profit of £803,000, more than double the previous year's figure.

The name Anglo Irish Bank Corporation plc appeared on the Irish Stock Exchange for the first time on 1 February 1987. A share price of 70p valued the bank at close to £1.6 million. Never one to miss a marketing opportunity, FitzPatrick said that the bank would offer scholarships in Anglo-Irish literature at UCD. It got him some favourable media coverage, though the bank's new academic connections did not prompt it to begin using a hyphen in its name.

'It wasn't a job for us in the early days,' FitzPatrick later recalled. 'It was a matter of pride and survival. We had a hunger to grow. There was just twenty of us when we floated. It was like we were lending our own money, not the bank's money. It was all smart, simple straightforward. It is like we used to say, we can't make money if we don't lend money. And unlike some others, we never employed people to tell us why we shouldn't lend.'

This was one of many reasons Anglo was doomed to fail.

2. 'You don't drink bottles at Anglo, you drink pints'

1987 – Anglo's value: €2 million

In its first full year as the publicly quoted Anglo Irish Bank Corporation, ending September 1987, FitzPatrick's institution made profits of £1.45 million. This compared with profits of £125 million at AIB and £80 million at Bank of Ireland around that time; Anglo was still a minnow in the Irish banking pond. It had a loan book of £92 million, and was well funded with deposits of £100 million. At this stage, the biggest individual loan on the bank's books was £150,000.

City of Dublin Bank was a mess when FitzPatrick took control of it, bedevilled by bad debts. FitzPatrick decided to get out of the small-fry hire-purchase business that had been City of Dublin Bank's bread and butter for two decades, but the bad debts already on the balance sheet were a drag on the performance of the new Anglo, and life at the bank in the late 1980s was about problem-solving.

Anglo lenders would come up with novel ways of recovering loans. One former executive at the bank remembers a lender calling to a restaurant whose owner was in arrears. The restaurateur said that he couldn't pay and he pointed to a painting on the wall, saying that the bank could take that if it wanted, not thinking that it would. The lender took the painting down and brought it back to St Stephen's Green. It remained hanging in a director's office for fifteen years.

One former colleague remembers FitzPatrick insisting that a customer sign a personal guarantee to ensure a loan would be repaid. 'If we get our toes wet, I want you to fucking drown,' he told the customer, according to the colleague's account of the meeting.

FitzPatrick's early moves to build Anglo included the acquisition of two old Dublin firms of stockbrokers. He had noticed that Anglo's customers were putting money on deposit and later withdrawing it to buy shares through stockbroking firms such as Davy's or Goodbody's. Why shouldn't Anglo earn similar fee income by offering its customers the same service?

Porter & Irvine was acquired in 1987 and came with an attractive list of private clients. Solomons & Abrahamson, long established with a solid client base of large institutions, was bought the following year. Anglo merged the two into Solomons Abrahamson & Irvine, and the new stock-broking division was based in the bank's head office on St Stephen's Green.

In 1988 Anglo acquired Irish Bank of Commerce, where FitzPatrick had got his start in banking, from Crédit Commercial de France. No other takeover would be as instrumental in shaping Anglo's future. Anglo adopted Irish Bank of Commerce's 'customer relationship' model of bank-ing under which, rather than 'churning' loans and focusing on one-off transactions as it had in the past, it focused on holding on to customers for years and lending to them repeatedly.

'That really was the ignition for what Anglo later became,' says a former executive. 'It was a powerhouse purchase for the bank, a real shot in the arm.'

That much is clear in retrospect, but at the time it wouldn't have been obvious. Irish Bank of Commerce had on its books a large number of builders and property developers – including Paddy Kelly, Gerry Gannon and Tom and Mick Bailey – who would go on to become big players in Ireland's development boom. In 1988, though, the property market was in the doldrums and developers were in trouble. Gannon's company, Thorn-ville Homes, was on the bad debt list at Irish Bank of Commerce when Anglo took over the loan book.

Also on Irish Bank of Commerce's customer books were Des and Ulick McEvaddy, whose company Omega Air bought and refurbished commer-cial aeroplanes for the US military. Media tycoon Tony O'Reilly also had a number of loans at Irish Bank of Commerce at the time, secured primar-ily on his shares in Independent Newspapers, publisher of the *Irish Independent* and *Sunday Independent* titles.

The acquisition was significant for another reason: it brought Bill Bar-rett, a former employee at AIB and Dutch bank ABN, into Anglo. Barrett had established long-standing relationships with many of the property developers on Irish Bank of Commerce's books and would become one of the best generators of new business for Anglo. Barrett rose to become director of banking and head of Anglo's Irish operation, its primary business, gain-ing a reputation for working late wining and dining the bank's customers.

Paddy Kelly's son Simon, a developer like his father, wrote in his 2010 book *Breakfast with Anglo* that Barrett was 'highly respected' by developers. By supporting struggling customers in bad times, he was repaid in good times and commanded their loyalty.

'I have never met a grey-haired developer who was not saved at some stage by Bill,' Kelly wrote. 'At the end of the 1980s he bailed us, and a number of other developers, out with some easy loans and the invitation to get started again. The bad loans were put aside to be paid in the future from new profits, and I think most or all of us eventually made the profits to pay them off.'

Another key banker who joined Anglo from the Irish Bank of Commerce stable was Padraic Murray. Murray had trained to become a priest after leaving school in 1969, then joined the Legion of Christ, a Mexican religious order whose founder had been expelled from the Jesuits. He would later tell friends that the seminary prepared him better for the world of banking than a commerce degree might ever have done. He remained with Anglo as a lender until his retirement in 2006.

Starting in 1988, FitzPatrick looked to build Anglo's loan business in the UK. To help fund this business, the bank started taking in sterling deposits in the Isle of Man. The island was regarded as something of a haven to hide money from the taxman. 'The Isle of Man wouldn't have been clean in today's terms,' FitzPatrick later told Tom Lyons. 'It was clean enough then, but it wasn't clean. There was nothing illegal but it was on the tax edge.'

Around the same time, Anglo opened a treasury business run by Tiarnan O'Mahoney, another of FitzPatrick's reliable lieutenants. While most banks had simple treasury operations that took in deposits, Anglo started offering customers the opportunity to trade in foreign exchange, government bond markets and more complex deposits. Over the next two decades, O'Mahoney would be instrumental in finding new ways to source funds to fuel the bank's lending.

FitzPatrick wasn't afraid to go out and hand-pick his bankers. Between 1987 and 1991 he poached forty-five staff from AIB, and by the early nineties about 90 per cent of staff in Anglo's head office was ex-AIB. The other defining characteristic of Anglo's staff was its youth: the oldest senior executive in the bank in 1988 was forty-two. The average age remained low as Anglo continued recruiting young bankers from rival lenders over the following years.

Employees remember FitzPatrick as an inspirational leader who stirred them into action with his speeches at staff meetings. 'He would have made a fantastic coach,' says one former executive. 'He would have you leaving the dressing room with your chest up ready to take on the world.' The executive remembers one of the bank's staff from Northern Ireland turning to him after one of FitzPatrick's rallying cries and saying: 'It would make you want to take up arms and cross the border.'

Colleagues also remember FitzPatrick being good with employees on a one-to-one level. 'Sean was very good with staff,' says Gerry Murphy. 'Back then they would have given blood for him. He was a good people person. He was thoughtful, remembering if a relative of a member of staff had been ill and would ask after them.'

Murphy recalls FitzPatrick as 'a very hard worker': 'He used to come into the bank at 7.15 a.m. every morning and he would be there until seven or eight in the evening.' Interestingly, in light of FitzPatrick's performance years later when Anglo's business went into dizzying decline, Murphy recalls that FitzPatrick 'would never defer something in the hope it would go away. He would always face up to it.'

Anglo approached every loan application on its own terms. Lenders were given an unusual degree of freedom to meet potential borrowers face-to-face and decide whether the bank should lend them money. Anglo was often proactive in initiating business relationships and relied less than other banks on unsolicited loan applications.

In media interviews in later years, FitzPatrick often cited one loan that exemplified Anglo's flexibility. The Goodman Group, the meat-processing empire run by Larry Goodman, had fallen into bankruptcy protection over a collapse in exports to the Middle East in 1990. The company could not secure a loan from any bank. FitzPatrick got a call from insolvency accountant Bernard Somers, an adviser to Goodman who had taken over the running of the business. Somers asked Anglo for a loan of £40 million at a time when the bank had a total loan book of £100 million. According to FitzPatrick, Somers told him that the loan would be guaranteed by the European Economic Community. FitzPatrick agreed to give the loan. It was repaid within four months when other banks started lending to the Goodman Group again, and Anglo enjoyed the benefit of a large fee for taking the risk.

Anglo's lending to a meat business was not new. The bank made large fees from meat companies on export credits in the late 1980s and early 1990s. In most cases, the bank didn't even give a loan – it just guaranteed the trade, covering delivery of the meat to the Middle East, and charged a fee. Anglo never lost one penny on these guarantees.

Unlike many of his peers in Irish banking, FitzPatrick had an entrepreneurial streak and liked taking gambles. 'Why go around the corner on four wheels when you can go around on two? Anyone who knew him knew that there was a bit of daring and risk-taking in Seanie,' says a long-serving former colleague at the bank.

Perhaps unsurprisingly, Anglo stepped on a few landmines in its early years. In 1988 it started a car-finance business with the largest independent motor dealer in the English Midlands, Swithland Motor Group. The business plan was simple: Anglo provided loans to customers to purchase cars from Swithland. But the business racked up large bad debts and Anglo closed it two years later.

Anglo's stockbroking business also blew up on FitzPatrick around 1990, leaving the bank with a loss of about £100,000. FitzPatrick had timed his foray into stockbroking badly. Stock markets still had not recovered from the October 1987 crash when Iraq invaded neighbouring Kuwait in August 1990, disrupting global markets further. Stock trading volumes were low, leaving brokers with low fees. Within a year of buying the firms, the newly merged business still had not made any money. Anglo got no business and was stuck paying large salaries to brokers.

FitzPatrick believed that Anglo's calamitous venture into stockbroking and his sacking of brokers caused damage to the bank's reputation. 'We didn't pay a heavy price financially but we paid a big, big price in the broking community. There was solidarity in the ranks and we suffered from a reputation point of view,' he told the *Sunday Tribune* in an interview in 2005.

Despite FitzPatrick's swashbuckling style and occasional gambles, Anglo was a pretty conservative bank. It had to be: it couldn't afford to lose money. His team had an entrepreneurial streak, were hard-working and took novel approaches to growing Anglo's business and attracting new customers from rival banks, but their core lending was cautious.

In the early 1990s Anglo focused on lending to hotels, restaurants and pubs in good locations, and industrial warehouses. With the property market languishing, it did not lend heavily to builders or developers. Anglo also avoided lending to farmers, new businesses or manufacturing. FitzPatrick's ideal loan was to a solicitor to buy a building leased to another professional firm. He described this as 'fabric of society' lending, believing it to be rock solid as it was based on the performance of the wider economy.

By 1991, Anglo's value on the stock market had grown to more than £30 million, but it was still very much in the shadows of the big banks. AIB was valued at £1.2 billion and Bank of Ireland about £1 billion.

To fund rapid expansion, FitzPatrick had tapped shareholders for cash in three rights issues in which shares were sold to raise funds. There would be a further four rights issues over the following six years. These fundraising exercises helped to grow the business, but they did not always send out strong signals about the bank.

'They looked bad,' says an ex-Anglo executive. 'The bank had just finished one when it started another. Anglo was growing so fast it was struggling to keep up.'

One consequence of the succession of rights issues was that the bank's share price went nowhere. Investors not already involved in Anglo had no interest in buying shares whose value was constantly diluted when the bank flogged new shares in rights issues. A languishing share price meant that the bank would always be constrained in the amount of money it could raise through those new share issues. But Anglo seemed to overcome this by selling its story well. Much of this was down to FitzPatrick's ability to talk a good game.

The stock suffered, too, from a general disbelief that Anglo could ever become big enough to compete with AIB and Bank of Ireland. Rivals felt Anglo's figures were too good to be sustained. 'Everyone thought Anglo was going to go bankrupt back in the 1990s,' said a senior banker at another institution. 'They were always thought to be about six months away from failing.'

Anglo did have major difficulties with loans in the early-1990s recession, particularly in the UK market, which had experienced a property crash. The UK loan book was full of property development loans originated by Irish Bank of Commerce. FitzPatrick had sent John Rowan over to run Anglo's UK business in London in 1988 after the UK management team walked out en masse to join a rival bank. Rowan had been shopping with his wife on Christmas Eve when he got a call from FitzPatrick. Did he want to take over the running of the UK office, FitzPatrick asked. He wanted an answer within hours. Rowan said he would do it for two years. He never came back.

Rowan hired David Murray as his right-hand man. They changed the focus of lending, moving from development to investment in good retail and office properties that were in secondary locations, away from the main high streets. This was lending to doctors, shopkeepers and pubs – mirroring Anglo's focus on this type of lending in Ireland.

In 1990 FitzPatrick had targeted the UK market for growth, intent on increasing Britain's contribution to Anglo's profits from 28 per cent to 50 per cent. But when the British property market crashed that same year, Anglo's UK business bombed. It lost between £5 million and £7 million out of a total loan book of about £110 million from 1990 to 1993. Peter Killen, Anglo's head of banking, scrutinized Anglo's UK book loan by loan and managed to lance many boils and contain the damage.

'Killen was a wise old owl,' says a former colleague. 'He went through all of that shit in the late 1980s, and when things turned sour in the UK in the early 1990s, he commuted over and back to London every week for two years. He was Mr Fix-It. Peter Killen is one of the reasons why the bank was still standing in 2002.'

FitzPatrick encouraged the bank's staff to live and breathe the job; they did not have the typical working day of the traditional banker who started at nine in the morning and left at five following a long lunch break. 'If things were going wrong, we looked under every stone. We did not sleep at night, wondering and worrying if we thought we were going to lose money on a deal,' said FitzPatrick.

He told his lenders to take their business personally, encouraging them to believe that it was their own money they were lending, not the bank's. In return, Anglo handed out share options to employees as rewards for their service. The options, which allowed employees to buy shares at a pre-agreed price below the market value, gave the bank's staff a sense of ownership over the bank and its business, and made them deeply protective of it.

The bank also watched costs. 'We never travel first class anywhere – we always go back of the bus,' FitzPatrick told Ivor Kenny for *Leaders: Conversations with Irish Chief Executives*. In the early days, there was no support staff inside the bank to carry out menial tasks such as clearing the coffee cups after a client meeting. Meetings outside the office were often in humble venues. One Anglo lender recalled having the first meeting of his lending team at McDonald's on Grafton Street.

One of the biggest projects backed by Anglo in the early 1990s was the purchase of Bartley Dunne's, a well-known Dublin gay bar, for £1.7 million, and its redevelopment. The brothers Liam and Des O'Dwyer paid what was at that time the highest price ever paid for a pub in Ireland. Liam went to the auction in July 1990 with just enough money to cover the deposit of £170,000. He won the bidding and immediately went to see Bill Barrett.

The O'Dwyers wanted to demolish the bar and build a seventy-five-bedroom hotel and 'super-pub' on the Stephen Street site in central Dublin. The construction costs were £8 million. Anglo agreed to cover the remainder of the purchase price – just over £1.5 million – and about £6 million of the construction cost; the O'Dwyers had to find the rest

'It was a big loan for Anglo at that time but they were great about it,' says Liam O'Dwyer. 'Bill Barrett was a very commercial banker – the heartbeat of Anglo – and a very social man. He always took time to ask what you did outside of nine to five.'

The timing of the project could not have been worse. The Gulf War broke out in August 1990, right in the middle of the O'Dwyers' construction schedule, causing interest rates on overnight inter-bank loans to rise to 100 per cent on an annualized basis and to 16 per cent (up from 10–12 per cent) on twelve-month loans. This almost crippled the project, but Anglo stood by the O'Dwyers.

The brothers hired a builder from Co. Clare by the name of Bernard McNamara to construct the bar and hotel. McNamara would go on to become one of Ireland's biggest developers and eventually one of its most indebted; but this was one of his first projects in Dublin.

The brothers' new bar, Break for the Border, and the adjoining Grafton Plaza Hotel, opened in November 1992. The venture made the O'Dwyer brothers a fortune and funded the growth of their business, Capital Bars, into the biggest pub chain in Ireland. It was floated on the stock market and grew to have a turnover of €43 million by 2001, when it was valued at €11 million.

The success of Break for the Border encouraged Anglo to finance further 'super-pubs' in Dublin, including the George, Café en Seine, the Dragon and Zanzibar, which became some of the most popular in the city. Break for the Border was the start of a beautiful friendship between the brothers and the bank.

'They were expensive but responsive – they didn't give you anything for nothing but they gave you a quick answer,' says Liam O'Dwyer. 'That was very important because you need to know pretty quickly whether you can get a loan if you are buying a property at auction.

'They were thorough, too – at that time they didn't just throw suitcases of money at you. The odd time they even said no.'

Capital Bars was to become another victim of the 2000s recession. It was de-listed in 2002 and eventually fell on hard times due to the downturn in a saturated pub market. The property crash killed off the company. A receiver was appointed in December 2009 by AIB, which was owed €26 million. The company owed Anglo €120 million.

FitzPatrick's willingness to tackle a problem head on – a quality cited by various colleagues from his early years at the helm of Anglo – was seriously tested for the first time in 1992.

The family of Belfast-born John Clegg Jr, a City of London lawyer and businessman, had ended up on Anglo Irish Bank's share register with a stake of 15 per cent through their investment in City of Dublin Bank. In

1988 FitzPatrick decided to invite the thirty-year-old Clegg to join the board 'in the belief that it was better to have a 15 per cent shareholder sitting around the table rather than sitting outside'. According to Gerry Murphy, he and FitzPatrick were not entirely comfortable having such a large shareholder on the bank's register. In 1990 FitzPatrick tried, unsuccessfully, to arrange for the sale of half the Clegg stake.

Clegg remained a non-executive director at Anglo until February 1992, when he resigned after his printing company, Wace, was linked with inaccurate reports alleging connections with money laundering for the IRA. Clegg had married into a Belfast family but there was no connection with the paramilitary organization. Clegg, who held 40,000 Anglo shares in his own name, strongly denied the allegations, but FitzPatrick believed the rumour was damaging the bank. Eventually Clegg agreed to step down from the board, but he and his family still retained their 15 per cent stake.

Clegg's large shareholding meant that there was virtually no trading in the stock. Other investors were reluctant to buy into the bank's shares knowing that a big shareholder might be forced to dump the stock at a fire-sale price if he ever got into financial difficulty. Such a scenario could cause the share price to collapse. It could also reduce the availability of stock to be bought and sold in the market, which would have a similarly negative effect on the share price.

The Clegg saga took another unusual turn in January 1993 when Jayne Riley, whom Clegg had described as his cousin but who was in fact his half-sister, and in whose name the Clegg family stake in Anglo was held, wrote to Anglo's institutional shareholders seeking to buy their shares in what appeared to be an attempt to take over the company. In a letter sent from an office in Chicago, from where she and her father, John Clegg Sr, appeared to operate, Riley asked Anglo's institutional investors at what price they would be willing to sell their total holding.

Nothing came of the overtures, but the letter was widely regarded in the market as an attempt by the Clegg family to put Anglo into play and attract bids. There was little chance that the Central Bank would have allowed the Clegg family to bid for or take over the bank, but the approach was seen as an attempt to flush out a counter-bid to take out the family's shareholding in the bank at a good price.

It was well over a year before FitzPatrick resolved the problem once and for all: in the spring of 1993 he flew out to South Africa to meet John Clegg Sr and convinced him to dump the shares. In July of that year the Investment

Bank of Ireland placed the Riley shares with institutions, most of which were already shareholders in the bank.

A later investigation by the UK Department of Trade and Industry found that Clegg had engaged in massive insider trading of shares in companies that had been taken over by Wace. The department's inquiry found that he had used bank accounts in his name at Anglo and Credit Suisse to benefit from substantial secret dealings in an array of companies.

With Clegg out of his hair, FitzPatrick took aggressive action to boost the bank's capital reserves to fuel the kind of lending growth that would sate his ambition.

Two years earlier he had tried to complete a big-ticket acquisition – the purchase of the Irish merchant bank Hill Samuel from Trustee Savings Bank. The bank was in a similar line of business to Anglo, with lots of pub, hotel and property loans, and there were personal ties as well: Michael Sheehan and Gerry Watson, who had hired FitzPatrick in 1974, had both worked at Hill Samuel. FitzPatrick had raised £26 million in a rights issue to fund the takeover, but the deal fell through after £500,000 was spent by Anglo on a due diligence examination of the company's books. The two sides could not agree on how much money should be set aside in the deal to cover potential bad debts, and the takeover fell through.

Anglo left the door open if Hill Samuel ever wanted to sell off just its loan book rather than the overall business, and eventually, in 1995, this is what happened. The acquisition pushed the size of Anglo's loan book over the £1 billion mark and made it the fifth largest in the country.

Along with the loan book, Anglo acquired from Hill Samuel a senior lender in Kieran Duggan who had strong relationships with builders and developers around the Dublin area. FitzPatrick recognized Duggan's value as a generator of business, and the two men became close. Duggan later became Anglo's 'Mr Big Deal', says a former executive at the bank. 'He was close to all the big property guys.'

Early in 1993 two Anglo managers, Pat Whelan and Owen O'Neill, interviewed David Drumm, a twenty-six-year-old chartered accountant from Skerries in north Co. Dublin, for a job as assistant manager. One of eight children and the son of a truck driver, Drumm had trained to be an accountant after leaving school. After completing his training, he worked initially on the liquidation of companies at an insolvency firm and later at one of the big accountancy firms, Deloitte & Touche. After four years with the firm, he left to work at Enterprise Equity, a state-backed company that invested in fledgling businesses. Drumm returned to work in accountancy in 1991 before applying to join Anglo.

Drumm went through two more rounds of interviews – with Tom Browne, a senior lender at the bank, and finally with Bill Barrett, the head of lending. On 13 May 1993 he received his letter of offer. Anglo would pay him £23,000 a year for a role reporting to a lending manager. In its letter, the bank noted that 'the current regulations of the company relating to share dealing ethics will apply to this appointment'.

Browne had started at the bank in January 1990, joining from AIB, like so many other employees at Anglo. Whelan had joined in October 1989. Drumm, Browne, Whelan and O'Neill made up the core of the Dublin lending team and were known as 'Bill's boys' outside the team, as they were all regarded as acolytes of Barrett.

The Anglo culture was very much like that of a boys' locker room. Senior lenders were encouraged to socialize to build team spirit. This regularly involved late nights out and big drinking sessions. '[One of the senior bankers] would bring you and insist on you getting pissed,' says one former lender. 'You might try to watch your drinking but you would always end up getting pissed.'

One former executive who wasn't a big drinker says it was noticed by his peers at the bank that he drank bottles rather than pints in order to limit his intake. 'You don't drink bottles at Anglo, you drink pints,' he was told. According to a former insider, FitzPatrick 'expected everyone to eat, sleep and drink Anglo. I have rarely come across a business with such a culture.'

In 1995 Tiarnan O'Mahoney, Anglo's head of treasury, spotted an opportunity for Anglo to make its first acquisition outside Ireland and the UK. Royal Bank of Canada wanted to sell Royal Trust Bank, a hundred-year-old Austrian institution. It had no loans but deposits of £235 million. Banks sometimes raised deposits in one country to fund lending in another. This is exactly what Anglo did, buying the deposit book in Austria to fund new lending in Ireland. O'Mahoney said at the time that acquiring Royal Trust Bank would give Anglo 'a cheap source of funding for future lending'.

Until then Anglo had focused on attracting deposits by offering high interest rates and targeting businesses, charities and credit unions. Retail deposits from everyday savers came in through the bank's small branch

network, but most of the business was done by phone and by post. This
was a steady business but it wasn't bringing in the quantities of money that
FitzPatrick wanted to fuel lending.

The Austria business was different. With one acquisition, Anglo could
fill its boots to the tune of £235 million. The average deposit was about
£120,000 and the customers were largely Americans, sourced through US
brokers and the bank's Canadian owners. The takeover pushed Anglo's
deposits to £1.1 billion, roughly matching the size of the loan book.

FitzPatrick continued on the acquisition trail. In December 1995 Anglo
bought a £66 million sterling loan book from Allied Dunbar, and the private Dublin bank Ansbacher Bankers, which had loans of about £80
million and deposits of £140 million. Ansbacher operated in a similar space
to Anglo, concentrating on lending to businesses. Donegal-born developer
Pat Doherty of Harcourt Developments, who would become a major borrower at Anglo during the property boom, accounted for a very large part
of Ansbacher's loan book.

The Ansbacher takeover brought Catherine Mullarkey – an experienced
lender who was also the daughter of Paddy Mullarkey, the former secretary general of the Department of Finance – into Anglo. She would go on to
become a highly regarded senior lender at Anglo, and ended up on the board
of the Dublin Docklands Development Authority, which would be drawn
into controversy over its relationship with Anglo and Sean FitzPatrick.

Another purchase in 1995 transformed Anglo's British operations. The
bank acquired UK lender Chemical Bank, whose American parent company had four years earlier merged with US banking giant Manufacturers
Hanover. The acquisition added loans of about £35 million sterling, bringing Anglo's UK loan book to about £150 million. But, more importantly,
like the Irish takeovers, the acquisition gave Anglo access to new groups of
customers. Chemical Bank had a combination of Jewish and Irish roots in
New York, and its UK business gave Anglo access to big-time property
investors in the Jewish community in north London.

Two of Anglo's new customers had survived Auschwitz and gone on to
establish large property businesses in London. Another ex-Chemical Bank
customer, Benzion Freshwater, was a property investor and an Orthodox
Jew who would be ranked 110th in the Sunday Times Rich List in 2009
with an estimated fortune of £473 million.

As a result of the bank's acquisition spree Anglo's loan book almost doubled in size between 1994 and 1996, to £1.5 billion.

FitzPatrick never felt the need to establish a substantial retail branch network that could attract ordinary depositors. He thought a chain of branches would be 'expensive baggage' and that by the mid-1990s there had been 'a fundamental change in the behaviour of depositors', who he believed were no longer interested in putting their money with the nearest bank but looking to play the market for the best deposit rates.

In January 1996 Anglo disclosed that it paid £1.4 million to six executive directors of the bank. It was a massive sum of money to be paid to the management team of a small specialized bank – particularly one whose share price was still languishing at around 60p – but chairman Gerry Murphy defended the track record of FitzPatrick and his team. The bank had enjoyed a decade of 'substantial growth' with the bank returning profits of £19.1 million in the year to September 1995, compared with £286,000 in 1985. Murphy said that the bank would try to grow at 30 per cent a year – an astonishing target for any bank to set itself. Then again, Anglo was different.

Ireland's property tide started rising in the mid-1990s. The land banks that many of Anglo's developer clients had been sitting on for years quickly became very valuable, and developers started scrambling to acquire new plots of land – often former farmland – to build on. Many of these developers had stuck with Anglo after the bank remained loyal to them during the currency crisis of 1992–3, when interest rates at which Irish banks borrowed their money jumped from 10 per cent to 50 per cent at one point and the punt was devalued by 15 per cent. Other banks passed the interest rate increases on to customers and called time on struggling borrowers; Anglo stuck with them.

'There was always a confidence among the bank's customers that Anglo would stay with you,' says one banker. 'Usually they say that bankers offer you an umbrella when it's sunny and take it away when it rains. Well, Anglo changed that and was willing to lend to customers when no other bank was interested.'

Anglo's loyalty to struggling developers would be repaid over the following fifteen years as both bank and customers were the first to milk the property boom.

To understand how prices in the Irish property market grew, it is important to look at how the economic landscape changed in Ireland. The economy grew by an average of 6 per cent a year from 1988 to 2007 and unemployment dropped from 16 per cent in 1994 to 4 per cent in 1999, with higher incomes creating huge demand for houses and apartments. The true

'Celtic Tiger' period lasted until around 2000, with spectacular export-led growth driven by foreign multinationals such as Intel and Dell. Wages increased but not excessively so before 2000 as they remained competitive with other European countries.

Immigration increased, emigration declined, and household sizes became smaller; all these factors fuelled demand for housing. But one factor above all drove the residential and commercial property boom: interest rates, which began to fall in 1998 in advance of Ireland adopting the euro as an accounting currency on 1 January 1999 and remained low for a number of years. Joining such a large single-currency area meant that Irish banks could borrow more cheaply in the international money markets without foreign exchange risks. For the first time they had access to a vast pool of money that they could draw on at a cheap rate to lend to customers back home. The banks passed their lower cost of borrowing on to customers and houses became more affordable because mortgages were cheaper. This meant that buyers could also afford to buy dearer properties, which pushed prices higher.

Property prices tripled between 1994 and 2006, making the Irish real estate boom the most dramatic of any advanced economy in recent times. Gradually, people started assuming that property prices would continue rising and that, given the benign economic conditions, would never fall. A speculative mania centred around property gripped the country. The media enthusiastically supported the Irish preoccupation with property ownership and supported the profit growth at the banks while generally dismissing warnings that the property market was growing out of control.

The average price of an acre of land more than doubled between 1994 and 1999. Land values jumped most where the demand for housing was greatest – around Dublin – and Anglo was the first bank to lend heavily into this market. Many of the bank's builder customers purchased land with a view to building on it seven to ten years later.

There was nothing more important to a builder's overall business than the development plans of the various city and county councils. These documents set out a council's long-term strategy for the growth of a particular area, deciding which land would be re-zoned from agricultural to residential or commercial. The builders would pore over maps, assessing where new infrastructure such as roads and rail lines would be built and where they could snap up agricultural land nearby with a view to developing the land over time. Typically, a developer would identify the land and offer to pay the owner, in most cases a farmer, a sum to secure an exclusive option to purchase the land at a later date. The developer would then seek planning permission to build a housing estate or an apartment block; if permission was granted, the developer would pay the farmer a higher price.

In the early days of the boom, when credit was still relatively scarce and memories of the recession still fresh, a developer might secure enough bank finance to build an entrance to his proposed estate, three roads and four show houses to try to entice buyers. If there was enough interest, he might agree the sale of ten houses, against which the bank would lend him enough money to complete them. As the property market took off, the process accelerated: developers might agree fifty house sales in one weekend, fast-tracking the entire development. Rising land prices meanwhile pushed the value of the original tract far higher than the original sum paid. The equity thus created would allow the developer to borrow more heavily from Anglo to roll the dice all over again on another project.

Anglo was quicker to enter this market than its competitors. 'Anglo benefited enormously between 1996 and 1998. Where AIB and Bank of Ireland wouldn't take risks, as they were still very conservative, Anglo had experience in property and took on a large amount of lending,' says a rival banker.

Anglo had no trouble finding customers willing to borrow at an interest rate of 3 per cent over the cost of the money to the bank – a premium that could be 1 to 2 points higher than at the other banks – or to pay large arrangement fees. This meant Anglo enjoyed much larger profit margins on property deals than other banks. Later, when the other banks piled into this market, Anglo was able to continue charging higher fees because it gave decisions and provided finance more quickly than its competitors, and because by that stage it had developed extremely strong relationships with its developer and builder clients.

The size of Anglo's loan book ballooned as property values rose, increasing from €1 billion in 1994 to €5.7 billion in 1999. For the first time, Anglo's capacity to attract deposits could not keep up. Deposits rose from just under €1 billion to €4.4 billion over those years, creating a gap of €1.3 billion between Anglo's loans and deposits. This was a break with the traditional rule of banking whereby loans should never exceed deposits.

Ireland's entry into the euro made it easy for banks to disregard this principle. Ready access to greater pools of cash in the international money markets, with no foreign exchange risk, meant that Irish banks could lend more than they took on in deposits, comfortable in the belief that they would have no problem borrowing the difference at favourable interest rates.

Borrowings from other banks, mostly for terms of a year or less, increased by almost €1 billion in Anglo's financial year to the end of September 1999. This money was then lent out the other side of the bank to customers.

Issuing bonds, which are effectively IOUs to investors, was another way to raise funding. Again, being part of the euro area meant that Irish banks could tap foreign lenders for cash with no currency risk for the lender. A series of upgrades in Anglo's credit rating from 2001 to 2004 to the top 'A'-ratings gave the bank greater access to sources of funding as international ratings agencies such as Moody's and Fitch viewed the institution as a solid bet for lenders. British, German and French banks and investors responded and were among the main lenders to Anglo during these years. (The strong endorsements from ratings agencies would continue until 2007.)

The value of bonds issued by Anglo soared to €928 million in the year to September 2000 from €128 million the previous year. The bank borrowed a further €1.6 billion from bondholders and other banks the following year and started relying more heavily on short-term deposits of three months or less to fund the loan book. Anglo was borrowing short term to lend long term. This meant that Anglo would be in a vulnerable position if the money markets ever shut down: it would face repayments on its short-term funding and would be unable to renew the borrowings. This risk was not taken seriously by Anglo and the many other banks that adopted this approach to funding.

One of the landmark projects for Anglo during the 1990s was the development of the Jervis Shopping Centre on the site of the old Jervis Street hospital in Dublin city centre. It pushed the bank into a new league.

The hospital had closed in 1987. The building was sold to a British property company, Trafalgar House, for £5 million. Trafalgar had planned to build a £35 million shopping centre but, frustrated by planning delays in Dublin and economic difficulties back in the UK, it sold the building in 1994 to Belfast-born property developer and investor Paddy McKillen, who had made his money in his family's motor repair business, DC Exhausts.

McKillen realized early on that there was more money to be made from building properties for new outlets for the company than fitting exhausts to cars. He had made contact with one of the Trafalgar executives several years earlier and the two hit it off. McKillen told him to give him a call if they were ever putting Jervis on the market.

Estate agent Aidan O'Hogan at Hamilton Osborne King, Trafalgar's representative in Dublin, called McKillen in early 2004 and said the company was thinking of selling the old hospital. Would he be interested? He jumped at the opportunity, beating major property developers to secure the property at a cost of £4.7 million, a purchase that was financed entirely by Anglo.

McKillen and his business partner Padraig Drayne drafted plans to build a massive 330,000-square-foot shopping centre with three main retail tenants, fifty smaller shops and a multi-storey car park. It was a ballsy scheme. Construction started on the project around August 2005. McKillen was building at a time 'when there was straw still blowing around Mary Street', says one person who was involved. McKillen approached Anglo, but the £60 million required for such a development project would have amounted to about 5 per cent of the bank's overall loans. (Typically, banks tried to limit exposure to any one borrower to a maximum of 1 per cent.) The plan would have to be financed by a syndicate of banks, which Anglo agreed to lead. The other banks involved were Irish Intercontinental Bank (later to become KBC Bank), ICC Bank (later to become part of Bank of Scotland (Ireland)) and Ansbacher (later to be taken over by Anglo). They all agreed to take a share of the lending, thereby spreading the risk, but Anglo provided the bulk of the money and did all the heavy lifting on the organizational side.

At the time it was the largest construction project ever undertaken in the country. It was said that McKillen worked the day shift on the project while Drayne worked at night. The project was dubbed 'Nervous Jervis': many observers believed the frenetic building activity was a sign that things were going wrong.

They weren't. Construction was completed in thirteen months and there were no major cost over-runs. Anglo was very closely involved with the project. Declan Quilligan, a senior manager at the bank who would go on to become an executive director and manage Anglo's UK division, liaised constantly with McKillen and provided regular reports to his boss, Tony Campbell, an associate director at the time who would rise through Anglo's ranks to set up the bank's wealth management division and to run its US operations.

Anglo's board admired how McKillen had lined up tenants for the shopping centre, guaranteeing a decent flow of rent and, by extension, repayments on the bank's loans. A year before it opened, more than 65 per cent of the centre had been let to retail businesses. This would have been enough to cover a large part of the interest payments on the loan. Anglo were proactive in signing up tenants: Bill Barrett, who by now had been rewarded for his service with a seat on the Anglo board, travelled with McKillen to pitch to UK retailers the merits of signing up as one of the centre's anchor tenants. Debenhams and Boots agreed to come aboard. The bank was comforted by McKillen's professionalism and thought he was something of a visionary, taking a gamble on an underdeveloped area of the city.

FitzPatrick's appetite for acquiring banks was still not sated. He told the *Sunday Tribune* in March 1998 that Anglo was looking at buying private banks in Germany, France and Italy. This was all part of a plan to increase earnings by 15 per cent a year for the next five years.

In July 1998 Anglo purchased the asset management and private banking arm of French bank Crédit Lyonnais in Austria for €12.8 million. The business was bolted on to Anglo's bank in Vienna. FitzPatrick was also very keen to take over one of the other small banks in Ireland. A good fit was ICC Bank, the state-owned business lender. A marriage of the two would make Anglo a much bigger and more diverse player in the business banking market. A takeover of ICC would also fulfil a large part of Anglo's audacious growth plan. FitzPatrick was watching his old accountancy buddy Charlie McCreevy, by then Minister for Finance, to see when he would put the state-owned bank on the market. McCreevy eventually did so in 1999, but it wasn't until February 2001 that it was sold.

As the bidding process reached the eleventh hour, FitzPatrick gathered a group of financial advisers in the boardroom of Anglo one evening to come up with a final bid. But FitzPatrick was beaten to ICC by Mark Duffy, a former Anglo executive who now ran Bank of Scotland's Irish operation. He turned Bank of Scotland (Ireland) into a lender that cut the cost of mortgages during the boom, thereby fuelling the surge in house prices; he also competed with Anglo in the market for development loans.

Losing ICC would have hurt FitzPatrick, who had never really forgiven Duffy for leaving Anglo for Equity Bank and taking another Anglo executive, Richard McDonnell, and two other staff with him. Anyone who left Anglo on bad terms ran the risk of incurring FitzPatrick's wrath. 'You were either with him or against him,' says one former executive. FitzPatrick would also have been sore over Duffy's role in the takeover of Smurfit Paribas in 1999. FitzPatrick wanted to acquire the entire business but was forced to settle for the banking part only, while Equity Bank acquired the leasing division.

Anglo reported a 56 per cent increase in profits, to €89 million, for the year to September 1999. The bank's loan book had grown from just €1 million when FitzPatrick took over in 1978 to €5.7 billion in 1999, backed by deposits of €4.4 billion. Apart from its Dublin premises, it now had branches in Cork, Limerick, Waterford and Belfast and offices in London, Birmingham, Glasgow, Manchester, the Isle of Man, Vienna, Boston and Düsseldorf.

FitzPatrick could count on one hand the number of staff employed at Anglo when he took charge; by the end of the 1990s the number on the payroll had risen to 538. Three-quarters of the bank's business was in Ireland.

Anglo's figures were well ahead of expectations. Analysts were now encouraging investors to buy the bank's stock, saying that it was undervalued compared with AIB and Bank of Ireland, and that the bank was in a unique position to make money for shareholders as it held the middle business market in Europe's fastest-growing economy.

At the turn of the millennium, Anglo was primed for a period of extraordinary growth.

3.   Riding the Tiger
2000 – Anglo's value: €650 million

'You have to keep the board on your side – there will come a time when you need them to back you against the odds.' Anglo colleagues would recall that this was Sean FitzPatrick's repeated advice to David Drumm after the younger man succeeded him as chief executive of the bank in January 2005.

FitzPatrick was speaking from experience. In 2000 he'd got a bloody nose when attempting an audacious acquisition of Ireland's fourth largest mortgage lender, First Active. It was to prove one takeover too many for Anglo.

First Active, formerly a customer-owned building society, had been floated on the Stock Exchange in 1998 and was heavily criticized by investors and the media the following year for losing ground in the home loans market to Bank of Scotland (Ireland). To compound its problems, First Active was left rudderless in January 2000 following the sudden resignation of chief executive John Smyth. He departed after the bank's shares halved in value within the space of a year, falling below the flotation price. The bank's chairman, John Callaghan, a former managing partner of accountancy firm KPMG, took over the running of the bank as executive chairman just months after joining the board. He was helped by the bank's chief financial officer Cormac McCarthy, who would later run First Active and its eventual owner Ulster Bank.

Sean FitzPatrick spied an opportunity. First Active was in a different part of the banking market: it sold home loans and investment products. But First Active had two things Anglo wanted – surplus capital on its books that it could lend on, and a network of retail branches that the bank could use to hoover up deposits from a wider customer base. FitzPatrick's interest in the First Active branch network was a departure: he had hitherto viewed high-street branches as more trouble than they were worth. But Anglo had grown, and FitzPatrick now eyed seriously the possibility of growing into a more comprehensive bank.

FitzPatrick called Callaghan and proposed a merger. They met, talked it through and agreed that a deal made sense. First Active was fighting a battle with trade unions over plans to cut 175 jobs and close twenty-five branches and was without a full management team to cope with its problems. After months of protracted discussions between FitzPatrick and Callaghan, a deal was agreed.

The market never really understood Anglo's interest. Taking over a branch network and a substantial mortgage book appeared to be a radical departure from the bank's commercial lending business. The board did not get the opportunity to explain FitzPatrick's thinking behind the transaction, as the two lenders hammered out a deal in private. When the details of the secret talks were leaked to the *Irish Times* and published on 13 May 2000, shares in both banks fell. First Active had already been subjected to horrendous criticism in the media, particularly from broadcaster and columnist Eamon Dunphy and *Sunday Independent* business editor Shane Ross, who were shareholders in the bank. Now critical questions were raised about the bank's interest in troubled First Active.

The leak and the negative reaction to the news meant that Anglo could no longer conclude the deal in private: it had to come out publicly to explain the reasoning behind the deal even as it was negotiating it. This complicated matters terribly. Anglo had to show credible reasons for the takeover and demonstrate that it would be backed by strong new management.

This is where difficulties arose. Both banks might have been happy for Anglo to take over First Active, but as a recently demutualized building society First Active was legally protected from takeover until 2003. The deal had to be a 'merger of equals'.

There were different interpretations of the rules governing how key management roles would have to be divided up between Anglo and First Active. Anglo's advisers Ernst & Young were of the opinion that it could claim the most powerful seats in the boardroom of the new entity, while PricewaterhouseCoopers and JP Morgan in London – a blue-blood bank hired by First Active to provide solid advice – said this was not possible. Under the proposed deal as negotiated by FitzPatrick, each side would appoint the same number of directors to the board of the enlarged bank. Callaghan would be chairman and FitzPatrick chief executive.

Anglo chairman Tony O'Brien wasn't happy. O'Brien, who had joined the board in 1997 and succeeded Gerry Murphy as chairman in January 1999, was a relative newcomer to Anglo and an outsider in the FitzPatrick culture, a gold-plated corporate guy who had won street cred in Irish business circles for building the drinks and snacks group Cantrell & Cochrane into a thriving business. He was the first 'outsider' to be appointed chairman at Anglo, and the contrast with Gerry Murphy – a lifetime banker who had plucked the young FitzPatrick from obscurity – was dramatic. One former board member recalls that O'Brien and FitzPatrick argued over everything and then made up afterwards over a pint. But the reconciliations were only temporary. FitzPatrick would never let go of contentious issues between the two. He would regularly badger O'Brien at dinner parties over the various plans that he had for Anglo.

O'Brien wasn't the only board member that FitzPatrick had a tempestuous relationship with. Another director from the 1990s recalls being invited to breakfast by FitzPatrick shortly after the announcement of the bank's excellent results. Over their meal FitzPatrick told him that he was the only director who had not congratulated him. The director thought it bizarre that a bank chief executive as well paid as FitzPatrick would be insecure enough to demand praise.

'FitzPatrick was arrogant,' says another former director of the bank. 'He wanted semi-yes-men around him. He didn't mind having arguments but he always wanted to win. If he didn't win the argument, he would think very badly of you. Sean FitzPatrick felt that it was Sean FitzPatrick plc and not Anglo Irish Bank plc – he felt that it was his bank, that he should call the shots to the board and the management . . . He didn't want a board at all.'

'He had an ego that liked to be lauded,' says a former executive. 'As the bank attracted more attention, the ego inflated. I think there was a lot of venerating at the altar within the bank.'

O'Brien felt that Anglo needed tighter controls and clearer reporting lines from management to board; FitzPatrick disagreed. 'For a banker it was unusual to want so much autonomy,' says the former Anglo board member. '[FitzPatrick] was very good at putting his case and if it was not accepted, there would be a lot of aggro.' O'Brien thought FitzPatrick acted as though he owned the bank and viewed boardroom decisions as little more than a rubber-stamping exercise. The chairman was hell-bent on controlling his headstrong chief executive and giving the board status, and the First Active drama provided an opportunity.

Under the proposed First Active deal, O'Brien was going to lose out. He felt that the executives at the bank had, characteristically, agreed the deal with First Active without checking with the Anglo board. For its part, the board felt that First Active was a 'yellow-pack operation' with low interest margins. It was also heavily unionized. Anglo had managed to keep the unions out of the bank and the board's view was that it didn't need the tricky industrial-relations problems that the First Active workforce would bring.

The deal was about a week away from being announced when details of the merger discussions were leaked. FitzPatrick had kept the board briefed on the merger talks, which had been going on since the previous January, but the board felt that he and the executives were on a solo run without the approval of the board to conclude the deal they wanted. The subsequent criticism in the media following the leak also stung the non-executive directors.

FitzPatrick made it clear to First Active following the press leak that he had a problem with his board. It was a deeply embarrassing position for FitzPatrick to be in. First Active had been told by him all along that the board of Anglo would not be a problem.

'Sean FitzPatrick was Anglo Irish Bank,' says a source involved on the First Active side. 'If you were talking to Sean, you were talking to Anglo. He had put across the view during discussions that we didn't have to worry about his board.'

While Anglo's non-executive board members weren't keen on First Active, they were happy to let a merger proceed, provided it was on the board's terms and that Anglo would take the most powerful boardroom and management positions in the enlarged bank. O'Brien and the non-executive directors on the board of Anglo proposed changes to the deal negotiated by FitzPatrick. O'Brien wanted to be appointed as chairman of the merged bank. FitzPatrick would be chief executive and Anglo's finance director Willie McAteer would hold the same position in the enlarged bank. Callaghan would be relegated to deputy chairman, and First Active offered only one executive position.

O'Brien travelled out to First Active's offices in Booterstown, south Dublin with Billy McCann, another non-executive director, to put the new proposals directly to Callaghan. He was having none of it, given that FitzPatrick and the Anglo executives had promised him the role of chairman of the enlarged bank. As a compromise, O'Brien suggested that Callaghan could be chairman for six months and then O'Brien would take over, but Callaghan did not bite. What was on offer now clearly was not a 'merger of equals'.

'Even if we wanted to accept it, we couldn't,' said Callaghan at the time. 'Anglo wasn't looking for a merger, it was looking for a low-price takeover.'

The deal collapsed at Callaghan's meeting with O'Brien and McCann on 22 May, just over a week after news of the merger talks was leaked.

FitzPatrick was uncharacteristically guarded over subsequent years when asked why the First Active deal had collapsed. Speaking in 2005, he said: 'It would have been a good deal for us, but it just didn't work out.' FitzPatrick later told Tom Lyons that he had asked O'Brien 'to do the big thing' and step aside, but that O'Brien had said that the matter was up to the board, and the board backed him to stay on as chairman.

The collapse of the deal was 'the first time Sean had been stopped in his tracks', says a former board member of the bank. 'It was a chastening experience for all the executives. It was the first time that they had been held back and brought to a quick halt. The boardroom was like a funeral parlour for weeks after that.'

The First Active debacle fell right in the middle of O'Brien's term as chairman. He was due to step down in January 2002 after three years in the role. It would not be unusual for an Anglo chairman to complete two terms but 'there was no way Seanie was going to let O'Brien serve another term as chairman after the First Active deal collapsed', says an Anglo insider. O'Brien, for his own part, had no intention of standing for another term.

About six months before the chairman's term was up, FitzPatrick told O'Brien that he wanted to be executive chairman of the bank, and to appoint O'Mahoney as his managing director. FitzPatrick said that he would hold the role for three or four years before becoming non-executive chairman and leaving the day-to-day responsibility of running Anglo entirely to O'Mahoney. O'Brien was aghast. As chairman of the board's nominations committee he was to have an influential role in choosing the next chairman. He was deeply opposed to FitzPatrick's plan, which would give FitzPatrick control over both the board and the management. O'Brien was so concerned that he spoke to the governor of the Central Bank, Maurice O'Connell, who was also strongly against the idea.

FitzPatrick brought the issue up repeatedly with O'Brien, but to no avail. The other non-executive directors shared their chairman's concerns. They saw the danger of vesting too much power in FitzPatrick and felt that he was trying to shut out the board. FitzPatrick knew he would have the support of the shareholders for his plan and regularly boasted about this. O'Brien was equally aware of the shareholders' adulation of the chief executive. At the four annual meetings chaired by O'Brien between 1999 and 2002, FitzPatrick received standing ovations from shareholders, thankful for the bank's strong performance.

'Shareholders were very keen to have FitzPatrick as their chairman,' says a former Anglo board member. 'He was the driver of the business and he brought added value. They publicly acclaimed him and Anglo, and they ridiculed the other banks for trying to emulate him and the bank.'

FitzPatrick eventually dropped his idea. It would be O'Brien's last victory over him.

Although O'Brien chaired the appointments committee, FitzPatrick managed to use his considerable power and influence within the bank to fill the boardroom with his own friends and favoured appointees. O'Brien encountered major opposition from FitzPatrick on suggested candidates and often found himself out-flanked by the chief executive and his supporters. As the senior member of the appointments committee, FitzPatrick selected the people he wanted to sit on the board, and the committee would meet to discuss them. The interview process was also led by FitzPatrick.

Peter Murray, who was close to FitzPatrick and a deputy chairman of glass-bottling company Ardagh, took over as chairman. Murray was very much regarded as FitzPatrick's man on the board, and it was believed that Murray was keeping the chairman's seat warm for when FitzPatrick's time came to step up to the role.

Anton Stanzel, a former director general of the Austrian Ministry of Finance and former head of banking regulation in the country, was appointed to the Anglo board on 19 April 2001. Stanzel had built up a strong relationship with Terry Carroll, the Anglo executive who ran the bank's Austrian operations, and one of Stanzel's staff had supervised Anglo during his time as the head of banking regulation. This was not the first time FitzPatrick had persuaded a former gamekeeper to turn poacher. Timothy O'Grady Walshe had joined the Anglo board in 1990 following his retirement from the Irish Central Bank. In 1994 the bank appointed Anthony Coleby to the board shortly after his retirement from his role in monetary policy and market operations overseeing bank supervision for the Bank of England; Coleby remained on the board until 26 January 2001.

Ned Sullivan, the former managing director of food company Glanbia, joined the Anglo board in November 2001, and in May 2002 FitzPatrick appointed his close friend Fintan Drury, the former RTE news journalist who had set up his own public relations firm, Drury Communications, which handled Anglo's media relations work.

The absence of women from the Anglo boardroom, and the shortage of female lenders, was conspicuous. Catherine Mullarkey, a lender who joined

Anglo through its acquisition of Ansbacher's Irish operations, was one of the few exceptions. She left the bank around 2004.

One male former senior lender recalls taking an ambitious female junior on a routine trip to a site being developed by one of their large customers. 'She had to go up a ladder in a short skirt and high heels. It was embarrassing. It was very different in lending as you had to go out, meet the clients and walk about on the building sites,' he said.

As part of his drive to improve corporate governance at Anglo, and under pressure from the Central Bank and the Stock Exchange, Tony O'Brien had tried to appoint a female board member during his time as chairman. One of his first preferred candidates was blocked by FitzPatrick. This had more to do with the testy relationship between them than any objection FitzPatrick had to having a woman on the board of his bank.

FitzPatrick himself recognized that Anglo needed a female board member. In January 2003 the bank appointed Patricia Jamal, a former managing director and head of global financial institutions at UK bank Barclays Capital. Jamal would serve on the board until 2006; in that same year Anne Heraty, chief executive of recruitment firm CPL Resources, joined the board. It would not be until the following year, when the former Citibank International Europe chief operating officer Noël Harwerth became a director, that the Anglo board contained more than one woman.

FitzPatrick had been acutely aware for many years of the potential to make money from the growing class of genuinely wealthy individuals in Celtic Tiger Ireland. In 1998 Anglo set up a private bank in Dublin to manage investments for rich customers – some of whom were getting richer with each Anglo-financed property deal. The business was run initially by Tony Campbell, who had worked closely with Paddy McKillen developing the Jervis Shopping Centre.

Anglo had an advantage over the growing private-client divisions of the stockbroking firms. The bank could take a lump sum from a group of customers, make it bigger with loans from the banks, and invest the money in properties – often shopping centres or office blocks – identified by its most successful borrowers.

Such was the success of the private bank that Anglo looked to expand this part of the business further. In 2001 the bank bought out a Swiss private bank, Banque Marcuard Cook & Cie, for €85 million. This was O'Mahoney's brainchild. The aim was to increase profits through fee income on stock and investment funds without having to expend valuable capital or funding.

★

By 2002, as the Irish property market really started to bubble, no bank was better placed than Anglo to make the most from it. The bank's client list included some of the biggest names in the business – house-builders Gerry Gannon, Seamus Ross of Menolly Homes, the Bailey Brothers and Sean Mulryan of Ballymore Properties; Treasury Holdings and its owners Johnny Ronan and Richard Barrett; shopping centre developer Joe O'Reilly; and Cork developers Michael O'Flynn and John Fleming.

Anglo's clients were particularly dominant in greater Dublin. Menolly Homes was prolific in west Dublin. Gerry Gannon and the Bailey brothers were prominent in north Dublin, while Joe O'Reilly and the Cosgrave brothers built housing estates in the south of the city. McGarrell Reilly, the company owned by Cavan builder Sean Reilly, was prominent around Ratoath in Co. Meath and Lusk and Malahide in north Co. Dublin.

One of the bigger projects that Anglo bankrolled for Gannon was a residential and shopping development styled as a new village centre being built at Applewood in Swords. Constructed between 1999 and 2005, the development was vast, involving close to 1,000 homes and 14,000 square metres of commercial space. After ferocious internal debate, the bank decided to lend Gannon 100 per cent of the cost of the project. Gannon offered the bank a share of the profits and a full personal guarantee. The bank was comfortable with the deal, given Gannon's track record in development and the size of his net worth and scale of his various assets, which at the time included large land banks in north Co. Dublin worth hundreds of millions.

Anglo was also happy that Gannon was to pay an interest margin of about 3 per cent – even higher than most other developers on Anglo's books – as well as the bank's usual 1 per cent arrangement fee. Unlike other borrowers, Gannon never complained to the bank about its high margins. By 2007, his company Gannon Homes was among Anglo's top five borrowers with debts of close to €1 billion.

Anglo was bullish about the Applewood development's prospects because the deal came at a time of huge demand for houses, particularly in north Co. Dublin. Tom Browne pushed hard for the 100 per cent loan, and won out. One former Anglo lender says that the success of the Applewood project was one of the reasons Browne's career took off at Anglo. The fees and share of the profits for Anglo amounted to at least €20 million, and Gannon paid substantial interest to Anglo on its loans.

In the late 1990s, 100 per cent lending on development projects was still rare. FitzPatrick was not comfortable with 100 per cent lending, and was still not as keen on development lending as he was on leased investment properties. With development lending, the bank would not be repaid until a project was completed, whereas a leased investment property generated income from rents and earlier repayments.

Bankers always want builders to put 'skin in the game': invest their own cash in development projects. But, in a quickly rising market, developers liked 100 per cent loans because they felt it didn't make sense to freeze cash in deals that were constantly generating profits.

Development finance normally involved two loans – one to buy the land and another to build the project. Anglo's policy was to insist that the customer put up 35 per cent of the land purchase in cash; the bank would provide the remaining 65 per cent. For the construction loan, the bank wanted cash amounting to 25 per cent of the loan from the developer in return for funding the remaining 75 per cent.

The construction loan was drawn down in stages. The developer might plan to sell fifty houses in a planned development of one hundred. Using the first draw-down of the loan, he would finish the show houses, the roads and the landscaping in the development and launch the project one weekend with some fanfare in the property supplements of the national newspapers.

The insatiable demand for houses among the general public – fuelled by the easy access to cheap mortgages at other banks – meant that developers often sold every house on the development during the launch weekend. With one hundred sales contracts signed and deposits paid, the developer would then be able to draw down the remainder of the construction loan using the paper profit on the project.

In some cases the profit was huge. For example, on a house sold for €500,000, the site cost might amount to €175,000 per house and the construction and other costs come to €215,000, leaving a net profit of €110,000 for every unit.

For the biggest borrowers who had multiple projects on the go, Anglo developed a different approach. In many cases, the bank waived the 25 per cent cash requirement on the next project, relying instead on an 'equity release' of the paper profit accumulated in the previous one. This meant that the bank was, in effect, taking 100 per cent of the risk in the next project, though it would claim that it had other security, such as the power to seize assets. As repeat customers came to account for an ever greater proportion of Anglo's development book, 100 per cent lending increasingly became the norm for the bank.

This was high-risk lending and far from best practice in banking. It was built on an assumption of ever-rising asset values and would leave the bank terribly exposed in the event of a property downturn. But as other banks began targeting Anglo's customers, its fear of losing business forced the bank deeper into 100 per cent lending.

'Equity releases were a real problem and were always frowned upon at credit committee, but too many exceptions were made because of competition,' says a former senior Anglo insider. 'If a client had equity tied up in a particular asset and you would not lend against it, you were forcing him to bring it to another lender who would easily give him the 75 per cent of value, so it was a real issue.'

Anglo increased its exposure to customers and the property market even further by offering to provide the equity component in both property investment and development deals through customers at Anglo's private bank. In many cases this share too was funded by loans from the bank, so the bank was taking 100 per cent of the risk.

Anglo believed it was protecting itself by taking additional security against all its customers in the way it approved loans. To get a few more hooks in a borrower, Anglo would require as collateral other assets, mostly properties, held by the borrower, and in many cases it would seek a personal guarantee. This was supposed to mean that if everything went belly up – if the property value collapsed, if the cash stopped flowing and if the business had no more assets to sell – the customer personally would have to cough up.

But while personal guarantees might have provided the bank with some protection against a rogue developer or a dud project, they would not be worth the paper they were written on in the event of a serious property crash. Most of Anglo's borrowers were so heavily into property that when the bubble burst, they had nothing left with which to honour a guarantee.

As the wealth of Anglo's developer clients grew, the stories of their exploits became more colourful. Johnny Ronan, the son of a wealthy Tipperary pig farmer, was the most ostentatious of the new band of Irish multimillionaires. He celebrated victory in a bitter planning battle over one of his development projects by flying fifty friends to Italy, where Luciano Pavarotti sang for them in the garden of Ronan's villa. On another occasion he sent a voucher to his business rivals telling them that they each had a Guatemalan pig named in their honour as part of a fund-raising effort by the charity Trocaire.

Most of these developers had started off very small, as bricklayers or plasterers or tilers, remortgaging homes to start their own businesses. Now they travelled in private helicopters and executive jets, purchased extensive art and wine collections, kept thoroughbred racehorses at their own stud farms, and amassed homes in major cities and tourist resorts. Anglo made a fortune lending to these people. It charged higher interest rates and applied higher fees than other banks – a price the developers were happy to pay in exchange for Anglo's quick responses and personal attention.

'Anglo's USP was its speed of decision,' says one former manager of the bank. It was quite common that a customer would approach Anglo on a Monday applying for a loan of several million euros for a property development project and receive approval by the end of the week.

In his book *Breakfast with Anglo*, Simon Kelly wrote that he often met his Anglo lender, Kieran Duggan, at the Shelbourne Hotel, a stone's throw from the bank's head office, for early-morning breakfasts to discuss loans for property deals which would be agreed in lightning-fast time.

'Your loan approval could be done and dusted at the first meeting,' says another developer. 'Simon Kelly was right – you could meet Anglo for breakfast, get an unofficial nod and off you went.'

'Of all the banks, Anglo kept closest to you,' says another property developer. 'They would talk to you on a weekly basis.'

One former executive at the bank who did not work on the lending side says the bankers 'were around the developers, looking for deals. They got there first. The property developers were full of gossip and they would tell each other, "The person you need to talk to is such-and-such at Anglo." After a while the business started coming.'

At a time when developers and builders were bidding for lucrative parcels of land or trophy investment properties, Anglo's ability to say yes quickly – or at least avoid a slow no – was hugely beneficial to buyers. Even though the loan might cost more at Anglo, borrowers were willing to pay extra because they'd get it quickly. They knew the profits they stood to make in a rising market would easily cover the increase. As a result of its approach, Anglo left AIB and Bank of Ireland in its wake when lending to developers took off as the property market boomed.

Simon Kelly wrote that for him and his father Anglo was 'the only show in town' when it came to financing speculative development. 'John Flynn [another developer] used to say that Anglo was the first bank to allow us to walk in the front door; Bank of Ireland and AIB sent developers to various sub-divisions and specialty sections. Developers were never invited into the old establishment banks, and Anglo built its whole business on dealing with them.'

The other banks recognized Anglo's success and struggled to compete. 'The other banks may have dropped their interest rates but Anglo was still charging 3 per cent and getting the business,' says a property lender at AIB. 'They charged through the nose but if you were getting a 150 per cent return on your project in a few short years, you didn't care about paying a 3 per cent margin.' Kelly called this the 'Anglo premium'.

Another developer says that he and his colleagues liked the buzz of risk that came with Anglo. 'You were in thinner air. It was more high-risk stuff with a quicker turnaround. Anglo perhaps felt that they had a better understanding of property. They seemed more like a buccaneer's bank than a "Steady Eddie"-type bank.'

Anglo took it personally when rivals tried to poach some of the better loans. One developer recalled trying to spread lending risk on his properties in England across a few banks. Anglo blocked him. 'They had control over the equity in your deals and if you tried to take that out, they wouldn't let you,' he says. Kelly wrote that the only time in his career that an Anglo banker became upset with him was when he repaid a loan with money borrowed from AIB. (The property crash left the Kellys with debts of up to €900 million.)

One senior Anglo banker recalls how AIB would try to cherry-pick the best loans of its biggest customers by offering an interest rate of 1 per cent over the bank's own borrowing cost, comfortably beating Anglo's own standard mark-up of 2.25 per cent. 'I would tell the customer that if you want to do that, then take everything to AIB – all the land, non-recourse and all the other bags-of-shit loans you have with us,' he says.

Another developer says that one senior banker at Anglo once told him that the bank never wanted him to repay capital on his loans. It always wanted him to roll up the equity from one completed deal – i.e. the difference between the value of the property and the debt on it – and use it to fund another one.

As a result, developers' borrowings just kept getting higher and higher.

The weekly Friday credit-committee meeting at Anglo is the stuff of folklore. In the early years, lending managers feared presenting proposals to senior lenders such as Bill Barrett and Peter Killen, who had cleaned up Anglo's loan book in its early years. The two bankers would regularly tear a manager's proposal asunder.

'If Bill took out the calculator during a credit-committee meeting, you were dead,' recalls a former senior lender at Anglo.

'A fellow like Bill wouldn't take any prisoners,' says another former executive of the bank. 'In my view Bill was probably the best lender we had.'

Killen, Anglo's head of risk from around 1991 until 2003, took over chairing the credit committee in the mid-1990s after Gerry Murphy left the role. Every loan application had to be run past the committee with a written submission and a verbal presentation by the lending manager. There were six lending 'directors' within Anglo's Irish operations and about twelve 'associate directors'. Three to four teams of lenders, comprising managers and assistant managers, worked with each director. Associate directors usually had two teams of lenders reporting to them. Each team managed on average about €700 million to €800 million in loans. This was at a time when the bank was at its biggest in 2008 with a total loan book of €73 billion.

The bank's lending division had what it called 'mini-credits', a preparation meeting held every Thursday among senior lenders before they presented to the full committee the following day. Mini-credits – a type of dress rehearsal for a loan presentation to the main committee – was usually chaired by a director or an associate director in the lending division. Associate managers were given an opportunity to present a loan application. They would go through the details and then the associate director would open up the case for discussion with all the lenders in the room. Unlike the credit-committee meetings, no executives from the risk or finance teams attended; it was just lenders.

Any problem that arose with a loan application at the Thursday meeting could be ironed out before Friday. 'Fridays went well because Thursdays didn't,' says one former manager at the bank.

There was no embarrassment if a lender got it wrong at 'mini-credits', but if they slipped up before the credit committee, 'they would be killed', he says.

The credit committee met at 8 a.m. every Friday in the third-floor boardroom. Some days the meetings would last well into the early afternoon. Lenders presented loan applications that had been put through the wringer the previous day and there would be a debate as to whether the loan should be given. One of the main questions asked by the chief risk officer on the Friday morning was: 'What were the key issues that arose with this application yesterday and how have those issues been addressed now?' according to one former senior lender.

At other banks the lender would usually present the case to the committee and then leave; if the application was refused, the lender would not necessarily know why. At Anglo the lenders could see what the credit committee liked and didn't like, and tailor the loan accordingly the next time.

The committee looked at the things that credit committees at every bank look at: the strength and track record of the borrower, the borrower's ability to meet loan repayments, and the collateral being provided. There were arguments about the value of a borrower's assets and whether the loan-to-value ratio was appropriate. 'Reputation risk' was also considered. Anglo finance director Willie McAteer once overruled a loan to a businessman who ran a profitable pub chain because he also had a couple of lap-dancing clubs.

The credit-committee meetings, which FitzPatrick attended regularly until the late 1990s, often became heated. Voices were raised, there were stand-up rows and lenders stormed out.

'It was a bear pit,' says a former senior lender at Anglo. 'If you didn't get your loans approved over a few weeks in a row, they would move you off to another area such as treasury or wealth management if you couldn't hack it.'

The banking model that FitzPatrick created, under which his lenders formed strong bonds with their customers, meant that many lenders passionately argued the case for the big borrowers.

Years later, when investigating the causes of the Irish banking crisis, the Finnish banking expert Peter Nyberg concluded that the bank found it hard to say no to applications from its biggest customers: 'The lending culture was such that when applications were problematic, the mindset was "there is a 'yes' in there somewhere",' he wrote in his report published in April 2011. 'Being a relationship lender, Anglo found it quite difficult to decline a loan to any of its traditional top customers.' Nyberg found evidence of loose record-keeping at credit committees and even looser credit decisions. No minutes of credit-committee meetings were taken until 2004, and then only at the behest of the Financial Regulator, he said, and reports on exceptions to credit policy began to be produced only in November 2005, again at the insistence of the Regulator. The level of exceptions was running at more than 25 per cent a month from the commencement of these reports.

Some staff felt that there was not enough general questioning of the bank's broader strategy and its focus on property, and that the testosterone-fuelled credit-committee meetings were set up to railroad through loans to the big borrowers, whose applications would never be refused.

'It was a cross between a Nuremberg rally and the half-time talk to an American football team,' says one ex-Anglo manager. 'There were between fifty and sixty people in the room . . . The whole system was set up wrong. No one was going to dissent in that atmosphere.'

In 2003 Killen was replaced by Pat Whelan as chief risk officer and the two men chaired the meetings jointly for a year until Killen's departure from the bank in 2004, when Tommy Walsh joined Whelan as a co-chairman. Killen had been grooming Whelan to take over as head of risk for a number of years. By that stage, the bank's loan book was growing so fast that Whelan, as chief risk officer, set up a separate credit committee in London in 2005 and moved Walsh there as chair. Back in Dublin, another manager, Niall Tuite, took over the co-chairing duties.

Although Anglo bankers often found it difficult to leave the 'lending pack', which was where the most exciting action was, colleagues believe that Whelan accepted the job of chief risk officer in the hope that this might ultimately lead to an appointment to the board – as it did, in 2006.

All new non-executive board members were encouraged to attend the Friday meetings to get a feel and understanding of how the bank approved loans to clients. Until 2004, all loans required 'noting' by a non-executive director before being drawn down by a borrower. This was effectively a sign-off by a board member of the bank. 'Noting' was rotated among the board so that every non-executive director would have the opportunity to see how loans were being agreed. The practice had been introduced back in the 1980s at a time when Anglo approved a loan or two a week. In a fast-paced approvals process, this had the potential to slow the process down, damaging Anglo's unique selling point.

Senior lenders, who had high-profile customers waiting for cheques, didn't like this. They felt the exercise was pointless in any case, as a non-executive director couldn't actually block a loan or send it back to the credit committee if they didn't like it. Most lenders viewed it as an unnecessary box-ticking exercise, particularly when non-executive director Michael Jacob, who had a habit of raising a multitude of queries on loans, was 'noting'.

As Anglo's lending growth soared, 'noting' – even though it was carried out relatively quickly – became an ever greater impediment to the operation of Anglo's frenetic lending machine. In 2004 Pat Whelan decided to establish a threshold of €25 million on loans that had to be passed to board members. This didn't help matters for the big borrowers who were demanding vast sums of money to fuel the increasing demand for housing, so Whelan then decided that only loans over a certain percentage of a client's existing borrowings had to go for 'noting'. This dramatically reduced the number of big-borrower loans going to board members, but Whelan still wasn't happy. In 2006 Whelan, then in his role as head of the Irish division, tried to get David Drumm to bypass the 'noting' procedure altogether. He made his case to the board but the idea was quickly shot down.

It is not clear how many loans of more than €25 million were being approved at the peak of the property boom. But given how property values spiralled, and that lending peaked at more than €300 million a week during 2007, it is likely to have been a very large number.

The change for the big borrowers meant fewer of their loans came to the attention of a board member. Either way, non-executive directors made themselves available to sign off loans quickly, knowing the importance of a 'quick yes' for Anglo's insatiable demand for business.

A number of non-executive directors had a broader oversight of the bank's lending, receiving six-monthly reviews of the loan book through their involvement in the bank's risk and compliance committee – a sub-committee of the board. The committee comprised two executive directors and two non-executive directors and its stated role, according to the bank's annual reports, was to review 'the key risks and compliance issues inherent in the business and the system of internal control necessary to manage them and present its findings to the board'. It met six or seven times a year.

Peter Killen, Pat Whelan and Willie McAteer reported to the committee in their roles as successive chief risk officers at the bank, outlining the bad or potentially bad loans at the bank and where they saw problems emerging. The committee was chaired by non-executive director Michael Jacob until 2007, then by former journalist and public relations executive Fintan Drury until June 2008, and then by management consultant Lar Bradshaw.

Peter Nyberg reached damning conclusions on the failure of Anglo's non-executive directors to exercise useful oversight. They were experienced and well regarded in their own fields of speciality but they were not experts in banking. 'Several . . . appear to have been dependent on senior management to assess the needs for the reporting systems and procedures necessary to contain the key risks identified,' he said in his report on the banking crisis. 'Accordingly, there is little evidence that board members at the time were active in challenging the bank's approach or its pace of lending growth.' The fact that the non-executive directors held a large amount of shares in Anglo showed their confidence in its operations and their assessment of the risks taken on by the bank, Nyberg said.

As that pace of lending growth soared between 2005 and 2007, the credit committee was increasingly bypassed, according to many former insiders. Lenders orchestrated so-called 'corridor credits', whereby loans were informally approved outside the credit committee to get deals done before being formally signed off later. In some cases, loans that were rejected by the credit committee in London were approved by the Dublin committee.

'It became too busy and loans did not get the same level of discussion when the loan growth really started taking off,' says a senior executive at the bank. 'We kidded ourselves that this system really worked – we just didn't have the time.'

Sometimes, to get loans away quickly, the bank did 'drive-by' valuations and back-of-the-envelope calculations. The assumption underlying this cursory scrutiny was that the borrowers were safe credit risks, having built up hundreds of millions of euros' worth of equity from rising property values.

Not every deal flew through the credit committee unopposed. One proposal that caused some discomfort was a loan to Roy McCabe, the owner of a pharmacy chain, to buy the 400-year-old Farnham Estate in Cavan for the development of a hotel and golf course. McCabe bought the estate for €6.35 million in 2001 before starting construction on the site in 2005. Some senior lenders argued that the project was outside McCabe's area of expertise and questioned whether an up-market hotel and golf resort in a rural area in the border county of Cavan could be successful. The bank also had a large number of high-end golf courses on its books. One lender argued in the credit committee that he felt the project was an ego trip for McCabe. A loan on the project was rejected three times by the committee. McCabe eventually got a hearing with David Drumm, and after the developer offered to provide additional security and sell off some sites for houses to be built on the grounds of the estate, Anglo agreed to fund his golf resort. Anglo gave loans of about €60 million to McCabe's holding company, which owned the pharmacy chain and the Cavan resort. A significant portion of the debt went on the Farnham project.

Anglo's lenders were also concerned about getting involved in financing businessman Barry O'Callaghan and his company, education software provider Riverdeep, later Education Media & Publishing Group (EMPG), to acquire publishers Houghton Mifflin and Harcourt in 2006. Some of Anglo's loans were secured on the debts due to the group from its customers. A former member of Anglo's inner circle describes the River-deep deal as 'so far outside our comfort zone'.

The bank was right to be concerned. Heavy borrowings amounting to $7 billion drawn to create EMPG (later renamed Houghton Mifflin Harcourt) were too great and the lenders to the group ended up taking control of the business and writing off about 60 per cent of their loans in a debt-for-equity swap in 2010. O'Callaghan ended up leaving the company the following year. His borrowings from Anglo were substantial and the bank had security only on his shares in EMPG, which were wiped out in the 2010 restructuring.

Concerns were also expressed at the credit committee in 2005 about the planned redevelopment of The Square shopping centre in Tallaght, Co. Dublin, by solicitor–developer Noel Smyth. The project carried a 100 per cent exposure for Anglo as the bank did not just give the main loan on the €320 million project, but it took a slice of the action. The redevelopment got bogged down in litigation, and during the court case it emerged that Smyth's companies had borrowed a total of almost €500 million in respect of The Square on an annual rental income of just €13 million.

The advantages conferred by Anglo's ability to move quickly on big loan decisions was perhaps best seen in the purchase of the luxury Savoy Hotel Group in London for £750 million in April 2004 by a group led by Derek Quinlan. The price paid equated to nearly £1 million for each of the hotel group's 772 bedrooms.

Quinlan, a former tax inspector, had grown his own business from a small practice in Dublin giving tax advice to investing his clients' money in property developments or commercial investments where there was a tax saving to be made. Quinlan Private, based in the leafy Dublin suburb of Ballsbridge, developed a particular expertise in doing the necessary financial and legal paperwork with lightning speed to gain an advantage over rival bidders. By the time of the Savoy purchase, Quinlan Private had €3 billion worth of assets under management. Within four years, this figure would soar to more than €10 billion.

Saudi billionaire Prince Alwaleed Bin Talal was initially in pole position to take over the Savoy group. Quinlan Private had a short time to out-manoeuvre him, getting the legal and financial paperwork together and securing the loans to show the vendors that it had the cash to buy the group. Anglo wanted to spread the risk and AIB was quickly brought on board. Anglo's loan on the project totalled €468 million. It was an astonishing win for Quinlan and the two Irish banks, and a sign that the Irish property investors, supported by the rising value of their properties and other assets at home, could compete with the richest investors in the world for trophy assets.

The equity investors and ultimate owners of the hotel group included the creators of *Riverdance*, Moya Doherty and John McColgan (who would later sell on their shareholding), stockbroker Kyran McLaughlin of Dublin firm Davy, property investor Paddy McKillen, Manchester businessman Peter Green, whose family interests were managed out of Dublin, and Quinlan himself.

Sean FitzPatrick was also an investor in the early stages of the group. He was approached by Quinlan after two of his backers, Lochlann Quinn and Martin Naughton, directors of the international electrical-appliance maker Glen Dimplex, pulled out. Quinlan needed €25 million. FitzPatrick agreed to invest in a personal capacity, and brought in fellow Anglo board member Lar Bradshaw and developer Pat Doherty, a customer of Anglo for almost a decade.

The initial plan was to sell off the hotels individually, leaving a tidy profit at the end of the process. But when the other shareholders decided to sell only the Savoy and retain the other hotels for redevelopment, Fitz-Patrick, Bradshaw and Doherty wanted out. Within months of investing they sold their shares, each netting a profit of €4 million.

Anglo's business grew out of all recognition as the property boom heated up. Overall lending increased by 39 per cent in 2000, another 39 per cent in 2001, 24 per cent in 2002, 44 per cent in 2003 and 35 per cent in 2004. This extraordinary growth was both a cause and a consequence of skyrocketing property prices. By 2004, the value of land and offices had tripled in a decade, while the value of shop space increased five-fold over the same period.

The loan book trebled in size from just under €8 billion in September 2000 to €24 billion in September 2004. Deposits increased at the same rate, rising from €6.5 billion to €19.5 billion. This extended the gap between loans and deposits, which was bridged by Anglo's heavy borrowing from bondholders. By 2004, Anglo owed €6.9 billion on bonds it had issued in the debt markets. A further €2.6 billion was borrowed from other banks. Also, most of the bank's deposits, some €16.8 billion, were short term in nature, either repayable on demand or within a term of three months.

It was an astonishing rate of growth, which should have sounded alarm bells in the financial and investment community. But the success story was believed, and cheered on, by the financial markets. Anglo's value on the stock market rose from €734 million in 2000 to €4.9 billion in 2004. Profits nearly quadrupled over the four-year period to break the half-a-billion mark, rising from €134 million in 2000 to €504 million in 2004.

Anglo rewarded its staff at levels well in excess of industry average. Pay was largely based on performance, and performance was fuelled by lending growth which in turned fuelled profits.

As a publicly quoted bank with a small staff, Anglo could offer share-based incentives to employees well down the chain. This helped Anglo poach senior lenders from Ulster Bank, where stock options in its parent Royal Bank of Scotland were not passed as far down the line.

Executives in the treasury team were paid lower salaries than lenders but could earn bigger bonuses calculated using a formula based on the bank's trading profits. It was different for lenders. They received larger salaries but smaller bonuses.

The annual meetings during which the executive directors and senior management decided how to carve up the yearly bonus pot often grew very heated. 'It was not unusual for very robust conversations to take place across the table as each division head defended his decision's loan proposals from criticism of being either too generous or even too harsh,' says a former senior Anglo figure.

In 2001 FitzPatrick received a performance bonus of €952,000 to reward him for the bank's 'exceptional performance' over the previous five years and for agreeing to sign on for another three years as chief executive. This was on top of a regular performance bonus of €559,000 for the year and a deferred bonus of €190,000 from an earlier year.

Board members at Anglo had heard rumours that, given Anglo's performance over the previous years, FitzPatrick might be seen as a candidate to replace Maurice Keane, who was due to depart as chief executive of Bank of Ireland in 2001.

'We didn't seriously expect that Bank of Ireland would poach him,' says an Anglo board member at that time. 'We agreed to pay him the additional bonus so he wouldn't have any bad thoughts such as leaving. Sean was not a man for a pat on the back if he was doing a good job – the only thing that made him feel appreciated was cash.'

All told, FitzPatrick cleared €2.3 million that year, making him Ireland's best-paid banker by some distance. Over four years of bumper lending growth preceding his move upstairs to the chairman's office, FitzPatrick earned just shy of €9.3 million, of which bonuses accounted for €5.9 million.

His senior executives were richly rewarded as well. Tiarnan O'Mahoney, the chief operating officer, made €5.2 million over the four years. O'Mahoney's pay included a take-home bonus of €1 million in 2004, his last year at the bank. John Rowan, head of UK operations, made €4.8 million as a reward for growing Anglo's British loan book from €4 billion, or 37 per cent of the bank's total, in 2001 to almost €10 billion, or 40 per cent of the total book, three years later. Finance director Willie McAteer earned €4.4 million over that time.

As the bankers at Anglo made fortunes, there was a real sense that the established banks were missing a trick. Anglo was regarded as cutting edge.

'Anglo – particularly in the Irish context from a political, financial and public relations perspective – was "the new bank",' says a former manager. 'It was thought that Anglo had found a new way of doing banking . . . it was like an Apple computers or Microsoft in software.'

But outsiders looking in failed to see the risks building in Anglo as its gamble on the fortunes of the property market became bigger and bigger.

4. 'David Who?'

2004 – Anglo's value: €6 billion

Anglo's success was the source of some puzzlement in the markets and among its competitors.

'I remember looking at Anglo's figures and saying, "How the fuck do they do it?",' says a senior executive at a rival bank. 'I had developers coming into me, saying, "You guys just don't get it."' The response of several banks was to try to emulate Anglo's formula, the executive says: 'There was a herd mentality in banking and we followed Anglo.'

Some investors and analysts, too, were perplexed by the astonishing share growth Anglo enjoyed. Len Riddell, a banking analyst at Goodbody Stockbrokers (owned by AIB) and a fan of the bank, wrote in a research note to clients in February 2004: 'It shouldn't happen to a bank – doubling your money, then doubling your money again, then gaining another 20 per cent in the space of just over two years. It is not what bank investors expect.' Anglo was Riddell's top pick among the Irish banking stocks.

FitzPatrick's bank was quickly creeping up on the €10.4 billion value the market had placed on AIB and €10 billion on Bank of Ireland – and it was doing so, in part, by winning business from former clients of the big two. In 2004 AIB chief executive Michael Buckley established a 'win-back team' as part of the bank's efforts to understand why the bank was losing business. The team comprised four people led by Catherine Moroney, a senior executive at AIB. It was charged with trying to understand 'the competitive dynamic', according to one source at the bank who describes it as an analytical exercise rather than a practical one to attract business. As late as 2007 consultancy firm Oliver Wyman presented Anglo, at an internal AIB seminar, as an example to which AIB should aspire.

Bank of Ireland, though more conservative than AIB, also started to warm up to the competitive challenge in 2004. There was even a concern within Bank of Ireland around this time that Anglo could secure enough support from institutional investors to mount a takeover of Bank of Ireland, so highly regarded was it. Bank of Ireland's new chief executive, Brian Goggin, and its recently appointed head of corporate business, Richie Boucher, led a move to lend more to property developers. Bank of

Ireland was regarded as being 'light' on property and Goggin developed a more coordinated approach between the bank's corporate banking business and its branches to agree more development loans. Boucher was on good terms with many of the developers, including one of the most prolific buyers of property at the height of the market, Sean Dunne.

For its part, Ulster Bank was spurred into action after seeing a lot of staff – including its head of property lending, Kieran Dowling, and another senior lender, Niall Tuite – poached by Anglo. Embarrassingly, Hugh McNally, whose father John was an Ulster Bank director and ran the bank's corporate banking business, moved to Anglo around this time.

'You must remember that at this time Anglo was racing ahead and my shareholders were asking what I was doing about this,' says a rival banker. 'Sadly, it all came down to the fact that it was a bunch of people trying to compete . . . The market were saying that this was a new paradigm, a new model in banking – the relationship thing. Why do you think every bank in town went with the same thing to a different degree or another? It wasn't about pay or bonuses. There was natural pride at stake.'

Long-established and loyal Anglo customers didn't always appreciate the approaches from other banks.

'I remember meeting one developer during the height of the boom and suggested that the bank was willing to do deals with him,' says a former senior manager at AIB. 'He went for me: "Who the fuck do you think you are? You're Johnny Come Latelys. Where were you when I needed you to lend to me? You can go fuck off with yourself. You want my business now that I have a fortune."'

Banker turned journalist Michael Murray noted in a column in the *Sunday Business Post* in February 2004 that Anglo's new loans in one year amounted to two-thirds of all Irish loans in long-established business banking division of Bank of Ireland. Murray took the view that this rate of growth was high risk, and that Anglo was on 'an unenviable and dangerous treadmill' of aggressive loans, a treadmill from which it couldn't get off. He believed that the bank had to keep lending to sustain its incredible earnings growth. If it stopped, earnings would plummet.

'Some Anglo competitors seem to believe that they are caught between a rock and a hard place,' wrote Murray. 'If they get on the treadmill and compete on the same terms, against their better judgment, then the whole banking sector, and with it the economy, will suffer hugely when economic waters get choppier. If they don't compete, they will continue to lose market share to Anglo and suffer financially in the short term.'

Murray's words proved to be prophetic, but at the time few were worried about the prospect of a slump. The other banks' main concern was to try to keep up with Anglo.

Bankers at rival lenders couldn't understand how FitzPatrick kept profit growth up.

Mike Soden, chief executive of Bank of Ireland from March 2002 until June 2004, remembers how he and some of the bank's executives regularly pored over Anglo's figures when it published its results. Soden used to telephone FitzPatrick, congratulate him and call him a 'cute hoor' because Anglo was reporting profits that Bank of Ireland could never achieve. But he could not understand how Anglo made so much money on its loans and earned such high fee income. 'I used to always say to him that I just don't know how you do it,' he says.

Soden says that while he was happy to acknowledge Anglo's success to FitzPatrick, he was sceptical about the bank's business model: 'I could not get to grips with Anglo. I said it in my own organization: if there was ever a downturn or a liquidity crisis, they were done for – they were gone.' Soden viewed Anglo as 'extraordinarily aggressive'. 'They were making decisions at a speed that we could not countenance – in some respects they were bringing deals to their customers.'

Soden's friendly relationship with FitzPatrick didn't stop the Anglo boss from poking fun at him when he resigned under pressure in June 2004 after accessing adult websites on his work computer. A short while later FitzPatrick invited him to Anglo's annual golf outing at Druid's Glen. In his usual Master of the Universe-style speech, FitzPatrick joked that Soden had flown in from Las Vegas – a reference to a website he had reportedly visited. There was nervous laughter in the room. 'People were a bit pissed off and taken aback,' says one banker who was in attendance.

'He had the small man syndrome,' says Soden of the speech.

The year 2004 was a momentous one for Anglo, for two reasons: a major changing of the guard, and a policy decision that the bank failed to follow through on.

In January FitzPatrick, then aged fifty-five, announced that he would be standing aside as chief executive after twenty-six years in charge. 'I want a change,' he told the *Irish Times*. 'This is no surprise. I didn't want to run

Anglo until I was sixty. I want to get out and do something else before I get too old.'

FitzPatrick had a policy of encouraging his most senior executives to leave once they reached their mid-fifties. The idea behind this was to help the bank retain younger staff by creating opportunities for advancement. Barrett had left the bank in 2003 and Killen in 2004, both at the age of fifty-six.

'Sean had this theory that you should go a few years before retirement [age] and not to be hanging around for the gold watch,' says a former Anglo insider. 'It showed the young guys they had a chance to see they could rise through the ranks. But the bank lost grey-hairs like Bill Barrett, Peter Killen, Kieran Duggan and Padraic Murray. They all came out of the lending side. There was a huge gap created.'

Anglo insiders believe FitzPatrick made a mistake by staging a very public race for his successor. At this stage, he had abandoned his master plan – as outlined to the bank's chairman Tony O'Brien – to groom O'Mahoney to succeed him, but O'Mahoney was seen externally as the front-runner. The candidates were whittled down to him and three others: Tom Browne, head of Anglo's wealth-management unit; John Rowan, the head of the UK division; and David Drumm, who had been in charge of the US operation but had returned to Dublin in June 2003 to take control of Anglo's lending operations in Dublin.

O'Mahoney was thought internally to be at a disadvantage because he had not been a lender at the bank, having been in charge of the bank's treasury operations. As the profit generators, lenders held the most power.

Browne was regarded as a good lender but there was a feeling that he would not be able to switch to a leadership role, filling FitzPatrick's boots. Rowan was at a disadvantage being based in the UK, and he was not regarded as dynamic, charismatic or a motivator of staff.

This left the dark horse, the thirty-seven-year-old Drumm, in a surprisingly strong position in the race to succeed Seanie. When he was unveiled as FitzPatrick's successor in September 2004, Anglo staff were stunned. So were investors. 'David Who?' was the almost universal response to news of his appointment.

The genesis of Drumm's rise within Anglo dated back to the mid-1990s, when the bank began to receive applications from existing clients and some new borrowers for loans to fund US property. The bank was reluctant to move into a market in which it had no real presence or knowledge, but loans on US deals started to be approved and by 1997 the possibility of setting up a US office was high on the bank's agenda.

A lender at the bank, Robert Kehoe, managed Anglo's small portfolio of US loans, but when he was asked to travel to the US to research the potential for a US office, he declined. Drumm, a senior lender at Anglo at the time, was asked instead. He agreed to relocate to Boston, which the bank considered a more 'manageable' market than New York or Chicago.

Drumm moved to Boston with his pregnant wife and two-and-a-half-year-old daughter in April 1998, renting an apartment in the affluent Back Bay area. He was instructed to report back in the autumn on whether there was a place for Anglo in the US market.

He drew up a list of the top twenty property development companies in the New England area and arranged to meet them one by one. He also met all the top bankers in Boston, starting with the two biggest players in the city – Fleet Bank and Bank of Boston (later to become part of Bank of America) – to see whether there were any gaps in the market. In October Drumm recommended that Anglo set up an office in Boston on the basis that he believed there was room in the market for a new commercial lender in property. He got the green light from the board, and his first task on his return to the US was to apply for a banking licence from the Federal Reserve Bank of Boston, a protracted process that ended in June 1999 when Anglo received a licence to operate in the US.

Drumm took a lease on a small office at 84 State Street in downtown Boston. His first appointee was Ronan Flynn, a former Anglo employee who had moved to the US. Paul Doyle and Paul Brophy joined from Anglo in Ireland, and Drumm poached staff from local banks in Boston. In 2002 Anglo opened an office in New York.

The bank's deals in the US were comparatively small during Drumm's four years there. They ranged from $1 million to about $30 million on properties such as offices, car parks, and retail buildings and shopping centres, and were concentrated in New England. Drumm's largest deal during his time in Boston was the loan for the new head office of New Balance, a manufacturer of running shoes, in the suburb of Brighton to the west of the city. It was a high-profile deal for Anglo as the building overlooked the busy Massachusetts Turnpike.

In Boston, Drumm created a carbon-copy version of the model that had made Anglo so successful back in Ireland: quick approvals of loans tailored for the specific demands of a customer and the hands-on 'relationship banking' approach. Word spread that there was a new bank in town willing to provide construction loans that could be tweaked to a customer's own situation. The bank developed a strong relationship with Fleet Bank and the two often worked together on deals.

By the time Drumm left Boston in June 2003 the US loan book had grown to about $1 billion. The successful setting-up of the Boston office marked Drumm out as 'one to watch', but few in the bank would have seen him as FitzPatrick's successor as chief executive of Anglo – and neither would Drumm himself.

The background to Drumm's appointment was more a testament to Fitz-Patrick's refusal to relinquish control of his bank than to Drumm's ability to do the job. After FitzPatrick had made it known within the bank in early 2004 that he wanted to leave, there was a frenzy of speculation as to who would fill his giant shoes. Drumm believed that FitzPatrick made sure that Peter Murray, the bank's chairman, and Michael Jacob, the second longest-serving director on the board, would insist that FitzPatrick move upstairs to become chairman. Murray's term was drawing to a close. Drumm confided to colleagues that FitzPatrick had become bored in the chief executive's job and was no longer focused on the day-to-day running of the bank.

FitzPatrick established a committee of the board to oversee the appoint-ment of the new chief executive by August or September. The committee comprised Murray, Jacob and Fintan Drury, three board members who were close to FitzPatrick. He also brought in accountant Donal O'Connor, the managing partner of PricewaterhouseCoopers and a long-time friend of FitzPatrick's, to join the committee as an independent member.

The committee sought the views of the senior executives at Anglo on what the bank was looking for and who the candidates were likely to be. Drumm believed this process was to find out who would be most favoured within the upper ranks of management and that this would put O'Mahoney at a disadvantage because he was not as popular as the others in the bank.

The British recruitment firm Whitehead Mann pointed to O'Mahoney as the best candidate for the job but they found he had a 'prickly, edgy approach' and was not well liked at the bank. O'Mahoney was seen as play-ing 'bad cop' to FitzPatrick's 'good cop', and it was felt that FitzPatrick had promoted him to the job of chief operations officer with a view to becom-ing chief executive. One source close to the bank described O'Mahoney as FitzPatrick's *consigliere* and a good counterpoint to FitzPatrick. Another says, 'Sean did not like to do any dirty work with staff as he wanted everyone to like him, so he just got Tiarnan to do it,' while a third recalls, 'If Sean fired someone, Sean and the employee would come out crying. Tiarnan was different – he had no problem putting the boot in.'

Drumm, like the other executives, was canvassed for his views on who might be suitable as the next chief executive. Speaking to Jacob and Murray, he identified 'the three amigos' – O'Mahoney, Rowan and Browne – as the main candidates but he warned them about O'Mahoney. Asked whom he would choose as chief executive, Drumm named Browne. When asked if he himself would be interested in the job, Drumm gave an emphatic no.

John Rowan had been given an early indication – before Drumm was aware of it – that FitzPatrick was eyeing Drumm as his successor. About a year before the succession race began, FitzPatrick and Rowan went for a walk around St Stephen's Green. FitzPatrick told Rowan that his wife, Triona, had said that she believed Drumm was the most like FitzPatrick. Rowan felt FitzPatrick was trying to talk him out of running by suggesting that Drumm was his chosen candidate.

Soon after Drumm spoke to the nominations committee, there began to be a lot of speculation within the bank that Drumm – who was not generally viewed as a candidate – was throwing his hat in. He was being asked about it openly. Drumm felt he had to do something. He asked FitzPatrick to breakfast one morning in the Shelbourne Hotel. He told FitzPatrick he didn't want the job or even to be considered. FitzPatrick said that was fine. But the talk of Drumm putting his name forward continued.

Several weeks later, FitzPatrick dropped in on a meeting at the bank one evening and called Drumm into his office. FitzPatrick gave Drumm his signature glare and asked him why he was 'playing hard to get' on the chief executive's job. He told him that he had to make up his mind once and for all. Drumm repeated that he didn't want the job. FitzPatrick told Drumm there was at least a 50 per cent chance of him getting it.

Drumm, feeling that this was 'classic Sean' and that FitzPatrick was trying to play him for whatever reason, told his boss that he would go home, talk to his family, and give him an answer in the morning.

Drumm thought FitzPatrick was picking him not because he was the best man for the job but because he was the man FitzPatrick would find it easiest to control, thereby keeping a strong hand in the running of Anglo.

The following morning, Drumm told FitzPatrick that he would put his name in the hat. FitzPatrick lined up psychometric tests for Drumm and interviews with Whitehead Mann. FitzPatrick told Drumm that Whitehead Mann had picked O'Mahoney as their preferred candidate but that he was working on 'rubbishing' the recruitment firm's report so it would be ignored. Whatever Sean wants, Sean gets, Drumm thought.

Drumm might not have had FitzPatrick's charisma or been Anglo's best lender, but he had a strong analytical mind. Former senior Anglo executives have said that he gave a stunningly strong presentation to the selection committee.

FitzPatrick worked his magic behind the scenes, and on 22 September 2004, two days after Drumm's interviews with the selection committee, the thirty-seven-year-old was appointed chief executive, effective the following January.

A half-hour after the other candidates were informed, all staff were emailed about the appointment. Rowan was upset. He took a walk around the Green to gather his thoughts. Drumm had to attend a board meeting at which the decision would be ratified. He had never attended an Anglo board meeting before.

The meeting lasted just fifteen minutes and Drumm followed Browne back to his office. He recalls Browne being in tears and punching the wall at one stage, telling him that he could not understand what had happened. Drumm figured that Browne, like himself, may have been told by Fitz-Patrick that he had the job wrapped up.

Browne and Drumm barely spoke for almost six months after the appointment. Browne had been Drumm's boss and hadn't seen him as a threat for the role of chief executive.

After the appointment, Browne went to FitzPatrick and said that he was happy to stay on as long as he was paid the same as Drumm and this was shown in the regular disclosures of executive pay at the bank in its annual reports. It was an astonishing demand. Willie McAteer, Anglo's finance director, offered to drop his salary to the same level as Browne's to make him feel better, but Drumm refused to let McAteer do this.

In his first year as chief executive, Drumm was paid €2.354 million, including a basic salary of €663,000, an annual bonus of €900,000, a deferred bonus of €600,000 from his performance in a previous year, and pension contributions and benefits totalling €191,000. This compared with a total pay package of €1.525 million for Browne, including a basic salary of €397,000.

Drumm later remembered the sequence of events leading to his appointment in a rare interview with the author for the *Irish Times* in January 2011. He believed FitzPatrick's appointment of his successor epitomized how he operated at the bank.

'Sean is a very capable, driven and fastidious operator and was unmatched in Irish banking,' said Drumm. 'But he was also very controlling – it comes with the territory I suppose. He could not have achieved all that he achieved by being laid back. Sean left nothing to chance and particularly not the appointment of his successor as CEO.

'I would not have allowed my name to go forward for the position if Sean had not pushed me to; Sean usually got what he wanted. I most certainly would not have been appointed as CEO if Sean didn't want that. He had total control of the board. I can only speculate on why he was so keen on me but I am certain he had his reasons. He was rarely on the receiving end of anything and liked to be in control of outcomes. For my part I was not positive toward taking the job because I did not want the public profile that came with it, and I knew following in Sean's footsteps would be very difficult.'

One former executive of the bank is critical of the very public way in which FitzPatrick staged the four-way succession race: 'It was Sean's decision to run it that way. He should have kept it tight and been much more discreet. It was typical Seanie to run something in such a public way, with a big song and dance.'

'The succession race was FitzPatrick's ultimate power play,' says another Anglo insider.

For FitzPatrick's part, he told Tom Lyons that he believed that Tiarnan O'Mahoney was passed over in favour of Drumm as he no longer fitted in with the culture of lending in the bank.

'I think what killed Tiarnan [was that] we needed to continue the culture,' said FitzPatrick. 'People on the board loved the culture within the bank, they would get presentations [from the executives] every board meeting and they would just go, Jesus Christ! . . . They were seen as a level above everyone that they knew in their own firms.'

One non-executive director of the bank, the former senior Austrian civil servant Anton Stanzel, says he would have preferred Tiarnan O'Mahoney, with his background in treasury and greater experience, to Drumm: 'I always had the feeling that Sean FitzPatrick would like to have [Drumm] in that position. Sean said that he was neutral in the appointment but my impression was that he wanted him as chief executive.'

Drumm was known within the bank for fighting his corner at the credit committee when fellow lenders at the bank tried to pick holes in loan applications from his big US customers. 'David did not take no for an answer,' says a former colleague who fell in and out of favour with him.

★

After stepping down as chief executive, FitzPatrick became Anglo's chairman, replacing his friend Peter Murray and completing the move that Tony O'Brien had rejected just over two years previously. The move raised some eyebrows. Swapping the chief executive's seat for the chairman's in the boardroom was not regarded as best practice at a publicly traded company.

The Irish Association of Investment Managers (IAIM), the representative body for large stock-market investors, had been canvassed by the committee set up to find FitzPatrick's successor. They felt that it ran counter to best practice in corporate governance for the chief executive of a publicly quoted company to move up to the role of chairman. While it was common in the US for executives to hold the roles of chief executive and chairman simultaneously, it was rare in Ireland. Michael Smurfit, who filled both roles at the same time at his paper and packaging company, was one of the exceptions.

FitzPatrick later told Tom Lyons that he had held a meeting with IAIM and acknowledged that the move he proposed to make was 'anti-good corporate governance'. IAIM secretary general Ann Fitzgerald told the *Sunday Business Post* at the time that the association was prepared to make an exception as long as Anglo appointed a strong 'independent' deputy chairman as a counter-balance. No such appointment was ever made.

O'Mahoney walked away from Anglo in December 2004. Relations between him and Drumm had always been frosty. Drumm felt that O'Mahoney went out of his way to make him look small at executive meetings. On one occasion when O'Mahoney visited Boston, Drumm booked them a table in a nice restaurant for lunch.

'I had it in my head that I was trying to get on with him,' Drumm told a colleague about the lunch. 'Pere-fucking-stroika. At the lunch, Tiarnan started, "What are we doing over here? You are going to lose your shirt over here. An Irish bank in the US? What is it going to do?" Perestroika? It was over within minutes.'

Rowan stayed on for another year, but he switched off after Drumm got the job. He insisted on negotiating his departure with FitzPatrick and not Drumm, and left with a payment of €1.1 million on top of the €4.5 million he was paid over his last three years at the bank. O'Mahoney's golden parachute had been €3.65 million plus a €250,000 top-up to his pension – this was on top of the €4.4 million he had earned in salary and bonuses over the previous three years.

These were astonishing sums, but characteristic of a bank inebriated by its own success. Golden parachutes were part of FitzPatrick's culture at

Anglo. If things didn't work out with a member of staff, the bank would negotiate their departure, pay them a large sum to secure their exit and throw them a party to show there were no hard feelings.

FitzPatrick often talked about the need to make staff 'good leavers' so they wouldn't bad-mouth the bank. 'I think Sean liked to be liked and that the payments were part of this so that it didn't become confrontational,' says a former executive.

As long-established executives departed, the new ones made their mark. After Drumm took over as CEO in January 2005, he was told by Fitz-Patrick that he needed to increase his shareholding immediately to show confidence in the bank. He had 37,000 Anglo shares, which were worth about €350,000 at the time – a fairly insignificant sum for the chief executive of a high-flying publicly quoted company. On 28 February 2005 he purchased another 50,000 shares, using a loan provided by the bank.

FitzPatrick took advantage of the buoyant share price to take some gains. He raised €27.6 million by selling 2 million Anglo shares, about half his shareholding, on the eve of his retirement as chief executive. Peter Killen, who retired as head of risk management, raised €9.3 million in 2004 by selling half his shareholding.

FitzPatrick was never shy about talking about the wealth he had helped create at Anglo: 'There are a lot of millionaires in this bank and so it's really a case of pointing them out and saying "this is what has happened to them",' FitzPatrick said in an interview in 2004. 'They are able to spend that money, send their kids to the best schools, live in a nice house, buy their big cars. They are held up as role models because it is possible for younger people to achieve that.'

In November 2004, two months after being named chief executive designate and two months before taking up the position, Drumm nailed his colours to the mast, saying that he would continue to push lending growth as FitzPatrick had in the years before him. The bank had enjoyed loan growth of more than 30 per cent per annum over the previous three years.

In November, as the bank announced lending growth of 35 per cent to €24.4 billion for the year to September 2004, and profits over the half-billion mark for the first time, Drumm said that there would be 'more of the same' in the future and boldly declared that Anglo would double its profits within the next five years under his management.

The first half of the bank's 2004 financial year marked the strongest period of profit growth in its history. Anglo was milking the property boom, generating most of its profits from the Irish market.

Around this time Anglo was making waves in the British property market, and Drumm envisaged that the bank's UK business would become significantly bigger than the Irish operations within three to five years.

One big UK deal for Anglo was the acquisition of the Earls Court and Olympia exhibition halls, music venues and conference centres in London for £245 million in May 2004 by the private property fund of businessmen Anthony Lyons, Simon Conway and David Coffer. This was the biggest loan ever handled by Anglo at the time – a fact John Rowan, head of Anglo's UK operations, was proud of.

Drumm also wanted the US business to grow significantly. Other banks were starting to lend more heavily to Irish property developers and this was squeezing Anglo's margins. The bank believed that Ireland could not provide the same growth that Anglo had enjoyed in the past. But although it concentrated more on overseas lending, Anglo wasn't significantly changing the *type* of lending it was doing. Property remained predominant. It was overseas, but it was still property. The bank's profit growth was inextricably tied to lending growth, largely in that one sector.

The investment community and wider market, failing to spot the dangers inherent in Anglo's hugely skewed loan portfolio, lapped up Drumm's ambitious aims. On the day he set out his five-year plan, the bank's share price climbed 5 per cent to €16.42, valuing the bank at about €7 billion. 'Anglo was getting plenty of encouragement,' says a former Anglo executive. 'David Drumm said the bank would double its profits and the investment community said they would buy more shares. Imagine a lone voice coming out publicly against that.'

One analyst, Seamus Murphy, then at stockbrokers Merrion Capital, raised his price forecast for the stock from €17.30 to €18.50 in November 2004, saying that Anglo remained the 'top pick' of the Irish banks on the basis that the bank's management team could deliver 'superior earnings growth'.

In April 2005 Anglo split its shares in two – offering each shareholder two shares for every one they had, at half the current value – to facilitate trading in the stock and to make it more accessible to retail investors. This helped to push the share price still higher.

One senior Anglo executive, who had witnessed the property downturn in the UK in the 1990s, felt that the bank should be making the most of what it had, managing existing loans to get the best return from them but not pushing for further dramatic growth in property. He had left the bank prior to Drumm's appointment still holding a large number of shares, and decided to sell them all when he heard Drumm say that he would double Anglo's profits within five years. If the executive had sold the shares while still employed by Anglo, the move would have been interpreted as disloyal.

The housing bubble – though not yet recognized as such in Ireland – was inflating at a dramatic rate. The number of new houses being built rose from 49,800 in 2000 to 57,695 in 2002 and 76,954 in 2004.

Anglo was bankrolling most of the builders responsible for this construction boom. The bank's deepening involvement in construction and property development projects had by this point raised red flags at board level and within the executive management team. The issue had been raised as a concern in most presentations to the board by Anglo's risk department since as long ago as 2002. Anton Stanzel says that he regularly warned the bank to spread its risk out of property lending when he was a non-executive director between April 2001 and January 2005. He suggested that the bank should look at growing its treasury and private banking businesses instead. He raised the matter during informal talks on the board's annual 'strategy days', when the board and executives would discuss Anglo's future direction.

'They listened, but the focus was just on property because it was so successful,' says Stanzel. 'It is very difficult to tell people that an area of lending is very, very dangerous when you have such success.' Stanzel admits, however, that he 'would never have foreseen a crisis' on the scale of the one that began to unfold in 2008.

Around the middle of 2004, Anglo's management team started to become particularly alarmed at the rate of growth in land values and some other sectors in Ireland, including the pub trade. Anglo's involvement in land and development – the higher-risk end of the property market where projects could take years to produce income – amounted to more than 20 per cent of the bank's loan book that year, according to the bank's own risk reports. But this gave only part of the picture: if investment property was included, the bank's lending to the real estate market accounted for well over 80 per cent of the loan book.

The internal risk team at the bank reported to the board in late 2005 that the twenty largest loans totalled €6.8 billion. Loans classified solely as 'property development' totalled €649 million, or less than 10 per cent of the biggest twenty while loans defined as 'property development/investment' totalled €5.8 billion, or 85 per cent. Based on these figures, it was clear that if the largest loans were reflective of the bank's wider lending – and Anglo executives confirmed they were – a crash in the property market would be enough to bring it down.

Drumm feared that the bank's exposure to land and development was too high and decided that it should be trimmed to 20 per cent as soon as possible and eventually capped at 15 per cent. The bank decided to accept no new customers in this area and changed its lending criteria so that lending to existing customers in this area would be limited.

However, the rules were largely ignored. The bank was entwined so heavily with its top borrowers that it was unable, or unwilling, to turn off the tap of new lending to them and break the banking mould that had brought such success.

When declaring its annual and half-year results the bank was always keen to stress to investors that it had a healthy 'pipeline' of new loans agreed; that its continually growing lending would, in time, feed into future profits. The pipeline was closely monitored by investors and bank analysts to gauge the bank's future profitability. Pulling back from one of the bank's biggest areas of lending – development – would have left the pipeline looking less bountiful and sent out a warning signal that the bank's future profitability was in question.

Simon Kelly recalled in *Breakfast with Anglo* that Joe McWilliams, a lending director in the bank, had been assigned to manage the loans to him and his father with a brief 'to slow down the juggernaut' and 'deliver a soft landing'. Kelly said that to this end he wanted to sell an office building the Kellys owned on Burlington Road in Dublin 4 but that McWilliams was uncomfortable with the idea.

'I was attempting to sell some buildings and pay [the bank] off, and they were still trying to hold loan assets and increase profits . . . To achieve and sustain growth, clients like me had to keep borrowing more and more money. This was fine in theory, but in practice the quality of the deals was getting worse. The growth was not compatible with prudent lending and cracks were appearing,' Kelly wrote.

In an interview in October 2010 with the *Sunday Independent*, Drumm said that he was haunted by the bank's failure to pull back from the most high-risk categories of property lending as it had planned to in 2004. 'One thing that goes around and around and around in my mind is that we made a decision in 2004 to reduce our land and development exposures, particularly in Ireland, because right at that time we saw intense competition coming in from other banks, we saw land prices going up at a ridiculous rate, and we made a conscious decision to pull back from it. We failed to execute on our own plan, and we never pulled back. That was because of the strength of the relationship, we just had very strong, long-standing relationships with our borrowers and we couldn't stand back from them. If I think back about that time and what we could have done differently – I can't get away from thinking about that quite frankly.'

It was an astonishing admission of failure. It shocked Anglo's former chairman Gerry Murphy, who says: 'What he was saying was that the bloody customers were running the bank – not the board of the bank. I thought that was an incredible statement . . .'

The nature of land and development lending meant that once Anglo had agreed to bankroll a project, it was very hard to pull back. 'If you give a developer money to buy a field and you give them money to put the infrastructure in place such as drainage and sewers, then you have to lend them money to build houses. You have to follow through,' one former senior Anglo manager explains.

In internal discussions, Anglo bankers tried to dwell on the difference between loans provided on development land where there was no immediate prospect of repayment and development where houses and apartments had been pre-sold and were awaiting completion before the developer could start paying down the loan. The bank saw different risks between the two – there would be little prospect of the loans being repaid in the short term in the former but a greater chance of an earlier repayment in the latter. The explanation was provided to try to convince themselves that the risks were not as great as many outside the bank later assumed.

While the decision to reduce the level of property lending may have been made at the highest level, senior lenders continued to seek approval for proposed development deals at the credit committee. Many were successful for a variety of reasons but most often because the deal involved a long-standing customer who had substantial net worth, a solid track record in development projects and a vast array of assets that the bank believed could be seized if the project ran aground. Others were approved because they offered Anglo big profits that would maintain Anglo's soaring growth rate – Drumm's objective for the bank.

'In 2004 they saw that they were too heavily into property and a flag went up,' says one former Anglo executive. 'But in 2004 you would have to stop the game completely for a bank not to have any problems now, given the crash that the country has experienced. Drumm would have lost his job overnight.'

Anglo, like the other Irish banks, had also woefully under-provided for defaulters. The bank's bad-debt provisions ranged from €36 million on a loan book of €5.7 billion in 1999 to €339 million on a loan book of €33 billion in 2005. Even if Anglo had anticipated a property crash down the tracks – and there is no evidence that anyone in the bank did so – accounting rules would have prevented it from making a general provision for possible losses; from 2005, provisions had to be linked to specific loans. If repayments were coming in on schedule on a loan, the bank could not set a bad-loan provision against it.

The bank's overall exposure to particular customers and to property generally was reviewed and discussed regularly by the bank's risk management section and by the board, but they believed that the large borrowers had long and diverse lists of assets, including significant assets outside Ireland, and that this meant that the risk of these clients defaulting was minimal. Its recklessness lay in its failure to step back, look at the history of property bubbles and change its business model before it was too late.

The few voices that raised alarms about the state of the Irish property market were being dismissed and ridiculed as cranks. The economist and newspaper columnist David McWilliams warned as far back as 2003 that future generations in Ireland were facing a massive debt burden due to the mounting borrowings that were being drawn to buy property. Outside Ireland, *The Economist* magazine predicted in May 2003 that Irish house prices would fall by up to 20 per cent over the next four years as part of a worldwide tumble in the property market and that there were clear danger signals 'flashing red' in cities such as Dublin, Amsterdam and London. The International Monetary Fund warned in August 2003 – albeit in a report full of caveats – that the Irish property market was in dangerous territory and there was a 'significant risk' of over-valuation on house prices, possibly by up to 50 per cent.

Such warnings were widely rubbished in Ireland. A large number of the people doing the rubbishing, unsurprisingly, were connected with banks, stockbrokers and estate agencies. Bank of Ireland's chief economist Dan McLaughlin said that the analysis by *The Economist* was based on a number of 'specious' arguments. Marie Hunt, then an associate director of estate agents Gunne Group, said the magazine was 'scaremongering'. Aidan O'Hogan, president of the Irish Auctioneers and Valuers Institute (IAVI), warned that in the Irish market 'sitting on the fence' was a very high-risk strategy. Marian Finnegan, chief economist with Sherry FitzGerald, said that *The Economist*'s arguments were too general and did not take local issues into account.

Government officials, too, played down warnings. Officials in the Department of the Environment wrote to their junior minister, Fianna Fáil's Noel Ahern, in late May 2003 in response to the *Economist* article, saying that there were many other commentaries suggesting a 'soft landing' in the market. The officials cited research by the Central Bank, the Bank of Ireland, AIB-owned Goodbody Stockbrokers and the IAVI.

Regardless of the ferocious debate about the property market at the time, rising land values meant that homeowners who were not even speculating in property were seeing the value of their houses and apartments rising in value. When everyone was seen to be doing so well, hardly anybody wanted it to end. 'From 2002 to 2004 you would have needed a benign dictator, who was good with predictions, to stop it, to say we were heading into a storm,' says a former banker at Anglo.

Having decided to reduce its exposure to the Irish property market, Anglo entered the three-year period that marked the peak of the property bubble doing exactly the opposite, with devastating consequences.

5. 'Paddy Kelly's net worth gives comfort'

2005 – Anglo's value: €8 billion

Anglo never followed through on its intention to reduce property development lending to 20 per cent, and eventually 15 per cent, of the overall loan book. Each time the bank was approached by a big client, it agreed to lend to just one more development project. Approval would always be justified on the basis that it was a one-off, that the customer was rock-solid, that the project was a sure thing. Anglo was like a junkie granting itself one last hit, again and again.

There was little chance of the Financial Regulator intervening. The Regulator had just three people supervising Anglo in 2005, and those three people were also responsible for monitoring Bank of Ireland, a bank that was at the time substantially larger than Anglo. The Regulator was under-resourced and out of its depth.

In March 2005 development loans briefly dipped just below 20 per cent of the overall loan book, but a previously unpublished internal report by Anglo's risk team shows that by December 2005 the figure was back up to 21.5 per cent. This should have been a warning. Instead the report rationalized the increase, saying that a number of the largest loans would soon be reclassified from 'property development' to the notionally safer 'property investment'. There was some logic to this: as a development project matures from a speculation on a greenfield site to the selling or renting of homes, offices or commercial premises, the riskiness of the bank's loan diminishes. If Anglo had allowed its development loan book to mature in this way, without making risky new-development bets, the character of the loan book would indeed have changed. But the focus remained on funding the next transaction, often with the rolled-up equity from the previous deal. Anglo continued to support its established clients' new development projects, and its exposure to a potential property crash only grew more extreme.

The bank was also breaking another of its key rules. Anglo was not supposed to lend more than 1 per cent of its total loan book, or 'risk assets', to any one borrower or linked group of borrowers.

Table 5.1 shows a list of the twenty largest borrowers at Anglo in

December 2005. They are ranked in order of approved loans, but the table also shows how much of that money had been drawn down. For the purposes of assessing the bank's exposure, Anglo took the loan limit as the more important figure on the assumption that the borrower would eventually draw down the full amount.

Table 5.1: Top twenty borrowers, December 2005

Borrower	Loan limit	Drawn	% of risk assets
Sloane Blackfriars	€614m	€527m	1.5
Castlethorn Construction (Joe O'Reilly)	€574m	€400m	1.4
Ballymore Properties (Sean Mulryan)	€564m	€249m	1.3
Gannon Homes (Gerry Gannon)	€537m	€501m	1.3
Gerry Barrett	€473m	€389m	1.1
Joe O'Reilly	€473m	€277m	1.1
Westark Properties	€468m	€461m	1.1
Somerston Hotels	€430m	€430m	1.0
Belfast Office Properties (Paddy McKillen and Padraig Drayne)	€423m	€416m	1.0
Vendart (David Pearl)	€418m	€418m	1.0
A. Brooks Properties	€378m	€364m	0.9
Dawnay Shore Hotels plc	€365m	€344m	0.9
Tiger Properties	€350m	€327m	0.8
AIAC – Whitgift	€343m	€328m	0.8
John Lally	€331m	€195m	0.8
Rambridge (Liam Carroll)	€330m	€195m	0.8
Kilquane	€318m	€293m	0.8
Q Hotels	€315m	€156m	0.8
Quinn Group Family Properties	€285m	€285m	0.7
Bernard McNamara	€284m	€259m	0.7
TOTAL	€8.273bn	€6.814bn	

The bank's risk team reported 'no issues' with the twenty largest borrowers.

As the table shows, the biggest borrower at the bank in December 2005 was Sloane Capital, the property-investment business set up by Limerick businessman Aidan Brooks and backed by racing and bloodstock tycoons J. P. McManus and John Magnier, two of the richest men in Ireland. (In the loan book, Anglo listed Sloane's debts under the name 'Sloane Blackfriars', a reference to the landmark corporate headquarters of consumer goods company Unilever on the Thames embankment next to Blackfriars bridge, which Brooks, Magnier and McManus purchased for £170 million in 2004.) Brooks had started out working at his father's television repair business in Limerick before renovating town houses and then embarking on larger projects in some of the more run-down areas of his native city, such as the Howleys Quay development. Surging property values made him a major player as, backed by McManus and Magnier, he snapped up other high-profile investment properties in the UK and the US.

Separate from Sloane Capital, Brooks's company A. Brooks Properties had a further €364 million drawn from the bank out of a limit of €378 million.

Developer Joe O'Reilly had €400 million drawn from the bank through Castlethorn Construction, the company behind the Dundrum Shopping Centre in Dublin. O'Reilly had drawn a further €277 million personally. These were the bank's second and sixth largest loans. Here again financial sleight of hand in Anglo's analysis kept O'Reilly's Castlethorn and personal borrowings separate in the risk report. Combined, the loans amounted to 2.5 per cent of the bank's risk assets.

Such manipulation on the part of Anglo wasn't restricted to its treatment of O'Reilly. The bank acted similarly regarding loans to Paddy McKillen. The norm at other banks was that any exposure to a single borrower – whether acting in a personal capacity or as a company owner or both – would be grouped as one exposure in any risk report. Anglo's distinction between personal and company exposures was highly unusual, particularly in a report whose notional purpose was to assess risks.

Sean Mulryan's Ballymore Properties was the third largest borrower on the Anglo list, with loans of €249 million and up to €564 million available to be drawn upon. Mulryan was followed by Gannon Homes, the housebuilding company owned by developer Gerry Gannon, which had loans approval for €537 million. Galway developer and former schoolteacher Gerry Barrett, owner of shopping centres in Galway and Drogheda and a chain of hotels, was Anglo's fifth-largest borrower with loan approval of €473 million, of which €389 million had been drawn down. Westark Properties, the company used by the investors gathered by Dublin financier Derek Quinlan to purchase the Maybourne Hotel Group in 2004, was the seventh largest borrower at the bank with loan approval of €468 million. At this stage, this was the only major exposure relating to Quinlan among the top twenty exposures. Quinlan would have been among the bank's most active customers but did not feature personally among the top twenty borrowers because most of his investments were made through partnerships or joint ventures.

Tiger Properties, a joint venture company co-owned by Cork developer Michael O'Flynn, was thirteenth on the list. Galway developer John Lally, fifteenth on the list, was at that time growing in prominence in the Dublin property market. He developed the Hilton Hotel in Kilmainham and owned the former stately home Humewood House, on 450 acres in Co. Wicklow.

Liam Carroll, famous as the most prolific builder of apartments in Dublin, featured at number sixteen through his company Rambridge, which had large tracts of land in the Dublin docklands, including on Sir John Rogerson's Quay on the south bank of the Liffey. Carroll's borrowings from Anglo would later increase to include loans for the construction of a new 236,000-square-foot head-office building for the bank on North Wall Quay in north Dublin docklands. Anglo had loaned about €40 million for this project and had agreed to provide a further €68 million to fund the construction of the building.

Carroll was a relative newcomer to Anglo, and when he won the contract to develop the bank's new head office in 2006, Treasury Holdings and Paddy Kelly – loyal and long-standing customers of the bank – were furious that they had lost out on a lucrative contract awarded by *their* bank to a developer who was not seen as part of the Anglo club. Carroll's site was picked by Anglo as its preferred location because he offered the bank an extremely keen rental deal (about €30 per square foot as opposed to a market average of about €60–65) and was willing to make an enormous contribution to the fitting out of the building.

One of the reasons Carroll had never previously done much of his financial business with Anglo was that he refused to pay Anglo's unusually high interest margin. He even considered borrowing from Bank of Ireland to complete Anglo's new head office – something that would have been deeply embarrassing for Anglo. The bank eventually agreed to drop its margin to a lower level to finance Carroll's construction of the building.

According to the internal risk report, the family of Sean Quinn had drawn €285 million in loans for the personal family investments, which included office blocks, shopping centres and warehouses in Turkey, Russia and India. Quinn, who had become an Anglo customer after the bank acquired the Smurfit Paribas loan book, was best known for his building materials and insurance businesses, but by 2005 he was also a major property player, as the Anglo list makes clear.

Belfast Office Properties was jointly owned by Paddy McKillen and Padraig Drayne, the developers of the Jervis Shopping Centre in Dublin city centre. Vendart, the tenth largest borrower, was a property company controlled by the London-based David Pearl, vice-president of English Premier League football club Tottenham Hotspur, who was estimated to be worth £233 million in 2009, ranking him in 241st position in the Sunday Times Rich List. Anglo financed 231 properties he owned in the UK with about 800 tenants.

Also among the top borrowers was Anglo's own property investment vehicle, Anglo Irish Assurance Company (AIAC), which had drawn €328 million from clients of the bank's wealth management division in a joint venture project with Frank Gormley's Howard Holdings to buy the Whitgift Shopping Centre in Croydon, near London, one of the biggest shopping centres in the UK. Several weeks after the list was drawn up, the Whitgift featured prominently in the bank's annual report for the year to September 2005.

Anglo was in breach of its own 1 per cent lending limit on the top seven borrowers, and a further three clients were right at the limit, but the bank's executives were unperturbed: 'We remain comfortable with the exposure as these deals are typically in very strong locations with good covenants and are supported by high net-worth individuals,' said the bank's December 2005 report. The risk report noted that the top twenty relationships at the bank accounted for 18.5 per cent or €6.9 billion of Anglo's loan book.

One figure jumps out of the report, showing the extent to which Anglo was bankrolling land speculation among its biggest borrowers. The percentage of the top twenty loans secured on land jumped from 4.8 in November 2004 to 12.2 in November 2005. This was a massive leap, but it did not seem to bother the bank's executives or the risk team. This was a dramatic explosion of lending for the most speculative kind of development during precisely the period when the bank had supposedly decided it must pull back in this area. The report should have set off alarm bells. It didn't.

Anglo's loan book was growing at a little under €1 billion a month. Loans had grown from €24.4 billion in September 2004 to €28.7 billion in

March 2005 to €34.4 billion in September 2005 to €36.9 billion in November 2005. By any measure, this was an extraordinary rate of growth.

As Anglo was circulating its internal risk report within the bank, David Drumm announced pre-tax profits of €685 million, an increase of 36 per cent on the previous year. Drumm said that the bank would be paying a 20 per cent increase in its dividend to reward the bank's shareholders.

The risk report showed that the bank was following Drumm's strategy of growing lending faster in the UK and the US than in Ireland. (In August 2005 he had said that he expected Anglo's UK business to become significantly bigger than its Irish operations within three to five years.) The fastest-growing region was North America, where Anglo had written an 86 per cent increase in loans over the past year. Reflecting the skyrocketing wealth of the bank's customer base, its wealth management division grew in percentage terms by more than any other in Anglo.

Table 5.2 lists the geographical breakdown of the bank's loan book at September 2005, according to the internal risk report:

Table 5.2: Loans by area, September 2005

	Loans	% increase over one year
Dublin	€13.4bn	31
Area offices in Ireland	€4.3bn	56
London	€8.6bn	25
UK area offices	€3.7bn	30
Wealth management	€1.9bn	100
North America	€2.5bn	86
TOTAL	€34.4bn	41

Anglo categorized €195 million of loans – or just 0.5 per cent of the total of €34.4 billion – as non-performing, meaning the borrower was not meeting loan repayments as agreed. The number of so-called 'watch cases' – loans which showed some signs of stress but which were still being repaid – stood at €517 million or just 1.4 per cent of the loan book, and this percentage had actually been falling. These figures confirmed 'the strong asset quality inherent in the book', the risk team said.

The continuing boom in the property market had made the bank complacent. Its thinking was that if the bank lost €1 million on a loan that was not fully repaid, it didn't matter because it had security over the property, which it could sell at a premium of at least €1 million in a rising market, covering the loss. 'Every bank had issues but in a rising market they will be covered by the increase in values,' says a former Anglo insider. 'It should have been a horrendous problem but it wasn't.'

One of the ways in which Anglo blinded itself to the big-picture dangers of a property downturn was by splitting hairs within its development portfolio. Willie McAteer, Anglo's finance director, always argued that there were different types of development lending and that some areas were riskier than others. For example, Anglo had backed many development projects in which the building had been pre-let to a blue-chip tenant such as a government agency or financial institution (then regarded as a solid tenant to have) or where a large number of houses or apartments had been sold off plan, and its loans towards such projects were considered rock-solid.

The bank's March 2006 risk analysis for the first time broke down its exposure to development lending into six categories:

land that had not been zoned for development;
land with zoning for development but no planning permission;
land with planning permission for development;
speculative development where construction was taking place and
    buildings had not been pre-sold or pre-let;
development where part of the project had been pre-let or pre-sold;
    and
development where the buildings were fully sold or pre-let.

Anglo wasn't completely heedless; it was just heedless of the big, existential threat of a property crash. The bank's lenders were very attentive to smaller, project-specific dangers. According to the December 2005 risk report, the bank reviewed a €4.8 million loan given to the Leas Cross nursing home in north Co. Dublin. Leas Cross had hit the headlines when it was the subject of a landmark investigation by RTE current affairs programme *Prime Time Investigates*, which showed sub-standard living conditions at the home amid allegations of abuse and neglect of elderly residents by care staff. The home eventually closed following a public uproar. Anglo noted that its owner, John Aherne, was meeting his loan repayments and that he would be able to clear the bank's debt in full once the property was sold, but the scandal at Leas Cross prompted Anglo to look at its wider exposure to the nursing home sector. It had loans of €38.9

million on thirteen nursing homes, and the review concluded that it should have no major concerns.

One property that haunted Anglo for years was a sixteen-storey office block called Pentagone Plaza in Clamart, just south-west of Paris. The bank had a loan of about €50 million on the property. It was discovered that there was asbestos in the building, which had to be removed at huge expense. Only seven floors of the building were ever let despite massive spending on marketing.

The loan was described internally as 'a poisoned chalice'. 'Everyone seemed to have dealt with it at some stage – you couldn't do anything with it,' says one former lender. Finance director Willie McAteer regularly referred to Pentagone Plaza as a loan that the bank should never have agreed as it was 'outside our comfort zone' and pointed it out to lenders like a 'bold child', a former executive recalls.

The loan had originally been rejected, but the decision was overturned when Kieran Duggan, one of the senior lenders at the bank, went to Sean FitzPatrick. 'Bill Barrett was furious,' recalls one Anglo lender. 'He was effing and blinding about it being overturned.' FitzPatrick was worried that news of the disastrous loan would leak out and that the all-powerful credit ratings agencies would get wind of it and start looking more deeply at Anglo's business model. They didn't.

The bank asked Galway property developer Brian Rhatigan to help fix this messy investment. In late 2005 the bank cut its losses, put the property on the market and wrote off €23 million of its debt. Rhatigan, who had been in ill health for some time, died soon afterwards. The bank agreed to make an ex-gratia payment of €5 million to Rhatigan's estate for the work he had done for the bank on the Pentagone Plaza loan.

Another problem loan for Anglo in late 2005 was the purchase and restoration of a super-pub in an old church, St Mary's, near the Jervis Shopping Centre. The bank had provided loans of €24.7 million to publican John Keating for the project, but it was hit by cost overruns. The risk team said that the bank would get at best €15.3 million for the pub, so it wrote off €8.4 million of the debt. By 2007 the debt had spiralled to €29.5 million but the sale of the pub in September 2007 reduced this by €15.9 million.

'The fit-out cost wasn't right and Keating didn't do his homework,' remembers one former Anglo insider. 'There were bodies from years ago found under it, and An Taisce and the heritage people got involved. It took two extra years to open that pub. It went to credit committee and it was approved. Keating had this plan to buy the building opposite, put the beer and kegs in the basement of the building opposite and pipe the drinks under the road into the pub. But the building across the road wasn't included – that was inexperience. It [the additional detail about the other building] should have gone to credit committee.'

Cost overruns on development projects regularly gave Anglo lenders sleepless nights. The price of financing a large-scale development would regularly spiral beyond what had originally been expected, and this would put back the day when the bank could start generating income on a project.

One of the biggest such nightmares for Anglo was the building of the five-star Ritz-Carlton Hotel at Powerscourt in Enniskerry, Co. Wicklow, by Treasury Holdings, the building firm controlled by Johnny Ronan and Richard Barrett. The bank pumped €120 million into the project. The development ran to twice the initially approved budget and had to go back to Anglo's credit committee when the façade of the building was changed. The problems with the project didn't stop the bank from running a picture of the hotel on the front of its 2007 annual report.

Another of the loans on 'watch' in November 2005 was the €16 million provided to property developer Paddy Kelly for the hotel and golf course at Tulfarris near Blessington in Co. Wicklow. The risk team reported that Kelly was trying to buy out the other shareholders and form a partnership with 'more significant, experienced and financially strong parties'. Kelly aimed to develop houses around the hotel, and Anglo believed that the repayment of the debt would depend on this rather than any money that was likely to be made by the hotel. The risk report noted: 'Paddy Kelly's net worth gives comfort.'

This was typical of Anglo. Whenever the bank had concerns about a loan, it would always allay them with the belief that the paper wealth of a developer meant that he could repay. It did not consider the fact that, in such a highly leveraged business, it would not take a very large drop in asset values to wipe out much of that wealth and leave developers unable to meet their obligations.

As part of Drumm's efforts to diversify the bank's loan book, Anglo decided to engage in more 'cash-flow lending' to corporate customers and small and medium-sized businesses. Cash-flow lending relates to businesses that produce relatively consistent streams of income. It is, in principle, less speculative and more predictable than asset lending, where the fate of the loan is dependent upon the performance of a property and the borrower may not expect to earn income from the property for a number of years.

Anglo hired Pat Walsh from Ulster Bank to develop the bank's run-of-the-mill business lending. Anglo's biggest corporate loan outstanding in November 2005 was to Topaz Energy, a private consortium backed by property developer Gerry Barrett, telecoms tycoon Denis O'Brien and executives at the private equity firm Ion Equity, which had purchased the petrol station network and distribution business of oil giant Shell using an Anglo loan facility of €212 million. Anglo would become an even bigger lender to Topaz when it acquired the Irish fuels business of Norwegian oil giant Statoil. This was one of Anglo's better loans.

The next two biggest corporate loans provided by Anglo were €154 million to Ardagh Glass, a UK bottle-manufacturing business owned by Dublin businessman Paul Coulson, and €104 million to Airtricity, a wind-energy company set up by businessman Eddie O'Connor. It would emerge in 2010 that Sean FitzPatrick was an investor in Airtricity. It was commonplace for FitzPatrick to invest on a personal basis in Anglo-bankrolled ventures.

Anglo also financed the management at stockbrokers Davy, the bank's own broker, in their €316 million takeover of the company from Bank of Ireland. It bankrolled Setanta Sports, the Irish broadcaster which took on Rupert Murdoch's giant BSkyB by acquiring the lucrative but expensive television rights to some English Premier League soccer matches. It also funded the purchase of TV3, the Irish television station which was bought by the UK private equity firm Doughty Hanson.

Although corporate hospitality was used by every bank to drum up new business and reward loyal customers during the boom years, Anglo had its own unique approach in this area. In the early 2000s, the bank put a select group of about twenty-five customers and their wives up in a hotel in Paris before taking them on the Orient Express to Venice, where they spent another night before flying home. Belfast businessman Peter Curistan, who developed the city's flagship Odyssey Centre, and Paddy Kelly were among those who went on the all-expenses-paid trip.

Bill Barrett would often say that if the bank was charging a customer a €1 million arrangement fee – which was not uncommon – then it had to give something back. This was not a question of fairness, but of good business: during a boom when every bank was clamouring for the business of the top developers, Anglo believed that generous entertainment encouraged customers to return again and again.

'You couldn't just offer them tickets to see Manchester United play,' says one senior Anglo executive who was involved in a number of foreign trips arranged by the bank. 'Many customers had their own private jets and helicopters, and some of them would even have had boxes at Old Trafford and other Premier League grounds.

'The guy who owed you €5 million was easy – you brought him over to Old Trafford. But for the larger borrowers, you had to offer them something different, something which they would go on. Otherwise they just wouldn't come. You can't exactly take Sean Mulryan to see Arsenal play; he could probably buy the club.'

According to Anglo documents relating to 2008, the bank paid €21,000 for Manchester United tickets and €19,000 for Chelsea season tickets; €42,000 to take clients to see Ireland's rugby Six Nations away games and €26,000 for tickets to the home games against New Zealand and Argentina; and €9,000 in August 2008 taking clients in the US to Boston Red Sox baseball matches. Ten-year premium rugby tickets for the then-unbuilt Aviva Stadium at Lansdowne Road in Dublin cost the bank €140,000.

The overnight trips helped the bank find out more about a customer: 'It gave you an opportunity to see them outside of the usual daytime business meetings – how they behaved if a good-looking waitress walked by or how they held their drink. It was a good way to see how the customer behaved and whether you could trust them with a loan,' says the former Anglo executive.

The trips could also create connections among the bank's clients. One Anglo banker recalled seeing a property transaction concerning a plot of land in Ireland being agreed over drinks between two rival developers on one such junket.

One of the most expensive fixtures in Anglo's entertainment calendar was the annual golf trip to Ireland for the bank's US customers. This dated back to 2001, when Drumm had brought a dozen or so Americans over. It was seen as a good way to build up business in a new market. The junket became so popular among businessmen in New England that a rival lender at Bank of America stood up at a property conference in Boston some years later and said that if customers banked with them, then they too would be taken on golf trips to Ireland.

The trip usually took place over the bank holiday weekend in early June at courses along the west coast such as Ballybunnion and Waterville in Co. Kerry, and Doonbeg and Lahinch in Co. Clare. Anglo eventually chartered a full-sized commercial plane rather than pay business-class airfares. Putting the customers on a single Anglo charter gave the bank good access to them for the duration of the transatlantic flights. In later years, certain Irish property developers were invited to join the US customers on the golf course. The bank decided to fly the US clients to Ireland on a scheduled flight rather than on a chartered plane for the June 2008 trip. The Aer Lingus tickets cost the bank €104,000, and the clients stayed at the five-star Aghadoe Heights Hotel in Killarney, Co. Kerry, costing €103,000. Anglo also purchased silver cufflinks from a Dublin jewellery designer as presents for the clients to commemorate the trip – they cost €7,000.

Tony Campbell, who succeeded Drumm as head of the bank's US operations, was a gregarious character who enjoyed socializing with Anglo's clients. Described by a former colleague as 'Mr Charming', the Donegal man played guitar and piano, having gigged in London during the 1980s.

Banking and golf went hand in hand at Anglo. In 2001 FitzPatrick was asked by the *Sunday Business Post* about his favoured sources of personal finance information. 'For information, one of the best sources is FT.com,' he said. 'For analysis, read *The Economist*. But for the real McCoy, you can't beat the nineteenth hole on the golf course.'

In September 2007 FitzPatrick questioned David Drumm on the merits of promoting Pat Whelan to replace Tom Browne as head of lending in Ireland. The reason for his doubts was simple: Whelan didn't play golf.

Many Anglo customers were not just avid golfers but developed or owned their own golf courses – Paddy Kelly at Tulfarris and Carton House (with the Mallaghan family), Joe O'Reilly at Killeen Castle in Co. Meath, Gerry Gannon, who co-owned the Ryder Cup course the K Club, and Sean Quinn with another Ryder Cup course, The Belfry, in England, and the Slieve Russell near his home in Co. Cavan. The bank had bankrolled the development of about thirty courses in total. Sean FitzPatrick himself invested in a Hungarian golf course after he stepped down as chief executive in 2005.

(In the year following the nationalization of the bank, the new management installed by the government discovered that the bank had spent a fortune on golf paraphernalia and other trinkets to give away to customers on its junkets. The total expenditure on such items came to a whopping €1.38 million between 2006 and 2009, more than €200,000 of it on golf balls alone. One *Irish Times* reader sent me a letter in response to the story after it first appeared in that newspaper. He had found two golf balls while playing a course in Portugal, one of which he enclosed, and explained how he had found them: 'It was errant second shots at the somewhat difficult 10th hole which brought about their early demise. It would seem that the Anglo clients are as wasteful as their benefactors.')

Table 5.3 provides a list of Anglo's expenditure on trips, client gifts and other paraphernalia.

Table 5.3: Hospitality expenditure, 2006–9

Category	2006	2007	2008	2009	TOTAL
Golf bags	€11,700	€6,700	€5,300	nil	€23,700
Golf balls	€74,900	€102,900	€30,600	nil	€208,400
'False bottom' Sports bags	€61,700	€4,200	nil	nil	€65,900
Golf – misc	€20,400	€97,900	€35,000	€1,700	€155,000
Golf day	€38,900	€40,900	€22,700	€262	€102,762
Hampers	€3,400	€3,500	€3,000	€1,178	€11,078
Jumpers	€3,300	€7,500	€19,000	€4,000	€33,800
'Other'	€25,900	€31,900	€10,900	€1,300	€70,000
Pens	€33,000	€38,200	€22,300	€5,600	€99,100
Piel bags	nil	€11,200	€7,700	nil	€18,900
Polo shirts	€20,700	€5,600	€5,100	nil	€31,400
Rugby tickets	€3,700	€3,900	€767	nil	€8,367
Ryder Cup	€39,900	€19,800	nil	nil	€59,700
Stationery	€16,300	€20,900	€14,800	€3,500	€55,500
Stock – golf	€6,100	€63,000	nil	nil	€69,100
T shirts	€5,000	€1,400	€966	€239	€7,605
Umbrellas	€111,700	€58,300	€48,500	nil	€218,500
Rain clothing	€41,000	€56,800	€2,895	nil	€100,695
Windtops	€3,100	€17,800	€2,600	nil	€23,500
iPods	€14,200	€1,700	€144	€376	€16,420
TOTAL	€534,900	€594,100	€232,272	€18,155	€1,379,427

In 2008 Anglo co-sponsored a golf championship with the *Financial Times*. The competition involved companies entering teams of four and playing thirteen of the best courses in Ireland and Britain, including Royal Birkdale, Sunningdale, Portmarnock and Gleneagles. The winning teams from each match went on to play in the final at a course in the Algarve in Portugal. The bank hired English golfer Lee Westwood as 'a brand ambassador' to promote the event. Anglo's spend on the championship in 2008 amounted to €304,000.

If the bank was profligate about entertaining its customers, it was just as wasteful when it came to bankrolling them in business. One deal more than any other epitomizes the bank's reckless lending and blinkered view of the Irish property market: the purchase and proposed development of the Irish Glass Bottle site in Ringsend, Dublin 4.

The twenty-five-acre site was the largest tract of land ever to come on the market in Dublin 4, the postal district that commanded the highest property prices in Ireland, when it came up for sale in October 2006. The market was at its most frenetic at this point and there was a huge interest in the site when it was put up for sale by the Dublin Port Company and South Wharf, a company established by the owner of the site, Ardagh Glass. Anglo had financed some of Ardagh's ventures in the past, and the company's owner, Paul Coulson – a bitter rival of Sean Quinn in the glass-manufacturing business – was well known to the bank.

Property developer Bernard McNamara, a former Fianna Fáil councillor from Lisdoonvarna in Co. Clare, was approached by Paul Maloney, the chief executive of the Dublin Docklands Development Authority (DDDA), the state body set up in 1997 to rejuvenate the decaying docklands. He wanted to see if McNamara would be interested in mounting a joint proposal to develop the land.

McNamara's company Michael McNamara & Co., which bore the name of his father, was the third largest building contractor in Ireland. It had a turnover of more than €400 million and employed 500 people. The company's branding was ubiquitous on the hoardings of construction sites around the city. McNamara was also one of the country's most prolific developers. The previous year he had been part of the consortium that bought the supermarket chain Superquinn for €450 million and of another consortium that acquired the Shelbourne Hotel for €140 million.

McNamara was not keen at first on the DDDA's proposal for the Ringsend site. He suggested that Maloney contact rival developer Liam Carroll, who owned an adjoining twelve-acre site, to see if he would be interested in combining the two sites and developing them as one. Maloney told McNamara that the DDDA would prefer to work with him. (Carroll later telephoned McNamara to see if he would sell his interest in the Irish Glass Bottle site after he did a deal with the DDDA. McNamara told Carroll that he would have to speak to the DDDA, as it was a shareholder. Nothing came of this.)

Maloney told McNamara that the Luas tram line from the city centre might be extended to the Irish Glass Bottle site and that the authority would sign off on planning permission to allow a high number of apartments per acre to be built. (The developer later claimed that Maloney's representations had led him to conclude that the project would be viable and that this dictated the price that he was willing to bid for the property. The DDDA later denied that it or Maloney had made representations to McNamara which induced him to become involved in a joint bid with the authority.)

The DDDA's own research on the site, carried out the previous year, had found that the land could be valued at more than €300 million, or €12.3 million an acre, based on the number of apartments that would be built on it. It had received advice that competition for the property could push the price up to €400 million.

Maloney also contacted another Anglo customer, Sean Mulryan of Ballymore Properties, but he wasn't willing to bid as much as McNamara. Mulryan was willing to contribute only €200 million to the purchase, while McNamara agreed to go to €300 million. The DDDA, for its part, was willing to contribute up to €127 million.

The authority had legal powers to fast-track any application for planning permission to develop sites within its bailiwick. For McNamara, this was crucial. Prior to being contacted by the DDDA, he had been in discussions with stockbrokers Davy about securing tens of millions of euros from the firm's private investors to part-fund the development of the Glass Bottle site. The involvement of the state-backed DDDA, with its planning powers, made it even easier for McNamara to attract cash from private investors who were clamouring to be part of a large and potentially lucrative development in Dublin 4. Interestingly, Derek Quinlan invested in the deal in a personal capacity after the investment committee at his firm, Quinlan Private, backed away from the project, feeling the land was overpriced.

McNamara set up a company called Becbay for the deal. Becbay put in an application to Anglo seeking a loan of €379 million to fund part of the purchase price. The loan application made it clear to the bank that the DDDA was a shareholder in the company with a 26 per cent stake.

Anglo was hot for the deal – and it knew that Bank of Ireland felt the same way. Here was a huge development site in the most desirable post-code in the country in a booming market, with a government body supporting the transaction as a shareholder. Perhaps most importantly, it was felt that there was no 'planning risk' – no danger that the proposed development would not gain planning permission, or would not secure the density of apartments or shops required for profitability. The DDDA was even offering a guarantee to pay the interest and some of the capital owing on its share of the bank's loan. The guarantee was written into Anglo's loan agreement with the state authority.

Paul Maloney took the unusual step of writing to Anglo saying that the DDDA could guarantee a high building density, that the Luas tram line would be extended from the Point music venue across the river from the Ringsend site, and that he could guarantee a fast-tracked planning permission so the development would not be delayed. The bank jumped at the opportunity, even though such a huge development loan would go squarely against its supposed new policy of minimizing its exposure to property development.

'We took huge comfort from the guarantee of the DDDA. We were lending against a huge tract of "raw" land at that point, so the loan was an exception to internal bank policy, but we had a state agency underwriting it,' says one former Anglo executive.

Anglo had wanted to share the risk on the loan with Bank of Ireland, but that bank was furious that Anglo had beaten it to the punch as the lead bank on the deal. Anglo instead turned to AIB, which was more than happy to grab a piece of the pie. The banks agreed to lend €293 million – €173 million from Anglo and €120 million from AIB. Anglo senior lenders Owen O'Neill, Paul Stephens and Gavin Wyley, managed the loan, while Tom Browne was instrumental in pushing the loan application through at a senior level.

This would not be the full extent of Anglo's lending to the project. The bank had also agreed to provide a further €898 million in loans to fund the construction of 2.6 million square feet of residential, office, retail and educational space on the site. This was more than twice the space in the Dundrum Shopping Centre in Dublin. It was a gargantuan development.

The DDDA put €32 million of public money into the deal, while Donatex, a company backed by McNamara and the private clients of Davy, ponied up €57 million and another company called Mempal, supported by Quinlan, invested €46 million towards the total price of €412 million – or €424 million including stamp duty.

In return for the private clients' investment, Davy got a loan note of €62 million and a personal guarantee from McNamara to repay them if things turned sour. In addition, McNamara agreed to guarantee €45 million of cash put into the deal, 41 per cent of all interest due by Becbay and 41 per cent of all cost overruns in relation to the development of the site. He also agreed to pay the Davy investors a return of 17 per cent on their loan note or a minimum of 40 per cent after two years.

The loan provided by the investors assembled by Davy was junior or subordinated debt; the banks' loans were the senior debt on the project. The banks would have first claim on repayment if the project failed. McNamara's decision to offer the investors so much security meant that he would lose out first. The fact that he agreed to such generous terms reflected his confidence in the project. He clearly felt this was a guaranteed winner for him.

The entire deal was built upon an overriding belief that the property market would continue booming. In the document sent out to investors to whet their appetite for the deal, Davy pointed to the fact that the number of new homes being built in 2006 would exceed 90,000, a record figure. Rather than view this enormous new supply as cause for concern about future values, Davy believed that supply was still lagging behind demand, and that it would take another four years of producing more than 75,000 houses a year to reach average EU levels of supply.

Anglo ran the figures submitted to it by McNamara and had a valuation of the site done by estate agents CB Richard Ellis (CBRE). CBRE reported that the project could generate sales and rent of €1.8 billion from 2,166 apartments and almost a million square feet of office, shop and other lettable space in the development. Total costs were estimated at almost €1.5 billion, which would leave McNamara with a profit of €326 million.

Costs included €142 million that would be paid to Anglo for funding the development of the site. These sums were based on McNamara selling 1,253 two-bedroom apartments for €625,000 each and 240 three-bedroom apartments at €850,000. At the time these prices were regarded by all involved in the project as reasonable for the booming residential market. (Property values in Dublin had declined so sharply by the middle of 2011 that €850,000 would be enough to purchase a five-bedroom period house in the upmarket suburb of Rathgar.)

A more conservative set of estimates drawn up by Davy – based on 20 per cent less income from property sales and rent – still showed McNamara emerging with a profit of €128 million.

The decision to finance the Irish Glass Bottle site deal might have seemed strange to some within Anglo, given the bank's own internally stated intention to reduce its exposure to property development. But as was well established by now, this rule was largely ignored. By late 2006 the bank's exposure to development stood at 28 per cent of the loan book, including Anglo's loans on the Irish Glass Bottle site.

'Exceptions were made to the 20 per cent rule because particular deals had to be backed,' says a former Anglo director. 'The big exception was the Irish Glass Bottle site. It looked good and Bank of Ireland was chasing it as well.'

In late 2007, about a year after the project was launched, McNamara gave the Davy investors an update. He was asked about how plans to build the country's first waste incinerator next to the site would affect the development. This was not a worry, he said, as there were incinerators beside major residential developments around the world. Anyway, the smoke would blow across Dublin bay towards Howth, he added, drawing some laughter.

Almost everything that could be wrong about a property development was wrong in the Irish Glass Bottle deal. There were serious problems with the site itself, and with transport links to it. The deal was far too debt-heavy: McNamara put up just €5 million in equity, for which he was getting a 41 per cent slice of the €412 million project. And the purchase was executed at the worst possible time – just months before the property market started turning.

But none of this was evident to the principals at the time. The day the Glass Bottle deal was completed, a member of the DDDA sent an email that was circulated to the directors of the authority. It said: 'Happy Days – our pension is now secured'.

Anglo's close ties to the DDDA long pre-dated the Irish Glass Bottle deal. FitzPatrick was appointed to the board of the authority in 1998 by the then Fianna Fáil environment minister Noel Dempsey. Lar Bradshaw, a non-executive director on the board of Anglo, was chairman of the DDDA from 1997 to 2007, and remained a board member at the authority until he and FitzPatrick resigned from Anglo in December 2008. Anglo board member Donal O'Connor succeeded Bradshaw as DDDA chairman. Furthermore, the DDDA had used its planning powers to grant planning permission to Liam Carroll to build Anglo's new headquarters on the site of the former Brooks Thomas timber yard in the north docklands in July 2007.

The ties between the bank and the development authority were both strong and open. In his later court action against the DDDA over the Irish Glass Bottle site deal, McNamara specifically pointed out the significance of the fact that Bradshaw and FitzPatrick took part in the authority's board meeting on 24 October 2006 where the proposal to participate in the purchase and development of the Ringsend site was considered. Typically, directors would have absented themselves from discussions due to the links between McNamara and Anglo.

McNamara claimed that FitzPatrick and Bradshaw had potential conflicts of interest as directors of Anglo sitting in on that decision. He pointed out that they had offered to withdraw from the meeting but did not actually do so. FitzPatrick later claimed that he never spoke to anyone in the bank about the loan to the McNamara-DDDA company. He also denied that he ever spoke to McNamara, a major customer of Anglo, about the DDDA or to his fellow board members at the DDDA about McNamara. 'There is no proof of any wrongdoing because there was no wrongdoing,' he said.

At around the same time that the DDDA was eyeing up a bid for the Ringsend site, one of Anglo's biggest borrowers, Irish property developer Garrett Kelleher, announced plans to build the tallest building in the United States at a cost of €1 billion. The Chicago Spire, to be designed by world-renowned architect Santiago Calatrava, would soar to 2,000 feet above a two-acre site where the Chicago river meets Lake Michigan.

Kelleher knew Chicago well, having moved there to set up a successful commercial painting business. He returned to Dublin in 1996 and founded Shelbourne Developments, buying prime properties in the city centre and redeveloping them with the fortune he'd made in Chicago. He refurbished a large building on St Stephen's Green, which formerly housed the Department of Justice, and landmark buildings on the Dublin quays.

The sheer scale of Kelleher's plans for the Chicago Spire raised major concerns within Anglo. The loan application was not just debated at credit committee but brought up at board level, with some directors expressing apprehensions. Anglo's finance director Willie McAteer was set against it but Tony Campbell, the head of the bank's US operations, liked Kelleher and thought the bank should help him.

The bank decided to back the Chicago Spire on the basis that the loan was secured on Kelleher's Dublin properties – another vote of confidence by the bank in the solidity of its core market.

'He was a good client and the loans on the Spire were secured against good commercial investment properties in Dublin – his buildings on St Stephen's Green, Dawson Street and Tara Street,' says a former Anglo executive. 'We never really wanted anything to do with the Spire but we lent on his equity in his Irish property.'

Kelleher recruited Hollywood couple Liam Neeson and Natasha Richardson to front a marketing roadshow to help sell apartments in the Spire, but his timing was terrible. Ground was broken on the Chicago site as the global financial markets began to wobble in 2007. Work on the site ceased in 2008, and the number of debts and legal actions arising out of the project led to the Spire being dubbed 'The Lien-ing Tower of Chicago'. Anglo – and in effect the Irish state – took formal possession of the site in October 2010 after Kelleher defaulted on loans of $77 million.

Incredibly, during a two-year period when the size of Anglo's loan book more than doubled, there was no one on the board of the bank overseeing risk.

The bank's long-time expert in risk, Peter Killen, had retired from the board in February 2004. Drumm did not appoint a banker with risk experience onto the board until he made Killen's successor as chief risk officer, Pat Whelan, an executive director in February 2006. This left a serious blind spot in the boardroom for a two-year period during which the bank's lending grew out of control.

Drumm clearly didn't think the role of chief risk officer was very significant. In September 2007, when Pat Whelan became head of Anglo's Irish business, Drumm gave the role of chief risk officer to Willie McAteer – who meanwhile kept his job of finance director. McAteer retained this dual role right up until just a few days before the bank was nationalized in January 2009. For a bank that was growing its loans by up to 45 per cent a year, doing without a dedicated head of risk was reckless to say the least.

The introduction of new international rules under a succession of Basel agreements – first published in 2004 – forced banks to set more cash aside to cover potential losses and to introduce new systems to mitigate risk. The rules required Anglo to spend more on its systems, but the risk department met huge opposition from senior executives at the bank when it tried to bolster the team. 'The bank didn't want to spend money on systems that was going to stop it doing business,' says an Anglo source. 'There was serious push-back from the guys in the finance department.'

Eventually the bank hired an experienced banking operations executive, Aidan Long, in 2005, as director of operations; but, in hindsight, it was too little too late.

The lack of attention to risk wasn't the only serious failing in the bank's structure. After Tiarnan O'Mahoney left in December 2004, the Anglo board did not include a single banker with experience in treasury. The bank's director of treasury Brian Murphy, a former executive at Citibank and Dutch bank ABN AMRO, joined in February 2003 but was never given a seat on the board even after O'Mahoney's departure. Murphy left in 2006 after just three years in the job. (He joined the National Treasury Management Agency.) Drumm never officially replaced him, though the role was in effect covered by the director of capital markets, John Bowe.

After Murphy's departure, four senior treasury executives were reporting directly to Drumm: director of capital markets John Bowe, head of credit investments Paul Somers, head of retail funding Peter Fitzgerald and head of trading Matt Cullen. (Somers left shortly after Murphy to join O'Mahoney's new company, International Securities and Trading Corporation (ISTC), and was replaced by Andrew Curtin.) To have four key reporting lines passing information directly to the chief executive was dangerous.

Declan Quilligan, a board member and the head of Anglo's UK business, advised Drumm to appoint a director of treasury so he would have one person reporting to him from this crucial area of the bank. Drumm ignored the advice.

'Drumm wasn't challenged enough as chief executive, as Sean Fitz-Patrick would have been before him by the likes of Peter Killen and Bill Barrett,' says a former Anglo executive. 'We should have challenged him more and certainly encouraged him to appoint a head of treasury.'

A bank's treasury operation should tell its lending side how much it can lend, but the opposite was the case at Anglo. The lenders threw out the money and the funding side of the business had to try to keep up. Bankers like to say that their institutions are likeliest to die not of cancer in their loan book but of a heart attack in their treasury operation. This would ultimately prove accurate in Anglo's case: the cancer would have got it eventually, but the primary cause of death was cardiac arrest.

With risk and treasury understaffed at executive level, and entirely unrepresented at board level, the dominance of the lending side of the business was complete. One former Anglo executive said that the lenders were like jet fighter pilots. 'If your army gets big enough, you need more cargo guys around to do the heavy-lifting, not just the jet fighter pilots,' he said.

Sean FitzPatrick put it even more colourfully when describing the difference between the treasury and lending departments at Anglo to Tom Lyons for *The FitzPatrick Tapes*: 'Treasury got the money in, and the lenders were centre forwards,' he said. 'Treasury was about full backs, centre-halfs, goalkeepers and wing-halfs. The lending guys were all about

Lionel Messi. They were all strikers. They were the pop-stars. They were the guys who were making the fucking money. They didn't worry about how the money was got to give to them.'

Serious concerns about weakness in the funding of the bank had been raised before the 'senior executive board' – the management team that ran the bank – as far back as 2003. It was pointed out at one meeting that the bank was running a big gap in how it was funding its loans. The average duration of the bank's loans was four years and nine months, yet the average duration of the bank's funding (including deposits, bonds and inter-bank loans) was eleven months. The bank was borrowing short to lend long, which would put it in a vulnerable position if interest rates were to rise or credit became harder to come by.

When the problem was raised with the executive team, there were blank faces, recalls a former executive. Anglo was run by lenders who didn't understand how a bank should be properly funded, he says. 'They all thought it was just about lending. They thought treasury was just an unnecessary overhead. Funding wasn't part of the equation or their thinking. They didn't have that all-embracing view of how banking works.'

One former executive believes that Sean FitzPatrick retired in 2004 in part because Anglo was growing beyond his understanding of banking. 'Sean treated the bank like his corner shop – he needed to know everything that was going on,' he said. 'As it got bigger I think he needed to hand over the reins.'

Meanwhile, in a race to keep enough cash coming in to fund its lending, the bank was offering some of the highest deposit rates in the savings market in Ireland and the UK. Deposits rose by 46 per cent to €36.9 billion, but there was still a gap of €13 billion between loans and deposits. The bank filled the gap by borrowing from bondholders in the international financial markets. This reliance on the bond markets was risky, because in the event of a financial crisis, the debt markets could seize up overnight and a bank like Anglo would not be able to fund itself. Without funding it could die of that heart attack.

Anglo was not the only Irish bank struggling to fund its runaway lending. In the final months of 2006 Drumm joined a growing chorus of bankers lobbying the then Minister for Finance Brian Cowen to push through legislative changes that would allow banks to use commercial property loans as collateral when borrowing money through the sale of 'covered bonds'. These were IOUs issued by the banks and supported by the bank's assets – i.e. its loans. It was effectively a means of selling loans on to investors to generate cash to lend again. The existing legislation only allowed the use of residential mortgages as collateral for covered bonds. This put Anglo at a serious disadvantage to those of its competitors that engaged in mortgage lending.

As part of a concerted lobbying campaign – orchestrated by the Irish Banking Federation (IBF), which represented the industry – Drumm wrote to Cowen on 10 October 2006 to express concern about delays in proposed changes to the legislation.

'From the bank's perspective, covered bond issuance has been identified as a key part of its funding strategy going forward,' Drumm wrote. 'Covered bonds are a cost effective and reliable form of long-term funding that would provide the bank with access to a new investor base.'

Correspondence obtained under the Freedom of Information Act reveals that Cowen's private secretary Paul Mooney wrote back to Drumm on 18 October 2006, saying that the minister shared his view that legislative changes to the Irish covered bond market would help attract business to Ireland and help the banks fund themselves. 'Further modernization of the legislative framework for covered bonds is critical to developing the competitiveness of Ireland as a base for the issuance of such securities and also as an alternative source of long-term funding of our banks,' wrote Mooney.

The intense lobby campaign by Anglo, the IBF and others ultimately proved a resounding success. Cowen introduced the requested changes to the legislation, which included an amendment that would allow banks like Anglo to use commercial mortgages – loans provided to buy investment properties such as office blocks and shopping centres – as collateral for bonds. This was despite the Financial Regulator's serious reservations, expressed to Cowen, about the use of commercial mortgages as collateral because of their 'greater inherent volatility'.

The legislation was passed in April 2007, two months after Cowen introduced it, in what would be one of his last acts as finance minister before the 2007 general election.

6.   The Best Bank in the World

June 2007 – Anglo's value: €13 billion

On the eve of the World Economic Forum in January 2007 in the Swiss ski resort of Davos, where the leaders of global capitalism go to network, financial consultants Oliver Wyman named Anglo Irish Bank the best bank in the world.

The ranking was based on the return it had made its shareholders. Anglo's share price had risen by more than 2,000 per cent in seven years as the market capitalization of the bank rose from €600 million in 2000 to just over €12 billion at the time of the Oliver Wyman survey. If you had invested €5,000 in the bank in 2000, your investment would be worth €101,000 by 2007. Over the same period Anglo's profits increased by 826 per cent.

The consultants praised Anglo's concentrated focus on 'business lending', which the bank had grown at a remarkable rate of 38 per cent a year for the past decade. They also referred to the bank's centralized loan approval process, saying that it maintained a high level of good loans and minimized lending risk by concentrating on a small number of borrowers. In other words, Oliver Wyman appeared to accept Anglo's view of its business hook, line and sinker. (Oliver Wyman was not alone in this: Anglo had been picking up gongs in Ireland and abroad for a number of years, and continued to do so well into 2008.) The 'business lending' referred to was, in fact, almost exclusively property lending, although no mention was made of this, and Oliver Wyman also apparently failed to notice something even Anglo understood: that the high concentration of loans among a small number of borrowers was risky.

The type of high-risk lending that Anglo engaged in to wrap up the Jurys Inns deal in June 2007, as described in the Prologue, typified the bank's approach to property plays during that year. But the bank did not just operate like this on big-ticket deals. It did so across its business.

In August 2007 Michael Daly, a former accountant turned property developer in Limerick, got a call from Anglo's office in the city. One of his lending managers in the office asked whether he would be available to meet the bank's chief executive David Drumm, who would be travelling down from Dublin. Daly agreed.

Daly and his business partners in their company, the Fordmount Property

Group, had spent more than €300 million on projects in the city – including Riverpoint, the tallest building in Limerick and third highest in Ireland when it was built; the Savoy Hotel and surrounding development in the downtown area; and the Castletroy Park Nursing Home, hotel and commercial development near the University of Limerick on the Dublin road. Daly had also spent a further €100 million buying a prime building on Munich's main shopping street in Germany where retailer H&M was the tenant. Anglo bankrolled almost all of it.

During a two-hour meeting at the Limerick Savoy on the morning of 15 August, Drumm offered to finance further investment and development opportunities that would bring the value of the property deals involving Daly and his business partners to €1 billion.

Drumm was interested in Daly's plan to redevelop a block right in the middle of Limerick city centre which housed the upmarket Brown Thomas department store. He was also keen for Daly to buy more properties in Germany. The bank was impressed by his commercial property investments in Munich and was also trying particularly hard to grow lending outside Ireland; Germany had been identified as a target. Drumm told Daly that he wanted him to spend a further €500 million – about €125 million a year – investing in more properties in Germany over the following four years and that Anglo was also keen to back his €150 million redevelopment of the Brown Thomas block.

Daly explained that he and his business partners had more German deals in their sights, including one landmark property with a rock-solid tenant, but they couldn't afford the €200 million asking price.

'We can land you more deals in Munich but our problem is that we don't have the equity to do the deals,' Daly told Drumm.

'Don't worry about the equity – we will get you the money to get the deals done,' Drumm replied.

This was the first time that Anglo was offering to become a partner in Daly's deals and not just a lender. Anglo had only financed the loan on the Munich property, but the bank liked the deal so much that it wanted Daly and his partners to find a similar property on which they and the bank would be partners in the purchase.

Drumm proposed that the bank would take a stake in any more prime German properties that Daly found, sell another stake to the private clients of its wealth management division in Dublin and offer Daly and his partners what was called 'sweat equity' – in effect, the final stake in the property – in return for bringing the deal to the bank.

It was not unusual for Anglo to use cash from rich customers in the bank's wealth management division to fund transactions. Earlier in 2007 the bank had joined forces with customers to fund the purchase of The Metquarter shopping centre in Liverpool with the family of property investor John McCormack and his Dublin-based company Alanis. Two years earlier the McCormacks also bought the Royal Exchange building in London for €78 million using cash from customers in Anglo's private bank.

All told, Anglo completed about €2 billion worth of deals using cash from its private clients. It was not uncommon for Anglo to provide loans to the customers of the wealth management division too, piling debt on debt. As long as the value of the property continued to rise, there was no problem. In 2005, lending to the wealth management division was the fastest-growing part of the loan book.

By late 2007 the credit crunch had squeezed bank lending and Anglo, like other financial institutions, started getting cold feet about new deals. Nothing ever came of Drumm's overture to Michael Daly to find another German property transaction. In the end, Daly's relationship with Anglo and heavy borrowings for his property deals would prove to be his undoing after the market collapsed. Like many of Anglo's borrowers he had agreed to provide personal guarantees on the bank's loans. When Anglo sued him in 2010 for their recovery he outlined his meetings with Drumm, claiming in court that he was regarded as a 'favoured developer' in the Limerick region and that he had 'easy access' to Drumm and FitzPatrick. He argued that he had been actively encouraged by Anglo in 2006 and 2007 to undertake massive property developments with the assurance that hundreds of millions of euros would be made available. He was firmly part of the Anglo inner circle.

Daly also claimed in court that he was assured many times by Anglo's senior executives that the personal guarantees they sought from him were 'regarded as a formality only by the bank' and that they would never be called in. At one point his personal wealth was valued at €50 million and the bank had accepted a guarantee of €160 million from him. The gap between these two figures shows exactly how seriously the bank took personal guarantees.

By the time of Drumm's meeting with Daly in Limerick, the financial markets had started to turn with the onset of the global credit crunch following the emergence of the US subprime mortgage disaster. But the bank was still lending money hand over fist: an average of €346 million a week during the 2007 financial year. This was up from €300 million a week during 2006 and €179 million a week the previous year (see Table 6.1).

Table 6.1: New net lending, 2002–7

Financial year	Amount
2007	€18.0bn
2006	€15.6bn
2005	€9.3bn
2004	€6.3bn
2003	€4.6bn
2002	€2.8bn

In September 2005 Anglo's US loans still stood at just €2.5 billion. Over the course of a 24-month period the US loan book jumped by about €7 billion, or roughly €60 million a week. By 2008 Anglo's US loans, managed by 100 staff working out of offices in Boston, New York and Chicago, accounted for almost 13 per cent of the bank's overall loan book, compared with less than 5 per cent in 2005. Almost 85 per cent of the bank's US loans were concentrated in New York, New England, Chicago and Washington DC.

The bank's big US move came just as the American property market was reaching its zenith. Anglo became viewed in the States as a bank that was willing to seek returns on riskier projects that other lenders would decline.

'They did deals that a lot of other banks shook their heads at,' says a senior banker at a large US bank in Manhattan. 'They were so aggressive and they wanted to be recognized as players, as a big bank, but they weren't. They were a small regional, foreign lender.'

'They hit the New York market at the frothiest time in the market,' says a banker from a rival lender in that city. 'They developed a reputation for agreeing to do deals that other banks would not touch. They were lending on some good projects but at a time when the prices were just too high.'

A banker who worked at Anglo in the US before moving on to join another lender said the bank had 'a more entrepreneurial' culture than other institutions. Anglo's New York office held weekly credit meetings on Tuesdays, but this wasn't like the credit approval process he experienced at other banks. This was 'more a committee of peers' – there was no senior executive in head office in Ireland casting a critical eye over applications or overruling loans the US lenders approved. Final credit approval from Dublin 'was just a rubber stamp', he says. Anglo's US business was 'a deal shop – they were deal junkies'.

★

While business was booming for Anglo in the US during 2007, the property market started coming unstuck at home. Irish loans accounted for €38 billion of the bank's overall €67 billion loan book in September 2007. The bank's net new lending into Ireland was €9.3 billion during the year, an increase of almost 33 per cent. This was a massive increase at a time when the economy was already overheated.

An internal report produced by the bank in December 2007 showed that Anglo had failed to reduce its exposure to property development. Anglo's lending to developers accounted for 25 per cent of the overall loan book, amounting to €17.5 billion out of loans totalling €68.7 billion at the end of November 2007. To get the development figure below 20 per cent of the loan book, Anglo would have to shed €3.4 billion of net loans (providing fewer loans than the amounts being repaid); and it would need to shed the same amount again to meet the long-term aim of capping this lending at 15 per cent. Instead, the bank had provided a further €2 billion in net new development loans over the previous six months at the peak of the market.

Table 6.2 provides a list of the top twenty 'group limits' – the biggest borrowers at Anglo at 30 November 2007. The bank listed the loans by sector: 'property development' (PD), 'property investment' (PI), 'hotel' (H), 'tourism and leisure' (T&L) and 'glass manufacturer' (GM). The list was compiled according to the same criteria that governed the previous top twenty list in 2005 (Table 5.1).

The top twenty borrowers accounted for €11 billion, or 16 per cent of the bank's overall loan book. Ardagh Glass is the only customer in the top twenty whose borrowings did not relate to property development or investment or hotels. Judging from this list, Anglo clearly wasn't disengaging from property development.

Joe O'Reilly had drawn down a staggering €1.22 billion either personally for property investment or through his company, Castlethorn Construction, for development. He had approval from Anglo to push these borrowings to €2.1 billion. He was the bank's biggest borrower.

The bank's report on exposures as of 30 November 2007 raised a significant caveat around the listing of the group exposures. It didn't include some of the bank's 'most active clients', including financier Derek Quinlan and developer Paddy Kelly. They did not appear on the list because their debts were spread across numerous different partnerships and joint ventures.

The decision by the bank not to include these names in a report on the risks facing the bank was a major failing. 'Anglo were trying to fool themselves,' says a former executive of a rival bank. 'Our approach was to lump

Table 6.2: Top twenty borrowers, November 2007

	Loan limit	Drawn	Type
Ballymore Properties (Sean Mulryan)	€1.474bn	€1.047bn	PD
Joe O'Reilly	€1.446bn	€636m	PI
Gannon Homes (Gerry Gannon)	€991m	€909m	PD
Vesway (Jurys Inns deal/Quinlan)	€817m	€778m	H
Quinn Group Family Properties (Sean Quinn)	€777m	€719m	T&L
Vendart (David Pearl)	€737m	€683m	PI
Somerston Hotels (UK hotels)	€651m	€410m	H
Castlethorn Construction (Joe O'Reilly)	€648m	€588m	PD
Gerry Barrett	€643m	€553m	PI
Ardagh Glass (UK) (Paul Coulson)	€609m	€450m	GM
Coroin (Savoy Hotel Group)	€585m	€544m	H
Q Hotels (UK four-star hotel chain)	€562m	€517m	H
Radora Developments (Bernard McNamara)	€560m	€495m	PD
Tiger Developments (Michael O'Flynn)	€546m	€507m	PI
John Lally	€543m	€414m	PD
Noel Smyth	€540m	€519m	PI
Dawnay Shore Hotels plc	€466m	€462m	H
Belfast Office Properties (Paddy McKillen and Padraig Drayne)	€464m	€140m	PI
Trinity Walk Wakefield	€460m	€218m	PD
Curzon Hotel Properties	€458m	€425m	H
TOTAL	€13.977bn	€11.014bn	

every connection that a borrower had into group exposures to see the overall gross exposure.'

Anglo noted in the internal report that it had abided by the Financial Regulator's rules when listing the top borrowers and the sums they owed in the way it did. In the case of the top three entities on the list, and that of Sean Quinn, the bank was breaking its rule against allowing any single borrower to have more than 1 per cent of the loan book. It had reached the limit on a further two cases, including the loan to Derek Quinlan's investment company, Vesway, to purchase the Jurys Inns chain in June 2007.

One intriguing note in the report says that the bank did not roll out a new system of credit scoring of development loans to all the lenders at the bank during 2007 as had previously been planned. Until that point, there had been no technical method of assessing the risks in development lending. The bank never introduced the system it had developed because it felt that it generated 'probability of default' grades that 'were not an accurate reflection of the bank's development portfolio'. In other words, Anglo's lenders were not getting the results they wanted from the grading system, so the system was shelved.

Some interesting names emerge on the bank's loan book to the corporate and small and medium-sized business sector as listed in another part of the report. They include Bannatyne Fitness, the chain of health clubs owned by entrepreneur Duncan Bannatyne, one of the 'Dragons' on the BBC business programme *Dragons Den*. He had drawn €207 million from Anglo at November 2007. Another addition to the list was a loan of €208 million provided to the investment company FL Partners, run by corporate financier Peter Crowley, for the purchase of the horseracing newspaper the *Racing Post* and its website.

Table 6.3 provides a list of the top ten borrowers in Anglo's corporate and small and medium-sized business loan book that month.

The report acknowledged a slowdown in the Irish property market, noting that slowing sales had caused 'cash-flow pressure for some developers' and that if there wasn't a recovery, 'we would expect further issues as well as deterioration in existing "problem cases"'.

But the report papered over the cracks. 'Our exposure to the [Irish

Table 6.3: Top ten corporate, small and medium-sized borrowers, November 2007

Name	Loan limit	Drawn	Sector
Ardagh Glass	€610m	€450m	Manufacturers/glass
Topaz Energy	€429m	€317m	Oil/petrol stations
PD Parks	€353m	€317m	Caravan parks
Green Note	€350m	€325m	Financial services
Acision	€248m	€228m	Mobile phone technology
Bannatyne Fitness	€237m	€207m	Health clubs
Racing Post	€219m	€208m	Newspaper/website
TV3	€162m	€129m	Television station
Airtricity	€159m	€131m	Wind farms
Acorn Care	€133m	€99m	Special needs schools

property] sector has reduced due to a combination of our own concerted efforts, and prudent scaling back of activities by our customers. In an overall sense, we remain comfortable with our lending in the sector, as our underwriting criteria has consistently been to back the right people in good locations.'

The Financial Regulator, meanwhile, had grown concerned about the exposure of the Irish banks to property developers. In December 2007 Patrick Neary, the chief executive of the Regulator, sent inspectors to look at how five banks handled five large borrowers in commercial property. It was known as the 'five by five big developer exposure inspection'.

The findings of the inspection were made public in a report by Central Bank governor Patrick Honohan in May 2010. They showed how much trust the banks placed in 'unverified assertions' by the borrowers on their personal wealth and how inaccurate the information used by the banks was. The banks had been unable to obtain a net worth statement from one big borrower while statements by another two had not been verified.

The inspection showed that the banks had only a sketchy understanding of the total debts of each borrower across all of the banks. One bank believed that one of its borrowers had debts of several hundred million, while another bank provided data to show that the borrower in fact had debts in excess of €1 billion. The Regulator found that one unidentified bank relied on management estimates of property valuations. One borrower had included as part of his net worth a loan of €100 million provided by one of the banks.

Honohan's findings were damning of the Regulator. 'Despite this catalogue of banking deficiencies, the full implications of the obvious lesson – that loan appraisal had been wholly inadequate and personal guarantees could not be relied upon – does not appear to have been taken on board by the regulatory system,' he said in his report. The Regulator did not understand that the solvency of the banks could be at risk given the declining value of collateral, which must have been clearly in prospect. But the findings of the 'five by five' did not appear to concern either the Regulator or the banks. Honohan found that they 'remained fairly relaxed' about them – the post-inspection meetings between the Regulator and the banks lasted just twenty to thirty minutes.

While the Regulator was looking, however half-heartedly, at the big development loans in late 2007, the focus of senior Anglo management was elsewhere.

7. The Richest Man in Ireland

11 September 2007 – Anglo's value: €10.3 billion

The Ardboyne Hotel in Navan, Co. Meath, is known for hosting local weddings and family functions, meetings of anglers and antique fairs, and for its nightclub, Liquid. But on the morning of 11 September 2007, this sleepy three-star hotel with its chintzy décor was the setting for one of the most spectacular disclosures in Irish financial history.

The first part of the hotel's name is derived from the Irish word 'ard', meaning a high or raised position. It overlooks the Boyne Valley and is not far from the Hill of Tara, the ancient seat of the high kings of Ireland. On that Tuesday morning in 2007 four kings of Irish business met for a candid conversation over pots of tea.

Sean FitzPatrick and David Drumm had driven from Dublin to meet Sean Quinn, a self-made billionaire and Ireland's richest man, and his lieutenant Liam McCaffrey, the chief executive of Quinn Group. Quinn and McCaffrey had travelled from Quinn Group's stronghold on the borderlands of Fermanagh and Cavan. The Ardboyne was neutral ground.

Drumm and FitzPatrick knew Quinn had been secretly building up a large stake in Anglo shares. But they had no idea exactly how large. Quinn portrayed himself as an ordinary man with a simple lifestyle who enjoyed playing cards for a few euros with friends at night, but as an entrepreneur he took massive gambles – and many had paid off handsomely. From humble beginnings digging gravel out of the family farm on the border with Northern Ireland, he had built a massive business with a staff of more than 6,000 people. He told the author in a rare interview for the *Sunday Business Post* in 2001 that he planned 'to live poor and die rich'.

Quinn's vast fortune was largely derived from his businesses manufacturing building materials, glass, plastics and radiators along a four-mile stretch of road between Ballyconnell in Co. Cavan and Derrylin in Co. Fermanagh, straddling the border. Quinn's method was to build a manufacturing plant to the highest specification, create the lowest cost for every unit he produced and then 'buy the market' by undercutting rivals' products. His skill was his patience. He would wait – covering losses – while he managed to corner a market and then he would increase his prices.

Quinn moved into insurance in the mid-1990s. The motivation for doing so was a practical one: he was angry at what he saw as the extortionate cost of insuring the trucks that carried his cement and building supplies. Quinn Insurance was set up in 1996 to offer motorists low-cost insurance premiums. The model was simple – charge less for premiums. To do this, he kept overheads low by avoiding insurance brokers and selling directly to customers (this was the root of the company's trading name, Quinn Direct), much as Michael O'Leary's Ryanair had cut out travel agents and other 'middlemen'.

The other expense that was kept low was claims costs. Quinn employed a panel of about 600 'self-employed' claims managers across the country who were immediately assigned to a claim wherever it was notified to the insurer. These managers included a substantial number of retired police officers. The aim of having so many claims handlers was that the company would get details of an accident quickly. Where the Quinn Direct customer was liable, the company aggressively sought quick and early settlement of claims so it could avoid seeing these brought to court.

The Sunday Times Rich List, published in April 2007, estimated that Sean Quinn was the twelfth wealthiest man in Britain or Ireland with a net worth of £3 billion sterling – close to €4.5 billion at the time. (The newspaper would rank him even higher the following year, and Forbes magazine's 2008 Rich List named him as the 146th richest in the world. Both agreed he was the richest man in Ireland.)

In the autumn of 2007 the Quinn Group was firing on all cylinders, generating large profits from its low-cost, low-price insurance business and from supplying cement and other building materials to the booming Irish construction sector. A report issued to bondholder lenders to the Quinn Group in May 2008 showed that the group's sales went from €597 million in 2003 to €2.1 billion in 2007. The company told the bondholders that the group's cash earnings – a measure of profitability before one-off costs and tax – rose from €202 million in 2003 to €492 million in 2007.

Two years previously, Quinn had started to make long-holding investments outside the business for the benefit of his five children, sources close to the businessman claim.

Quinn's five children were not exactly impoverished. Quinn would frequently tell his bankers at Anglo with some pride that each of them was a billionaire, as they each owned an equal share of his group of businesses and the group was worth €5 billion at the peak of its fortunes. Quinn had passed on the ownership of all the shares in the group to his son and four daughters around 2004. He himself held no shares in the main ownership company of the business, Quinn Group (ROI). Quinn's son, Sean Jr, worked in the business, along with three of his daughters – Colette, Aoife and Brenda.

Quinn began to build a stake in Anglo shares in secret, by investing in the bank through CFDs – contracts for difference. CFDs, a form of investment based around the movement of a company's share price, had become hugely popular for investors looking to turn a quick profit in boom-time Ireland. It is possible to use CFDs to go 'long' on a share, i.e. bet that its price will rise, or to 'short' the share, i.e. gamble that its price will fall. The investor taking a long position has to pay only a small deposit – known as the margin – and borrows the remainder of the cost of the shares from the broker-dealer. If the stock rises, the investor may sell the CFD and pocket 100 per cent of the increase. In this respect, CFD investments are no different from an ordinary share investment. The added appeal of CFDs, to the investor with an appetite for big returns and a willingness to live with big risk, is that in a rising market the use of debt to fund CFDs amplifies the investor's gains dramatically. If you invest in a share via a CFD and put down a cash margin of 20 per cent, and the value of the share increases 20 per cent, you can sell the CFD, repay the 80 per cent of its price that you borrowed, and reap a profit of 100 per cent over your original investment. Spending the same amount of cash on a direct share purchase would have yielded a gain of just 20 per cent. Of course, leverage works the same way if the share price falls: the investor's losses, as a percentage of the cash margin, are amplified. When the share price falls significantly, the investor has to deposit more cash to cover the loss. This is known as the 'margin call' so dreaded by investors.

Significantly, in CFD positions the shares themselves are not bought or sold by the investor – they are instead held by the broker-dealer – so it is possible to build up a large investment anonymously, and this would have appealed to the publicity-shy Quinn. But Quinn's main reason for investing in Anglo through CFDs was that he didn't need to put up the full amount of cash to get the full benefit. He simply couldn't have afforded to take the same scale of investment in Anglo through conventional share buying. He was greedy – he wanted to gamble big-time on the stock but avoid putting up the cash by buying the shares directly. In October 2005 Quinn had CFD positions in Anglo, AIB and Bank of Ireland as part of a much wider investment portfolio that included stakes in Ryanair,

Deutsche Telecom and Tullow Oil. From late 2006 Quinn started reducing his investments in these other companies to increase his bet on Anglo.

Quinn might never have gone as far as he did with Anglo CFDs had the Revenue Commissioners followed through on their intention, in March 2006, to apply stamp duty to the investments. The Irish Stock Exchange and stockbrokers quickly began lobbying Minister for Finance Brian Cowen and officials in the Department of Finance, warning of a collapse in trading volumes if tax was applied to CFDs. Cowen duly bowed to the pressure and intervened to prevent the taxation change.

Newspaper reports in early 2007 estimated that Quinn held a large stake, about 5 per cent, in Anglo through CFDs. In a rare public speech in March of that year, Quinn had expressed admiration for Anglo. Quinn said that whenever the Quinn Group considered expanding into a new area of business, it would assess the competitors in the particular field. 'If it was a David Drumm or a Michael O'Leary of Ryanair that were in that business, then we would try to avoid it,' he said, prompting laughter in the audience. 'If there was somebody else that was in it, we might take that to be a healthy challenge.' Some took Quinn's praise of Anglo as confirmation that he was a big investor in the bank.

By June of that year there was more chatter in the market about further stake-building by Quinn, as the bank's share price reached an all-time high of €17.53. Estimates were putting his stake at well over 5 per cent. There was some speculation in the market that Quinn was up to something bigger, that he was building a large financial services group. Given that he owned a major insurance company and part of NCB stockbrokers, this was not an outlandish idea.

By the end of the summer, speculation about the size of his stake in the bank had reached fever pitch. This was unsettling for Anglo. The bank was receiving regular inquiries about Quinn from investors, market analysts and, most crucially, credit rating agencies who were hearing the rumours and reading the news stories. Media speculation in late August put Quinn's stake at about 11 per cent, valuing his investment at about €1 billion and leading to speculation that he was about to make a bigger move on the bank.

Gary McGann, chief executive of paper and packaging group Smurfit Kappa and a non-executive director at Anglo, pushed the matter at a board meeting in early September. By now the directors felt that it was time to speak to Quinn directly. The bank needed to know exactly what the size of his stake was and what his intentions were.

The bank's concerns centred on the fact that if Quinn's investment was too big, the bank could be badly exposed. If Quinn ever got into financial trouble, he would have to unwind his investment, so if Quinn's stake was as big as was being rumoured, a drop in the share price could be enough to put Quinn into difficulty. After years of dramatic rises, the share price *was* falling: from a peak of over €17.50 in June, the share was now trading at around €13.50. If Quinn had to unwind the CFDs, the brokers who had sold them to him, and who held the Anglo shares on his behalf, would have to dump the shares if he could not cover his losses. A sudden fire sale of a large percentage of the bank's shares could cause the share price to plummet.

Even short of this nightmare scenario, the very existence of a large secret shareholding is potentially destabilizing. If word got out that Quinn's stake was really big, Anglo shares could come under attack. Shareholders might sell out, and send the share price plummeting. This could lead to a run on the bank by nervous depositors. It was just about the worst position a bank could find itself in. At least, this is what the bank was so terrified of, particularly as the global credit crunch started to bite in the autumn of 2007. At a time of stress in the international financial markets, Anglo executives viewed the share price as a proxy for funding – every heavy fall in the share price would be matched by a large withdrawal of deposits. This gloomy analysis would prove to be correct.

Anglo executives were uncommonly obsessed with the movement of the bank's share price, possibly because they themselves held such a large number of Anglo shares. The bank's executive directors and non-executive board members held 12 million shares – or 1.6 per cent of the total – in September 2008. This compared with 0.15 per cent of Bank of Ireland stock held by its executive directors and board members and 0.14 per cent at AIB.

At the end of the summer of 2007 the Anglo board felt it was time for a face-to-face encounter with Quinn. Drumm broached the subject with Liam McCaffrey, and the Ardboyne meeting was arranged. Quinn knew the hotel well – he had owned it up until three years previously.

FitzPatrick and Drumm had flown into Dublin airport that morning after attending a private dinner for Anglo clients at a London hotel. The former president of the Soviet Union, Mikhail Gorbachev, had been the guest speaker at the dinner. He spoke about the collapse of the USSR in 1991 and the upheavals that followed in Russia.

FitzPatrick and Drumm had driven to the airport the previous day, each in his own car, planning to travel on to Navan to meet Quinn after the London trip. They took the M1 to Julianstown before driving along the back roads through the village of Duleek to Navan. FitzPatrick didn't have a clue about the geography of north Co. Dublin and Meath, but Drumm had grown up in Skerries and before joining Anglo he had worked this territory for a state-owned venture-capital business helping companies to secure investment and advising them on how to develop their businesses. Drumm led the way in his Range Rover Sport, with music blaring as usual; FitzPatrick followed in his Mercedes.

The bankers arrived in the lobby of the Ardboyne in plenty of time for the 9.30 a.m. meeting; Quinn and McCaffrey turned up shortly after. Quinn led the way into a private meeting room he had booked towards the back of the hotel where they would not be noticed. FitzPatrick described the room to Tom Lyons as 'pretty spare but with a table and chairs'. The introductions were informal, with the two bankers sitting on one side of the table and Quinn and McCaffrey on the other. Before they got down to business, they ordered tea.

Before the meeting, Quinn and McCaffrey had discussed whether they should disclose the exact scale of Quinn's stake in Anglo or just tell the bankers that it was 'large'. Quinn wanted to be absolutely upfront with them on the size of the stake, and so he and McCaffrey spent a little time working out the percentage beforehand.

Undeterred – or indeed emboldened – by the falling share price, Quinn had spent the previous three months snapping up a large amount of Anglo stock through CFDs. He believed that the price would rise again.

For their part, FitzPatrick and Drumm knew the Ardboyne meeting would be awkward. FitzPatrick later claimed that Drumm brought him along because Quinn was more likely to react favourably to him. 'David was more up to speed about the activities of CFDs,' FitzPatrick told Tom Lyons. 'He was bringing me because he always felt that Quinn regarded me as a superhuman, as a superhero. He wanted Quinn to see how disappointed I would be.'

FitzPatrick got an impression of Quinn as 'a real 1960s Irishman'. 'He was one of those hail fellow well met, ah sure I will go down there and play the old cards, five or six lads for 10 bob, or whatever it was,' he recalled. 'He was always producing all that and would be nearly blessing himself. Everything will be all right. He was very human but . . . I didn't easily like him.'

*

The conversation started off like a meeting of a mutual appreciation society. FitzPatrick told Quinn how much he admired what he had achieved in business. Quinn responded, paying tribute to FitzPatrick's success in building Anglo into one of the biggest companies on the Irish stock market with one of the best-performing stocks in the world. He spoke about how much he respected Anglo and its management, and remarked on how it had broken the mould in banking by building a new business model.

After the volley of compliments between Quinn and FitzPatrick, the four men got down to the real business. FitzPatrick and Drumm asked the question: how big was Quinn's CFD stake in the bank? He replied that he held a stake of about 24 per cent of the shares.

FitzPatrick and Drumm were gobsmacked. FitzPatrick physically recoiled in his seat. Drumm later told colleagues that it was the only time he ever saw FitzPatrick rendered speechless.

FitzPatrick later told Tom Lyons that their reaction was measured but stern. There was 'no banging the table or anything like that' but voices were raised. 'I was physically shocked,' he recalled. 'I wasn't expecting that.' The bankers had thought that Quinn had a 10 per cent interest in Anglo through CFDs, or possibly 12 per cent.

Quinn seemed to turn to FitzPatrick, a man he admired, for approval. But instead he saw utter dismay. This was evident from the shock on both of the Anglo men's faces. FitzPatrick and Drumm knew that the size of Quinn's stake spelt big trouble for the bank.

Within the space of a few minutes, Quinn's demeanour changed, mirroring the reaction of the bankers. Everyone in the room now realized the gravity of the situation they were in. Seeing Quinn's reaction, FitzPatrick and Drumm felt that for the first time he understood the size of the hole he had dug for himself. The fates of Ireland's third largest bank and the country's wealthiest man were now deeply entwined.

Drumm, the forty-year-old banker, told Quinn, the sixty-one-year-old billionaire, that if word got out about the size of his stake in the bank, the share price would most likely collapse, with damaging consequences for the bank's funding and deposits. Quinn was asked what his intentions for Anglo were and whether he planned to take the bank over completely. He ruled this out, saying that he liked the bank's style and operation.

The two bankers thought Quinn looked like a child who had been scolded. They have claimed that Quinn tentatively agreed not to increase his stake any further, though the Quinn camp says that no such promise was made – that Quinn's intention was to hold his stake in the bank as a long-term investment and that he made that clear at the meeting.

The four men finished their cups of tea and the two sides went their separate ways. The meeting had lasted about forty-five minutes.

FitzPatrick and Drumm knew they had a serious problem. As they stood at the boot of FitzPatrick's car, the chairman went into a soliloquy about what they had just heard and what they needed to do. They had to tell the other directors of the bank and ring round to organize a board meeting back in Dublin that night. The two agreed to drive back towards Dublin and stop to discuss a plan of action at the first restaurant or café.

They drove off, FitzPatrick following Drumm. Fifteen minutes down the road they pulled in at the County Club in the village of Dunshaughlin. After pulling into the car park, Drumm went over to FitzPatrick's car. He could see the chairman was on the phone and assumed he was talking to Anglo board member Gary McGann, with whom FitzPatrick was close.

They went inside and ordered more tea.

Drumm and FitzPatrick spoke about what might be in store for the bank as a result of Quinn's secret stake-building and how they should deal with it from here. They decided that after the board was informed, the Financial Regulator should be told.

Their minds were racing. Drumm kept thinking about how the bank had for years travelled the world trying to encourage major financial institutions to invest in its shares. Anglo might, if it was lucky, encourage a blue-chip bank, insurer or pension fund business to buy up to 1 per cent of the bank. But even then it would be only after months of hard selling about the merits of investing in an Irish bank.

Now they would have to sit in front of those very same international investors in New York, Toronto and San Francisco, and explain how a single businessman controlled about a quarter of the bank's shares.

Quinn's investment would destroy the credibility that Anglo had spent years building up among super-wealthy institutional investors, they believed. These are the very investors who sit on the share registers of the biggest and best companies around the world. How would they feel about being in bed with Sean Quinn? If they found out, they would be asking difficult questions of Anglo. Can Quinn hold on to such a large stake? What if he has to dump the stock? Has he used his investment as security to borrow from other banks? Can another bank force him to sell? Will he be forced to sell at some point in the future?

At this stage, Drumm and FitzPatrick weren't worried about Quinn's own personal finances. He was, after all, Ireland's richest man. His businesses were generating huge amounts of cash. As a result, Quinn was felt to be 'beyond any sort of financial strain', FitzPatrick later told Tom Lyons. 'It was felt that it was a dealable deal; in other words, it was sortable out.'

Their brief crisis meeting over, FitzPatrick and Drumm hopped in their cars and headed for Dublin. FitzPatrick called all the non-executive directors from his car on the way back. The board members, excluding the executive directors, met either in person or over the phone on a conference call that evening at 6.15 p.m. in Heritage House, the Georgian building the bank owned two doors down from its head office on St Stephen's Green.

There was a discussion among the directors about whether they should tell fellow board member Tom Browne, who had handed in his resignation a week earlier, about the Quinn situation. The board concluded that Browne shouldn't be told, because he would be leaving the bank soon and Anglo wanted to keep this information within the bank's inner circle. Drumm immediately informed the other executive directors about the Quinn stake.

That night the non-executive directors agreed at the dinner in Heritage House that the Financial Regulator had to be 'brought into the loop' about the extent of Quinn's holding. Three directors – Ned Sullivan, the chairman of food group Greencore; Gary McGann of Smurfit Kappa; and Fintan Drury, the former journalist and sports event manager – could not attend the dinner. Drumm and FitzPatrick met Sullivan on the afternoon of 20 September in his office to update him. McGann and Drury were briefed by Drumm at Smurfit's head office in Clonskeagh on the south side of Dublin at a meeting on the evening of 24 September.

Drumm also arranged to see Pat Neary, the chief executive of the Financial Regulator, in his office on the seventh floor of the Central Bank and Regulator's building on Dame Street in Dublin. The Anglo chief executive broke the news about Quinn's investment and the concerns of Anglo's board. Neary was dismissive. It wasn't an issue. He lectured Drumm about how CFD investments worked and that they are really only derivatives with no real shares behind them. Neary saw the Quinn stake as 'just a bet'.

Drumm was stunned. The bank had a major crisis on its hands and the country's top banking regulator did not seem to grasp the scale of the problem facing them both. Neary was wrong on CFDs. Although the shares were not owned directly by Quinn, every share covered by the CFD was owned by a broker, and any unwinding of Quinn's position could involve the sudden arrival of a quarter of Anglo's shares on the market.

Despite Neary's initial dismissiveness, the Quinn issue was discussed over the following weeks and months by the boards of the Financial Regulator and the Central Bank as well as at meetings of the government's financial war cabinet, the Domestic Standing Group, whose job it was to assess threats to the financial stability of the country. The group comprised the secretary-general of the Department of Finance, the governor of the Central Bank and the head of the Financial Regulator. Later, as the crisis deteriorated, the Regulator's prudential director Con Horan, who was responsible for the health checks on the state of the banks, attended meetings of the group.

Brian Cowen later admitted that he was briefed by the governor of the Central Bank, John Hurley, on the issue when he was Minister for Finance and by FitzPatrick himself in a phone call while Cowen was away on official duty in the Far East in March 2008.

In the months after the Ardboyne meeting, Quinn did not reduce his stake in Anglo. On the contrary, he gambled even further, increasing his holding to 28 or 29 per cent at its peak during 2008. Quinn clearly didn't take Anglo's concerns about the size of his investment seriously.

'I think he also felt listening to David, and possibly me as well, that things were going well within the bank,' FitzPatrick recalled in *The Fitz-Patrick Tapes*. 'Therefore the rest of the world had got it wrong. Sean had got it right and time would show that he had got it right, and the share price would come back again.'

How could Quinn, a veteran businessman, not see the risk he was taking by investing so heavily in one stock?

'Someone who has a lot of conviction does tend to take risks that they should not take,' says a close associate of Quinn's. 'That goes with the territory. An entrepreneur's instinct is to see things go right. Did he feel that Anglo would be the same? Lots of our businesses had issues and they have been overcome. But this was different – it was not under Sean's control.'

Anglo consulted with the Financial Regulator to see if the bank was legally obliged to let the stock market know about Quinn's stake. It was advised that because the investment was held in CFDs, the bank did not have to issue a statement to the Stock Exchange to make it public. Despite the advice of the Regulator, the bank also approached Tom Courtney, a solicitor at one of the country's top legal firms, Arthur Cox, to seek his advice on the same question. (Curiously, on this issue Anglo chose not to consult its own corporate lawyers, Dublin solicitors Matheson Ormsby Prentice.) Anglo did not divulge to Courtney what it knew about Quinn.

The bank didn't want too many people knowing what it believed was highly sensitive information. Instead, it asked the solicitor simply to explain what CFDs were and what investors who held stakes in public companies through these instruments were obliged to disclose about them. Anglo also asked Arthur Cox to advise on how it could find out whether an investor held a secret stake through CFDs.

The bank asked its lawyers these two general questions and drew its own conclusions indirectly from the responses it got. Although Arthur Cox never said as much (not having been asked), Anglo concluded that it was not obliged to disclose the scale of Quinn's CFD interest.

Anglo later believed that Quinn himself and his stake-building in Anglo, trading around 215 million shares, or more than a quarter of the bank, was one reason the bank's stock reached the heights it did through 2007. The irony is that Quinn thought market demand was pushing up the share price because investors, like him, believed in the bank when in fact his own investing may have been behind it.

The scale of his investment might give the impression that Quinn had a sophisticated financial team managing his investments. He hadn't. He employed a few managers in the company's offices in Cavan who worked outside the Quinn Group overseeing the family's investments. They were just administrators. Quinn called the shots.

Quinn had made serious investment mistakes before. He invested heavily in technology stocks in the late 1990s and when the dotcom bubble burst in 2001 he was left nursing heavy losses. But he recovered. The fact that Quinn had overcome obstacles in business in the past probably contributed to his sanguine view of the Anglo situation. When the value of his investment in Anglo fell in the summer of 2007 he felt it was time to buy more, not sell, to recover some of his losses.

The close relationship between Anglo and Quinn wasn't new. It dated as far back as 1998. The bank had funded the construction of the Slieve Russell Hotel in Ballyconnell, Co. Cavan, a five-star hotel near a small border-region town. It was widely dismissed as a white elephant, but despite its critics it traded well. Anglo also funded Quinn's purchase of the Hillgrove Hotel in Monaghan and the Ambassador Hotel just outside Dublin to the tune of about €30 million in the early 2000s.

In January 2003 Anglo gave Quinn a loan of £9.5 million to finance the purchase of the Holiday Inn in Nottingham. At the end of that year, the bank provided another loan of €24.4 million to refinance Quinn's loans from other banks on Buswells Hotel opposite Leinster House in Dublin – a popular haunt of politicians and the people who surround them – and the various pubs owned by the Quinn Group in Dublin.

By the middle of the 2000s, buoyed by rapidly rising property values at home, Quinn decided to expand into Europe. Anglo advanced €140 million allowing him to acquire the Hilton Hotel and the Ibis Hotel in Prague in January 2005.

From 2005 onwards Anglo continued lending to the Quinn Group, towards the purchase of properties and sites in Ukraine, Russia and Turkey. The properties were office blocks, shopping centres and large warehouses for distribution businesses, and by late 2007 Quinn had loans of just over €1 billion with Anglo. The loans were nothing out of the ordinary for a big Irish property buyer, and certainly not for the man viewed as Ireland's richest. Anglo felt that it had a low-risk customer in Quinn. The loans themselves were structured conservatively, amounting to no more than 70 per cent of the value of the property it was secured on. The bank also had an added layer of security which it believed would make it bulletproof – it had the full personal guarantee of Sean Quinn on all of his loans. This would cause him problems three years later when it came to repaying loans of €2.8 billion to Anglo.

8.   Falling Back to Earth

Late September 2007 – Anglo's value: €9.9 billion

Quinn's disclosure could not have come at a worse time for Anglo. In September 2007 the financial world was in chaos. Investors feared that financial institutions had built up unknown exposures to the collapsing US property market and to toxic subprime mortgages. Global funding markets had seized up and credit was now very hard to come by. This left the weakest and most reckless banks exposed.

On 13 September 2007, just days after the Ardboyne meeting, the BBC's business editor Robert Peston reported that Northern Rock, the UK's fifth largest mortgage lender, had run out of liquidity and been forced to turn to the Bank of England as the lender of last resort to keep its doors open. The report led to the first run on a British bank in more than a century.

Northern Rock, which specialized in mortgages, funded its lending by borrowing in the international money markets, which had been awash with cheap and easy cash. The subprime crisis quickly caused this tap to turn off, and Northern Rock, unable to find alternative funding, couldn't continue.

Liquidity – i.e. available cash – is the oxygen that keeps a bank alive. It allows it to repay its debts as they fall due. A bank can have a healthy balance sheet – and Anglo's balance sheet still looked very healthy at this point – but if it cannot source liquidity it cannot trade. Now, with the credit markets seized up, Anglo's ability to find cash started to come under the microscope. The markets were also starting to get concerned about the bank's balance sheet.

During the first half of 2007 a slow decline in house prices had been the first indication that the Irish property boom was over. Hedge fund managers started to sniff around the possibility of betting on Irish bank stocks falling. They did this by short selling, or 'going short' on a stock. Short sellers 'borrow' shares from long-term holders of the stock and sell them in the hope that the price will fall. This then allows them to buy them back more cheaply, return them to the original lender of the stock and make a profit.

Anglo's position as a bank with more than 80 per cent of its loan book in property meant that it was in the cross-hairs of short sellers at a time of

declining property prices. It had been the biggest beneficiary of the boom
in property, growing its market share from 3 per cent of Irish banking to
18 per cent over the past decade. But now Ireland had a property bubble,
and by this stage the more clued-in overseas financial analysts and
economists – and a minority of domestic commentators – knew it. The
Irish banking sector – not just Anglo – was horribly over-exposed on land
and development lending: lending funded by outside borrowing on a massive scale. The banks owed overseas lenders the equivalent of 60 per cent of
Ireland's GDP by 2003.

One Dublin stockbroker recalls meeting a few London hedge fund managers who were eager to understand more about Anglo. They were
particularly interested in the scale of the bank's exposure to Sean Quinn, he
says. They wanted to know about the 'overhang' in the shares from Quinn's
position – in other words, the extent of his large stake in the bank. The
hedge fund managers recognized that if the share price started to fall,
Quinn could go bust. A sudden and disorderly fire sale of Quinn's Anglo
shares would, in turn, push the share price even lower, putting further
pressure on the bank. Anglo could find itself in a dangerous downward
spiral.

The broker said that the fund managers also asked about Anglo's liquidity and funding pressures. They made careful notes, gathering intelligence
for their attack.

One of the few economists to foresee the impending problems facing the
Irish economy and the banks was Morgan Kelly, an economics professor at
University College Dublin. In December 2006 he wrote an article in the
Irish Times warning that sudden prosperity and easy credit had driven house
prices to absurd levels, and that those prices could halve in value over the
next several years. The article was largely ignored and Kelly privately ridiculed as something of a Jeremiah. He was accused of 'talking down the
economy', a phrase regularly used by government ministers and the powerful Irish property and banking lobby.

Kelly, whose research specialisms had nothing to do with house-price
bubbles (he was working on medieval population theory at the time, he
later said), had started looking at the banks and the property market when
he saw former students appearing on television as bank economists and
telling the nation that the country was in for a soft landing.

In a paper published in July 2007, Kelly predicted that house prices
could drop by 60 per cent. A few days later, Taoiseach Bertie Ahern tackled

the economic naysayers in one of the most controversial comments of his entire leadership. 'Sitting on the sidelines, cribbing and moaning is a lost opportunity, I don't know how people who engage in that don't commit suicide,' he said. (This wasn't the first time Ahern had criticized pessimists and cheered on the property boom. In April 2006 he called for an examination of 'why so many people got it so wrong' in warning about an overheated construction sector and advising people about the possibility of a downturn in 2005 and 2006. 'My view is there's not a great problem. Really, the bad advice of last year given by so many has maybe made some people make mistakes, that they should have bought last year,' he said.)

When, in another article in the *Irish Times* in September 2007, Kelly linked his thesis on the collapse of the property market to heavy lending to developers and potential bad debts worth tens of billions held by 'Bank of Ireland, Anglo Irish Bank and other builder-friendly banks', the bankers didn't like it. Matt Moran, chief financial officer at Anglo, called Kelly at his UCD office to give him an earful. 'He went on about how "the real-estate developers who are borrowing from us are so incredibly rich they are only borrowing from us as a favour". I wanted to argue, but we ended up having lunch. This is Ireland, after all,' Kelly told *Vanity Fair*'s Michael Lewis in 2011.

The lunch took place at the Town Bar and Grill on Kildare Street. It was a fitting place to meet: property developer Johnny Ronan, one of Anglo's biggest customers, financed the restaurant. The banker told the economics professor that he simply didn't understand the bank. Moran said that Anglo had such a close relationship with its wealthy borrowers that it was fully aware of any problems and could easily handle them. Kelly didn't believe a word of it.

Moran, who had been a member of the local boxing club while growing up in Castlebar, Co. Mayo, was a key figure on the bank's investor relations team. He dealt with queries from shareholders and helped to present the bank's financial results to the media and the investment community every six months. He was also the bank's pit bull, charged with chastising bank analysts, financial journalists and anyone else who spoke or wrote negatively about the bank. He would regularly telephone critics of the bank to give them a piece of his mind.

Former colleagues describe Moran as 'a know-it-all' and as 'ambitious and arrogant', someone with a reputation as a fighter. Much to Moran's amusement, Drumm nicknamed him 'Fallujah' because of the manner in which he went about his business. (Another lender at the bank became known as 'Chopper' after he was sick in a helicopter owned by one of the bank's big clients.)

'Matt didn't do subtle,' says one former Anglo executive.

Another former Anglo executive who worked with Moran at the bank, reworking an old formula, jokes, 'Half the broker community thought he was a bollix; the other half hadn't met him yet!'

FitzPatrick hired Moran in 2002. He had worked in the US for Arthur Andersen, the disgraced accountancy firm that was broken up after the Enron financial scandal, before joining a corporate finance company. Fitz-Patrick had met him in New York on a business trip, liked him and promised him a job. 'Put it in writing and I'll think about it,' was Moran's reputed response. FitzPatrick admired Moran for standing up to him – something that didn't happen much, one of their former colleagues at Anglo says.

The bank had hired Moran as chief financial officer to expand the financial management structures, knowing that finance director Willie McAteer, part of the older generation, would soon retire. Anglo executives say that Moran performed this task well. Despite his manner, Moran's work ethic was highly regarded and some saw him as a potential future CEO.

Moran was one of FitzPatrick's favourites. The day before senior Anglo executives made presentations to the board at an annual strategy day in the K Club, they performed a dress rehearsal for FitzPatrick. He listened and proceeded to tear their presentations apart to improve them for the board the following day.

'After you spoke, Seanie said stuff like: "Jaysus, that was terrible, I want to kill myself after hearing that . . . we'd want to close the bank after what you just said,"' says one executive. 'Matt got up and walked up and down the room, like a weatherman and using his hands during his presentation. The rest of us had just sat down. When Matt finished, Sean sat back in his chair and started applauding. The rest of us didn't like it. It wasn't good to be the teacher's pet in Anglo.'

Another target of Matt Moran's wrath was Seamus Murphy, a trader at Davy stockbrokers who sold to institutional investors. Murphy had tipped Anglo in 2004 during his time as a banking analyst at rival firm Merrion Capital. He moved to the trading room at Davy in 2006, and by early 2007 he had grown deeply sceptical about Anglo's prospects. He started telling his clients that he believed the stock was worth €5 to €6 a share, about a third of its actual price at the time. But Murphy was a lone voice in the crowd. In those days the market couldn't get enough of the stock.

In summer 2007 Moran met Murphy for a coffee in a hotel in Dublin and lambasted him for his negative assessment of Anglo.

Murphy was regarded as one of the smartest brokers at Davy. Colleagues say he had a great ability to foresee how markets would move and to read trends. He knew Anglo inside out, having followed the bank as a broker for eight years. As a result, his analysis of the bank attracted a great deal of international interest. Many large investors coming through Dublin sought him out to discuss his views.

He advised large clients, including hedge funds in London, that the falling property market and the rising cost of borrowing would be a problem for Anglo. As a result, hedge funds went short on Anglo and shareholders who had held the stock for the long haul sold out. Ronan Hurley, another trader at Davy, took a similar position and gave the same advice to clients. Murphy and Hurley's advice on Anglo would end up making and saving Davy's clients a lot of money. As Anglo's share price kept falling through the summer of 2007, more and more investors became interested in what Murphy was saying.

In September 2007 Anglo received a call from one of its institutional shareholders in London, who reported that Murphy was 'shitting all over the bank'. Moran's intervention over coffee clearly had had no effect.

Later that month the bank held one of its regular 'financial site visits' for the investment community – a presentation to about 200 people, mostly international investors but also some traders and analysts from Davy. Just as the meeting was about to start, Moran asked Murphy to leave the third-floor boardroom: he wasn't welcome. Harsh words were exchanged as Moran escorted Murphy from the building.

The episode was deeply embarrassing for Murphy. His colleagues were surprised to see him back in the office so quickly. The story was soon a hot topic of discussion.

Davy always thought it strange that Anglo, more so than any other public company, seemed both to be obsessed by the performance of its share price and to believe that it could be defended by tackling stockbrokers. In Davy's view these attitudes stemmed from the fact that Anglo's management were such large shareholders in the bank.

Drumm contacted the deputy chairman of Davy, Kyran McLaughlin, and arranged a meeting at the bank. McLaughlin denied that Davy had been involved in spreading rumours about Anglo and said there was nothing vindictive about the position that Davy took. The firm was passing on to its clients legitimate misgivings about the bank's exposure to the property market. He explained that it was not brokers who were responsible for the share price falling but the bank itself – the business the bank had been doing was giving investors cause for concern.

By this stage, Davy had grounds for suspicion that a major bad-debt problem was building up at Anglo. The stockbroking firm had a busy private-clients division, which packaged up property investments for wealthy customers. Davy turned down a number of property deals that were subsequently snapped up by Anglo for customers in its own wealth management division. The firm couldn't see how some of these deals would work.

The row continued at the highest levels. At a subsequent meeting, Drumm angrily told McLaughlin that he would watch his business go down the tubes, as corporate Ireland would never forget what the firm was doing. The Anglo board even passed a resolution that FitzPatrick would write to McLaughlin to express the bank's disapproval of the behaviour of Davy staff.

One former senior Anglo executive says that he regretted the aggressive action taken by the bank against critics of its business model: 'There was an arrogance in Anglo – we thought we were masters of the universe,' he says. 'There was a sense that we felt these people didn't know what they were talking about because we believed our own press.'

At the start of October 2007 Anglo shares were trading at just over €14, about 20 per cent off their peak level earlier that year. The talk in the market was that it had sought funding from the European Central Bank (ECB) – a lender of last resort for struggling banks. There was also a rumour that Ryanair had pulled a large deposit from Anglo, though this was later denied by the airline.

Investment bank Goldman Sachs suggested in a report on 2 November that the Irish banks were facing heavy losses from a slowdown in the housing market. Goldman singled out Anglo, saying that the bank faced a different and large range of problems with commercial property prices falling in Ireland, the UK and the US. Anglo became a short seller's favourite stock. Hedge funds took particularly robust short positions against Anglo. Always on the offensive, Moran believed he could convince the hedge fund managers that they were wrong about the bank, and he felt Drumm should go out and meet them. Drumm refused, believing that such an initiative would only add fuel to the fire.

Anglo was making regular complaints to the Financial Regulator about 'rumour-mongering' by stockbrokers. The bank contacted those who were advising clients to bet against the bank to inform them that their conversations were being recorded.

Anglo also contacted international stockbrokers to reassure them that the bank was not running out of cash. This was a risky approach. The bank was in a so-called 'closed period': it was not allowed to reveal price-sensitive information to the market until its annual results were published in late November. Breaking silence during a closed period to dismiss a rumour could backfire, adding to the speculation that it might be true.

Analysts at the German investment bank Dresdner Kleinwort circulated a note on 6 November telling investors that they had met Anglo management the previous day. They were assured that Anglo had not turned to the ECB or the Irish Central Bank for emergency funding and that the bank had sufficient resources to lend more to other banks than it took in. The analysts said Anglo sourced almost two-thirds of its funding from customer deposits – this compared with just over a third at Northern Rock – meaning it was less reliant on inter-bank lending. The market appeared to be convinced. The share price climbed. But the positive vibes around Anglo did not last long.

On Monday, 12 November 2007 an opinion column by *Irish Times* business editor John McManus rattled a few cages at Anglo. McManus said that the bank's decision to come out openly to dismiss market rumours was a brave move by David Drumm: 'It is a very risky strategy for the senior management – even indirectly – to come out and tell the market that all the rumours floating around are not true. When you do that you put your credibility on the line and if it does not work, then you have lost your credibility,' wrote McManus. His view was that Anglo did not have 'a natural deposit base' as, unlike the other big Irish banks, it had no network of branches; as a consequence it was over-reliant on the international money markets for its funding.

McManus was right. Anglo secured most of its retail funding by paying over the odds on rates for deposits. In a credit crunch, offering the highest interest rates to savers was interpreted as a sign of weakness: of being desperate for cash.

McManus's article prompted the governor of the Central Bank, John Hurley, to contact Drumm. Hurley told him that the bank could really do without this kind of reporting at a time of growing crisis in global banking. The chief executive responded by telling journalists that Anglo was enjoying strong growth in its deposit base, contrary to the rumour in the markets that the bank was struggling.

★

In an odd twist in the Anglo story, the first Irish victim of the global credit crunch was Tiarnan O'Mahoney, the man responsible for making sure Anglo was well funded for a twenty-year period.

After missing out on the chief executive's job to Drumm and his departure from the bank in December 2004, O'Mahoney set up a specialist lender called International Securities Trading Corporation (ISTC). He brought Paul Somers, a smart operator in Anglo's treasury department, with him. ISTC borrowed money in the international debt markets, investing in complex debt instruments such as bonds and other IOUs, and lent the money on as capital to banks and financial institutions. It also brokered and managed debt transactions for financial institutions.

In what was seen as a parting gift to his long-serving lieutenant, FitzPatrick is said to have opened his contacts book for his former head of treasury and helped O'Mahoney tap investments from Anglo's major customers. Telecoms tycoon Denis O'Brien, property developer Paddy Kelly and builder Seamus Ross were among the investors who pumped about €150 million in cash into O'Mahoney's venture. Sean Quinn was also among the investors when ISTC was established in 2005. O'Mahoney described his share register as 'a who's who of Irish business'.

It was typical of the times that many of the investors who helped fund the start-up of the company didn't really understand its business model. But they were willing to invest in it because of O'Mahoney's standing as one of the brightest guys at Anglo Irish Bank and FitzPatrick's support and encouragement. FitzPatrick himself put up €1 million.

The catalyst for the collapse of the firm was the downgrading of the credit ratings on about €210 million worth of debt instruments known as structured investment vehicles (SIVs) held by ISTC. When the US subprime crisis broke, investors dumped complex instruments like SIVs, fearing that they could be contaminated with subprime debt.

The downgrading of ISTC's SIVs triggered margin calls from the investment banks that did business with it. These calls could not be met. On 12 November 2007 ISTC suspended trading in its shares, postponed publication of its financial results and scrapped plans to raise €150 million through a bond issue in a last-minute rescue attempt by financier Dermot Desmond.

In February 2008 investors in ISTC were forced to write off losses of €820 million, at the time the biggest cash loss for an Irish company. The firm had just €57.8 million of assets to cover liabilities of €878 million.

★

Anglo's own problems continued to mount. In November, rival AIB cut off its credit lines to Anglo. AIB had been providing Anglo with loans of up to €700 million on a short- to medium-term basis. Colm Doherty, the head of AIB's capital market division, felt uneasy with what he was hearing about Anglo in the market and the bank's financial position. FitzPatrick phoned Doherty and tried to convince him to maintain funding support, but to no avail.

Anglo was also coming under pressure from other banks in different ways. The bank's customers were regularly reporting back that officials in AIB and Bank of Ireland had told them that their money wasn't safe in Anglo. This was hard to prove, and no customer was willing to allow Anglo to put their name forward and to bring the matter to the attention of the Financial Regulator. On one occasion Drumm found a customer in Cork who was initially willing to testify for the bank but later changed her mind. The bank was never able to gather enough evidence to make any such allegation against another bank stick. Paranoia may also have been at play at Anglo, but the bank genuinely believed that its rivals were going out of their way to undermine it.

As the financial crisis intensified, the other banks could also exert pressure on Anglo through simple day-to-day transactions. Property developers did not operate current accounts through Anglo but through the main banks, particularly AIB and Bank of Ireland. Repayments on Anglo loans had to be made through these accounts and some officials at rival banks would delay a payment to Anglo until the following morning or, if due on a Friday, until the following Monday.

On 23 November, a week before Anglo presented its annual results, Patrick Neary tried to reassure the markets that the Irish banks had plenty of funding and that their businesses were sound.

The country's top banking regulator told a gathering of the Institute of Chartered Accountants in Ireland at the Druid's Glen golf resort in Wicklow – a regular haunt for Anglo's annual corporate hospitality outings – that the banks had significant medium-term funding and a wide range of options available to them for getting through the credit crunch.

'Irish banks are solidly profitable and well-capitalized' and had one of the lowest rates of non-performing loans among banks in all European Union countries, he said.

Neary was more like a mouthpiece for the banking sector than a financial watchdog. One of his former colleagues went so far as to describe him as a ' "how high" merchant – you know, asked to jump, he'd say "how high?" '

Fire-fighting what it believed was scaremongering was taking its toll on the bank's executives. Prior to announcing Anglo's results for the year to September 2007, Drumm visited the dentist and later said it was the most relaxing forty-five minutes he had in a month. The results themselves were excellent: the bank announced a 46 per cent increase in profits to €1.243 billion – the first time Anglo's profits broke the €1-billion mark. But the results were for the bank's performance during the best year of the property boom – a boom that was now clearly over. This was eaten bread.

By 2007, loans to customers exceeded deposits by €13 billion and the bank's own borrowing from bondholders had soared to €23 billion – a massive 60 per cent increase on the previous year. Anglo's borrowing from other banks stood at €13 billion. Anglo had got itself heavily in hock to investors and other banks, primarily overseas.

The bank wrote off just €335 million to cover bad loans – less than 0.5 per cent of a total loan book of €67 billion. Such figures did little to reassure the nervous markets. They were equally nervous to see that the bank had provided €18 billion in new loans – an astonishing figure in a year when the property market started to go bad.

Announcing the results, Drumm said that banks had been unfairly hammered for their exposure to property when the growing financial crisis was really about funding. He was bullish about the bank's future, believing that the financial results might contradict some of the rumour-mongers targeting the bank. 'Our stellar results are not going to fix the market, but it might silence a few people,' he said. It did, for two days. The share price rose briefly but then continued its steady decline.

In a show of support the senior management team and board members purchased tens of thousands of shares in the bank at prices ranging from €10.60 to €11.33 a share. This was typical – Anglo putting its money where its mouth was. Sean FitzPatrick spent almost €500,000 buying 47,000 shares, pushing his overall shareholding to just under 4.6 million. This made him the biggest individual investor in the bank after Sean Quinn.

Among the non-executive directors, FitzPatrick's close friend and associate Lar Bradshaw was the next biggest buyer of shares after the results. He spent €451,000 buying 42,600 shares. Drumm, Pat Whelan, Declan Quilligan, Tony Campbell, Matt Moran, John Bowe, Peter Butler and Peter Fitzgerald all purchased shares under options they held as rewards from Anglo.

Shortly after announcing its results, Anglo brought a case against a developer over a failed property venture. The bank had loaned €84 million to a company called Maryborough Construction Holdings to build a shopping centre and offices in the centre of Portlaoise, about an hour outside Dublin. The loan fell into arrears and the bank didn't like the way the project was being managed, specifically the developer's protracted negotiations to secure a major anchor tenant. Anglo pulled the plug just before Christmas 2007. The property was dumped on the market for €25 million and the bank later sued a director of the company, Tony Browne, over personal guarantees he gave on the loans. It secured a judgment against him for this entire amount.

It was the first time the bank actually moved against a borrower on the back of a personal guarantee. It was only the beginning.

In the autumn of 2007 I met a casually dressed FitzPatrick in Anglo's lobby on St Stephen's Green. When I had called him requesting a chat about Anglo and the state of the Irish banks, he had stressed that he had a non-executive role and that the man in charge was David Drumm. I said I knew this but would like to meet him and hear his views.

We walked down the Green to a coffee shop at the top of Dawson Street. It was a nice afternoon so we sat at a table outside. FitzPatrick started from scratch, describing Anglo's business model. He pointed across the road to the building on the far corner, using it as an example of how the bank wasn't a property lender but a lender on the cash flow from rock-solid tenants in the building.

'There could be a major shop on the ground floor, one of the biggest accountancy firms on the first floor and one of the biggest law firms on the second floor,' he said. 'Anglo was covered on its loan, not just on the value of the property but on the strength of the businesses in the building. The strength of the bank loan on the building was a sign of the strength of the economy.'

It was FitzPatrick's stock presentation. It tripped off his tongue from years of practice. As he was elaborating, Anglo non-executive board member Fintan Drury, a close friend of FitzPatrick's, walked past, noticing FitzPatrick in full flow. Drury leaned over the railing next to our table and interrupted him. 'I'd say there's a lot of shite being talked here,' he said. We all laughed.

Drury may have been joking, but with hindsight he was right – the FitzPatrick banking model *was* shite. It took a property crash to expose just how flawed it was.

9.   The Comfort Zone

November 2007 — Anglo's value: €9 billion

In mid-November 2007, Anglo's share price dropped below €9, about half its value just six months previously — and, perhaps more significantly, a third below the average price at which Sean Quinn had purchased his CFDs. That month Quinn approached Anglo for a working-capital loan.

Working-capital facilities are usually provided to companies to fund their day-to-day expenses. Relative to the size of the bank's property loan book, Anglo did only a small amount of working-capital lending to businesses. In Quinn's case, Anglo had given loans primarily for the family's hotels, office blocks and shopping centres outside of the main Quinn Group businesses.

In the following months, Anglo would lend considerable sums of money that were described internally at the bank as 'working capital'. In reality, they were nothing of the kind. The loans were advanced to make sure Quinn had enough cash to cover the margin calls on his Anglo CFDs that had been triggered by the falling share price.

Quinn and his executives were surprised that Anglo did not force him to sell assets or to reduce his stake in the bank during November and December 2007, but Anglo's reluctance to follow that path is not hard to understand. If Quinn sold assets, that could be taken as confirmation of the truth of rumours in the market about Quinn's stake in the bank, send the share price into free-fall, and potentially spark a run on deposits.

On 14 January 2008 Quinn attended a private dinner with David Drumm at Buswell's Hotel. Drumm brought Pat Whelan, and Quinn brought Liam McCaffrey. Quinn was adamant that the bank was under-valued by the market and that Drumm and the bank were not doing enough to argue Anglo's case against the rumour-mongers.

A subsequent internal Anglo report found that Quinn took CFD positions on a further 24 million shares in Anglo during 2008. Despite already facing potentially enormous losses on a share whose price was plummeting, Quinn added to the size of his bet. This was the classic behaviour of a blinkered gambler.

*

In the first days of 2008 Anglo sent shareholders its full annual report for the year to 30 September 2007. The report revealed that Drumm had been paid just under €3.3 million for the 2007 financial year, including a €2 million performance bonus. This amounted to an astonishing €63,000 a week, an increase from the €58,000 a week he earned the previous year. Drumm made in three and a half days the same amount that someone on the average industrial wage would earn in a year. Drumm's pay for 2007 was later revised upwards to €4.6 million to take account of an additional cash payment of €1.38 million received in lieu of a payment into his pension after the government changed pension rules taxing retirement funds over €5 million. This made Drumm Ireland's highest paid bank chief, earning more than the €4 million made by Bank of Ireland chief executive Brian Goggin in the year to March 2008 and the €2.1 million wage packet of AIB boss Eugene Sheehy in 2007.

Fifteen executive directors and board members at Anglo shared €9.6 million for the year, compared with €8.8 million the previous year. Bonuses to executive directors totalled almost €5 million. The report also showed that the executive directors and non-executive board members held more than 11 million shares in the bank and had options to buy a further 5 million. This gave the senior executive team and board more than 2 per cent of the bank's stock, an unusually high figure for a bank.

Drumm claimed in private briefings around this time that Anglo's profits would not be affected by the decline in new lending because the bank was still profiting from 'an annuity effect', making money from the repayment of old loans. This was true – provided Anglo's customers kept their repayments up. In a turning property market, that could not be taken for granted.

The annual report also showed that directors of the bank had borrowed a total of €41 million from Anglo, or an average of €3 million per director. This was a high figure by Irish standards: directors and senior executives at AIB had borrowed €18 million at the end of 2007, while the corresponding amount at Bank of Ireland was €11 million.

Over the course of the first three months of 2008, the Irish stock market kept falling. At their peak, Irish bank shares had been worth more than €50 billion; by early March 2008 they were worth about €30 billion.

Fears that the banks would collapse under the strain imposed by the international credit crisis forced the government into planning for such a financial disaster. A so-called 'scoping paper' was drafted by the Department of Finance outlining the powers that the Minister for Finance had to save an illiquid bank (one that had suffered a run on deposits) and an insolvent bank (one whose liabilities exceeded its assets and no longer had enough cash to meet losses on loans).

The paper pointed out that the government's financial war cabinet, the Domestic Standing Group, had to develop a national contingency plan and carry out a crisis simulation exercise. The paper said that there was just €455 million available at Irish banks to pay out to depositors, whose savings were guaranteed by the government up to €20,000, and it was likely that much more would be needed. Anglo alone had deposits of about €50 billion at the time.

The department considered the possibility of introducing a larger guarantee. The scoping paper suggested that the government might also have to consider guaranteeing inter-bank lending to stop the international markets from withdrawing loans to the Irish banking system. It also expressed concerns that if the Central Bank gave 'exceptional liquidity assistance' – emergency loans to a struggling bank – and this became public, it could create a perception that the bank was 'in trouble and at risk of collapse'.

The report was largely a discussion paper intended to assess the options available to the government, given the legal powers and financial resources available, to save or close a bank. No concerns were raised about any particular bank. However, the paper did raise the possibility of contagion, or a 'domino' effect: if one Irish bank failed, then others could follow and the entire Irish banking system could be in trouble.

Government officials said in the report that a financial institution could be deemed to be 'too big to fail' if its demise is likely to provoke 'systemic' failure of the financial sector overall. The officials pointed out that the government could not publicly define any bank as being 'too big to fail', as this could encourage 'moral hazard' – whereby the bank might take on higher risks and engage in reckless behaviour in the knowledge that it was going to be bailed out.

At a secret presentation at the Department of Finance on 8 February it was agreed that legislation should be drafted empowering the minister to introduce guarantees for banks and to nationalize financial institutions. Again, no bank was mentioned specifically in the department's presentation.

Anglo's board met on 31 January 2008. The first item on the agenda was the pressures that the bank was coming under in terms of funding and liquidity. John Bowe, the bank's director of capital markets, briefed the board on what was happening in the market, the shape of the balance sheet and how the Financial Regulator and the credit ratings agencies were reacting.

FitzPatrick later claimed in *The FitzPatrick Tapes* that he was not aware of the bank's critical problems until August 2008. 'It wasn't belted home to the board,' he said. In an interview conducted for the *Irish Times* in January 2011 in response to the publication of the book, David Drumm told me he was astonished by FitzPatrick's claim. He said that all of the directors of the bank were being apprised of the difficulties with the bank's funding as far back as the start of 2008. He offered the January board meeting as an example of one such briefing, adding that throughout 2008 Anglo executives had kept the board, including FitzPatrick as chairman, up to date on the bank's precarious funding position. At each board meeting the directors would be presented with details of funding flows in and out of the bank and any credit lines that had been won or lost, said Drumm. There was usually an update from John Bowe about the state of the markets, whether the bank was attempting to sell any bonds to raise funding and whether there were any major loan repayments by the bank coming up.

'We had our usual scheduled board meetings but Sean FitzPatrick called countless ad-hoc meetings and board conference calls often at short notice throughout 2008 specifically to deal with the funding crisis,' Drumm said. 'If any board member did not understand how banks fund themselves when they joined the Anglo board, they had a PhD in funding by the end of 2008.'

Anglo's January board meeting was attended by recruitment specialist Ffion Hague, a corporate governance adviser and the wife of the Conservative politician William Hague. Ffion Hague specialized in evaluating the boards of companies and helping businesses improve the quality of their non-executive directors. As a headhunter, she helped companies find new non-executive board members – people usually in the latter stages of their careers with wide-ranging experience in business suited to a particular company.

Hanson Green, the London-based firm at which she worked, had been hired by Anglo the previous November to evaluate the bank's board and make it more compliant with what was regarded as 'best practice' in the industry at the time. Hague had sat in on a board meeting on 19 November and had gathered information over the following two months by asking questions of the board members.

She reported on her findings at the January meeting, telling the directors that they were a 'good to great' board. It was 'universally felt that this is a good board with high-calibre individuals providing effective leadership to the company'. The culture in the boardroom was 'open, rigorous and professional with mutual respect among members'. Comparing it with other boards, she said there was 'depth of experience but not breadth'.

Hague's 'master scoresheets' on the performance of FitzPatrick scored him highly across a range of areas. The scoresheets were marked based on conversations she had with members of the board. She discovered that the senior independent director, Ned Sullivan, and another non-executive director, Fintan Drury, had spoken to shareholders about FitzPatrick's change of position from chief executive to chairman in 2005, and that the shareholders had raised no objections.

'If they had thought it was a bad idea, he would not have stayed as Sean is not one to impose himself on others,' Hague reported. She found that FitzPatrick had 'a good, respectful but challenging relationship with the CEO'.

The lowest score FitzPatrick received – eight out of twelve – was on the question of whether he was 'independently minded'.

'By the nature of his personality he is independent-minded but I have yet to see evidence of a major challenge of the CEO. Perhaps this is done behind closed doors,' Hague said. Her report found that FitzPatrick was more aligned with the non-executive directors at the bank than with the bank's executive team, and that 'the independent directors can be in awe of him'.

The observations in her report on FitzPatrick's 'unique contribution to the board' are revealing about the board's view of him. Among the phrases used by the non-executives were 'sets an open and honest tone', 'sets a lovely light tone and uses humour to great effect' and 'makes it easy for people to ask the dumb question'.

Among the responses regarding FitzPatrick's 'greatest contribution during the year' were 'being the chairman and resisting the temptation to play the role of CEO at a time of difficulty for the bank', 'being a superb mentor for David [Drumm]', 'management of credit risk' and 'being a real person of unbelievable humanity and integrity'. He also won praise for his 'assertive handling of one of our large shareholders' – Sean Quinn, of course, though Quinn was not named. FitzPatrick's board members obviously held him in a high and fond regard.

Asked if they were ready to tackle a crisis, the board members told Hague that there was 'no formal plan in place – reactions are instinctive when crisis strikes', that 'an exercise in simulating a catastrophic episode would be worthwhile' and that the board needed to move 'up a gear' to ready itself for any problems ahead.

Hague noted the board's concerns that it included no executive from the treasury and capital markets side of the bank and there was a need for 'another woman to redress the gender imbalance'. Her assessment of the audit committee found that there was no member with risk experience. She recommended greater transparency around appointments to the board and that appointments should be made to fill skills gaps among directors.

Anglo's risk and compliance committee – a long-standing subcommittee of the board set up to assess risks at the bank – had not held a meeting since the credit crisis erupted, but this didn't seem to matter to the board. 'We have no serious issues or problems – there was no need to change direction or do anything differently,' Hague quoted one board member on the committee as saying. 'David [Drumm] met with the NEDs [non-executive directors] over dinner on a couple of occasions and they were happy.' The committee seemed unaware of the problems facing the bank.

In her summary, Hague told the board that it was in a 'comfort zone': there was a 'cosiness' around the boardroom table. She reported that the non-executive directors were frustrated that they were not contributing more to the strategy of the bank. All the overseas-based board members 'mentioned to one degree or another that they felt outside the club'. In light of the fact that the bank's business was becoming more international, Hague recommended that the board should spend more time abroad discussing issues arising from Anglo's business in foreign countries.

After hearing Hague's report at the January board meeting, the directors agreed to discuss it in detail at their next meeting, in March. That evening they enjoyed a lively dinner with Hague at which there was good-natured banter about her husband's politics and the likelihood of his party ever seeing power again.

The minutes of the board meeting on 7 March 2008 state: 'It was proposed, given time constraints, and agreed to defer the discussion on the findings of both the chairman's individual performance evaluation and the external board review to a future board meeting.' In other words, the Hague report was shelved.

'The report was a box-ticking exercise,' says one former director, who added that it wasn't taken seriously. 'I left it in my drawer.' It was never mentioned in the boardroom again.

★

The day after the January board meeting, Sean FitzPatrick gave his usual stirring performance at Anglo's annual meeting in the Mansion House in Dublin. Despite the uncertainty in the market and a declining share price, shareholders were still in awe of the man whose bank had made enormous returns for so many of them.

FitzPatrick oozed confidence as always, giving no sign of the stresses that the bank was experiencing. In his speech to shareholders, he acknowledged that Anglo was living in dangerous times in the financial markets.

'We are living in a period characterized by significant global economic uncertainty,' FitzPatrick told shareholders. 'The more prudent reappraisal of risk will ultimately benefit the long-term well-being of most economies. I also believe that those who have managed their businesses tightly and have carefully underwritten risk will differentiate themselves over time.'

Like many commentators at this time, FitzPatrick parroted the stock phrase widely peddled by Irish business leaders and politicians whenever concerns were raised about the economy: 'The fundamentals of the Irish economy remain sound and provide a base for relative economic strength in the future, albeit at lower growth levels.'

While FitzPatrick was publicly singing Anglo's praises, privately he continued to encourage his senior executive team and the non-executive board members to demonstrate their belief in the institution by purchasing shares in the bank. In the days following the annual meeting, the heads of the bank's Irish, UK and US lending divisions – Pat Whelan, Declan Quilligan and Tony Campbell – all exercised share options to purchase between 65,000 and 71,000 shares. Finance director Willie McAteer bought 80,000 shares. Most dramatically, David Drumm agreed to exercise 500,000 share options. The shares cost €3.98 million and there was tax of €414,000 due on the transaction, which cost Drumm €4.4 million in total.

Anglo agreed to provide a new loan of €7.65 million to Drumm to renew an existing loan he had received to buy shares in the bank. The interest rate due on the loan was just 1.4 per cent. This was a very low rate for a loan provided to buy shares. No ordinary bank would have agreed to provide a loan on as risky and volatile an investment as shares. But then Anglo was different.

On 22 February 2008 Pat Whelan wrote a letter to Sean Quinn's lieutenant Liam McCaffrey. The subject was not Quinn's vast stake in Anglo shares, but rather his vast borrowings from the bank.

'In seeking visibility for debt reduction of these facilities we note that you have agreed to a disposal of assets within the property portfolio,' Whelan wrote. 'The attached schedule is a list of the assets that you agree that [sic] will be placed on the market for immediate sale. Furthermore it is agreed between us that the target debt reduction from the disposal of these assets is approximately €500 million.'

Anglo was concerned that Quinn had started to draw down 'working-capital' loans in November and December 2007 to cover his share losses and wanted him to cover these losses. While the bank wrote to Quinn urging him to sell the assets, it did not apply any real pressure. Again, Quinn's associates felt that the bank was reluctant to force Quinn to put assets on the market for fear that this would send out a dangerous signal that he was in financial trouble.

At the February meeting of Anglo's nominations committee, board member Fintan Drury raised a concern. Drury's term as a non-executive director was due to end in June 2008. He had told Sean FitzPatrick the previous December that he didn't want to serve a third three-year term.

Drury felt that non-executive directors shouldn't outstay their welcome. Although he and FitzPatrick were very close, the two men had in the past clashed over the bank's decision to retain its longest-serving director, Michael Jacob, on the board. Jacob had joined the board in 1988. Drury felt the board needed new blood.

Drury's concern at the nominations committee meeting related to another matter. The committee would be considering new appointments to the board and, following his retirement from it, they also needed to fill his own position as chairman of the risk and compliance committee. He had been a member of the committee from May 2002 and chairman from April 2007, succeeding Michael Jacob. While he thought appointing 'generalists' or non-bankers to the boards of banks was important, he said that the role of chairman of the risk committee was too complicated for a generalist. It involved understanding complex and evolving international banking rules around the Basel agreements. The volume of information was enormous. Drury, whose own expertise was in public relations, had no personal experience of dealing with these matters. The other members of the risk committee were Lar Bradshaw, a management consultant, and Ned Sullivan, who ran a food business.

Non-executive board member Anne Heraty chaired the nominations committee, which also comprised Lar Bradshaw, David Drumm and Sean FitzPatrick. Drury's concerns were noted by the other board members.

The bank subsequently tried to recruit a number of high-profile non-executive directors with wider experience in financial services in September 2008. They included Paul Manduca, who had a long career in fund management, former investment banker Jonathan Asquith and George Mitchell, a former senior banker at UK lender NatWest. FitzPatrick and Drumm met prospective board members at the offices of Ffion Hague's company, Hanson Green. However, the dramatic events in Irish banking that month proved a distraction and no new appointments were made to the board. FitzPatrick's friend Donal O'Connor was the last appointment to the board under FitzPatrick and Drumm when he replaced Drury in June 2008.

Irish Life & Permanent's boardroom on the seventh floor of the Irish Life building on Middle Abbey Street, north of the River Liffey, has stunning views – among other landmarks visible to the south are the head offices of Bank of Ireland in Dublin 2 and, further off in Ballsbridge, Bankcentre, the head office of AIB.

On the morning of Wednesday, 27 February 2008, at the presentation of the company's 2008 results, Denis Casey, the chief executive of IL&P, was trying his best to reassure financial reporters that the company could fund itself. IL&P had a profitable pensions and investments business in Irish Life, the biggest in Ireland, but all eyes were on the performance of Permanent TSB, the banking division, which had borrowed heavily in the international markets to become Ireland's largest mortgage lender with an Irish mortgage book of close to €30 billion.

Casey, who had moved into the corner office as IL&P chief executive just six months earlier, had driven Permanent TSB's lending during the long housing boom. Permanent TSB had avoided lending to property developers, preferring to focus on home loans. Its problem now was its unusually heavy dependence on inter-bank funding and borrowing in the wholesale money markets. When the credit crunch squeezed the funding markets on which the bank had drawn so heavily to finance its lending to customers, the business model came under extreme strain. As the bank's own borrowing costs in the markets rose and bond investors became less keen to lend to Irish institutions, IL&P was forced to turn to the European Central Bank for funding.

Borrowing from the ECB was not unusual, but it was regarded as a temporary measure to tide a bank over if it couldn't raise money on its own. Relying too heavily on ECB borrowings sent out a signal that a bank was weak. As the credit crisis deteriorated through late 2007 and early 2008 IL&P was forced to rely more heavily on the ECB.

At the results presentation, a truculent Casey adopted a defensive position as he fielded awkward questions from reporters. He was flanked by his finance director Peter Fitzpatrick, who said the company had borrowings of €5.3 billion from the ECB at the end of 2007 but had since reduced this to €4.6 billion. This still accounted for well over 10 per cent of the company's funding.

On Monday, 3 March – five days after the results presentation – Peter Fitzpatrick along with IL&P's head of treasury David Gantly and head of credit Frank McGowan met two senior Central Bank officials, Tony Grimes and Brian Halpin, and the prudential director at the Financial Regulator, Con Horan. They expressed concern and surprise that Fitzpatrick had referred to the size of the ECB loans at the company's results presentation. They told him that this might be regarded in the markets as a weakness and not the strength that IL&P had tried to portray it as during the results presentation. The Central Bank and Financial Regulator made it clear to the IL&P executives that other Irish banks were borrowing from the ECB, though they avoided making direct reference to it publicly.

Fitzpatrick was gobsmacked. He reported back to Casey – who was abroad on 3 March – what he had been told. He felt the Central Bank and Financial Regulator were hypersensitive about Irish banks borrowing heavily from the ECB and the loans being publicly disclosed.

Upon his return to Dublin, Casey telephoned the chief executive of the Regulator, Patrick Neary, to find out more about the concerns that had been raised with Fitzpatrick at the 3 March meeting. Neary told him that there was a sensitivity to an increased level of borrowing from the ECB. At the end of their conversation, Neary suggested that they meet along with the governor of the Central Bank, John Hurley. Neary wanted to discuss a strategy whereby Irish banks would help each other out with funding problems. He referred to this as the 'green jersey agenda'. It was the first time Casey had heard the phrase.

On 11 March 2008, shortly before the Casey–Neary meeting took place, the *Daily Telegraph* published an article by columnist Ambrose Evans-Pritchard under the headline 'Irish banks may need life-support as property prices crash'. The article quoted Morgan Kelly: 'We are going to see banks on life support with very big bail-outs. The precedent for this is what happened in the Nordic countries in the early 1990s when they had to take over the banks. We may have to do something similar.'

The previous January Kelly had written another deeply pessimistic article for the *Irish Times* about the dire state of the property market and the risk of losses facing the banks. 'For their part, banks are now in a position of throwing good money after bad: having lent money for land which has depreciated in value, they are lending more money to build on it in the hope that they can recoup their losses, or at least delay the inevitable change in value that may leave some of them with solvency problems of their own,' he wrote.

Kelly, by now the bête noire of the Irish banks and property lobby, was centre-stage again following the controversy stirred up by Evans-Pritchard's article. One banking analyst, who was compiling his own research on the Irish banks, emailed Kelly to ask if he could see more detailed analysis of his findings.

Kelly emailed back, saying: 'I was just spouting off: I have not had a chance to work on it systematically.' Soon afterwards Kelly received an email from Matt Moran at Anglo that consisted entirely of a copy of Kelly's email exchange with the analyst. Moran wrote no message of his own. He was clearly trying to make a point to Kelly.

The *Irish Independent*'s business editor, Tom McEnaney, ran a story on the emails, naming Kelly under the headline 'Banking collapse economist was "just spouting off"'. The newspaper quoted another economist, Jim Power, who had been chief economist at Bank of Ireland and was now at Friends First, describing Kelly's analysis of the banks as 'ridiculous' and saying that the Irish banks were 'very well capitalized'.

Deeply concerned that the Irish banks' borrowing from the ECB was getting too much attention, John Hurley and Pat Neary arranged a series of meetings with the chief executives of the banks.

Denis Casey met Hurley and Neary at 4.30 p.m. on 13 March 2008 – two days after the *Telegraph*'s article. In a boardroom on the top floor of the Central Bank building on Dame Street, Hurley and Neary spoke about how funding across the Irish banking system was vulnerable and how the Irish banks needed to 'circle the wagons' to support each other. They told Casey that they recognized that AIB and Bank of Ireland enjoyed the benefit of the perception that they were too big to fail. The other banks – Anglo, Irish Life & Permanent and two building societies, EBS and Irish Nationwide – did not have the luxury of implicit government support.

'The two big banks just weren't playing ball,' recalls a senior executive at one of the smaller Irish lenders. 'AIB and Bank of Ireland had a limited appetite for funding arrangements with the other Irish banks. This was not a figment of our imagination. In a liquidity crisis when the oxygen is removed, the smaller canaries go first. The two big banks thought that their credit ratings were strong enough that they could stand on their own. If they didn't, they would be supported so they felt they didn't need to support the smaller Irish financial institutions.'

In an affidavit sent to the Garda investigation into the collapse of Anglo, Casey stated: 'In March 2008, the chief executive of the Financial Regulator and the governor of the Central Bank requested the Irish Life and Permanent Group to participate in a "Green Jersey Agenda" under which Irish financial institutions were asked to provide each other with mutual in-market support at a time of unprecedented turmoil in global financial markets in order to maintain financial stability.'

After meeting Hurley and Neary, Casey reported back to the IL&P board members the Regulator's directive that the 'green jersey agenda' be handled with absolute discretion as this kind of support would be viewed negatively in the international markets and also because the Central Bank was very concerned about negative press coverage on Ireland in the UK media.

At his own meeting with Hurley and Neary, Drumm received the same message that Irish banks should help each other with funding. In response he emailed Anglo's head of treasury John Bowe and the rest of his executive team on Sunday, 16 March: 'John, will you put some thought into what the govenor [sic] asked us to look at – how the Irish banks could help each other? Firstly who are we talking about? AIB, Bank [of Ireland], Anglo, IL[&]P, INBS [Irish Nationwide] and EBS.' Drumm told the executives that he wanted to 'get into dialogue with CB [Central Bank] and other CEOs on this soon rather than later'.

Matt Moran forwarded Drumm's email on to Matt Cullen and Ciaran McArdle in the treasury department. 'Let's think what assistance we can give JB on this,' he said.

Meanwhile, in his discussions with AIB, Hurley specifically raised the issue of providing funding to Anglo. In one meeting with Colm Doherty, the head of AIB's capital markets division, Hurley said that the banks were helping each other out in innovative ways and that AIB could be doing more innovative things with its funding. But Doherty wasn't biting. He wanted to protect AIB. Concerned about the financial state of Anglo and the rumours in the market, Doherty had cut off funding to Anglo in November 2007. Doherty had general discussions with Eamonn Hackett, the head of global treasury, and Nick Treble, the head of treasury within Doherty's division, about Hurley's request. He later responded, saying that AIB would consider helping Anglo if the bank received a letter from Hurley approving the arrangement. Doherty was looking to Hurley for some kind of written but unspecified sanctioning of AIB support for Anglo. No letter was ever provided by the Central Bank, and so AIB refused to provide Anglo with funding.

The absence of any specific directions from Hurley and Neary about the operation of the 'green jersey agenda' allowed the banks to interpret the instruction as they saw fit. Anglo and IL&P took that interpretation far further than AIB was willing to.

10. Under Attack

March 2008 – Anglo's value: €5 billion

On 13 March, as the chief executive of the Financial Regulator and the Central Bank governor were telling Irish Life & Permanent boss Denis Casey about the 'green jersey agenda', an analyst at the London office of investment bank Merrill Lynch published an explosive report. It analysed the most aggressive lenders in the UK commercial property market. The report started a few fires at Anglo.

The analyst, Phil Ingram, had based his report on a simple straw poll of the main commercial property valuers in the UK. It was more anecdotal than scientific, but the answers were fascinating and showed how the Irish banks had piled into the UK property market, applying the same loose credit standards that they had at home. Anglo and AIB – along with the UK banks Halifax Bank of Scotland (HBOS) and Royal Bank of Scotland (RBS) – were cited by the valuers as among the most aggressive lenders. Irish Nationwide Building Society, the 'boutique' lender-to-developers run by Michael Fingleton, was also mentioned.

The report noted that the bubble in the UK commercial property market was 'bursting' and that the banks in this market were going to lose money. Anglo was cited as the bank with the biggest credit risk in the UK commercial property market. Ingram said that the banks that were 'late arrivals to the party' were regarded as being 'especially aggressive'. These banks had taken 'more risk for less reward' and were expected to take the biggest losses. Anglo was among the late arrivals. The bank had grown its UK loans significantly over the previous two to three years as it expanded aggressively outside Ireland.

David Drumm was hopping mad over the report, which he viewed as a piece of research blatantly 'placed' to suit Merrill Lynch's own trading desk. Drumm contacted Kevan Watts, who managed Merrill Lynch's operations in Asia and had had some recent dealings with Anglo, to complain. Drumm told him that Ingram's study wasn't just sloppy but that it was cynically biased towards the position Merrill Lynch's trading desk had taken on Anglo.

Later that same day, one of my contacts at Anglo told me that the report was being withdrawn by Merrill Lynch. I contacted Merrill Lynch's communications department, where a spokeswoman informed me that Ingram's report had been released 'before being edited' and would be re-issued, but that there would be 'no material change' in its findings.

In the March 2011 edition of *Vanity Fair* Michael Lewis referred to the Merrill Lynch note in an article on Ireland's economic crisis. Lewis reported that Ingram's bosses had 'hauled him into meetings with in-house lawyers, who toned down the report's pointed language and purged it of its damning quotes from market insiders, including its many references to Irish banks. And from that moment everything Ingram wrote about Irish banks was edited, and bowdlerized by Merrill Lynch's lawyers. At the end of 2008, Merrill fired him.'

Merrill Lynch and the other leading investment banks had bigger things on their mind that week than the sensibilities of Anglo Irish Bank. On Monday, 10 March rumours began to circulate around a nervous Wall Street and the wider financial markets that Bear Stearns, an eighty-five-year-old institution and America's fifth largest investment bank, had liquidity problems and was having difficulties repaying its lenders. Bear Stearns had $18 billion in cash, but this didn't reassure the panicked markets. Breathless media reports on business channel CNBC suggested that Bear Stearns could be the first big American institution to fail in the crisis arising from the securitization of US subprime debt. Other banks stopped lending to the bank, in effect causing a run on it.

Over the following weekend, the US Federal Reserve stepped in with an orchestrated rescue by its rival JP Morgan in a deal that valued Bear Stearns at just $236 million, or 1.3 per cent of its value a year earlier.

The big news breaking from the US startled Dublin traders, though few could yet believe that an Irish bank would end up in the cross-hairs of frazzled investors. The following Monday was St Patrick's Day, and although the Irish stock market remained open, Ireland's main stockbroking firms all had skeleton staffs working, for 17 March is usually a very sleepy day of trading. Not in 2008, however.

That morning, the influential Lex column in the *Financial Times* suggested that investors should examine three key areas in banking: liquidity – do banks have enough to meet their day-to-day repayments and avoid insolvency; capital – have banks set aside enough in reserve to cover potential bad loans and investments coming down the tracks; and asset quality – just how bad are their loans and investments? 'Even minor prejudices gain significance in a panic sell-off,' wrote the anonymous columnist. 'For example, nobody wants to have anything to do with banks with commercial property exposure (Anglo Irish Bank and HBOS) or buy-to-let lending (Bradford & Bingley).'

The singling out of Anglo, the only Irish bank mentioned by Lex, was akin to marking the bank's door as among the most contagious in a financial plague. Traders in Dublin watched their computer terminals in horror as share prices of the Irish banks nose-dived in the first three hours of trading. They had never seen anything like it. Irish bank stocks were flashing red, signalling dramatic falls. Anglo's share graph was descending almost vertically.

'We were caught in the headlights,' says one Dublin trader. 'There were only a few of us in the office that day and when we saw the share prices fall, we were like: "What the fuck is happening?" There was no Irish news flow that day because it was St Patrick's Day and there were no Irish investors in the market. This was international investors, particularly in London, and the hedge funds were making a strong statement about what they thought about Anglo and Ireland.'

Rumours began to circulate in the market that Lehman Brothers was not far off becoming the next big Wall Street bank to collapse. Worryingly, from an Irish perspective, Lehman held about 5 per cent of Anglo stock. If the US bank was forced to dump this holding, Anglo would come under even more pressure.

Anglo's share price dropped 23 per cent before ending the day down 15 per cent at €6.96 – some distance off its €17.53 peak in June 2007. Almost €1 billion was wiped off the value of the bank in a matter of hours – about €1.6 million for every minute of trading that day. Investors had made a strong statement about what they thought of Anglo. Suddenly, Anglo found itself on an unwelcome global stage, facing even more questions around its financial health.

Senior managers at Anglo were shaken by the catastrophic collapse in the share price. But rather than ask whether investors had legitimate concerns about the bank's exposure to property or its funding position, Anglo executives went looking for a bogeyman. They believed they were the victims of intense bad-mouthing in the market and a one-day short-selling raid by hedge funds. They also suspected that the scale of the CFD positions held by Quinn had leaked out into the market and that the hedge funds had got wind of it.

★

As the St Patrick's Day disaster unfolded, the board of Anglo held a conference call to consider the day's events. One of the non-executive directors suggested that they should be planning what to do in the event that a queue of depositors started to form outside the head office on St Stephen's Green and there was a run on the bank. It was even suggested by a non-executive director of the bank that the management team should have rope barriers ready to corral depositors demanding their money.

With images of queues outside Northern Rock's branches the previous September still fresh in people's minds, Peter Fitzgerald, who was in charge of customer deposits, was instructed to come up with a contingency plan in case the same thing happened to Anglo. Staff were told to be at work at 6 a.m. the next morning to manage any gathering crowds; customers were to be kept off the street in front of the bank at all costs.

The bank's management were even worried that some hedge fund managers would try to boost their profits by placing plants at the branches to encourage queues, so putting further pressure on the bank. Staff members were primed to 'smoke them out' by demanding identification and account details from those in line. Paranoia seemed to be getting the better of Anglo's executives.

A further conference call was held at 1 p.m. the following day. Just three directors were in Anglo's boardroom for it: finance director Willie McAteer and non-execs Anne Heraty and Ned Sullivan. On the phone were David Drumm, Sean FitzPatrick, Pat Whelan, Declan Quilligan, Lar Bradshaw, Fintan Drury, Michael Jacob and Gary McGann. Another non-executive director, Noël Harwerth, couldn't participate.

Drumm did most of the talking. He told the board that the bank was receiving an unusually high number of calls from concerned depositors in light of the share price collapse the previous day and the negative commentary about the bank. He confirmed that the bank had lost some deposits as a result. There was a discussion concerning whether a public statement from the state's top banking authorities about 'the robustness of the Irish banks' would allay fears. The board felt this was a good idea, and agreed that the bank should seek a meeting with Hurley and Neary.

Next on the agenda was Sean Quinn. The official minutes of Anglo's board meetings never mentioned Quinn by name but rather referred to 'a large CFD position connected to the bank's shares'. The bank was afraid that a leaked minute of the meeting could confirm market rumours about the issue.

At the second meeting on that Tuesday, at 3.30 p.m., the board considered several options for dealing with Quinn, who would be facing stiff margin calls from his broker-dealers in the wake of the big drop in the Anglo share price. Holding two board meetings in one day was highly unusual, but warranted, given the trouble facing the bank. The board decided that the best plan was to find a long-term shareholder to acquire the shares supporting Quinn's CFD position.

During these panic-filled days, Anglo board member Fintan Drury got a phone call from Sean FitzPatrick. The Anglo chairman asked the non-executive director, who was a personal friend of finance minister Brian Cowen, whether he should call Cowen to tell him about the problems Anglo was experiencing. Cowen was away in the Far East on a St Patrick's Day ministerial trip.

Cowen's ministerial diary over the period he served as Minister for Finance – September 2004 to May 2008 – shows twelve appointments with Drury. This was a significant number, given that Cowen met the governor of the Central Bank, John Hurley, seventeen times over the same period and officials from the Financial Regulator seven times, including just two meetings with its chief executive, Pat Neary.

Some of the meetings may be explained by the fact that Drury occasionally helped Cowen to write his speeches, including the eulogy Cowen gave at the graveside of former president Patrick Hillery on 15 April 2008. It was a landmark speech for Cowen, who had just been elected leader of Fianna Fáil and was due to take over as Taoiseach just weeks later.

Following the St Patrick's Day Massacre, Drury thought it might be worthwhile for FitzPatrick to talk to Cowen. Drury rang Cowen to ask whether he would take a call from the Anglo chairman. Cowen called John Hurley, the governor of the Central Bank, to see whether Hurley had any objections to him speaking to FitzPatrick. Hurley didn't, and Drury was told to give FitzPatrick the go-ahead. FitzPatrick phoned Cowen on his mobile. He told him about the collapse of the bank's shares and how he believed it was connected to the shareholding built up by Quinn.

As he later told Tom Lyons, FitzPatrick informed Cowen that 'what was really happening was that pressure was coming from the shorters, these guys, the hedge funds, trying to get Quinn'.

The Anglo board met again at noon on Wednesday, 19 March. The board discussed the announcement of an investigation by the UK's banking regulator, the Financial Services Authority (FSA), into rumours about and short selling of the shares of HBOS, whose share price had collapsed

17 per cent the previous day. Like Anglo, HBOS had an enormous property exposure.

The FSA wanted to discover whether certain investors, namely hedge
funds, had orchestrated the share price declines by spreading rumours
about the bank. Anglo believed that something equally sinister was at work
in the Irish market and wanted the Financial Regulator to investigate and
punish those responsible.

The board also discussed an article in that day's *Irish Times* which questioned the bank's funding position, linking concerns about deposits to the
massive share sell-off. 'The bank was cursed by the general lack of trust in
the banking sectors, fears that deposits were walking out the door and
rumours that troubled US investment bank Lehman's was placing a 2.4 per
cent stake in the company with a third party,' wrote reporter Laura Slattery. 'Even, as one dealer said, if there was "probably not" any truth in any
of it, the sickness in the financial system following the collapse of Bear
Stearns is enough for investors, from institutional giants to small-time
fund managers alike, to cut Anglo out of the picture, while hedge fund
managers took the opportunity to short the stock.'

Slattery's report was accurate, painfully so for Anglo. It touched a nerve
with the bank's board of directors, particularly the reference to the lost
deposits, which they felt could trigger further withdrawals. For a bank, it's
a vicious circle: reports about customers withdrawing deposits lead to
more customers withdrawing deposits. Responding to concerns raised at
the Wednesday board meeting about the bank's deposits, Drumm said
Anglo's funding remained solid: despite withdrawals, the bank could still
meet repayment demands on deposits.

Drumm reported to the board on a meeting he had had with John Hurley and Pat Neary earlier that day. (The bank was in contact with the
Central Bank and Financial Regulator by phone every day, sometimes several times a day, following the share price collapse.) They had discussed the
board's concerns about short selling in the bank's stock, he said. The board
agreed to retain advisers from investment bank Morgan Stanley to see
whether there was enough appetite in the market to find a long-term
investor to take Quinn out of the picture.

One of the dangers that exercised Anglo was that every share held by a
broker-dealer in respect of a Quinn CFD could be lent out to short sellers
looking for a quick profit. Quinn's 215 million CFDs made the bank highly
vulnerable. At one point during 2008, on Anglo's urging, Quinn asked his
CFD broker-dealers not to lend out the underlying shares on his CFDs.

His requests were ignored – his brokers could do as they liked with the stock and they were in business to make money, not to protect Quinn's position.

On Thursday, 20 March, Anglo's board met again by conference call at 2 p.m. The directors agreed that they needed to push the Regulator to take some action to protect the bank from what they believed were speculators making big money betting against it. Later that afternoon Drumm placed a call to John Hurley and pleaded with him to release a statement on the health of the banking system to avoid a run on Anglo's deposits. Hurley told Drumm that the Central Bank was considering all options. The following day was Good Friday and the start of the four-day Easter holiday weekend. Drumm told Hurley that if the Regulator didn't do something at once then there could be a major run on deposits when the bank reopened the following Tuesday. Unusually, Hurley agreed to run past Drumm a draft statement the Central Bank was going to issue. The Anglo chief executive approved it and asked the Central Bank governor to release the statement as quickly as possible.

The first statement came later that day from the Financial Regulator: 'The Financial Regulator is concerned that false and misleading rumours circulating in financial markets in recent days are connected to unusual trading patterns in Irish shares,' it said, adding that the office would be examining 'certain transactions in this regard'.

Then Hurley issued his own statement in which he 'strongly' supported the Regulator's actions in relation to 'investigations into trading in financial shares over recent days'. He also said: 'The Irish banking sector remains robust and has no material exposures to the sub-prime market.'

The interaction between Hurley and Drumm shows how cosy the relationship was between the bank and the state. Drumm had pleaded with the governor for a statement to protect the bank's share price; he'd got two.

The strong statements from Dame Street hit the mark: Anglo's share price jumped 14 per cent to €7.85 on the Thursday. Short sellers in the bank rushed to buy long in the stock in a move known in the market as 'short covering' to protect themselves. All told, Anglo lost €1 billion in deposits over the course of the week of the St Patrick's Day Massacre, but the statements from the Financial Regulator and Hurley on the Thursday stopped further haemorrhage of funding from the bank – for the time being.

On Good Friday, 21 March, with the stock markets closed, FitzPatrick and Drumm went down to the Central Bank to meet Hurley, Neary and

Horan to discuss the flow of deposits out of Anglo. Hurley was particularly concerned about what the bank was going to do the following Tuesday when it reopened its doors. Drumm assured him that the bank would have senior staff in the branches at 6 a.m. to watch for any sign of a queue forming and to be prepared to bring people inside if necessary to prevent images of queuing depositors appearing in the media.

The media's reporting of the St Patrick's Day Massacre and coverage of the bank's difficulties over the previous months was a source of much frustration to the bank. Drumm felt that media reports were encouraging depositors to withdraw their money, and even suggested to Hurley at one point that he should call the editors of the national newspapers to explain the gravity of the situation facing the banks and the country at large, though Hurley never did so.

Later on Good Friday, Anglo's finance director Willie McAteer drove out to Neary's house in south Dublin to go through what the bank believed were the margins on Quinn's CFD positions and the effect of the share price losses on Quinn. The Regulator wanted to familiarize itself with the Quinn issue after the 'bear raid'.

Privately, David Drumm told colleagues that he didn't believe the Regulator's investigation into alleged rumour-mongering about the bank would go anywhere. But he wasn't really concerned about an investigation. He just wanted some public statement from Dame Street that would stop the avalanche of rumours that was driving down the share price.

The previous autumn Anglo had clashed with Davy over the bank's view that the stockbrokers were 'talking down' their shares. In the early months of 2008 Anglo had another stockbroking firm, Merrion Capital, in its sights. The bank had received reports back from property developer Sean Mulryan, who had an account at Merrion, that an investment adviser there had been rubbishing the bank.

The adviser, Ken Costello, reportedly told Mulryan that there had been a small run on Anglo, with about €30 million to €40 million being withdrawn, and advised him to get his money out of the banks. 'They're fucked – the Irish banks are fucked,' Costello reputedly said. Clients liked Costello's straight-talking manner – he generated good business and was one of the best-paid people at the firm – but Mulryan didn't agree with his assessment. He told Costello that he knew the Anglo guys had plans to raise money in the US and that the bank would be fine.

Merrion had never been a great supporter of Anglo, believing the bank was over-exposed to property. Merrion's CEO John Conroy had been at an investment conference in New York some years earlier at which Fitz-Patrick sat alongside the chief executives of two other Irish public companies during a panel presentation on Irish companies. If you want to buy the Celtic Tiger, forget about these two other companies and buy Anglo, FitzPatrick told investors. The other company executives were furious. Conroy was stunned by FitzPatrick's chutzpah.

Drumm and other executives at Anglo knew Costello of old. He had worked in the bank's wealth management division until 2002 but had fallen out with Tony Campbell, who had helped set up the division, and left the bank a short time later.

Costello's would not be the only departure from the division. During subsequent years there were always tensions between investment advisers in Anglo's private bank and the lenders in the main bank. The lenders feared that if the advisers encouraged the bank's big customers to invest in a project that failed, their lending relationship with the bank might be ruined. 'If you were in lending at Anglo, everyone outside that area was regarded as second-class citizens within the bank,' says a former executive.

FitzPatrick got on to Conroy. He wanted Costello fired; he also tried to smear the broker, claiming erroneously that Costello had been fired from Anglo years before for fraud – an allegation he later withdrew and apolo-gized for making.

In response to FitzPatrick's charge that Merrion was undermining Anglo, Conroy argued that the firm was simply taking the same negative view of the bank that the market had taken and which was reflected in the falling share price. Conroy felt Costello was simply relaying the concerns in the market to Mulryan.

On 26 March Pat Neary called Conroy. He reassured him that the Regu-lator was not targeting Merrion in particular with its investigation but that it was asking all stockbroking firms whether there were any unusual share trades in Anglo or whether any rumours about the bank had been received or passed on since the start of March.

The Regulator also looked into the activities of Seamus Murphy and Ronan Hurley, two traders at Davy who had been targeted by Anglo the previous autumn for advising clients to sell the bank's stock. The Regula-tor sought emails and other communications from Murphy and Hurley. Davy handed over everything. It had nothing to hide. The firm gave the Regulator details of the investors who had bought and sold the stock and showed that no brokers were doing their own dealing. The evidence proved that there was no conspiracy against Anglo.

There was a sense among stockbrokers that Anglo and the Regulator were working hand in glove. A letter sent to Merrion by Anglo's lawyers Matheson Ormsby Prentice, on Drumm's instruction, threatening the firm with legal action over Costello's comments to Mulryan and demanding a retraction of what he had said was copied to the Regulator. Neary insisted that his investigation was separate from Anglo's representations, but Conroy was not convinced.

The Regulator and Anglo wanted to find out if Merrion was spreading – or was the source of – a rumour that Merrill Lynch had withdrawn a $2 billion credit line from Anglo. The rumour, which was incorrect, appeared to originate from instant-messaging communications between brokers and their customers via their Bloomberg news wire machines. It had started with a US fund management client of Merrion's sending a message to a broker at the firm, asking about Merrill Lynch pulling a credit line from an unnamed bank. The message was then circulated within the firm and to outside investors and other brokers. At some point in the forwarding of the message, the instruction to 'hold' Anglo stock, meaning do not buy or sell Anglo shares, was added, leading people to believe that Anglo was the bank in question.

Anglo filed a complaint in the London High Court claiming that an employee of the London stockbroking firm Mirabaud Securities, part of a private Swiss banking group, had sent an email on 29 February saying: 'Anglo-Irish, ML pull a $2bln credit line? Rumor.' The bank wanted the names of everyone who had either sent or received the email and a copy of all communication between Mirabaud and other parties between 25 February and 7 March 2008. Anglo was trying to trace the email back to the original author, believing that there was a major conspiracy against the bank. Nothing ever came of Anglo's complaint.

The Regulator did not find a jot of evidence to show that Merrion had spread rumours about Anglo or profited on the back of them. Conroy was incensed. The firm spent the equivalent of two weeks' work by eight people, worth in the region of €50,000, with a further six-figure sum paid in legal fees to one of Dublin's biggest law firms, William Fry, to defend itself from Anglo's suspicions. It was a huge management distraction and didn't help Merrion's reputation either.

Merrion's chairman Ray Curran and FitzPatrick met and agreed to bury the hatchet. Drumm was furious, feeling that FitzPatrick had caved in. He felt that Anglo should have made an example of Merrion by suing them and that this would have sent a signal out into the wider market.

Costello's language on the call to Mulryan might have been better chosen, but this was how some brokers spoke. 'They were swimming against the tide and going against the culture at the time,' says a source with intimate knowledge of the episode. 'Anglo was one of the darlings of the Celtic Tiger and if you went against them, they would come out fighting.'

Costello's, and Merrion's, view of Anglo would eventually be vindicated, although, as the source says, 'It took nine or ten more months to show Anglo for what it was.'

As Anglo's share price fell, the bank continued to supply Sean Quinn with 'working-capital' facilities to enable him to meet his margin calls. The board approved the loans, and the Financial Regulator was notified.

An internal report compiled almost two years later shows the rapid growth of Quinn's borrowings from the bank as the value of his investment in it fell further and further. Over a six-day period around the St Patrick's Day Massacre Quinn drew down €367.5 million – an average of €60 million a day – to meet the mounting losses on his investment, according to the Anglo report. He borrowed €67.5 million on Friday, 14 March, followed by €20 million and €220 million on two separate loans the following Monday, 17 March, and €60 million the day after that. As 17 March was a bank holiday in Ireland, a UK branch of Anglo provided the loan that day. (In June 2011 Quinn's finance director Dara O'Reilly would testify during a court case involving the bank that as Anglo's share price fell and Quinn's own resources became 'extremely limited', O'Reilly would call the bank and give a 'rough calculation' of how the margin call had been determined. Documents were then drawn up saying that the loans were purportedly for 'property development', O'Reilly testified, and O'Reilly would then obtain the necessary signatures so that the loans could be transferred. 'When I rang the bank on a very frequent basis in 2008, it was very clear it was for margin calls,' he told the court.)

On 18 March Quinn Group chief executive Liam McCaffrey fired off a letter to Michael O'Sullivan, the Anglo lender who managed Quinn's account at the bank, in relation to that day's €220 million draw-down. The letter was astonishing. Writing on behalf of Quinn, McCaffrey effectively signed over potential control of the Quinn Group, a business he had built up through hard graft over a thirty-five-year period. In return for the latest loan, Quinn agreed to hand over the share certificates in the main company

at the apex of the Quinn Group corporate pyramid. It covered the ownership and ultimate control of his many and varied businesses. He was putting
his life's work on the line.

In truth, Quinn had no choice. He had to meet the margin calls and the
only way to do this was to borrow more and more from Anglo. He also
offered the bank personal guarantees in his name and the names of all of his
children to cover the new loans, as the bank had requested.

'I can confirm that as additional comfort in relation to the security on
this facility the Quinn family are prepared to support their personal guarantees by giving Anglo Irish Bank Corporation plc physical custody of
their shares in Quinn Group RoI Limited,' said McCaffrey in the letter to
the bank.

While the added security helped, Anglo was still in a weak position.
Besides its debt to Anglo, Quinn Group owed €1.3 billion to a syndicate of
Irish and UK banks and investors, and the debts were structured in such a
way that the syndicate was ahead of Anglo in the queue to be repaid.

The St Patrick's Day Massacre had come close to breaking Anglo; it had
taken the intervention of the Central Bank and Financial Regulator to halt
a sell-off of shares that could have sparked a fatal run on the bank. Anglo
believed that any public disclosure of Quinn's shareholding and a disorderly unwinding of his investment in the bank could cause the same sort of
chain reaction – and it could not necessarily count on the regulators to turn
the tide a second time. The Quinn situation had to be resolved.

11.   The Quinn Fixation

April 2008 – Anglo's value: €6 billion

Drumm felt that FitzPatrick, after initially standing back following his move to a non-executive role as chairman in 2005, was starting to muscle in to the running of the bank as the financial crisis worsened.

In his interviews for *The FitzPatrick Tapes*, FitzPatrick claimed that during 2008 he left the running of the bank to Drumm: 'David was chief executive now at this stage for the guts of four years. He was running his own show. He was clearly the boss and he was seen as the boss.'

In an interview for the *Irish Times* in January 2011, Drumm challenged this recollection, saying that FitzPatrick, even though he was chairman, had actually played a much more significant and leading role in events at Anglo during 2008 than FitzPatrick had described. Drumm agreed that FitzPatrick did step back after becoming chairman in 2005. In his first two years in the role FitzPatrick left Drumm to his own devices while he focused on personal investments and travelled extensively – 'If anything, he probably over-corrected,' said Drumm – but FitzPatrick was 'not a back seat kind of guy', Drumm told me. He said that the chairman would have found it hard to maintain a hands-off approach after being chief executive for eighteen years and growing the bank into a €13 billion company, and that 'when things started to get difficult in 2007 he started to come back into the picture. I had no difficulty with that and frankly I was glad of all the help and advice I could get. When Bear Stearns collapsed and we had the mini-run on the bank in March 2008 Sean more or less took charge again.'

FitzPatrick had an office on the third floor of St Stephen's Court, just down the hall from Drumm, and he began to come in every day. 'Perhaps his instincts kicked in and he could see trouble and couldn't just stand by and be a spectator. Whatever his reasons he became more and more involved and began to interfere in the day-to-day executive decision-making,' said Drumm. 'It was not only affecting me it was also causing significant frustration among the executive directors and senior executives as they were getting constant calls from him, second guessing their actions and decisions. The reason it was damaging to the bank is it undermined the management function within the bank as people began to wonder who was in charge. It also created uncertainty in people's minds as Sean's increasing involvement in the day-to-day operations naturally created concerns about what was happening at the bank.'

Drumm felt this was harming the bank. By April 2008 he was so concerned that he raised the matter with Ned Sullivan in his role as senior independent director. Drumm felt that he could not do his job properly with FitzPatrick behaving as if he was Anglo's chief executive again.

Sullivan was not as close to FitzPatrick as some of the other directors were, but he was nervous about meeting Drumm behind FitzPatrick's back. 'What's our alibi for meeting?' Sullivan asked Drumm when they met. When Drumm outlined his problem, Sullivan told him that he must somehow make FitzPatrick change his behaviour. Sullivan suggested asking him to take an office outside the bank. A week later Drumm put the idea to his chairman. FitzPatrick baulked, saying that it was normal for the chairman to have an office in the bank. Drumm replied that the circumstances at Anglo were far from normal: FitzPatrick had been chief executive for eighteen years before becoming chairman. FitzPatrick said the office was convenient and he had everything there he needed. Drumm offered to move his files and provide him with a PA. FitzPatrick said he would think about it and give him an answer by June.

Several weeks later Drumm received a call from the bank's former chairman Peter Murray, who was very close to FitzPatrick. They agreed to meet for breakfast in Carluccio's café on Dawson Street on 3 June. Murray said that FitzPatrick had mentioned Drumm's proposal that he move out of the bank. Murray thought that, as chairman, FitzPatrick should have an office in the bank, but that he should not be there every day. Drumm pointed out that FitzPatrick was no ordinary chairman. Murray did not comment. The breakfast ended, FitzPatrick never moved, and 'the relationship between us did not improve', said Drumm.

About a week and a half after the St Patrick's Day Massacre, Drumm and FitzPatrick had another meeting with Quinn and McCaffrey at Buswell's Hotel. The purpose of the meeting was to encourage Quinn to agree to an orderly unwinding of his Anglo CFDs. The bank wanted Quinn to cut his holding in the bank by half, and to 'go long' on the other half, about 15 per cent of the bank's shares, holding that amount directly in ordinary shares. Anglo wanted Quinn to sell as much as he could but believed it could only realistically place between 10 and 15 per cent in the market. At this stage, the bank had not raised the prospect of lending money to Quinn to help him take a long position in the stock.

Anglo's board felt that if some of Quinn's CFDs were placed with other investors and he went long on the remainder, it would bring certainty to Quinn's investment in the bank and end the market rumours and short-seller attacks once and for all.

Quinn was completely against this. To buy the stock outright, Quinn would have to pony up cash to cover 100 per cent of the value of the stock. He would be crystallizing losses on his CFD positions – losses he still believed would be reversed.

Anglo was desperately trying to convince Quinn that he was a big part of the problem – that *his* investment was among the forces that were caus-ing the share price to fall. Drumm felt that McCaffrey understood this but that he was struggling to make his boss realize that he had to do the right thing.

The discussion went round in circles until FitzPatrick asked Drumm to leave the room. Quinn motioned to McCaffrey to do the same. Drumm and McCaffrey went into an adjacent conference room and waited. When they were called back in about twenty minutes later FitzPatrick announced that they had agreed a deal whereby Quinn would sell CFD positions in 9.4 per cent of the bank's stock, leaving him with about 20 per cent. He would 'go long' on about 15 per cent of this, holding it in ordinary shares as a long-term investment, and the remainder would be left in CFDs to be unwound at a later date. It wasn't what Anglo wanted – FitzPatrick and Drumm had been hoping to get Quinn out of CFDs entirely – but Drumm felt it was a good start.

What Drumm didn't discover until later was that FitzPatrick had agreed to lend Quinn even more money 'to tide him over'. Drumm felt that Quinn, being a skilled negotiator, knew FitzPatrick would agree to further lending just to get the share deal done.

Much to the surprise of the other parties at the meeting, FitzPatrick was later quoted in *The FitzPatrick Tapes* saying that he had not been aware that the bank was lending to Quinn to cover the margin calls on the losses on his investment in Anglo. He said that he had no idea how Quinn was fund-ing his losses on the bank's stock: 'I am not trying to be evasive with you,' he told Tom Lyons. 'I just don't know. I wasn't close enough to it. I was a hundred million miles away from it. I just didn't get involved in any of the lending. I had no idea what money we had lent to the guy at that stage in general terms.'

FitzPatrick's statement on this point is not credible. At the time of the Buswell's meeting, Quinn owed the bank close to €1.6 billion, of which €367 million had been lent over six days following the St Patrick's Day Massacre. The Quinn issue had also been discussed at length during five board meetings, all attended by FitzPatrick as chairman, over that frenetic period. Board members were regularly asking how Quinn was covering his losses. Anglo executives maintain that the board was fully aware of the heavy lending to Quinn.

FitzPatrick's statement of ignorance regarding Anglo's loans to Quinn surprised Quinn's people too. 'Of course he knew about the loans,' says one of the businessman's close associates. 'To me it was inconceivable that anyone would go into the meeting without knowing the exposure to Quinn.'

On the evening of the Buswell's meeting, the board met by conference call. FitzPatrick recounted the details in his usual dramatic fashion. He told the directors that Quinn had hugged him and even cried when McCaffrey and Drumm were out of the room. Drumm felt that his role in the day's events was more that of a bystander than chief executive of the bank. Fitz-Patrick had called the shots.

On Monday, 31 March, Anglo's chief financial officer Matt Moran emailed Con Horan, the prudential director at the Financial Regulator, to report that the bank and Quinn had agreed to a deal to unwind part of his CFD stake. The email was sent at 6.01 p.m. Moran copied his colleagues Fiachre O'Neill, head of legal, tax and compliance, and Willie McAteer, the finance director. Moran told Horan that he was forwarding a copy of the agreement reached between Anglo and Sean Quinn, the Quinn Group and any affiliates of the business as requested, pointing out that it had been signed by both sides that afternoon.

The letter discloses that Quinn's direct 15 per cent shareholding would be split among Quinn's five children – his son and four daughters – so that no one individual would hold more than 3 per cent of the bank. This would prevent the triggering of an immediate public disclosure under stock market rules.

The bank also wanted reassurance that the Regulator would agree to allow each of Quinn's children to hold the shares individually and to acknowledge that they were not acting in concert, which would be against stock market rules.

Horan was sent the legal agreement reached between the bank and

Quinn that day. It stipulated that the placing of the CFDs would be done at a discount of no greater than 5 per cent of the current share price. Anglo had to strike a balance in the pricing of the deal. In order to attract a buyer for such a large and 'distressed' shareholding, it had to offer a discount; but the discount couldn't be so great that Quinn would object to selling at a price that was lower than he could theoretically get in the market.

Morgan Stanley, Anglo's investment banking advisers, and Matheson Ormsby Prentice, the bank's corporate lawyers, gave advice on the transaction. The Financial Regulator encouraged the bank to complete the placing of the shares as quickly as possible. The bank said that it would fund Quinn's purchase of the shares, to which the Regulator raised no objection.

Then came the hard part. Anglo had to find investors to take a stake of almost 10 per cent of a bank that was heavily exposed to Irish property at a time of falling prices and that had shed more than €6 billion in value in less than a year during a time of severe strain in the financial markets. It was an impossible task, but Anglo's management, with their can-do attitude, believed they could find investors.

In the first half of March the bank had organized a three-day trip to the Middle East. Drumm, Willie McAteer and Matt Moran were chaperoned by Morgan Stanley as they travelled to Dubai and Abu Dhabi for a series of meetings with sovereign wealth funds, multibillion-dollar companies owned by the oil-rich states and ruling families of the Middle East. Anglo were at the back of a long queue. Every major US bank had approached sovereign wealth funds for help as the financial crisis deteriorated. They were regarded as white knights.

Anglo's approaches to these cash-rich funds proved unsuccessful. It was hardly surprising. Why would they buy into a small bank based in Ireland with a heavy exposure to a country and property market that appeared to be on the brink of a downturn from one of the biggest booms in modern economic history?

While in the Middle East, Drumm received an email from Pat Whelan to let him know that Quinn was 'panicking a bit because he wanted to know if we are planning to issue a new statement to counteract the negative commentary'. Drumm replied a few minutes later, slightly frustrated. 'He rang yesterday and I called back, didn't get him – will ring hiim [sic] today, tell Liam to calm him down he's [Quinn] done enough damage – I'm out here up to me bol##x in sand because of that f++ker.'

On 1 April Drumm gave a presentation at an investor conference run by Morgan Stanley at the Hilton Hotel in London's Park Lane. His seven-slide presentation to the conference repeated the points made in the bank's detailed trading update from 6 March. The bank expected to grow loans by 10 per cent in the first half of the year and earnings by 15 per cent.

The presentation made no reference to the traumatic middle week of March. The bank had experienced 'strong customer deposit growth' and enjoyed an 'excellent liquidity position'. Anglo was 'well resourced' in terms of funding and capital, and there was 'significant organic growth potential' in the bank's markets. To anyone listening in, it would appear that there was nothing wrong at all.

The bank's intention was to 'soft sound' a few investors on the possibility of taking up part of Quinn's holding. But the mood was far more negative than anyone expected. There were still major concerns about the future of Lehman Brothers and uncertainty as to whether major European banks had declared all of their losses on the US subprime crisis. Investors wanted to sell financial stocks, not buy more.

While in London, Drumm got a call from Neary, who was keen to know if any of the Quinn stock had been offloaded. Drumm reported that the mood at the conference was poor. Neary was disappointed.

Morgan Stanley named the plan to resolve the Quinn situation 'Project Maple'. One theory is that this refers to the Anglo logo's resemblance to a maple leaf, but in documents 'Maple' was sometimes used as code for 'Quinn'. The choice of a five-letter code name was not, in any case, coincidental: investment banks often choose pseudonyms containing the same number of letters as the client's real name so that the alias can easily be replaced in documents if confidentiality is lifted from the project.

Anglo's advisers identified the Dutch Rabobank as a potential strategic partner that might be interested in buying up the 9.4 per cent Quinn CFD stake. Better known as a prudent lender to the agricultural and food industries, Rabobank had found itself in difficulty with its Irish subsidiary, the Agricultural Credit Corporation (ACC), the former government-owned bank which it purchased for €165 million in 2002. During the property boom ACC had followed Anglo, AIB, Bank of Scotland (Ireland) and Ulster Bank into the property market. It joined the party at the very end, providing some of its biggest loans to the likes of property developers John Fleming and Liam Carroll after the property market had begun to turn. ACC's loan book was already in a dire state, with about a third of its borrowers in default.

Morgan Stanley believed that if Anglo was willing to take over the struggling ACC, which had a loan book of about €5 billion (compared with Anglo's €70 billion at that time), Rabobank might be willing in return to buy some or all of the shares backing the Quinn CFDs that the bank was trying to sell.

An alliance with Rabobank would help Anglo for another reason. Rabobank was the only private bank in the world that had managed to hang on to its top 'AAA' credit rating during the crisis, as its Irish radio adverts attested. The bank protected this prized rating zealously, as it was a magnet for deposits. Anglo believed that its own standing – and possibly its credit rating – would improve if it had the backing of a large investment from a Dutch bank regarded as one of the most careful lenders in the world.

'Neither side of it made sense but put together it made sense,' says a former Anglo director. 'ACC was a bag of shit – it had come to the property development market very late and Rabobank were scared to death that ACC would have an impact on their credit rating. We said we would take ACC, and we will pay you with Anglo stock and you will take a bit of this Quinn stake.'

Drumm and his executives travelled to Rabobank's base in Utrecht a number of times to try to sell the plan to the Dutch bank. The two banks kept talking until July 2008.

Meanwhile, a number of US institutional shareholders in Anglo were asked if they would be interested in increasing their stakes by taking some or all the 9.4 per cent. Only one, the Boston private equity firm Bain Capital, responded. Drumm met them with Tony Campbell, the head of Anglo's US operations, in June.

Bain is best known for having been co-founded by Mitt Romney, a former governor of Massachusetts who had recently withdrawn from the race for the Republican nomination in the 2008 United States presidential election. The firm was a long-term shareholder in the bank and Drumm knew its people well from his Boston days. Anglo sent Declan Quilligan, the head of Anglo's UK operations, to Frankfurt to meet some of Bain's European representatives.

On 24 April 2008 Anglo hosted a special private dinner at Heritage House for Minister for Finance Brian Cowen. Fintan Drury had organized the dinner so that Cowen could meet Anglo's board members and executives after a meeting of the board earlier that afternoon.

The timing for Anglo could not have been better. Cowen had just been elected leader of Fianna Fáil without challenge, succeeding Bertie Ahern who had resigned in the face of a financial scandal. Earlier that day Cowen had led the tributes to Ahern on his last day in the Dáil as Taoiseach; Cowen would soon assume that office himself. The timing of the dinner was a coincidence. Drury had been trying to plan it for six months and it had been postponed on a number of occasions.

Drury met Cowen at the Department of Finance that evening and they walked the short distance to Heritage House. On the way, Cowen told Drury that he didn't want the dinner to last any longer than ninety minutes as he wanted the two of them to go for pints afterwards.

After introductions and drinks, the bankers and the incoming Taoiseach sat down to dinner. Cowen, seated to the right of Drumm, was 'lorrying into the wine', says one former executive at the bank. After they finished eating, FitzPatrick gave a short speech and then asked each executive and a few of the non-executive directors to give Cowen an update of how business was doing in their respective areas.

Pat Whelan spoke about Ireland, Declan Quilligan the UK and Tony Campbell the US. Because there was no one on the board specifically representing treasury, Drumm spoke about the state of the funding markets.

Gary McGann, Ned Sullivan, Anne Heraty and Drury, all non-executive directors, also spoke. The new Taoiseach was told about the pressure in the property market as a result of the credit crunch and how the bank had funding problems because of the turmoil in the international financial markets, but that it wasn't a major issue.

There was also a general chat about the bloodstock industry. Non-executive Anglo director Noël Harwerth had connections with Kentucky and the bloodstock industry there, and Cowen, a big racing fan, had plenty to say about it, as did a few of the bankers. There was general banter about Drury's ignorance on the subject, given that he was chairman of bookmaker Paddy Power. 'Sure you don't know anything about horseracing,' Cowen joked with Drury during the conversation.

In November 2010, during a conference call with Anglo customer and property developer Garrett Kelleher and *Irish Independent* journalist Bruce Arnold, David Drumm recounted details of his conversation with Cowen that night. An *Irish Daily Mail* journalist, Jason O'Toole, was also present at Arnold's house in south Dublin and listening in on the conversation. The call had been set up by Kelleher to find out from Drumm just how involved Cowen and the government had been in the events leading up to the collapse of Anglo Irish Bank and how much they knew about the Quinn stake. Kelleher, a critic of the state's response to the banking crisis – particularly with regard to the effect of the National Asset Management Agency (NAMA) on the property market – wanted to get some dirt on the government.

The *Irish Daily Mail* subsequently reported Drumm's comments on the call in January 2011. According to the report, Drumm told Kelleher and the others gathered in Arnold's house that he had asked Cowen at the dinner whether he could speak to the National Treasury Management Agency (NTMA) about putting more money on deposit with Anglo.

The NTMA managed the government's finances and borrowings in the debt markets. At any one time it held cash of about €20 billion in reserve and spread it around about 100 banks and financial institutions worldwide, trying to get the best rate without compromising the safety of the money.

Michael Somers, the chief executive of the NTMA, and some of his senior staff were never comfortable with Anglo's business model and its lack of a traditional deposit-collecting base. Accordingly, Somers limited the NTMA's exposure to Anglo, placing a deposit of €40 million with the bank in August 2007 for a year, while at the same time placing up to €200 million with AIB and Bank of Ireland.

Speaking to RTE's *Today with Pat Kenny* radio programme in January 2011, Somers said: 'When we began to look at banks and withdrawing deposits and putting them with the Central Bank, I was somewhat dismayed to discover that we were stuck with Anglo, as it were, for a year because my inclination would have been at that stage possibly to take the money off them.'

After the financial crisis struck, the NTMA refused to place any more money on deposit with Anglo. This infuriated the bank. At a time of severe financial difficulty, the government's own debt management agency, which was flush with cash reserves, was not helping out an Irish bank in its time of need.

Drumm told Kelleher and the others on the conference call that at the Heritage House dinner he and Cowen 'had a long conversation about our funding worries and that not only would we like the money, that that would help, that it would send out the right signal to the market – that the government was supportive of the bank. So when I asked had anything happened with it, he got annoyed and said that he had – quote – "I told those fuckers." He said: "I told those fuckers." There's no real proof, unfortunately.'

Drumm's phrasing – 'I asked had anything happened with it' – implies that Anglo had previously made representations to Cowen or to his department seeking deposit support from the NTMA; Cowen's response, as quoted by Drumm, seems to have been that he made representations to the NTMA on the matter but that they had not been acted upon.

As recently as two days before the Heritage House dinner, senior Department of Finance officials had spoken to senior staff at the Central Bank and Financial Regulator about discussions they had had with the NTMA about the possibility of giving liquidity assistance to the Irish banks. While the NTMA may have been asked to support the Irish banks generally, there is no record of any specific request being made by Cowen or the department to assist Anglo specifically.

Drumm told Kelleher et al. that he wasn't surprised that Cowen had readily agreed to help Anglo because 'Sean was in there'. FitzPatrick used to brag to Drumm that he was part of Cowen's 'kitchen cabinet', a group of senior figures with backgrounds in economics and business whom he could call on for advice.

'Sean was probably giving smart advice to Brian Cowen. He had very, very smart people around him,' said Drumm. The kitchen cabinet meetings were 'ad hoc, on demand, not scheduled, weekly, evening time, no real set tone'.

'Sean attended these informal meetings. I cannot confirm that a meeting of the kitchen cabinet was ever held in the bank. In fact, I think they were usually in Government Buildings. The whole purpose of the cabinet was to get a broader brief.'

To date there has been no corroboration of Drumm's view that FitzPatrick was part of a 'kitchen cabinet' of advisers to Cowen. FitzPatrick may well have embellished his role in his conversations with Drumm. A source close to Cowen disputed any characterization of a group of advisers in existence around the politician, saying that Cowen may have met prominent business figures for discussions from time to time but there was certainly no formal or informal grouping that could be described as a 'kitchen cabinet'.

After the Heritage House dinner came to light in January 2011, Cowen denied that he had made any request to the NTMA to help Anglo during 2008. Somers also came to his defence, saying that he received no request for further funding into Anglo from Cowen. The strength of the denials seemed to be enough to rubbish Drumm's claims.

It also emerged in January 2011 that Cowen as Minister for Finance had asked the NTMA to deposit additional funds in the Irish banks – in all of them, not just in Anglo – in December 2007 because of the serious liquidity pressures they were under at that time. Somers had sought legal advice before agreeing to the request. He said that he had got 'a bit of heat' from Department of Finance officials not to reduce the NTMA's deposit levels in general across the Irish banks, despite his own personal concerns about Anglo. The advice said that he should get written instructions from the minister before depositing any more of the NTMA's funds with the Irish banks. In the end the NTMA placed the deposits.

Through April and May Drumm received regular phone calls from Pat Neary and Con Horan, asking how he was getting on with finding an investor for the Quinn stake. Drumm felt that the regulators were not prepared or able to resolve the situation, so they were trying to get Anglo to do it. He believed that the Regulator should have used its supervisory relationship with Quinn Insurance as an avenue to put pressure on Quinn directly to sell down his stake in Anglo.

On 8 May 2008 Pat Whelan and Michael O'Sullivan, the Anglo lender who managed Quinn's account, met Con Horan, who advised them that Quinn's auditors, the accountancy firm PricewaterhouseCoopers, would not be in a position to sign off fully on the 2007 accounts of the Quinn Group because of guarantees held by Anglo that were affecting the calculation of the ratio between the group's debt and earnings. Unless Anglo released the group from the guarantees, the accounts would trigger a breach of loan agreements or covenants with the group's other lenders and bondholders. This in turn could lead to the lenders taking much more aggressive action against Quinn Group. If the lenders demanded the immediate repayment of the group's loans, Quinn could find it difficult to meet the margin calls on the losses on the Anglo shares. This could in turn result in the CFD broker-dealers dumping his Anglo stock in the market, leading to a rapidly falling share price and panicking depositors in the bank.

Horan asked Anglo to release Quinn Group from the guarantees. (The bank had already refused the same request from Quinn Group.) Horan's request puzzled the bank. On the one hand, Horan was expressing concern at the size of the bank's exposure to Quinn through his loans. On the other hand, Horan wanted the bank to surrender its security, thereby increasing the risk of those loans. The bank felt that the Regulator was pushing two opposing agendas: it had an interest in protecting Anglo, but it also had an interest in the survival of a business that owned the country's second largest insurer.

The issue proved academic. Anglo concluded that it could accede to Horan's request to release Quinn Group from the guarantee because the bank had a much stronger form of security: a charge over the group's shares. This gave the bank the potential to take ownership of Quinn's businesses if he couldn't repay his loans.

The Regulator was right to be concerned about Quinn's insurance business. Quinn Group issued a confidential report to its bondholders in May 2008 which disclosed a web of dubious financial transactions relating to the Anglo losses.

The group admitted to its bondholders in the 77-page report that during the second half of 2007 and the first three months of 2008 'certain equity investments outside Quinn Group (part-financed by inter-company loans from Quinn Group) incurred losses triggering margin calls'. This was a reference to Sean Quinn's CFDs on Anglo shares. The report said that Quinn had taken €398 million out of the group to cover losses on Anglo but had reduced this to €288 million by May 2008. The money had been routed through Quinn Insurance to Quinn Group and lent on to the family.

The group admitted to bondholders that 'an element of these inter-company loans were treated originally as cash deposits in respect of Quinn Insurance'. The tens of millions lent to Quinn to pay his brokers had been treated as though it was cash at hand for Quinn Insurance that could be used to show its solvency against potential claims from customers.

PricewaterhouseCoopers rejected this accounting treatment and said that the Financial Regulator should be notified. 'On arriving at this conclusion, the company immediately notified the Financial Regulator,' the group told bondholders.

Bondholders were told PricewaterhouseCoopers began discussions with the Quinn Group during April and May 2008 about whether these loans could be repaid. One consequence of this drama was that the accounts would not be signed off by the deadline specified in their loan agreements.

Quinn Group agreed a plan with the Regulator to repay part of the €288 million at a rate of €15 million a month over nine months from July 2008 to March 2009 and to pay the remaining €153 million with dividends from the business.

In addition, the report disclosed that the Quinn family had sold some of their properties to Quinn Insurance for a total of €300 million without independent valuations being carried out on the properties. Pricewater- houseCoopers, upon learning of this, had insisted that independent valuations be carried out; these valued the properties at €211 million. Quinn attributed the €89 million difference in valuation to falling property prices. There was a difference of almost 30 per cent between the two valuations, which could not be explained by the falling market given that the valuations were made within months of each other. In any case, it was highly unusual that no independent valuations were carried out.

In an interview for the RTE television programme *Prime Time* in June 2010, Quinn was asked whether his family had been overpaid for assets purchased by the insurance company to cover losses on Anglo.

'There's no doubt that we looked to cover Anglo losses in many ways . . . including buying assets or borrowing money from Anglo Irish Bank,' Quinn replied. 'As regards any assets transferred from Quinn Group or Quinn Properties or the Quinn family, they were transferred at true value, at an honest value.'

The report said that management at Quinn Group had accepted that the decision to lend company money to the family – and the accounting treatment of those loans – 'was not undertaken with proper due diligence on the regulatory impact of the transactions'. This was caused 'to a significant extent', according to the report, by the fact that the investment committee 'was not operating effectively since the middle of 2007' as Paddy Mullarkey, chairman of the investment committee, had resigned from the board for personal reasons; as a result, 'the investment committee did not formally sit and examine these transactions and thus they were not subject to board approval'.

For dipping into the cash reserves of the Quinn Group to cover his investment on Anglo, thereby damaging the solvency of Quinn Insurance, a regulated entity, Sean Quinn was fined €200,000 personally by the Regulator in October 2008, and Quinn Insurance was fined to the tune of €3.25 million. At the time these were the highest fines ever levied against an individual and a company, respectively. Quinn was forced to step down as chairman of the insurance company and from its board.

At the beginning of May Anglo published six-month accounts to the end of March. The bank reported a 17 per cent increase in profits to €647 million for the half-year and, in a very bullish move, stood by its forecast that it would grow profits by 15 per cent over the full year. The bank wrote off just 0.1 per cent of its loan book against problem debts. But it was, finally, applying the brakes to its lending. It had provided €6 billion in new loans during the six months compared with almost €9 billion for the previous half-year and €9.3 billion for the six months before that.

In his public statements Drumm tried to distance Anglo from the large global investment banks that were losing massive sums of money. He said that there were now opportunities for 'an old-fashioned relationship banker like ourselves' because the competition from 'Wall Street types' had disappeared during the credit crunch.

Asked about the collapse in the share price, Drumm replied: 'Rumours are very damaging and the only thing you can do about rumours is produce the facts and that's why results [day] is always a big day for Anglo.'

Despite the stress on the bank, and despite the run on deposits in the three weeks leading up to the end of the six-month accounting period, deposits were up €5.6 billion on a year earlier. It would later emerge that Anglo was helped by short-term deposits of €750 million from Irish Life & Permanent over the end of the half-year to make the bank's deposit figures look better.

An internal investigation at Anglo following the bank's nationalization in January 2009 found that it had similar short-term deposit arrangements with a large number of other financial institutions in the UK and the rest of Europe, including Lloyds, Credit Suisse, Rabobank, RBS and HBOS. These arrangements helped the bank improve its deposit figures at key reporting dates such as over the end of the March 2008 accounting half-year and the September 2008 full-year report. No exact figures on the scale of the lending were provided in the internal report, but Anglo insiders said that they ran to hundreds of millions of euros in short-term deposits. This helped to make the end-of-March deposits appear much better than they actually were.

Anglo's share price continued to fall through the second half of May; Sean Quinn received further margins calls on his CFDs and the bank continued lending to him.

Matt Moran emailed Drumm and McAteer on 28 May to give them the latest update on the Quinn situation following a phone call with Liam McCaffrey. Moran said that he had tried to get McCaffrey to put pressure on Quinn to sell more shares. McCaffrey had said that Quinn had sold 500,000 shares but Moran told him that this would not be well received by the Regulator, which was seeking a far larger sell-off. Moran said the Regulator was putting the bank 'under significant pressure'.

Moran also told McCaffrey that while Quinn would take a 10 to 20 per cent reduction if he sold a big block of CFDs now, he would have to do this anyway in a few months' time when the share price would be lower. He had to act immediately.

'[I] said he needed to speak to Sean so we can decide on a deal that will protect us all given [the] massive downside risk. [I] shitted him up significantly and no doubting his own deep concern,' Moran said in his email to Drumm and McAteer. He also reported that McCaffrey felt that Credit Suisse and Lehman Brothers would be interested in financing Quinn to 'go long' on his investment in the bank.

In early June, at Quinn's request, Drumm had yet another meeting with Quinn and McCaffrey at Buswell's. Quinn told Drumm that, despite having been released from the Anglo guarantee, the group was still at risk of breaching its loan agreement with its other banks and bondholders. If the covenants were breached, the banks could investigate transactions outside the group involving the Quinn family. This would mean that the bondholders and lenders to the group could find out all about Quinn's investment in Anglo. This wasn't good for either Quinn or the bank as it would expose his disastrous gamble on the bank's shares and Anglo's decision to cover his losses.

Quinn wanted a cash facility of €200 million to allow him to meet the agreements in his loan covenants with the syndicate of banks and bondholders who had loaned €1.3 billion to the Quinn Group. If he got the cash, the bondholders would back off and there would be no investigation.

Drumm refused to provide the cash facility, but Quinn did not give up. He told the lead bank in the syndicate of lenders to the Quinn Group, Barclays, that he was at risk of breaching the loan agreement. Barclays advised that the bondholders would require a full independent investigation into the activities of both the group and the Quinn family, including the Anglo CFD positions.

Barclays and the bondholders were aware of the Quinn CFDs, but Quinn believed that involving outside investigators would be a disaster because the details of the actual size of his stake in Anglo – and the unusual financial transactions within his group to fund the losses on that stake – could leak out, causing him greater problems. He urged Anglo to reconsider its decision not to lend him the €200 million cash facility.

The share price shed almost a third of its value in June, declining from €8.40 to €5.77. Anglo continued to cover Quinn's margin calls with 'working capital facilities', via nine draw-downs totalling €232.35 million during the month, bringing his debts to the bank to a staggering €1.9 billion.

During one of the bank's regular meetings with the regulator in June, Neary took Drumm aside. He was concerned that details of the Quinn Group's May 2008 confidential report would leak out. It had after all been circulated to a wide group of bondholders and lenders, including other Irish banks. Neary also told Drumm that one of the members of the board of the Regulator had heard about FitzPatrick discussing the Quinn situation at a dinner and wanted the loose talk to stop. It was dangerous for the bank and the financial stability of the country.

'Tell that fella to keep his trap shut,' Neary said, according to Drumm's account of the conversation to colleagues.

Anglo held one board meeting a year outside Dublin, and over the previous three years the board had met in Geneva, Vienna and London. Wives were always invited. On the 2007 trip board members and senior executives stayed at the Dorchester, the legendary five-star hotel in Mayfair. Some stayed on until the Sunday – at the bank's expense.

On Friday, 27 June 2008, the board of Anglo gathered at the Sheraton Hotel in Fota Island, Cork. The hotel and golf resort had been built by one of Anglo's biggest clients outside Dublin, property developer John Fleming, who was based in Bandon, west Cork. In attendance at the board meeting were Sean FitzPatrick, Lar Bradshaw, Noël Harwerth, Michael Jacob, Willie McAteer, Gary McGann, Ned Sullivan, Pat Whelan, Declan Quilligan and company secretary Natasha Mercer. Drumm was with his family at their holiday home in Cape Cod, though it was far from a holiday for him: he had travelled to the US for an operation to remedy a chronic sinus condition that made sleeping difficult. He flew into Boston a few days before the operation on 19 June. He had intended to return to Ireland six days later but there were complications following the operation and his surgeon would not permit him to fly. He spent most of his time during his recovery in the US at the end of the phone at his Cape Cod house participating in conference calls with the Anglo board and executive management, and sounding out potential investors for the Quinn stake.

At the board meeting FitzPatrick confirmed the resignation of his close friend Fintan Drury, which had been announced a fortnight earlier. Drury had flagged to FitzPatrick the previous December his intention to leave and the nominations committee had discussed new board appointments in February.

His departure was unusual in that FitzPatrick didn't mark it with a farewell dinner of the board. In fact, Drury wasn't even present at the Fota meeting. He had a family holiday booked to start on the day of the meeting and was due to fly out of Dublin that afternoon.

The Fota board meeting was the first attended by Drury's replacement,

Donal O'Connor. Over breakfast in May 2007 he had been asked by Fitz-Patrick and Drumm if he would join the board of Anglo after he retired as managing partner of PricewaterhouseCoopers in September 2007. The two bankers wanted to secure him for the Anglo board before he was approached by another financial institution.

Anglo was right to move quickly. O'Connor was offered a high-profile board position by another financial institution in early 2008. When he mentioned the other offer to Anglo, FitzPatrick put his foot down and made it clear that Anglo had asked him first.

O'Connor knew FitzPatrick well. They sat on the board of the Dublin Docklands Development Authority along with another Anglo board member, Lar Bradshaw.

Drumm dialled in to the meeting by conference call from Cape Cod. The chief executive spoke about the idea of 'buying something', such as ACC Bank, which could bring in its owner Rabobank as an investor in Anglo. He suggested that Anglo should try to bring in a large shareholder such as the Spanish bank Santander – a fantastical idea given the state of banks internationally and the perceived risk associated with the Irish banks. He ended his review by addressing the Quinn problem.

'Of course every path leads back to the one great looming issue for us: Quinn,' he said. 'It is a big issue for the bank and our shareholders. It is also a banking issue because it is a large exposure, the loans are badly structured and now Quinn is coming under pressure from his other lenders.'

Drumm handed over to William Chalmers and Alex McMahon of Morgan Stanley to address the board on the options available to resolve the Quinn situation.

In a slide headed 'The Maple Issue', Chalmers and McMahon said that the situation 'continues to be sensitive' and that 'there is no immediate answer without significant risk attached'. They assessed the pros and cons of the options available to Anglo but made no novel suggestions. Every possible approach was difficult to execute, for the simple reason that nobody wanted to buy a big chunk of Anglo shares. The investment bankers were not really outlining anything new to the board; the options were fairly obvious. The difficult part was trying to make any of the options work.

On the bank's finances, senior executives told the board that Anglo could cope with a 'stress' or 'worst case' scenario over the years from 2009 to 2011 as it had enough cash in reserve. This view would prove to be absolute claptrap: Anglo's loan book was in a dire state. Borrowers were struggling to make interest repayments because the property market had frozen and their cash flow was drying up. Further loans were being given to struggling borrowers by way of 'equity releases' whereby they could borrow more money against the strength of the cash position built up in their property investments to tide them over. Anglo was also 'rolling over' interest payments for borrowers: in effect, allowing them to miss payments.

But despite the stress in the market, the Fota Island presentation to the board showed that the number of impaired loans – those on which borrowers had missed repayments – remained low, rising from €308 million, or just 0.49 per cent of the loan book, to €360 million in March 2008, or 0.52 per cent, and €361 million, or 0.51 per cent, in May 2008. Reassuring but entirely meaningless noises were made to the board by the top executives. The non-executive directors were told that impaired loans were still 'within acceptable parameters' and that the loan quality remained 'strong' against a 'challenging' local and global backdrop. The board was briefed about the 'proactivity and vigilance of management and their clear strategy for managing the loan book in the current economic climate'. The number of 'watch cases' had grown a bit more noticeably than the impaired loans, but the figures gave no indication of the intensity of the disaster that was brewing in the loan book.

Scott Rankin, a banking analyst at Davy stockbrokers, and the firm's economist Rossa White wrote a prescient report in May 2008, saying that it could take up to two years after the peak of the housing boom for non-performing loans to show up in banks' figures, due to the duration of interest roll-up facilities. They said that on development loans there was a willingness among the banks to 'roll with it' in the hope that the market would recover. 'We met recently with banks, valuers and a number of the largest developers. We think that the banks will tread softly in this market, and do what it takes to help clients work their way out of trouble,' they wrote.

Anglo was certainly operating on this basis in mid-2008.

In a highly unusual move, after making the presentation on the quality of the bank's loans at the Fota Island board meeting, the management team asked for a handout circulated to the board members to be returned afterwards. They didn't want the information being leaked outside the boardroom, because even though the figures didn't paint an accurate picture they were still considered potentially damaging to the bank.

The board also discussed Quinn's latest request for another €200 million loan. This was a hugely significant request because if the loan were advanced it would push the bank over a crucial regulatory threshold. A bank was not allowed to lend more than 25 per cent of its 'own funds' – essentially the bank's cash reserves and shareholder funds – to any single borrower. The rule was in place to prevent a bank becoming too exposed to any one borrower or group of borrowers. Anglo was now on the brink of breaching this rule at a time when the Regulator was putting huge pressure on the bank to reduce Quinn's borrowings.

The bank approved Quinn's request. Following the meeting in Fota Island, the board agreed that in return for providing the additional €200 million that Quinn was seeking, the bank should obtain full power of attorney over Quinn's CFD positions in Anglo. This was in addition to the bank's security over Quinn's shares in Quinn Group and his personal guarantees to the bank. The board felt that this would give Anglo the capacity to unwind the CFD positions as it saw fit. The suggestion was relayed to Quinn through Liam McCaffrey. Despite Quinn's concern about the price at which Anglo would trigger a sale – he worried that the bank could land him with even heavier losses than he had expected – he accepted the condition and Anglo gave him the €200 million loan.

Gaining power of attorney over Quinn's CFDs was significant for Anglo, but not decisive. The fundamental problem with the shares underlying the Quinn CFDs was that nobody wanted to buy them.

12.   Rounding Up the Golden Circle
July 2008 – Anglo's value: €4.4 billion

On Friday, 4 July at 2.28 a.m., Drumm, still in the US, sent an email to a colleague at the bank outlining a 'long and detailed' conversation he had had with Con Horan at the Financial Regulator. He said that he had informed Horan that the bank's lending to Quinn had reached €2 billion following the latest loan of €200 million. 'I told him we are up to 2.2bn but really that nets back to 2[bn] in that the latest 200k [*recte* €200 million] is just window-dressing as asked for bondholders and cash stays in the group,' Drumm wrote. 'I told him that absent the share issue SQ would not be our biggest lending worry given profits and ability to service debt.' He was simply making the point that Quinn was – or anyway appeared to be – in a healthier financial position than some of the bank's other big customers.

Drumm referred to a letter sent by Pat Neary, Horan's boss, on Wednesday, 25 June. Neary said that when Anglo's loans to Quinn had hit €1.5 billion, the Regulator had told the bank that it did not want to see any further increase in lending to Quinn. In fact, it had asked the bank to reduce its exposure to Quinn, he said. Querying Quinn's further request for €200 million, Neary asked Drumm whether he considered 'such a large facility appropriate'.

Drumm felt that Neary's letter was a classic exercise in ass-covering. The two men were in almost daily contact over Quinn, and Anglo had informed the Regulator about each new loan. In his internal email to the executives, Drumm said that he told Horan the bank was working on a reply to Neary's letter and that 'we would go down to talk it thru next week'. Drumm concluded the email by asking whether a copy of the legal advice obtained by the bank from Dublin law firm Matheson Ormsby Prentice on the Quinn transactions could be sent to the Regulator. 'I already said we would and he [Horan] reminded me,' said Drumm, 'plus its [sic] suits that they are party to it.'

Later that day Drumm wrote to Neary, explaining the additional €200 million loan and how he felt the bank was protected by the security it had, based on the value of Quinn's assets. The €200 million loan, he wrote, would be held on deposit at Anglo.

He told Neary that Anglo's board and credit committee had agreed to approve the €200 million on the basis that Quinn had assets of €4.6 billion and debts of €3.6 billion. This included the €2.1 billion of debt due from Quinn and a further €200 million that Anglo was willing to lend to him. The group had earnings of €492 million in 2007, which provided enough cover to meet his loan repayments.

Outlining how Anglo would be repaid, Drumm said that Quinn had agreed to sell properties by the end of 2008, from which the bank expected to raise €500 million, while the sale of shares 'as soon as possible' would raise another €500 million. The bank would see the temporary facility of €200 million returned once the group satisfied the loan agreements with the Quinn Group's syndicate of banks and bondholders.

The letter was stunning in its optimism. Quinn's earnings were falling in 2008 and the construction industry, on which Quinn's business was largely based, was on the verge of collapse. If Anglo found itself in trouble on the Quinn loans, would it be able to secure €3 billion for the Quinn Group and €900 million for his properties? It would be highly unlikely, given the mounting turmoil in the financial markets. But on paper everything looked rosy. Or at least that's what the bank wanted the Financial Regulator to think.

At 8.54 p.m. on 8 July Drumm fired off an email to Matt Moran, the chief financial officer of the bank. The subject of the email was 'Maple'. 'Matt, I spoke to Willie [McAteer] about moving the game forward tomorrow with a select group of clients – he will brief you. Time for action.'

Anglo's various efforts to place the Quinn stake had come to nothing. It was becoming clear that neither a major institutional investor nor an existing shareholder would be found to buy the Quinn stake. The bank decided to ask long-standing and loyal customers of the bank to buy the shares.

The idea of placing the Quinn stake with private individuals was not new. The board had raised it in discussions over the previous months. There had also been speculation in the press about it. In late April Shane Ross, business editor of the *Sunday Independent*, had written an article saying that a group of Anglo clients, including big builders and entrepreneurs, were planning to set up a €500 million fund to buy shares in the bank to squeeze the short sellers. Ross was not quite on the money – he named Sean Quinn as one of the businessmen who were planning to contribute to the fund – and it is not clear whether the idea Ross referred to was a separate share-boosting scheme that never came to fruition, or a garbled version of early discussions of the scheme to place the Quinn stake.

Board member Gary McGann later told John Purcell, a special investigator, that the board realized that investors could not be found among US institutions or Middle Eastern sovereign wealth funds. 'The view was expressed that an approach to high-net-worth Irish people may well be the most sensible proposition and so it was agreed that they would be approached,' McGann told Purcell. McGann said that he had spoken to FitzPatrick and Drumm on a number of occasions to make sure the bank was 'being adequately advised about how to do it and the manner in which it was appropriate to execute'.

According to McGann, various parties were aware of the bank's efforts to resolve the Quinn situation. 'Morgan Stanley were retained and obviously the company's lawyers MOPs [Matheson Ormsby Prentice] were obviously all over it,' McCann claimed. It was his position that 'the board were assured that they [the law firm] were all over it and that the Regulator was fully au fait with what we were trying to do and how we are trying to do it. And indeed the feedback consistently was that the Regulator was quite anxious that we get on with it, that we get the issue addressed.'

Drumm had floated the possibility of the bank lending against its shares to facilitate such a transaction as far back as 19 March, just after the St Patrick's Day Massacre, in an email to Matt Moran: 'If we had the approval of the regulator would there be any legal issue (company law) with lending against our own shares? As I understand it we have an out under Section 60 if our loan is in the "ordinary course of business" – in our case that means lending. Let's look at this option tomorrow.'

Under Section 60 of the Companies Act a company can lend money to an investor to buy shares in itself if lending is the company's ordinary course of business. The bank would later secure legal advice saying that such a transaction was permitted for Anglo for the reasons identified by Drumm.

In the absence of an external investor, Drumm felt that the bank had to act. Everyone in the market knew Quinn was a big shareholder in Anglo but no one knew exactly how big. No investor would want to buy into Anglo or increase their shareholding in the bank while there was a large but unknown exposure to a major shareholder. In fact, this exposure was another reason for selling Anglo shares. Uncertainty was killing the bank.

Con Horan called Drumm down to the Regulator's office on 8 July for an update on the placement of the Quinn stake. He warned Drumm again that the Regulator would not tolerate any further increase in lending to Quinn.

The next morning Drumm and Whelan sat down and drew up a list of about twenty-five of the bank's wealthiest clients. The initial list included the likes of Dermot Desmond and Denis O'Brien, two of the wealthiest people in Ireland. Other clients of the bank who were on the longlist were the developers Bernard McNamara, Sean Mulryan, Paddy Kelly and Michael O'Flynn.

In narrowing the list down to ten, Drumm and Whelan were guided by three criteria: financial firepower, discretion and loyalty to the bank. Drumm and Whelan wanted people they knew well, whom they could work with, and who would feel a sense of obligation to help the bank in its hour of need. The ten customers – who would eventually become known as the Maple Ten – were all wealthy developers with a track record of completing multimillion-euro projects with the bank's support. Each would be asked to buy 1 per cent of Anglo's shares from Quinn's CFD broker-dealers (thus did the portion of the bank's shares encompassed in the deal rise from 9.4 per cent to a round 10 per cent). Drumm decided that the bank would have to lend money to the individuals to help them buy the shares: few if any of them would have €45 million in spare cash for a transaction that needed to be concluded quickly, and even if they'd had the cash they would not likely have been keen to risk it on a plummeting bank share. And the bank would ask for recourse over just one-quarter of the value of the loans – meaning, in effect, that the borrowers would face the prospect of personal losses only if the shares lost more than 75 per cent of their value.

Drumm believed that the transaction would be enough to reassure investors about Quinn, which would in turn cause the share price to rise. The ten investors would then be able to sell the shares at a profit and repay the bank. Even though the 15 per cent that Quinn would retain would still be a large shareholding, Anglo thought the deal would satisfy the markets as Quinn was the owner of a large insurance company, the second largest in the country, and so a substantial stake in another financial services company would not be out of the ordinary for him.

This was a very optimistic reading of the situation. Drumm missed an important point: while Quinn's investment was one of the worst-kept secrets in the market, investors were also deeply concerned about the bank's massive exposure to the declining property sector and the flagging Irish economy. The Quinn problem was distracting Drumm from the bigger picture: that Anglo had far too many property loans.

Drumm called FitzPatrick and told him what they were thinking of doing. The chairman was ecstatic. He had a number of discussions with the bank's non-executive directors about the matter. FitzPatrick later told Tom Lyons that Drumm did not discuss with him the names of the ten clients: 'David told me that there was no need for me to know.' FitzPatrick claimed that all he was interested in was whether they were investors of substance.

Drumm disputed FitzPatrick's account when I interviewed him for the *Irish Times* in January 2011. 'He absolutely and utterly was told the names – he knew who they were,' Drumm said. According to another source familiar with the transaction, Pat Whelan also told FitzPatrick some of the names when they spoke on the telephone around the time of the transaction.

In preparation for the transaction, Anglo added a call option to the deal sheet for each of the investors in favour of the bank. This gave Anglo the power to force the investors to sell on the stock to institutional investors at a later date of its choosing. The paperwork was handled by Morgan Stanley, which was also organizing the unwinding of Quinn CFDs and the purchase of a direct stake of 15 per cent by the Quinn family.

Matt Moran and Willie McAteer dealt with Morgan Stanley. Fiachre O'Neill, head of the bank's legal and compliance department, worked with Robert Heron, a partner at Matheson Ormsby Prentice, the bank's corporate lawyers, on the legalities of the transaction. Drumm coordinated the deal, while he and Whelan briefed FitzPatrick, who kept the non-executive directors informed.

Anglo began contacting the ten chosen clients on 9 July to outline the proposal and set up meetings over the following weekend. Drumm meanwhile telephoned Horan to say that the bank had decided to place the shares with a group of individuals well known to the bank. Horan later told special investigator John Purcell that the bank had told him that institutional investors were lined up and ready to buy the stock, but if any of them proved unwilling at the last minute, the bank had a group of high-net-worth individuals ready 'almost as a back stop' for the deal. According to Horan, Drumm also told him that if any of the investors had a problem with cash flow, the bank would provide very short-term financing. Horan also says he was told that, for the financing of the long position taken by the Quinn family on 15 per cent, Anglo would provide a loan on the day of the transaction to execute the deal but that Quinn had Credit Suisse and another bank lined up to fund the purchase over the long term. (Eventually, the Credit Suisse deal fell through and Anglo ended up providing loans of close to €500 million to the family to buy the stake.)

Drumm and Whelan, according to sources close to the bank, would claim that Horan was told at least some of the names of the Maple Ten investors during a telephone call around the time of the Anglo transaction to demonstrate the potential borrowers' creditworthiness. Horan and other staff of the Regulator have vehemently denied the claim and have consistently maintained that they were never given any such names or the details of how they were funded with loans from the bank.

At around midday on 9 July Drumm and Whelan held a conference call with Sean Quinn and his chief executive Liam McCaffrey. It was a difficult conversation. Drumm told Quinn that the bank believed that 10 per cent of his stake could be placed and that it wanted to proceed. This was the time for action, time to trigger their March 2008 agreement.

The conversation was tense. Quinn was very unhappy. He felt the bank was forcing him to sell the shares. He had agreed with the bank on 27 March to sell a 9.4 per cent stake that would be placed by Anglo, but that agreement was reached when the bank's share price was €9.20 following the St Patrick's Day Massacre. The stock had since slumped to €4.85, which meant he was now staring at a much bigger loss on the deal. There was a feeling within the bank that Quinn never believed the bank could find buyers for the shares amid the growing fears about the stability of the Irish banking sector.

Drumm explained to Quinn that the Regulator had told the bank not to lend any more money to him under any circumstances and not to breach the regulatory guideline whereby no single customer should be granted loans exceeding 25 per cent of a bank's 'own funds' – i.e. its cash reserves and accumulated profits. Quinn's borrowings by now were very close to this limit.

Drumm told Quinn that part of the reason for the decline in the share price was speculation around the exact size of Quinn's investment and until that was resolved, the share price would not recover. He told Quinn that the transaction had the support of the board. Quinn wanted to meet the board, but Drumm refused. Quinn said that he didn't like the deal and that he wanted time to think about it; Drumm felt Quinn was hoping to wriggle out of it, but by this stage Anglo had full power of attorney over Quinn's CFDs. It could act with or without his consent.

At 2.13 p.m. that Wednesday Drumm emailed Declan Quilligan, Anglo's head of UK lending, with no message, just a subject line: 'Regulator squared.' Quilligan replied a minute later: 'Excellent! Hope he was grateful!' Drumm responded: 'Excited I would say – I think he's lying awake at night like the rest of us.' Quilligan pointed out to Drumm that Janus, an investment company based in the US, had increased its stake in Anglo to 5 per cent. Drumm replied that Janus was 'on the short list' of investors that the bank would try to place the shares with.

At 2.19 p.m. Matt Moran emailed Willie McAteer: 'Project Maple – Regulator conversation done & went fine.'

The next day, Thursday, 10 July, Drumm travelled to Utrecht in the Netherlands to see whether Rabobank would be interested in taking a stake in Anglo in return for Anglo taking over its struggling Irish subsidiary, ACC Bank. Drumm believed that Rabobank might come in following the Maple Ten transaction to take a large stake in Anglo. Drumm had been 'like an expectant father waiting to hear that the baby had arrived – that Rabobank had agreed to the deal', says an Anglo insider. 'It had got exciting. We had got into valuations and term sheets had been swapped. But then they came and said no – "it is not you, it is us". They shot us right between the eyes, Dutch-style.'

Drumm later emailed the executives to say that the investment was hard to move, given conditions in the financial markets. Rabobank felt that Anglo's funding model wasn't robust. Also, judging from its own experience of the Irish market through its subsidiary, it believed that Anglo's bad-debts problem would get far worse and that the bank did not have sufficient capital.

After months of hard graft and discussions with the Dutch, Anglo's overture had been firmly rebuffed. When Drumm emailed his executive team to say the deal was off, one of his management team replied: 'Bad news. But we will keep going and prove them wrong.' Drumm replied to him, saying simply: 'No surrender!' The colleague emailed back, saying: 'Orange bastards – they're all the same!' Drumm replied: 'Windmill-lovin', clog-wearin' MOFOs.'

At 6.16 p.m. on the evening of 10 July Anglo board member Gary McGann sent Drumm an email, saying that he had been speaking to FitzPatrick 'on a couple of occasions on the plan execution'. He offered Drumm words of encouragement, saying that he and his team were 'doing fantastic work in very trying circumstances' and that 'we are all rooting for you!'

In a follow-up email at 6.48 p.m., McGann seemed more concerned. He said that Drumm might have to explain the totality of the transaction at some point in the future. 'Given the number of parties that will have a sense of some part (if not all) of the total picture, we need to have a credible explanation for how we got where we were, what we have done about it, and whether the problem is solved (the ultimate judges of that being the depositors and investors),' he wrote.

Drumm replied at 6.53, thanking him for his support: 'The entire transaction has been explained to our regulator, is the subject of legal advice and is being handled by Morgan Stanley who must pass their own compliance regime.'

McGann replied at 7.01 saying that 'the only other potential audience is the media in the event/when it leaks'. Drumm responded at 7.13, telling McGann: 'We are handling each customer separately and they are our closest personal relationships going back fifteen years and handpicked mostly for that reason – me and Pat [Whelan] particularly and in one case Tony [Campbell]. None of them knows who else or how much is involved. It's the best we can do but Pat and I both feel good about it.'

On Friday, 11 July Drumm and Whelan started meeting the clients. Four of the businessmen on the list – Seamus Ross, Gerry Gannon, John McCabe and Sean Reilly – were seen separately that day at the bank's head office on St Stephen's Green. Ross was one of the biggest house-builders in Ireland through his company, Menolly Homes, and owned a number of hotels. Gannon was a prominent house-builder in north Co. Dublin and a co-owner of the K Club golf resort and housing development in Co. Kildare with Michael Smurfit. John McCabe was a prominent builder with a business dating back four decades. He was a business partner of another major Anglo borrower, Paddy Kelly, on various deals. In the mid-1990s, as property started to boom, he packaged up tax-based deals for Derek Quinlan's investment firm Quinlan Private. He also owned a number of development sites in London, including one next to the Ritz Hotel. Sean Reilly was a successful house-builder from Cavan. He had built a number of housing estates around the greater Dublin area in Lusk, Ratoath and Stepaside. He also developed the Marina Village in Malahide, Co. Dublin.

Two executives from Morgan Stanley walked the investors through the transaction, reassuring them that everything was above board. (Anglo's loans to the investors would cover the fees owing to the investment bank.) The investors would be personally liable for only 25 per cent of the loan drawn to buy the shares. The remaining 75 per cent would be secured solely on the shares. Some asked detailed questions about the state of Anglo. Drumm pointed to the profitable half-year results reported by the bank two months earlier.

Seamus Ross Jr came along with his father and asked questions about the deal, including how long the investors would have to hold on to the shares for. After the proposal was put to Sean Reilly he scribbled some figures on a piece of paper and realized that the most he could lose was about €12 million – i.e. a quarter of the value of the loan. He said that such a loss would hurt him badly but wouldn't wipe him out. He agreed to sign up, as did the other three.

Drumm asked Tony Campbell, the head of Anglo in the US, to contact Paddy McKillen and Gerry Conlan, both of whom were in the US at the time. Conlan was a property investor and owner of a number of private hospitals. Both he and McKillen agreed to take the loan and buy 1 per cent of Anglo's shares.

On Saturday, 12 July, Drumm and Whelan flew to Nice to meet Patrick Kearney, a Belfast-based property developer who owned shopping centres in Northern Ireland and England, and Gerry McGuire, the owner of the Laurence Centre, a shopping centre in Drogheda. The two men, who were on holiday in different parts of the French Riviera, both agreed to sign up to the transaction. The bankers then flew on to Portugal to meet Joe O'Reilly, the developer of the Dundrum Shopping Centre in Dublin, where he was holidaying on the Algarve. O'Reilly agreed to sign up too.

On the Saturday night, Horan received a call from Anglo. The bank told him the deal was going ahead. He asked whether the bank required the Regulator to approve any part of the deal. He was told no, there were no regulatory approvals required.

This exchange runs to the heart of the Regulator's involvement in the Maple Ten transaction and, more broadly, its relationship with the Irish banks. The Financial Regulator worked on the basis of 'principles-led regulation'. This put the onus on the bank to seek approval rather than on the Regulator to probe a deal. This is why Horan asked the question. This approach to banking regulation did not forbid regulators from asking other sorts of questions, but, incredibly, Horan did not ask who the investors were or how the deal was being financed. The fact that Horan was told about the deal on a Saturday night didn't help, as it would have been difficult to get a team together to examine the transaction as it was being executed. Still, given that it centred around the unwinding of a massive stake in the country's third largest bank, it seems strange that Horan didn't ask more probing questions.

Horan took comfort from having an investment bank of the calibre of Morgan Stanley involved. In an interview with special investigator John

Purcell, Horan said that he had told Anglo that it was 'important that Morgan Stanley kept everything right in terms of the markets, etc.'. Horan also spoke to Morgan Stanley himself.

Horan felt he didn't need to ask for the names of the ten investors, according to a source familiar with his thinking. The booming economy had created many multimillionaires and most rich investors could buy 1 per cent of the bank from their own resources and could do so in the market any day of the week without having to disclose it publicly.

On Monday, 14 July Drumm met the final name on the list of ten in Malahide, Co. Dublin. Brian O'Farrell was an auctioneer and owner of the Northside Shopping Centre in Coolock, Dublin, which he planned to redevelop. Like the other nine businessmen approached by Anglo, O'Farrell agreed to the deal.

It is remarkable, given the scale of the request, the deteriorating state of the property market and the sustained decline in Anglo's share price, that none of the ten refused to participate. Drumm believed that they all agreed based on their long-standing relationship with the bank; if so, it is an index of how powerful Anglo's 'relationship banking' model was. But this was not the only factor at work. The investors were putting up no cash of their own, and the bank was claiming recourse over just 25 per cent of the loan. And presumably none of the investors believed that the share price would fall much further.

Anglo never told the individual investors the identities of the others, or even how many others there were. (If one of the ten asked, Drumm would say there were three or four.) The transaction involved loans of €451 million to the Maple Ten, €45.1 million each. Declan Quilligan, a board member of Anglo, told investigator John Purcell that it was made clear to him by Drumm that Anglo was lending the full amount required for each of the ten customers to buy a 1 per cent stake. 'If a client decided, "I would prefer to put my own equity into it and do it," then that would have been fine too. But the bank was willing to do it and what made me comfortable was the Financial Regulator's awareness of it and acceptance of it and encouragement of it,' he said.

Quilligan thought Drumm had done well to get the investors to agree to recourse on even part of the loan. 'The main issue here was de-risking the bank from Quinn as opposed to the terms,' he said. 'The terms, whether we had recourse or didn't have recourse, the significance of that didn't register with me at that time.'

The loans carried the standard 2 per cent interest margin for the bank but there was no repayment schedule – the interest was 'rolled up', accruing on the loan.

Once the transaction was agreed, FitzPatrick rang the non-executive directors to let them know. The newest appointment to the board was Donal O'Connor. 'I got a call then from Mr FitzPatrick, who I think firstly was a bit apologetic in that he had – I can't remember the precise words – but the substance of it was that he had actually maybe forgotten that I was a director and [he] needed to [tell me],' O'Connor told Purcell.

One of the Maple Ten later told me how he became involved in the deal. He said a senior Anglo executive, whom he would not name but whom he knew well, called him to say that an issue had arisen over Quinn having built up a large stake in the bank.

The banker said that it was not just Anglo that was in trouble but the country, given how Anglo was a big part of the economy and how Quinn was a big player in the insurance industry. The banker told him that he would be doing the bank a favour and reminded him that he and the bank had come a long way together through the projects that they had been involved in. The banker also pointed out that Iceland was in economic meltdown and that if Anglo didn't execute this transaction then there could be a similar chain reaction for Ireland.

According to the investor, the banker said Quinn had agreed to sell part of his shareholding and that Anglo was looking for six customers to take some of it. Morgan Stanley processed the transaction and Matheson Ormsby Prentice had looked it over from a legal perspective, he was told. The Anglo customer was also told that the Stock Exchange had been notified about the transaction and that it 'goes all the way back to Merrion Street' – the Department of Finance.

He didn't even look at the documents – he just signed. He had never bought shares before. He trusted the bank and wanted to help it out because it had been so supportive of him over the years. He was in and out of the meeting with the two Morgan Stanley executives at the bank's head office in about thirty minutes. No Anglo bankers attended the meeting.

The investor said he never imagined at that point that Anglo would collapse.

Several weeks later he got a shock. After the deal was done, the share price almost doubled and he wanted out as quickly as possible. He was sitting on an unexpected profit of tens of millions of euros, but he didn't want to make a profit from the deal, he told me – his motivation was to assist Anglo because he had been asked for help by a bank that had been loyal to him over the years. It was only when he attempted to sell the shares that he discovered he had signed power of attorney over them to Morgan Stanley acting for Anglo. (It is not clear whether any of the other Maple Ten investors ceded power of attorney to the bank.)

Anglo was reluctant to sell, fearing that releasing 1 per cent of the bank's stock into the open market could damage the share price. The bank also faced the added difficulty that no institutional investors were willing to buy any shares. The investor argued that if he wasn't permitted to sell, then he shouldn't be on the hook for the 25 per cent he was personally liable for. The bank revised its agreement with him on the existing loan, waiving the 25 per cent recourse.

'If I was asked again, I would do it again,' the investor says. 'My motivation was that the bank was in trouble and the country was in trouble.'

But that was not the only reason: 'I also thought to myself that if I hadn't done what I did, what would have happened at the next loan review? I felt that my head was in the lion's mouth.'

The Maple Ten transaction was executed over the weekend of 12–13 July. Anglo executives Matt Moran, Fiachre O'Neill and Willie McAteer worked through the weekend with Morgan Stanley. The bank's finance, risk and compliance departments were also heavily involved. The Quinn team was cooperating but the bank sensed that Quinn himself was not keen on the deal and could yet create problems. Not that he could do anything about it – the bank had power of attorney over his CFDs in the bank and could proceed with the transaction as it saw fit. But the bank didn't want a rogue shareholder whom it could not control. He could blow the cover on the transaction and publicly disclose the nature of the deal, which could unravel the transaction entirely and lead to the ten investors backing out.

At 9.30 a.m. on Monday, 14 July Pat Whelan and Willie McAteer joined Drumm in his office on the third floor in St Stephen's Green for a conference call with Quinn and McCaffrey. Quinn was extremely unhappy. He felt he was being taken for a ride and threatened to back out of his March agreement with the bank. He told the bankers that the agreement had been reached when the share price was considerably higher and that the stock had fallen more dramatically in recent times. Drumm felt Quinn was suggesting that the bank was manipulating the stock down in order to force Quinn into making a decision. Furious at what Quinn was trying to suggest, Drumm walked out of the room. McAteer told Quinn the transaction was happening whether he liked it or not as the bank had power of attorney over his CFDs.

Relations between Drumm and Quinn had become seriously strained. Quinn had been waging a long-running campaign to lower the interest margin the bank was charging on his loans. The margin was 1.75 percentage points over the bank's cost of funds – i.e. slightly below its standard 2-point margin – but whenever they met, Quinn would tell Drumm that Quinn Group had a 0.8-point margin with Barclays and why would Anglo not lower theirs? Drumm steadfastly refused each time. Quinn regularly referred to 'that young pup Drumm' in conversations with Michael O'Sullivan, his lending manager at Anglo.

A few minutes after the Anglo–Quinn call ended, McCaffrey called Whelan on his mobile phone. He said that Quinn was willing to proceed with the transaction. Whelan asked for written confirmation. At 10.23 a.m. McCaffrey emailed Whelan: 'Please treat this mail as authorization to go ahead with the transaction which has been discussed to dispose of 102m shares in Anglo Irish Bank which we hold through CFD contracts. Our team are instructed to engage fully with Morgan Stanley to complete this deal.'

Anglo gave Morgan Stanley the go-ahead to launch the transaction. Over the following weeks the investment bank unwound the CFDs as the loans totalling €451 million were drawn down by the ten investors. The unwinding of the CFDs was complex; some of the shares behind Quinn's investment had been loaned out to short sellers betting against the bank and it took time to get the stock back. Drumm was surprised that Quinn had not realized that his brokers were taking his stock and lending it out to short sellers, thereby contributing to the fall in the share price. If he had not taken such a large CFD position, there would have been less stock available to borrow, and borrowing would therefore have been more expensive.

On Tuesday, 15 July the Quinn family released a statement through their spokesman, Brian Bell of the public relations firm Wilson Hartnell, saying that they were unwinding their CFD interests in Anglo and taking a direct shareholding of almost 15 per cent. The statement had been run past the Financial Regulator, not for approval but out of courtesy. Despite all he had gone through, Quinn was still optimistic that there would be growth for the stock and complimented 'Anglo's ability to outperform the banking sector in terms of profit growth' over the previous years.

The announcement of the unwinding of Quinn's CFDs initially had the opposite effect to that expected by the bank: the share price fell 6.5 per cent to €4.08. This valued the bank at €3.1 billion. It had lost more than €10 billion in market capitalization in just over a year. The conversion of a 15 per cent stake from CFDs to shares held by the family and the purchase of 10 per cent of the stock by the Maple Ten crystallized a loss of about €955 million for the Quinns, Anglo later estimated. The family's direct shareholding in the bank was worth about €465 million.

Anglo later requested that Matheson Ormsby Prentice record the advice it had given the bank concerning the transaction. In a letter dated 22 July 2008 the firm stated that the bank had not breached company law or corporate-takeover or Stock Exchange rules in the Quinns' share purchases, although there was no reference to the Maple Ten. The advice letter noted that the bank had kept the Regulator informed of the transaction. Anglo, seeking to cover itself, furnished a copy of the lawyers' letter of advice to the Regulator.

The Regulator was unhappy that Anglo had given €169 million in loans to Quinn to finance the family's purchase of shares. On 25 July a penalty was imposed on the bank, forcing it to deduct this amount from its capital reserves until it was repaid. The Regulator also said that it expected the bank to force Quinn to refinance this loan with another bank within two to three weeks. Neary later said that the board of the Regulator agreed to make the capital charge 'as penal as they could on Anglo'.

In fact, the Regulator's sanction was not nearly penal enough. The total figure advanced to the Quinns, including money channelled through six Cypriot companies owned by the family, was close to €500 million, or about €300 million more than the figure disclosed by the bank.

In the wake of the Quinn deal, Drumm turned his attention to another matter. He wanted to lift the spirits of staff whom, he felt, were feeling the brunt of the negative comment about the bank in the media and the general pessimism about the economy and the property market. Drumm decided to organize a party. He sent an email to all the bank's staff in Ireland on 22 July: 'Dear colleague, the stock markets are down. They say the economy is in recession. It rained most of the "summer". The holidays are over. This is Anglo so there is only one thing to do – party!' Drumm invited staff to join him on the evening of Friday, 5 September for food and drinks at the Mansion House for what he called the 'Back To School Doombuster Party'. There would be a live band to entertain them until late, he said.

★

Morale was also low in the Quinn camp. Sean Quinn was deeply unhappy about the unwinding of his CFDs. There was feverish speculation in the media about the extent of his losses from it, which were reported at about €1 billion. This raised serious questions about the effect on him personally and on his business, which employed about 6,000 people.

Angry at the bank's decision to force through the share process, he wrote a letter to David Drumm on Saturday, 26 July.

Dear David,

I am writing to express my concerns around the events which took place between 9th July and the evening of July 14th when we completed the transaction on the Anglo shares.

I am very aware and appreciative of your support over the past year during a difficult period for us. However I am not sure that we were treated fairly during this period which represented a five year low in the Anglo share price. We were in effect forced to sell the shares regardless of market price on the downside whilst the purchasers were given a maximum price. In other words the placing was to proceed regardless of price, the shares could have been sold for €1 whilst the purchasers were protected against the increase which would accrue from a market rally. This was at a time when Anglo was clearly underperforming its peers, in particular Bank of Ireland.

When I suggested an alternative scenario of selling enough shares to provide €100 million in cash it was discounted without any analysis or consideration. Even without disposing of shares the additional debt you advanced on the transaction could have covered a fall in price to €3.34, while advancing this debt in addition to realizing the €100 million in cash would have covered a fall to €2.42.

I know that this was a difficult period for all involved given the downturn in stock prices however. [sic] I feel that the bank's insistence on a sale was detrimental to our position and the longer term development of this group. Whilst I accept your right to sell in a controlled fashion, the process should have had some regard to price, timing and some consideration of my alternative proposal. I am sure that your motivation was to protect the bank, and by definition our remaining holding in it, however, I hope that equal emphasis was placed on our right to maximize our position and potential for recovery.

Over the course of those few days I tried very hard to get the bank to consider my perspective, however I received no hearing whatsoever.

This is in total contrast to our meetings in March when we spent considerable time discussing the potential placing. On this occasion there seemed to be a degree of panic driving the process, which I feel did not reflect a proper considered action plan.

Some of the actions indicative of the panic are as follows:

1. I was told of brokers particularly Goodbody's reducing your forecasts by increasing the bad debt provision;
2. From the date the transaction was first mentioned until it completed the Anglo price lost 23 per cent against Bank of Ireland, yet the transaction was forced through;
3. Despite our requests we were given no visibility on who the purchasers were;
4. After a heated discussion on Friday I called you back to say we should all consider it over the weekend, however the approach from Anglo on Monday morning was just as aggressive and you walked out of the telephone call;
5. I called you later on that day but my call was not returned.

In addition, I asked for an opportunity to meet the board and express my views but this request was disregarded.

I am writing this letter to you personally without the benefit of advice from my colleagues or legal advice. I strongly believe the actions of the bank were ill advised and will have a considerable impact on our wider group for many years. I would therefore ask you to consider the content of this letter carefully and I look forward to hearing from you.

Yours sincerely,
Sean Quinn
Managing Director

The bank felt that Quinn's alternative plan was nonsensical. He had been unwilling to take steps to deal with the situation himself, so the bank never believed that he would actually drip-feed stock into the market. They believed that he would never have been able to get a sufficient amount of stock away to make a meaningful difference without the market thinking that he was a forced seller. This would create an even bigger problem, as other shareholders might dump their stock in response. The hedge funds would then short Anglo shares further. Anglo's executives believed that they had solved the problem the only way they could.

But the letter made the board and management of the bank fearful of what Quinn might do next. They were right to be worried. They learned that Quinn had approached White & Case, a London law firm specializing in financial matters, and was considering suing Anglo.

On Monday, 28 July, two days after Quinn's letter, FitzPatrick had a special outing. Fintan Drury, who had stepped down from the board of the bank a month earlier, had arranged for FitzPatrick to play a round of golf with the new Taoiseach, Brian Cowen. The course was Druid's Heath, next to Druid's Glen, at the foot of the Wicklow Mountains overlooking the Irish Sea. Druid's Heath is known for its undulating greens and troublesome bunkers which trip up even the best golfers.

After the round of golf, FitzPatrick, Drury and Cowen were joined by Anglo board member Gary McGann and economist Alan Gray for dinner in the Marriott Hotel next to the course. Gray had been appointed to the board of the Central Bank by Brian Cowen in January 2007 when he was Minister for Finance.

FitzPatrick said in an interview for *The FitzPatrick Tapes* that there was no discussion that day about Anglo or the Quinn situation, despite the fact that the bank had just unwound the Quinn investment – a transaction that everyone from the Central Bank to the Financial Regulator to the Department of Finance had concerns about. The discussion centred on 'the world, Ireland, the economy', said FitzPatrick. When details of the golf outing were disclosed publicly for the first time in January 2011, Cowen similarly claimed that Anglo's problems with Quinn were not discussed during the golf or at the dinner afterwards.

Alan Gray later said that he was invited to provide ideas to stimulate economic growth and to reduce unemployment. The previous day Gray had drafted an economic action plan, entitled 'Building on Achievement', that ran to several pages. The memo, which was used to guide their brainstorming session after the golf and before their meal, contained no reference to Anglo. It did include a timeline through August and September of how to bring the plan to fruition and advised Cowen to hand-pick advisers to help him execute it. The document was used to direct the discussion. One copy was passed between Drury and Cowen, and both men annotated it heavily.

After his golf outing with Cowen, FitzPatrick set about trying to repair Anglo's relationship with Sean Quinn. The bank felt that it couldn't have an adversarial relationship with Quinn and his family, the bank's largest shareholders and borrowers. If Quinn sued, Anglo's placement of the shares with the Maple Ten would be disclosed and investors might take fright at the way the bank had orchestrated the transaction. The board agreed that FitzPatrick should be the man to meet Quinn and try to calm him down.

In August FitzPatrick rang Quinn to gauge the lie of the land. Fitz-Patrick reported back to Drumm that Quinn was angry, particularly at Drumm. Quinn wanted to get back all the money he'd lost on the shares and he also wanted the shares back. FitzPatrick told Drumm that he let Quinn rant. According to FitzPatrick, Quinn told him that he couldn't sleep and that it was the worst time of his life.

Drumm later gave a detailed account of his telephone call with Fitz-Patrick to an associate. In it, Drumm captured FitzPatrick's salty language and machine-gun delivery. 'Seanie phoned me after meeting Quinn. I was in London City Airport. Sean said: "Right, I met your man, right, and first of all, right, he's fucking unhappy with you . . . fucking hates you, he does, right. Fucking thinks you sold his shares on him, right. I had to agree with him. So this is how we're going to fucking play it, right. You'll be the bad cunt and I'll be the fucking guy who reaches out to him. I will rein him in, right. He's in awe of me."'

The bank's share price rose from €4.36 at the time of the transaction to almost €7 by 11 August. Three of the Maple Ten investors sold parts of their shareholdings, collectively amounting to about 1 per cent of the bank, at a profit. From mid-August on, the bank's share price started to decline again as the global financial crisis hit Irish bank stocks once more.

During the summer of 2008 real signs of strain were starting to show within Anglo's loan book as property values continued to decline.

An example of one stressed case came before Anglo's credit committee in July 2008. Galway developer John Lally was Anglo's fifteenth largest borrower as of late 2007. Early the following year he was moved to the bank's 'watch list'. The bank referred to this list internally as 'A&E' loans – if they improved, they could 'go home' to the performing list; if they deteriorated further, they were moved into 'intensive care'. Lally, who had been a client of the bank since 1993, had been involved in numerous devel-opments and property investments in the west of Ireland before concentrating on the Dublin market in recent years. In July 2008 he owed the bank €445.5 million – €66.6 million personally and €378.9 million through 'related' borrowings, including his companies' debts. This was in addition to borrowings totalling €126 million with AIB, Ulster Bank, Irish

Nationwide and Bank of Scotland (Ireland). He was placed on Anglo's 'watch list' in early 2008 as his developments in Dublin city centre – at Percy Place near Baggot Street Bridge and Eden Quay – had coincided with the property slump. Construction work had not yet started on the sites. To complicate matters further, one of his companies was being sued by Irish Life, the vendor of the property, for the payment of €60 million for his agreed €74 million purchase of a six-acre site in Sandyford, Co. Dublin.

Lally had paid a whopping €13.7 million for the quarter-acre site at Percy Place in December 2005. This amounted to almost €55 million an acre – slightly higher than the then-record price Sean Dunne had paid for the Jurys Ballsbridge site. But he believed he could turn a profit with a development of shops, restaurants and eleven apartments, one of which – a third-floor penthouse – he thought he could sell for €1.8 million.

In July 2008 the Anglo credit committee was asked to approve a renewal of his existing personal loans of €66.6 million until December 2008, which included €18 million owing on the Percy Place development. The committee was asked to approve 'interest roll-up' – the accrual of interest, as he wasn't repaying the bank – of almost €1 million on loans totalling €30 million, until the end of the year. 'We have indicated that no further development funding will be provided until the bank has conducted a detailed review of the overall Lally connection, and have devised a debt reduction strategy for the borrower,' his lenders said in the application to the credit committee.

The new loans of €66.6 million were related to properties whose value had fallen to €60 million – amounting to a loan-to-value ratio of 109 per cent, well in excess of the bank's limit. Nevertheless, his application was approved and marked down as an 'exception to credit policy'.

On 9 September, Drumm, FitzPatrick and Ned Sullivan, Anglo's senior independent director and chairman of the bank's audit committee, met Pat Neary and Con Horan. Neary later described the encounter to special investigator John Purcell as 'a strange meeting'. Anglo had asked the regulators to meet them in the bank because it was a sensitive time and they didn't want to be seen going into the Central Bank building on Dame Street.

The bankers informed the regulators that the Quinn Group had asked for more loans and was challenging Anglo on its handling of the unwinding of Quinn's Anglo CFDs. Horan later told Purcell that the bank

expressed concerns that Quinn would reveal the details of the deal publicly. Neary asked at the meeting if Anglo had any reservations about the
way the transaction had been handled. According to the account given by
Horan to Purcell, Drumm reassured them that the bank was happy and that
the transaction was 'pristine'. Neary told Purcell that the bank had wanted
to lend more to Quinn but that he gave this suggestion an emphatic no. 'I
mean I have to say I was on a short fuse and I just said, no,' he told Purcell.
'I was not going to engage or find reasons or whatever. I just told them no.'

The meeting lasted a mere ten minutes.

Quinn's borrowings to cover his share losses continued to rise, eventually spiralling to €2.34 billion, despite Neary's insistence that the bank not
increase its exposure to him. Including the family's property loans, the
Quinns owed the bank about €2.8 billion, making them Anglo's largest
borrowers by some distance.

13. 'Two bad banks don't make a good bank'

1 September 2008 – Anglo's value: €4 billion

On the afternoon of Sunday, 7 September David Drumm was at home in Malahide, north Co. Dublin, reading that day's newspapers. Drumm, his wife and two daughters lived in a multimillion-euro house in Abington, a gated estate where his neighbours included pop stars Ronan Keating and Nicky Byrne of Westlife, whose wife Georgina was the daughter of former Taoiseach Bertie Ahern.

He was enjoying a quiet weekend after hosting the 'Back To School Doombuster' party for about 600 staff. He had tried to lift staff spirits with a speech, saying that the bank's stock had been unfairly targeted during the St Patrick's Day Massacre and that he believed the bank was being dramatically under-valued by the stock market. The party cost the bank €80,000, excluding overnight accommodation for staff who travelled from the bank's regional offices for the night. The drinks bill alone was €24,000, which included €31 bottles of Prosecco, €30 bottles of Pinot Grigio and €24 bottles of Merlot. This kind of spending was not unusual for Anglo. The bank had spent €272,000 on Christmas staff parties in Dublin, London and Boston the previous December and €229,000 on three Christmas parties for clients in addition to €87,000 spent on Christmas hampers and wine for customers. But the expenditure was at best peculiar at a time when the bank was struggling to fund itself and to convince the markets that it was not going bust.

On the Sunday after Drumm's 'Doombuster' party another financial institution was making the news. The front page of that day's *Sunday Independent* featured a photograph of a smiling Michael Fingleton, the veteran chief executive of Irish Nationwide, casually dressed and standing outside the building society's head office on the Grand Canal in Dublin. The photograph had been taken the previous day. The accompanying article appeared under the headline: 'Reuters backs down on false INBS report'.

The news agency had been forced to withdraw a story posted on the wires at 6.14 p.m. the previous Friday as the Anglo party was about to start. The story said that Irish Nationwide was in talks with its lenders 'to avoid insolvency'. The report even went as far as to say that London accountant

Neville Kahn of Deloitte had been lined up as a possible administrator for the building society. A story like this at a time of extraordinary fear in the financial markets could bring down a financial institution.

The story reappeared on the wires at 8.31 p.m. This time it included a strong denial from Irish Nationwide. At 10.45 p.m. the story was removed. Reuters said that 'material elements' in the report were incorrect. The *Sunday Independent* quoted a spokesman for Reuters saying that the error occurred because a reporter had misinterpreted a source.

It had been a bad week for Irish Nationwide. Ratings agency Moody's had downgraded its credit rating because of concerns about the large amount of commercial property loans on its books.

As he was perusing the Sunday newspapers, Drumm's mobile phone rang. It was Pat Neary and Con Horan, on a conference call. They were going to their board later that evening as they were worried that, despite having been withdrawn, the Reuters report would cause a run on Irish Nationwide when the building society opened the following day. They wanted to be ready. They asked Drumm whether Anglo would be interested in taking over Irish Nationwide. Drumm replied that it would. But he stipulated conditions: Anglo would pay no premium above the value of the building society's net assets, the government would have to underwrite any losses on Irish Nationwide's loans and the Central Bank would have to provide funding support to the merged bank until it could stand on its own. Drumm was aware that if Anglo took over Irish Nationwide, the bank would be adding to its funding problems and to its exposure to property. Neary and Horan asked Drumm if they could take his proposal to their board. He said they could. Drumm was able to give such a firm expression of interest because Irish Nationwide had been on the market since 2007, and Anglo had considered buying it.

Irish Nationwide Building Society was a very strange financial institution. It had started life as the Irish Industrial Benefit Building Society in 1873. Sligo-born banker Michael Fingleton became chief executive in 1974 and spearheaded a move into commercial property lending starting in the late 1980s. By the time of the property crash, Irish Nationwide had strayed far from its original identity as a mortgage lender: 80 per cent of its €12 billion loan book was in speculative land and development or commercial property.

While Anglo had decided against trying to acquire Irish Nationwide in 2007 on the grounds that this would only increase Anglo's exposure to high-risk property lending, a takeover in September 2008 was a different prospect: it brought with it the possibility of government support. Anglo spied an opportunity.

Irish Nationwide was seen as the weakest link in the Irish financial system. In a secret internal memo on 5 September William Beausang, a senior official at the Department of Finance, told Minister for Finance Brian Lenihan that the building society expected to lose €200 million in deposits as a result of the credit-rating downgrade, and that there was potential for more difficulty if there were further downgrades. The Regulator had already asked both AIB and Bank of Ireland whether they would take over Irish Nationwide and both had refused. Bank of Ireland had, like Anglo, looked at the building society previously and didn't like its property loans or the quality of its mortgage book, which had the home loans and buy-to-let loans of many subcontractors and builders who worked for the developers it banked.

As soon as he got off the phone to Neary and Horan, Drumm called FitzPatrick to tell him about the approach. FitzPatrick thought it was a great opportunity; he later recalled that he told Drumm, 'This could be a great chance for us of actually getting the government to back us.' Another upside for Anglo was that it could get hold of Irish Nationwide's €5 billion in deposits, use its fifty-branch network to gather more deposits and use the building society's €2 billion residential mortgages as collateral to borrow from the European Central Bank. Anglo's ability to borrow from the ECB was limited because it had no residential mortgages, and residential mortgages were the only loans eligible for use as collateral by a bank to borrow from the lender of last resort in Frankfurt.

When Drumm got to his office on Monday, 8 September he drafted a paper for the Regulator outlining his proposal for Irish Nationwide. It was effectively a letter of offer to take over the building society with the conditions he had set out the day before.

FitzPatrick told Drumm to get in touch with Irish Nationwide's chairman, Dr Michael Walsh. Walsh had been a non-executive director of Anglo in the mid-1980s when it was still a tiny bank, and he and FitzPatrick had remained close ever since. Walsh was the right-hand man of financier Dermot Desmond, another good friend of FitzPatrick's, and a director of Desmond's firm, International Investment and Underwriting (IIU).

Drumm telephoned Walsh and told him about his plans for an Anglo/ Irish Nationwide tie-up. Walsh invited Drumm down to IIU's offices in the International Financial Services Centre in Dublin. They met twice over subsequent days. At the first meeting – at 5 p.m. on Monday, 8

September – Drumm gave Walsh his proposal. He brought along Willie McAteer, his finance director, to go through Irish Nationwide's books. Drumm met Walsh again the following day at 2 p.m., just prior to a meeting with Pat Neary and Con Horan in his office at Anglo to discuss his merger proposal.

FitzPatrick described these contacts with Walsh in an interview for *The FitzPatrick Tapes* as having taken place 'behind Fingleton's back' and recalled that there was 'tension' between Walsh and Fingleton. 'Michael Walsh saw us as the obvious people to do it because we had a better knowledge of their loan book than anybody else and we wouldn't be as scared of it and therefore wouldn't write off as much and more importantly we would be able to handle it,' FitzPatrick told Tom Lyons. An advantage of the deal for Anglo, in FitzPatrick's eyes, was that his bank would be seen as the white knight, answering the government's call to rescue a weaker institution; this, he felt, would make Anglo look stronger. 'On the other hand, the negative was that you were going to actually get a concentration of borrowers. For instance, Sean Mulryan was a big one of ours [and] a big one of theirs.'

At around 7 p.m. on Friday, 12 September Drumm picked up the phone to Denis Casey, the chief executive of Irish Life & Permanent, and asked for a meeting. The Irish Nationwide possibility was still alive but seemed to be lacking the necessary official support. Drumm needed another plan.

Casey agreed to meet the following Monday. After getting off the phone to Drumm, Casey called the company's head of treasury, David Gantly, to see if there was anything he should know about Anglo before the meeting. Gantly told Casey that Anglo had requested a loan of €5 billion from IL&P for a brief period including Anglo's financial-year end date, 30 September. Anglo had suffered deposit withdrawals during the month and wanted to boost its corporate deposit levels to make them look healthier than they were on the day the snapshot was taken of its books for the bank's annual report.

Drumm and Casey met for breakfast on Monday, 15 September in the five-star Westin Hotel in Dublin city centre. Drumm proposed a merger between the banks. Casey heard Drumm out and then went to consult his board. The two men met again at the Westin that same evening.

Between the meetings, Casey consulted his board about the merger approach. The board wasn't interested. IL&P had avoided lending to property developers and on commercial property, Anglo's main business, and had stuck to home loans, an area in which it led the Irish market. As the property market was turning, Casey and his board felt a tie-up with Anglo could create more problems than it would solve. IL&P had funding difficulties – it had lent almost three times as much as it had taken in on deposit and was heavily reliant on the international money markets to finance its €40 billion loan book – and there was nothing Anglo, which had its own serious funding problems, could do about that.

Casey knew, though, that the Regulator was looking at various mergers as a means of strengthening the smaller and weaker Irish banks. While he was against a marriage with Anglo, he felt IL&P needed another partner, and he proposed a merger with a smaller rival, the building society EBS. His board authorized him to make an approach.

On the same day that Drumm and Casey discussed a possible merger, a rather more seismic event took place in New York: Lehman Brothers filed for bankruptcy. The money markets, where the Irish banks sourced funding for about half their balance sheets, shut down and any financial institution regarded as shaky was quickly destabilized as anyone with cash on deposit there sought to find a safer home for it. Anglo's already unstable funding position became even more precarious. The bank started losing individual deposits of between €50 million and €200 million as the terms of deposits from large companies and financial institutions expired and they withdrew their money rather than 'roll it over' on a new deal. This was the start of a severe run on the bank, worse even than anything Anglo had seen following the St Patrick's Day Massacre. Over the next two weeks the bank would lose €500 million in funding on a good day, twice that on a bad day. Anglo wasn't going to survive long at that rate.

All the focus at this stage was on the Irish banks' liquidity problems – their ability to source funding and repay deposits on demand. Hardly anyone within the banks or the state was raising concerns about potential solvency problems. But there were good grounds by this stage to anticipate that bad debts would impose a crushing burden on banks' balance sheets – a burden that would remain even if the funding crisis was weathered. On the day of Lehman's collapse, *Irish Times* business editor John McManus wrote in his column that the real issue for the Irish banks was 'whether the banks are refusing to face up to the problems in their property loan books, and whether the Central Bank is letting them away with it'.

A research report by investment bank JP Morgan the previous week had shown that 75 per cent of lending by Irish banks since 1999 related to property. The report said that half of that lending had been done over the previous three years, i.e. at what was now known to have been the peak of a market that was clearly in decline.

The days following the collapse of Lehman Brothers were frenetic within Anglo, with daily meetings among the executive directors to discuss the weakening funding position of the bank as well as regular meetings with the Central Bank and Financial Regulator. There were also meetings with Morgan Stanley to see if they could find white-knight investors to pump cash into the bank. Nevertheless, Anglo management found time for other things. Drumm managed to make three sessions with his personal trainer in the gym of the five-star Merrion Hotel around the corner from Anglo's head office. He made sure that his Range Rover went for a service two days after Lehman's failed – 'wheels are squeeking [sic],' read an entry in his diary.

FitzPatrick meanwhile had several golf outings booked during the month, including tee times at top courses such as Wentworth in Surrey, Portmarnock and Royal Dublin. FitzPatrick's diary was always kept up-to-date with upcoming Sunday 'rumbles' and 'shotgun starts' at his local course.

In the late afternoon of Thursday, 18 September, with deposits flooding out the doors of Anglo, FitzPatrick sat down with Brian Lenihan, who had been appointed Minister for Finance the previous May when Brian Cowen had succeeded Bertie Ahern as Taoiseach. FitzPatrick had flown in that morning from a three-day trip to Brazil for a meeting of the board of credit-check company Experian. This was his first meeting with Lenihan. They were joined in the minister's private office by the secretary-general of the Department of Finance, David Doyle. Kevin Cardiff, the second secretary at the department in charge of banking policy, sat in on part of the meeting.

Lenihan later told an Oireachtas committee that at the meeting FitzPatrick outlined a proposal to merge Anglo with Irish Nationwide, a plan that would require state support. The minister gave the notion short shrift. Given that it was Neary who had floated the idea of the Irish Nationwide takeover initially, FitzPatrick had thought Lenihan would be interested; but, he recalled in *The FitzPatrick Tapes*, 'I never grabbed his attention.'

Lenihan and senior department officials doubted both Anglo's ability to complete the transaction and the bank's motives. Officials believed that it was a try-on, a Trojan horse to secure government backing for Anglo. The attitude within the department about the proposal was 'two bad banks don't make a good bank'. (The economist Colm McCarthy would put it even more succinctly in a conversation with the author: 'You tie two stones together – they'll still sink to the bottom.') Officials also felt, accurately enough, that Anglo wanted to be seen as 'the state's preferred solution provider'.

FitzPatrick's case wasn't helped when, just as his meeting with Lenihan was drawing to a close, I called the minister's spokesman, Eoin Dorgan. Word had spread around Dublin business circles that Anglo was pitching a takeover of Irish Nationwide with state support and I called the department to ask whether there was any truth in the story. After receiving my call, Dorgan spoke to Lenihan, who told him that FitzPatrick was just leaving after their meeting and cheekily suggested that Dorgan could put the query to the chairman of the bank directly. Dorgan approached FitzPatrick in the hallway of the department and asked him if Anglo had made an approach to take over Irish Nationwide and was seeking government support for the move. FitzPatrick feigned surprise and said no.

The *Irish Times* ran a report on the Anglo/Irish Nationwide proposal the following day. Michael Fingleton angrily denied the back-room dealings described in the story. In reality, the story was true, but Fingleton's chairman and the other major players were keeping him out of the loop. There was a sense among senior Department of Finance officials at this time that they couldn't work with Fingleton. They felt that he was continuously blaming everyone else for Irish Nationwide's problems.

The following day Lenihan issued a similar denial, although at the Oireachtas committee hearing the following February he confirmed that FitzPatrick had raised this proposal in their meeting.

Around the time of Anglo's approach to Lenihan, David Doyle received a note from Irish Nationwide chairman Michael Walsh. The note, which was later released by the Department of Finance to the Oireachtas Public Accounts Committee, outlined the options facing Irish Nationwide to protect its 180,000 depositors. The note shows that Walsh was most keen on the idea of a merger with Anglo. He also suggested the possibility of the state providing 'covert funding' to the building society so that it could run itself down over time. Walsh also acknowledged that merging Irish Nationwide into Anglo would be 'publicly seen as a bailout' and that because Anglo would require a guarantee from the state to execute the takeover, the other Irish banks might be opposed to such a 'sweetheart deal' for a competitor. He warned, too, that the state would be 'seen to be taking on a much bigger and more complicated problem than was necessary'.

On the day that FitzPatrick met Lenihan, Drumm and McAteer made a presentation to the Department of Finance, claiming that Anglo had 'no requirement' for cash from external sources. The bankers told the department that Anglo would make profits of €1.4 billion in 2008 and €1.1 billion in 2009 after writing off €100 million and €300 million, respectively, in bad debts for those years. Anglo still did not believe it had a solvency problem; the crisis was all about liquidity.

Anglo's view of potential losses on loans would prove to be a dramatic underestimate. The bank was either deceitful or deluded about the scale of its problems. Either way it was tragically unprepared for the property crash. At the time property values were falling but few bankers believed the market was heading for collapse.

Some within Anglo had concerns about the quality of its loan book and the exposure to the property market. By the summer of 2008 Lar Bradshaw was worried that the bank had more bad debts on its books than it was actually acknowledging. FitzPatrick encouraged him to carry out his own research to put his mind at ease.

Bradshaw and Donal O'Connor examined 82 per cent of the €43 billion Irish loan book, including forty-five development loans and five property-investment loans. They looked at what they thought were the potential 'stress cases' for loans based on possible falls in property prices. They assessed write-downs of up to 50 per cent for loans on land with no zoning bought for development and up to 40 per cent for loans on zoned land with no planning.

They determined that Anglo faced a potential loss of €797 million in 'an extreme case' and €424 million in a 'base' or expected case. The bank's management was 'all over' notable or 'watch' loan cases, they said, and the lenders had an 'intimate knowledge of situations/borrowers'. Bradshaw and O'Connor reported back to the board that they were 'pretty comfortable' that 67 per cent of the loans were performing, but a key risk was that some customers had 'limited further breathing space' and that 18 per cent of the loans were not reviewed.

'While we could argue at the margin on a few conclusions, the book is well provided for in [an] "extreme case" scenario,' they said in their report. But they warned that the impact of a 'black swan' event – a once-in-a-lifetime economic depression – or a 'long deep recession [was] difficult to factor in'.

Anglo's executives took comfort from their report and referred to it during internal presentations to demonstrate that the bank had a handle on the problems in the loan book. In reality, this was not the case. No one in the bank envisaged the extent of the property crash.

O'Connor later took the view that the executives placed too much reliance on their review of the loans, and that they didn't spend sufficient time on the review to understand fully the scale of the problems, according to sources with knowledge of his thinking. 'If you ask me, Could Lar Bradshaw and Donal O'Connor have got a handle on the problems in the bank at that time? It would have been impossible for them to get under the bonnet,' says a former executive.

On the same day, PricewaterhouseCoopers (long-time auditor to Bank of Ireland) was hired by the Financial Regulator to assess the true scale of the bad debts at Anglo Irish Bank and the other Irish banks. The government authorities clearly felt that they had to carry out their own independent analysis of Anglo's figures, which seemed highly optimistic at the very least.

On the night of Thursday, 18 September the Financial Regulator – as usual not acting on its own initiative but following the lead of its counterpart in the UK – introduced a ban on short selling in financial stocks. The following day, Anglo's share price jumped almost 30 per cent from €4.35 to €5.60. The increase in the share price, however, didn't stop the run on Anglo's deposits; and the shares of Anglo and other Irish banks resumed their decline within days.

Stockbrokers believed that the impact of short selling on the share prices of the banks, and particularly Anglo, had been largely overstated. Share prices were falling because long-holding shareholders had lost confidence in the banks and were selling out.

'There was a total naivety about this,' says one stockbroker. 'We didn't see that short selling was causing any problems. In fact, banning it reduced the level of share buying and selling, and did not improve the stock generally.'

On Saturday, 20 September staff of the Financial Regulator and Central Bank organized a series of intelligence-gathering meetings with the chairmen and chief executives of the six Irish banks. The regulators were concerned about the continued run on deposits. The previous Thursday RTE's afternoon phone-in show *Liveline* had featured call after call from listeners who had withdrawn money from Irish banks. One nervous caller spoke about money being safer stuffed in a mattress or buried in a garden.

In the aftermath of the programme, the banks were reporting to the Regulator large numbers of deposits flowing out of the system. Everyday conversations in taxis, pubs, restaurants and hairdressers were fuelling the withdrawal frenzy. Minister for Finance Brian Lenihan telephoned the director-general of RTE, Cathal Goan, to express his outrage at the trouble *Liveline* had caused in the Irish banking system.

On the following Saturday – the day of the Regulator's intelligence-gathering meetings – Lenihan announced that the state's guarantee on deposits in the Irish banks, which had covered the first €20,000 of any deposit, was being raised to €100,000. The banks were told that the minister's statement would contain 'generous wording' indicating that the government would stand behind the banks. The government said in the statement that it wanted to 'protect the whole financial system'.

These were reassuring noises in the absence of specific commitments. 'It was never quite clear what the government was saying but it was so ambiguous that it could be seen constructively by the market,' says one senior banker.

Later that Saturday evening Gillian Bowler, chair of IL&P, received a number of calls from Sean FitzPatrick. The Anglo chairman wanted one more chance to plead with IL&P to consider a merger. FitzPatrick believed that a marriage would protect both institutions from the chaos in the financial markets. He told Bowler that she needn't worry about who would fill the top jobs at the merged bank: effectively an offer by FitzPatrick that IL&P board members and executives would hold on to their positions in the enlarged entity.

Bowler called Denis Casey several times that night. He was at a dinner party and had to walk around the garden of his friend's house to get a better phone signal so he could talk to her. Casey and Bowler agreed that they would hear Anglo out one last time at a meeting on the Monday.

FitzPatrick's approach to Bowler was not the only effort Anglo made to rekindle the IL&P merger following Casey's refusal. During a social meeting, McGann asked his friend Kieran McGowan, a non-executive director of IL&P, whether there was any merit in a few non-executive directors from both banks getting together to discuss a possible merger. McGowan mentioned McGann's suggestion to Casey but not to the rest of the IL&P board. Casey wasn't happy about one of his board members being approached separately and felt that Anglo were trying to undermine him.

When Casey and Bowler met Drumm and FitzPatrick the following Monday, 22 September, again in the Westin Hotel – this time in the private Shilling Room at 11 a.m. – the atmosphere was frosty. The previous day's *Sunday Tribune* had suggested that IL&P would be the next bank to be part of 'a wave of consolidation set to sweep Irish banking once the deal between Anglo Irish Bank and Irish Nationwide is officially consummated'. Another story in the *Tribune* that day said: 'The pursuit of Irish Nationwide by David Drumm's Anglo Irish is to be welcomed, although one wonders if a deal with IL&P would make more sense.' Bowler had telephoned Fitz-Patrick on Sunday. She was furious. She believed that Anglo was behind the stories in the *Sunday Tribune*. Casey later told Garda investigators, in an affidavit submitted in June 2010, that he took the same view. Executives at IL&P were furious, as one consequence of the article was that it made depositors nervous about placing money with the company and negated the confidence-building effect of the increase in the deposit guarantee on the Saturday.

According to one account of the meeting at the Westin, Casey 'had a head on him'. He didn't want to be there. Bowler was described as more 'presidential' about it. She was willing to hear the Anglo bankers out. Drumm gave a PowerPoint presentation on Anglo's view of the merger. He said that they could form a more universal bank that offered a rounded banking service to a greater number of customers. Anglo had a commercial business (albeit almost exclusively in property), while IL&P had savers, home loans and a network of branches. Casey and Bowler rejected Anglo's overture again, saying dismissively that perhaps the two should talk again in eighteen to twenty-four months' time. Bowler was taken with Drumm's exuberance but concerned about Anglo's property-heavy business. A merger with Anglo was not a Plan L, M or N for IL&P, never mind a Plan A, B or C, she thought as she walked back to her offices after the meeting.

As their discussion about a potential merger drew to a close, FitzPatrick made a request, according to Casey's account of the meeting to special investigator John Purcell. 'As that meeting broke up, Sean FitzPatrick said, "Look, notwithstanding our falling out on that matter, could we neverthe-less continue to cooperate as we had been doing in providing support to each other?" The chairman [Gillian Bowler] and I confirmed that that could happen.'

'Can we still be friends?' was how Casey paraphrased FitzPatrick's request at the end of the meeting to Purcell. 'Let's let bygones be bygones, and we accept the position that you're taking in relation to the merger, but we are continuing, as I understand he said, to work well together, on a kind of day-to-day basis, things are very tough out there, we have our year-end coming up, can I take it that, you know, that that kind of inter-course will not be interrupted.'

Despite his fury at the appearance of the *Sunday Tribune* story, Casey was acutely aware that IL&P would almost certainly require support from Anglo in order to reduce its level of ECB borrowings at the company's next reporting date of 31 December 2008. The funding relationship between Anglo and IL&P dated back to the previous March, when Pat Neary at the Financial Regulator and John Hurley at the Central Bank encouraged the Irish banks to 'don the green jersey' and help each other out by funding one another if they couldn't source deposits in the money markets. Anglo and IL&P acted on this almost immediately, though perhaps not in the way Neary had in mind.

In advance of Anglo's half-year financial results, which would be calculated as at 31 March, IL&P placed a deposit of €750 million with Anglo through Irish Life Assurance. This was a circular transaction: the money had in fact originated with Anglo as an inter-bank deposit. IL&P would only agree to advance money to Anglo if it received money from Anglo first as cash collateral for the transaction. As far as IL&P was concerned this was to be the basis for their funding arrangements as it believed this meant zero risk for the company. The net effect for Anglo was that its corporate deposits figure increased because the Irish Life money originated with a pensions company, not a bank. The financial markets liked corporate deposits better than inter-bank deposits as they were regarded as more secure. This was important for Anglo, particularly after losing deposits following the St Patrick's Day Massacre. It wanted to make its books look as healthy as possible.

The March transaction had approval at the highest levels within IL&P. On 28 March Peter Fitzpatrick, the company's finance director, emailed Gerry Keenan, the head of Irish Life Investment Managers (ILIM), the company's fund management business which helped to process the transactions. The purpose of the email was to approve the €750 million transaction formally. Fitzpatrick said that he had a mandate from the company's chief executive, Denis Casey, and that the transaction didn't need to go through the company's internal assets and liabilities committee (Alco), which oversaw funding arrangements, as it was an overnight loan with no risk due to the collateral.

'To be absolutely clear, this is something which the Central Bank is encouraging us to do, along with other players in the banking sector and, at 30 June, we will be the beneficiaries of this kind of support,' Fitzpatrick told Keenan. 'Accordingly, we will be keeping this transaction tight to senior management and I would ask you not to advertise it widely within

ILIM. For that reason, Denis and I will sign off whatever is required, but we will not be bringing it through Alco as it is an overnight facility.'

As envisaged in Peter Fitzpatrick's email, Anglo returned the favour in advance of IL&P's half-year accounts in June. The Financial Regulator and Central Bank had put pressure on IL&P to reduce its borrowings from the European Central Bank, which were regarded as a sign that the bank could not source adequate funding on its own in the markets. IL&P and Anglo later agreed to a transaction wherein Anglo would lend €3.33 billion to IL&P for a short period before 30 June 2008 so that IL&P could reduce its borrowings at the ECB. This was not a circular transaction like the one in March, but rather a short-term inter-bank loan.

At a meeting on 3 July with Pat Neary and Con Horan, IL&P chair Gillian Bowler and chief executive Denis Casey showed that, having received the €3.33 billion in funding from Anglo, the company was able to reduce its ECB borrowings from about €7.5 billion in mid-April to about €4 billion at the end of June. As late as 22 August the Regulator was made aware that after the short-term Anglo loan was repaid, IL&P's ECB borrowings had gone back up to about €7.5 billion by the end of July.

The nature of the funding relationship between Anglo and IL&P – and the motivation for Anglo to keep the relationship going – is best illustrated by an internal Anglo email dated 30 April. The two banks had talked earlier that morning about a €1 billion funding deal whereby Anglo would lend cash to IL&P. Mike Nurse, head of risk management in Anglo's treasury department, emailed Willie McAteer, Matt Moran, and treasury executives John Bowe and Matt Cullen to say that the funding would be for one month. The motivation for IL&P was 'to reduce its reliance' on the discount funding from the European Central Bank, he said, while 'The motivation for Anglo is to acknowledge past assistance from the counterpart and to position us for future potential arrangements.' It was a symbiotic relationship – we scratch their back; they scratch ours.

Now, with Anglo's 30 September end-of-year accounting date fast approaching amid a worsening crisis the bank was in need of some serious scratching. It sought to tap IL&P for another circular transaction that would make the bank's figures look better in the year-end accounts.

McAteer and Drumm held meetings with the Financial Regulator on 17, 20 and 24 September to discuss the bank's deteriorating funding position over the month. According to a memo compiled by Anglo's legal advisers in January 2009, McAteer told the Regulator at the 24 September meeting that the bank would be 'managing the balance sheet at year end'.

Neary responded: 'Fair play to you, Willie.' Former colleagues who worked with Neary said this was just the kind of phrase he would use.

At the 17 September meeting Drumm met Neary and Horan in Dame Street. The bank was haemorrhaging deposits worth up to €1 billion every day, and was now in breach of the liquidity ratios specified by the Regulator. Drumm asked Neary and Horan if they would provide a 'backstop' credit line – effectively an emergency loan facility. Drumm proposed that Anglo would put aside part of its loan book as collateral for this facility. Anglo at this stage calculated that it needed about €7 billion in back-up liquidity to be able to meet the repayment of deposits as they were demanded or fell due.

According to an account of the meeting by one of those present, Neary told Drumm that he was 'somewhat embarrassed' as even though Anglo had been dealing with him directly all along on liquidity problems, he did not have the money and that he would have to speak to the Central Bank. Drumm felt this was 'hand-washing' by Neary: he believed that the regulator had the authority to sanction such a loan.

Drumm and Bowe met Hurley and other Central Bank officials to discuss the possibility of an emergency credit line. Anglo was told that there was only €4 billion 'in the system' for back-up liquidity in this kind of situation, that the €4 billion was in 'various pots', and that Anglo wasn't the only bank in difficulty. Drumm was shocked that the 'lender of last resort' for the Irish banking system had such a limited amount of cash available to it – less than 1 per cent of the country's bank assets – to save a bank experiencing a run on deposits. He would later describe this to friends as his 'oh Jesus' moment.

FitzPatrick recalled in an interview for The FitzPatrick Tapes, 'Leading up to the 29th of September things were real bad. I mean real bad. It got real bad treasury end and financial end, meaning our liquidity. The Central Bank might have been thinking of giving us money but they said they didn't have money to give us. They could only lend so much because they couldn't get it. We said don't be so stupid, will you not get the ECB to lend money to us?'

The Central Bank would later maintain that there was no limit on the loans it could make to support an Irish bank under its so-called exceptional liquidity assistance (ELA) facility. Hurley might have been playing a delicate game with Drumm and Bowe. The disclosure of the Bank of England's emergency loans to Northern Rock the previous year had led to a run on the troubled UK bank, and as a consequence of this there was a nervousness around providing such funding. A leak could make a bad situation even worse.

Not for the first time, Hurley urged Anglo to seek help from other banks. Anglo had tried this, and had got the cold shoulder from Bank of Ireland and AIB. Drumm told Hurley that there was no chance of the 'big boys' of Irish banking helping Anglo. They'd prefer if Anglo collapsed, he said. Hurley encouraged him again to approach AIB and Bank of Ireland. Drumm suggested to Hurley that he had the power to order them to cooperate.

AIB had, in fact, been asked to support Anglo, but said that it would only do so on the basis of a letter from the Central Bank governor. No letter ever materialized.

Drumm told Hurley that the bank had a good relationship with IL&P and that they had helped each other out over the end of their financial reporting periods.

Anglo had another problem to deal with throughout September. The UK banking regulator, the Financial Services Authority, was growing very nervous about the scale of British customer deposits in the Icelandic banks, which were now in serious trouble. This nervousness on the part of the FSA soon extended to other non-UK banks, including Anglo, that held substantial deposits from customers in the UK.

Anglo held about €11 billion in such deposits. As the financial crisis deteriorated in August, the FSA started probing Anglo's solvency and liquidity ratios. In the first half of September, as chaos reigned in the Irish, UK and European banking systems, economic nationalism kicked in and governments started protecting their own. The FSA sent a letter to Anglo demanding a so-called liquidity waiver to protect UK depositors.

Such a waiver would allow the FSA to call on Anglo at any point to place sufficient money in the UK to cover the deposits it had taken from UK customers. Given that this amounted to €11 billion, Anglo could go bust if the FSA were ever to make such a demand. On the other hand, if the bank didn't sign the letter, the FSA could withdraw its licence to operate as a bank within the UK. It was a gun to the head. The bank had no choice but to agree to the waiver provision.

The cash crisis at Anglo was causing problems for the bank's borrowers, too. The hotelier and publican Hugh O'Regan, best known for setting up the Thomas Read chain of pubs in Dublin, said in a High Court action taken by Anglo Irish Bank the following year that in September 2008 the bank had withdrawn a €26 million loan offer to buy a building at No. 8 St Stephen's Green that he wanted to turn into a philanthropic networking club. 'The atmosphere within the bank in September and October 2008 was frenetic and filled with panic,' O'Regan said in an affidavit to the court.

On Monday, 22 September high-ranking state officials met to see how they could create 'a war chest' of loans to help fund the floundering Irish banks. Oliver Whelan and John Corrigan were there from the National Treasury Management Agency, Kevin Cardiff and William Beausang attended from the Department of Finance, and Tony Grimes represented the Central Bank.

The officials had to come up with something. Goldman Sachs, the investment bank hired by Irish Nationwide to find solutions to its growing crisis, told officials that the building society was in danger of running out of funds in eleven days. The officials assessed how much money they could cobble together from various sources to help fund the banks. Grimes told the meeting that Anglo had already asked for a loan of €7 billion in an asset-swap deal with the Central Bank. He said that the Central Bank would not agree to this 'unless absolutely necessary'.

The following day, 23 September, the Department of Finance carried out a brainstorming session to consider more radical options to save the Irish banks. Various forced mergers and takeovers were suggested, including the takeover of Irish Nationwide by Anglo; given that these two institutions were the weakest in the system, the fact that state officials were thinking along these lines illustrates just how desperate or lacking in real ideas they were. A merger of the two biggest banks, AIB and Bank of Ireland, was also considered, as was a tie-up of Irish Nationwide, IL&P and EBS. AIB and Bank of Ireland had each been asked over the previous weeks whether it could take over Anglo, but the idea wasn't a runner. With a balance sheet of €100 billion, Anglo had grown too big for either AIB or Bank of Ireland to save.

On the same day, Sean FitzPatrick and fellow Anglo board member Lar Bradshaw purchased €1.1 million and €196,000 worth of the bank's shares, respectively. FitzPatrick thought they were good value at €3.92 and described the purchases to Tom Lyons as having been 'an announcement of our confidence'.

As the banks, and particularly Anglo, continued to weaken, the government's crisis management moved up a few gears. On Thursday, 25 September there was a major meeting at Government Buildings. Taoiseach

Brian Cowen and Minister for Finance Brian Lenihan met with their officials, John Hurley and Tony Grimes from the Central Bank, Michael Somers and John Corrigan from the NTMA and the Attorney General. The meeting was also attended by investment banking adviser Henrietta Baldock from Merrill Lynch, who had just been hired by the government to advise it on the banking crisis. PricewaterhouseCoopers also attended, as did Eugene McCague from law firm Arthur Cox, which was also working for the government. Irish Nationwide's adviser Basil Geoghegan from Goldman Sachs attended part of the meeting.

Neary told the meeting that the issue was liquidity, not solvency. There was 'no evidence to suggest that Anglo is insolvent on a going-concern basis', he said, 'it is simply unable to continue on the current basis from a liquidity point of view'. He felt the same way about Irish Nationwide.

David Doyle, the secretary general of the department, wasn't so sure. He said that the government would 'need a good idea of potential loss exposures within Anglo and INBS'. They could be €2 billion at Irish Nationwide after it used up its existing capital, he said, and €8.5 billion at Anglo. Given that Anglo had about €4 billion in capital, this implied that the bank was facing losses of €12.5 billion. This is the only documentation that has yet come to light to indicate that any state official had serious concerns around this time about the solvency of the banks.

'They were looking at options,' says one banker in the thick of the crisis. 'The focus was exclusively on liquidity and for the most part they had not jumped to some of the what-ifs around solvency.'

Incredibly, PricewaterhouseCoopers told the government on Sunday, 28 September that under a 'stressed case' Anglo, Irish Nationwide and IL&P would have just €5 billion in bad loans. (The subsequent collapse in the property market would ultimately leave Anglo and Irish Nationwide with bad debts of more than €40 billion. PwC's idea of a 'stressed case' was evidently a very benign one.)

Kevin Cardiff would tell an Oireachtas committee in July 2010 that he first realized that the Financial Regulator was out of its depth on understanding the problems at the banks when the Department of Finance had to rely on PwC and Irish Nationwide's advisers for information on Anglo and the building society. The limited resources at the Central Bank and Financial Regulator had been stretched to breaking point. Regulatory staff were monitoring everything from making sure there would be enough cash in branches to ringing round to see that the bank had sufficient amounts of foreign currency for customers. It was all hands on deck.

Considerable time and resources were spent dealing with the deepening black hole at Depfa, the Dublin-based bank owned by the German lender Hypo Real Estate. Depfa, a €200 billion bank, moved its head office from Germany to Dublin in 2002, making it the largest bank in Ireland. It specialized in 'borrowing short' from the money markets to 'lend long' on public infrastructure projects. When credit was readily available in the money markets, this was fine, but as soon as the credit markets stopped functioning, a bank with this kind of business model could quickly run out of cash – and this is what happened to Depfa in September 2008.

Matters were complicated by the confusion over which regulatory authority was responsible for Depfa. The bank was German owned but its head office was in Ireland. Ultimately, Hypo's €5.7 billion takeover of Depfa in October 2007 meant it was the German regulators' problem. The Irish authorities were lucky in that instance – but the Depfa crisis occupied much of their attention none the less at a time when they had not got to grips with the domestic banking crisis.

'The fear at the time was that Depfa could have become Europe's Lehman Brothers,' says a high-ranking source at the Financial Regulator.

At a meeting with Brian Lenihan, David Doyle, Kevin Cardiff and Con Horan on Friday, 26 September advisers from Merrill Lynch, which had been appointed to advise the government two days earlier, outlined a range of options to tackle the deteriorating situation at the banks. One option was a blanket state guarantee of the banks' liabilities – its deposits, bonds and other borrowings – but Merrill Lynch said that such a move could damage the creditworthiness of the state and threaten its AAA credit rating. In any case, they asked, could Ireland really afford to guarantee the combined €500 billion balance sheet of the Irish banks? Another possible drawback of a blanket guarantee for all the Irish banks, according to an internal Department of Finance note of the Merrill Lynch presentation, was that it could 'allow poorer banks to continue'.

Merrill Lynch also suggested other options to the government. It raised the possibility of Anglo and Irish Nationwide being nationalized, the creation of a special liquidity fund of €20 billion from which the state would lend the banks money secured on loans, and the setting up of a 'bad bank' to take problem loans out of the banks. In the end, though, Merrill Lynch described a blanket guarantee of bank liabilities as the 'best, most decisive, most impactful' solution from the market's point of view.

14.   Guaranteed

29 September 2008 – Anglo's value: €2 billion

By Sunday, 28 September Anglo was at the edge of a cliff and just days away from falling off. Merrill Lynch warned the government that day that Anglo had exhausted all sources of liquidity available to it. Anglo had enough cash to meet Monday's demands, but at the rate it was losing deposits it would not be able to open on the Tuesday.

The Cabinet met for an emergency meeting that Sunday to discuss the crisis at Anglo and the options that were on the table to deal with it. John Gormley, the Minister for the Environment and the leader of the Green Party, the junior party in the coalition, said on *Tonight with Vincent Browne* on TV3 in February 2011 that the idea of a bank guarantee was discussed at the Cabinet meeting that Sunday afternoon. He described this as the 'David McWilliams option'.

McWilliams, an influential economist and newspaper columnist, had written three articles encouraging the government to introduce a guarantee – in the *Sunday Business Post* on 21 September, in the *Irish Independent* on 24 September and again in the *Sunday Business Post* on 28 September, the day of the Cabinet meeting. In his last article he said that a blanket guarantee of liabilities should be introduced for the Irish banks. 'The only option is to guarantee 100 per cent of all depositors/creditors in the Irish banking system,' he wrote. 'This guarantee does not extend to shareholders who will have to live with the losses they have suffered. However, it applies to everyone else.'

Unbeknownst to the reading public, McWilliams had discussed his idea for a guarantee with Lenihan before publishing any of these pieces, when the Minister for Finance called to his Dublin home unexpectedly the previous week, late on the night of Wednesday, 17 September. According to McWilliams's 2009 book, *Follow the Money*, he advised the minister 'to guarantee everything for a limited period'. (Lenihan said of McWilliams's contribution, 'I don't think he has a unique patent on the government decision to give the guarantee but he was arguing for that course of action.')

The idea of a guarantee was certainly not novel. Governments regularly issued guarantees to banks as a first response to banking crises. Sweden used one in the early 1990s when its banks collapsed. The use of a guarantee had been considered by Irish officials before McWilliams wrote about it. Much earlier in the year, the Department of Finance had considered measures to deal with the growing crisis, including the possible need for a larger guarantee extending beyond the state's existing deposit protection scheme to cover inter-bank deposits. The Domestic Standing Group had met on the morning of 17 September – hours before the meeting between Lenihan and McWilliams – to discuss, among other subjects, a solution for 'underpinning the stability of Irish banks' with 'a state guarantee for all deposits'.

On Monday morning, 29 September, panic spread across the European financial markets. During the day, four European governments acted to prop up banks: Bradford & Bingley in the UK, Hypo Real Estate (with its Dublin subsidiary Depfa) in Germany, Glitnir in Iceland and Fortis in Belgium. In the US, the giant Citigroup took over its troubled rival Wachovia, America's sixth largest bank.

Anglo's share price began to sink amid fears that it would be the first Irish bank to fall as the wave of collapses was spreading across Europe. Fitz-Patrick and Drumm sat in Drumm's office on the third floor of Anglo's St Stephen's Green HQ. Executives were coming in and out and board members were dialling in to conference calls to keep up to date with the events of the day. As all this was going on, Willie McAteer entered Drumm's office. He had a problem.

McAteer had a loan of €8.25 million from Bank of Ireland, which he had drawn to exercise share options to buy stock in Anglo over the years. Bank of Ireland held a charge over 3.5 million Anglo shares owned by McAteer as collateral for the loan. The loan agreement stipulated that the shares had to be worth at least 1.4 times the value of the loan. Anglo's share price had collapsed to such a degree that this ratio had been breached, and Bank of Ireland was demanding repayment of the loan, which McAteer was unable to do at such short notice. Bank of Ireland threatened to seize his Anglo shares and dump them in the market to recover its money. Alternatively, McAteer himself could sell the shares, the value of which just about covered what he owed. McAteer asked Drumm what he wanted him to do.

Drumm could not allow Bank of Ireland to dump McAteer's shares *that* day and there was no way Anglo could allow the finance director of the bank – the second-highest-ranking executive in the bank – to sell out. It would send a devastating message on a day when the bank's share price was already under severe pressure. Drumm didn't hesitate. He sanctioned a loan from Anglo for the same amount and a cheque for €8.25 million was issued to McAteer to repay Bank of Ireland. Drumm later described this to an associate as 'a battlefield decision' that was necessary, given what Anglo was going through.

'We had to do that loan,' says a former lender at the bank. 'It just had to be done. The share price was a proxy for funding. Any bad news had the potential to knock the bank over – it was about cash flow. There was no way 3.5 million shares belonging to the bank's finance director could be sold on that day. It would have collapsed the bank. Giving him the loan was not a case of two wrongs making a right but it was the lesser of two evils.'

Pat Whelan organized the loan paperwork for McAteer. The letter of offer used a template from a similar loan letter given to the directors the previous January. Only the date was changed. The letter said the loan was non-recourse, meaning that the bank could only call the shares as collateral if the loan went bad. At the time, the share price was collapsing so the bank's security was disappearing in front of its eyes as the bank agreed to lend out a further €8.25 million to one of its directors.

In much the same way that the aim of the Maple Ten transaction was to prevent the Quinn shares being dumped in the open market, the McAteer loan was also sanctioned on the basis that it would stop the stock falling further. It was another type of support for the bank's flagging share price.

As the share price continued to fall, FitzPatrick and Drumm racked their brains about what to do next. The bankers had failed to convince the Central Bank to provide emergency credit, and felt that they never knew where they stood with the Regulator or the government. Officials just listened to what they had to say, took notes and left.

FitzPatrick believed that the bank should lobby Alan Gray, the economist and Central Bank board member with whom he had dined in the company of Brian Cowen at the Druid's Glen post-golf dinner in July. Gray could talk to the government on Anglo's behalf, they thought. FitzPatrick knew that Gray and Cowen were close. (Indeed, Cowen had been picking Gray's brain for economic advice for years. Cowen's appointments diary as Minister for Finance shows that he had been meeting Gray as far back as 14 October 2005. A private diplomatic cable sent on 1 October 2004 by the US ambassador to Ireland, James Kenny, back to Washington DC after Cowen became Minister for Finance, said: 'Cowen is currently being coached by Irish economist Alan Gray and is positioning himself to become a future Taoiseach.') Earlier in September FitzPatrick had called to the offices of Gray's economic consultancy business, Indecon, on Fitzwilliam

Place, hoping to discuss Anglo's difficulties; Gray had advised him to use normal channels with officials in the Central Bank, and the meeting had lasted just minutes.

Undeterred, or just desperate, FitzPatrick and Drumm tried again, arriving unannounced at Indecon on 29 September; Gray recalled the bizarre encounter in response to queries from the *Irish Times* in January 2011. The bankers told him that Anglo was experiencing extremely severe liquidity difficulties. This was not news to Gray – the bank's plight was well known in the markets – and he told them, as he had told FitzPatrick earlier in the month, that they needed to discuss this with Central Bank officials, not him. The bankers said that they had already done this and there had been no response.

Drumm carried a printed presentation with him and used it as speaking notes. He told Gray that Anglo was looking for a 'bridging' loan secured on the bank's loans and a promissory note or IOU from the bank. About €1.5 billion would allow Anglo to meet repayments falling due on 30 September, he said.

For a 'big-picture' solution for the overall banking system, Drumm suggested that the government should set up a special liquidity support fund. This was essentially a pool at the Central Bank from which the banks could borrow, using types of collateral that were not accepted for borrowings from the European Central Bank.

Incredibly, in Drumm's presentation to Gray, the bank claimed to have no solvency problems. Drumm said there were only €500 million of bad loans on Anglo's overall loan book of €73 billion. The bank was on course to make profits for the year ending 30 September of €1.6 billion before bad-debt provisions of €130 million and other one-off costs. Bad debts could rise five-fold in 2009 and Anglo would still make profits of more than €1 billion, he said.

Gray later said that FitzPatrick and Drumm did not ask him to make any representations to any other parties. Gray ended the meeting after about five to ten minutes and sent the bankers packing. Drumm reported to colleagues that Gray seemed fidgety and 'scared to death' about being in a private meeting with the two Anglo bankers.

Gray said in his statement to the *Irish Times* in January 2011 that he did not discuss his meeting with Drumm and FitzPatrick with any other parties and 'at no stage ever made any representations of any kind on behalf of Anglo Irish Bank'. He said that he did not discuss the meeting with the Taoiseach or anybody else.

★

Drumm and FitzPatrick returned to St Stephen's Green deflated, not knowing where to turn next. They phoned the bank's directors and held an impromptu board meeting by conference call – something they sometimes did several times a day at this stage in the crisis. The meeting drifted into silence as the directors tried to figure out what to do. Then FitzPatrick suggested that Anglo should reach out to AIB and Bank of Ireland to see if they would be interested in taking over the bank or merging with it. Drumm agreed instantly, saying there was no other option. The bank had to swallow its pride and do it. The Central Bank had left Anglo to fend for itself. Now it had no other choice but to go to its biggest rivals for help. The board agreed that it would be best if the approaches came from the chairman.

This was a difficult moment for FitzPatrick. Here was a man who had spent three decades carving out a niche at Anglo, competing ferociously against the two big banks. Now he was going, cap in hand, to grovel for help. First FitzPatrick called Richard Burrows, Bank of Ireland's chairman. Burrows agreed to meet immediately. FitzPatrick then called Dermot Gleeson, the chairman of AIB and a former attorney general, but got his voicemail. He left a message, saying that he needed to talk urgently.

Drumm and FitzPatrick drove in FitzPatrick's car to Bank of Ireland's head office on Baggot Street. They had been told to drive into the basement, take a back elevator to the seventh floor and head for the boardroom to avoid being seen entering the building. After arriving in the boardroom, they were joined by Burrows and Brian Goggin, the bank's chief executive.

Drumm asked if Bank of Ireland could lend Anglo money to help with its liquidity, enter into asset swaps to allow Anglo to tap the ECB for borrowings, or indeed consider some kind of merger. Burrows and Goggin listened intently and were gracious in their replies. They explained that Bank of Ireland had its own problems and that if things continued the way they were going it too might run out of money. Drumm suggested that they had a good 'liquidity backstop' in their mortgage book and that if Anglo and Bank of Ireland agreed to swap assets, Anglo could then use Bank of Ireland-issued mortgages as collateral to borrow from the ECB. Goggin said that they had tapped this already and there was a limit on how much they could use. With regard to a possible merger, Burrows asked FitzPatrick who the bank's advisers were. 'Morgan Stanley,' he replied. The meeting ended with the Bank of Ireland executives unwilling to contemplate a merger.

When FitzPatrick and Drumm returned to St Stephen's Green, FitzPatrick received a call back from Gleeson. The AIB chairman said that he was not prepared to meet and that the bank was 'not in a position to help' Anglo. It was a short, curt, 'sorry for your troubles'-type call.

'Gleeson was very uptight,' FitzPatrick later recalled to Tom Lyons. 'Obviously bothered . . . He was more or less saying we are all in difficulties here . . . The whole market has dried up. The international money market, it is just gone . . . So lookit, Sean, we all have our problems so you are on your own. So that was that.'

While FitzPatrick was speaking to Gleeson, Drumm received the latest update on the bank's cash position. It was bad news. Anglo would be short at least €1.5 billion the next day. The bank would not be able to open the following morning. He had no choice but to approach the Central Bank again for help. Drumm said that Anglo would not be able to open its doors the following morning, and the Central Bank agreed to support it with a loan of €900 million. This would buy some time – a day, at least.

By the time the stock market closed that Monday afternoon Anglo's share price had dropped by 46 per cent from €4.28 to €2.30, the largest fall, in both percentage and monetary terms, in a single day since the Anglo name first appeared on the Dublin Stock Exchange in 1987. Overall, Irish companies suffered their biggest one-day sell-off in more than a quarter of a century.

FitzPatrick later said that after leaving the office he went to the home of his old school friend, Jack O'Driscoll, in Bray, where he had dinner, and that he was at home and in bed by 11 p.m. He said that he did not make any further attempts to influence the government on a course of action to save Anglo.

Drumm stayed in Anglo's offices to complete the paperwork on the emergency loan from the Central Bank before going home to Malahide. He sensed that he had done all he could at that stage and handed over Anglo's fate to the Central Bank. Drumm felt that the Central Bank would not let Anglo fail on its watch, but in the back of his mind he worried about where the next day's cash requirement would come from.

Following Anglo's overtures, Bank of Ireland and AIB made contact with each other. They felt that, given the extraordinary approaches from Anglo, they needed to let the government know just how severe a crisis the Irish banks were facing. The banks' own treasury departments were able to monitor the level of deposits flooding out of Anglo. They felt that Anglo was on the verge of collapse and feared that if the government did nothing, the crisis could spread and they could be next.

Bank of Ireland asked government officials to arrange an urgent meeting with the Taoiseach and the Minister for Finance; AIB agreed to attend. Cowen and Lenihan accepted their request.

Around 6 p.m. Cowen and Lenihan met at Government Buildings. They were joined by the secretary general of the Department of the Taoiseach, Dermot McCarthy, and by David Doyle, Kevin Cardiff and William Beausang from the Department of Finance. Neary and Hurley also attended, and Attorney General Paul Gallagher joined the meeting later on.

At 6.37 p.m. Cardiff emailed Merrill Lynch executive Henrietta Baldock seeking a document she had drafted setting out the options facing the government. Cardiff's message was confined to the subject line: 'In meet with Taoiseach – need note on pros and cons of guarantee a sap [sic]'. Minutes later, Baldock replied with an attached fourteen-page document she had prepared the previous day.

The Merrill Lynch document shows that the focus was still on liquidity and not on solvency at Anglo and Irish Nationwide. It repeated Anglo's view that just 3 per cent of its loan book was impaired, though it warned that falling property prices could affect loans, particularly speculative development loans. Anglo's most pressing need was for liquidity owing to the 'sustained outflow' of corporate deposits and overnight funding, according to Merrill Lynch. Anglo would be down €100 million by Tuesday and the bank would not be able to open. At the rate it was losing deposits, Anglo would be down €4.9 billion within weeks.

The investment bankers said that the government could nationalize Anglo and Irish Nationwide by taking them into 'state protective custody' and it could generate 'a capital cushion' of €7.5 billion to protect against potential bad debts by wiping out Anglo's shareholders and the lowest rank of subordinated bondholders. But Merrill Lynch advised that a guarantee should be given to all depositors and senior bondholders, and all but the lowest rank of subordinated bondholders. The document contained just ten lines on Merrill Lynch's view of this option. It warned that the scale of the liabilities covered could be over €500 billion. 'This would almost certainly negatively impact the state's sovereign credit rating and raise issues as to its credibility,' said the government's advisers. 'The wider market will be aware that Ireland could not afford to cover the full amount if required. It might also be poorly received by other European states if they come under pressure to do the same.'

At 8.40 p.m. Denis O'Connor, a partner at PricewaterhouseCoopers, sent an email to Kevin Cardiff, Brendan McDonagh at the NTMA and

1. A young Sean FitzPatrick at the launch of Anglo's safety-deposit boxes in 1983

2. FitzPatrick with the man who hired him to run Anglo Irish Bank, veteran banker Gerry Murphy

3. Two of FitzPatrick's key early hires: Tiarnan O'Mahoney (*left*), who ran Anglo's treasury department for two decades and was the front-runner to succeed FitzPatrick as chief executive, and John Rowan (*below*), who ran Anglo's UK business from 1988 to 2005

4. Ned Sullivan, the food executive who joined the Anglo board in 2001 and was the bank's senior non-executive director when its crisis started unfolding

5. David Drumm (*left*), shortly after being appointed to succeed FitzPatrick as chief executive in 2005, with one of the other contenders for the post, Tom Browne

6. John Hurley, who served as governor of the Central Bank from 2002 to 2009 – the years of Anglo's dizzying rise and catastrophic fall

7. Pat Neary, who as chief executive of the Financial Regulator was the state official most directly responsible for supervising the banks

8. Ireland's richest man, Anglo's biggest headache: Sean Quinn at one of his cement plants

9. Donal O'Connor was appointed to the Anglo board in mid-2008; by the end of the year he had succeeded the disgraced FitzPatrick as chairman, and at the bank's e.g.m. in January 2009 he faced shareholders a day after the bank was nationalized

Matt Moran
Group Finance Director

Noël Harwerth
Chairman of Risk &

10. Matt Moran, one of Anglo's most combative executives, and Noël Harwerth, who headed the board's risk and compliance committee, on the podium at the e.g.m.

11. Gary McGann, a close ally of FitzPatrick's on the Anglo board from 2004, resigned along with the other remaining non-executive directors after the January 2009 e.g.m.

12. Declan Quilligan, an executive director of Anglo, was effectively acting chief executive after Drumm's resignation, but the board's attempt to appoint him to the post permanently was not approved by the Financial Regulator

13. Alan Dukes, appointed to the Anglo board by Minister for Finance Brian Lenihan after the September 2008 bank guarantee, became chairman of the bank in its zombie phase

14. 'How did you know I would be here?': an angry David Drumm, back in Dublin in October 2009 to talk to Anglo's new management about the millions of euros he owed the bank

15. Mike Aynsley (*left*) took over as Anglo chief executive in September 2009, and was joined by Maarten van Eden as chief financial officer in January 2010; the two had no success in their efforts to carve a working bank out of the mess they inherited

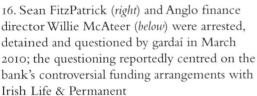

16. Sean FitzPatrick (*right*) and Anglo finance director Willie McAteer (*below*) were arrested, detained and questioned by gardaí in March 2010; the questioning reportedly centred on the bank's controversial funding arrangements with Irish Life & Permanent

17. Taoiseach Brian Cowen – whose political downfall would be triggered by revelations about his contacts with Sean FitzPatrick – and Minister for Finance Brian Lenihan at the publication of two reports on the Irish banking crisis in June 2010

18. Patrick Honohan, the academic turned Central Bank governor whose *Morning Ireland* interview in November 2010 confirmed that the state would be accepting high-interest bailout loans from the EU and IMF

19. Ghost HQ: the shell of Anglo's new building, abandoned when the bank imploded

20. The Anglo Irish Bank sign is removed from the bank's former headquarters in St Stephen's Green in April 2011

Brian Halpin at the Central Bank. Anglo had run out of cash, he said. The bank had lost €1.8 billion in deposits over the course of the day and did not have any reserves left. The bank had borrowed €900 million from the Central Bank and there was more than €2 billion of debt which had to be repaid by the bank the following day. If depositors came knocking on Anglo's door in the morning to get their money back, the bank would not be able to pay them.

While the Taoiseach, the Minister for Finance and their top regulatory and finance officials deliberated, the AIB chairman Dermot Gleeson and chief executive Eugene Sheehy, together with the Bank of Ireland chairman Richard Burrows and chief executive Brian Goggin, waited for two hours in the Sycamore Room in Government Buildings. Eventually the bankers were called in. Incredibly, the chief executive of the Financial Regulator, Pat Neary – the man responsible for supervising the banks – was not present at the meeting with the bankers.

Gleeson spoke first, arguing that Anglo and Irish Nationwide were the two delinquents on the Irish banking block and needed to be taken out by the state. The fact that nothing was being done about them suggested that there was something wrong with the entire Irish banking system, he said. This was having a damaging effect on AIB and Bank of Ireland. It was paralysing the markets where the two banks borrowed: investors who usually lent to them thought that all the banks were in the same situation as Anglo and Irish Nationwide because they had not been treated any differently by the government.

Sheehy and Goggin spoke on the more technical problems that their banks were facing because of the difficulties at Anglo, but the emphasis was the same. The two banks asked the government to nationalize Anglo and possibly Irish Nationwide and to guarantee the liabilities of the other Irish banks. The bankers took the view that the government couldn't take a bank into state ownership midweek with the markets open; it could not be done any sooner than the following weekend. The bankers had the sense that Lenihan was in favour of nationalizing Anglo that night but that Cowen was against it.

Lenihan was the main speaker on the government side but the meeting was chaired by Cowen, who, with his jacket off, was very much in charge.

After they had said their bit, the bankers were shown into separate rooms – AIB in one, Bank of Ireland in another – to allow the Taoiseach and Minister for Finance to consider what to do next. They had had about forty-five minutes to state their case.

The Department of Finance had prepared a draft piece of legislation the previous May that would allow them to nationalize a bank. This was the result of several months of planning following the collapse of Northern Rock the previous year. So the government had the legislative wherewithal to nationalize Anglo that evening.

Taking one bank into state ownership was ruled out, however, because of what had happened in the financial markets that day. The part-nationalization of Belgian bank Fortis had not stopped investors from rounding on the Belgian-French bank Dexia. Government officials felt that to nationalize Anglo would set off a chain reaction: they'd also have to nationalize the next weakest, and then the next, and so on.

That night, as the crisis meeting was taking place at Government Buildings, the US Congress voted down the Troubled Asset Relief Program, the proposed $700 billion bailout to take the most toxic assets and loans out of the US banks. It was believed that Irish bank shares would nose-dive again the following day if the government didn't come up with a convincing plan to cover the entire Irish banking system.

The Taoiseach telephoned Alan Gray to ask him how he thought the markets might react if the government introduced a bank guarantee. According to his account of the conversation, Gray told Cowen that it was important that the government considered whether it would be breaching any of the EU Commission's stringent rules on state aid to companies by guaranteeing the banks and suggested that if there was any guarantee, the government should charge a fee for it and that it should be limited to a certain period of time. A short while later the Taoiseach decided that a guarantee of all deposits and most bonds at the six Irish banks was the best option. Only undated subordinated bonds across the six institutions, worth about €8 billion, were excluded.

The senior AIB and Bank of Ireland bankers were informed later that night that the government had chosen a guarantee, but that it could be implemented only if the banks requested it. This was, they believed, for technical reasons related to EU state-aid rules. 'It was like, "Here's the sweet jar, but you have to ask for the sweets,"' says a well-placed source.

The two big banks were asked what funds they could provide to Anglo to tide the bank over. AIB and Bank of Ireland both agreed to provide €5 billion until the weekend. The two banks thought that the money would only be needed for the short term as they were led to believe from the discussions that night that Anglo would be nationalized the following weekend. They were in any case worried that Anglo wouldn't last the week, even with a state guarantee, and so they sought a specific guarantee from the government that they would get their money back by the end of the week. In the event, no request was ever made to AIB or Bank of Ireland to draw down the €5 billion each bank pledged; Bank of Ireland was irritated to have incurred about €1 million in costs cobbling the €5 billion together.

The Central Bank agreed on Monday night to lend Anglo a further €3 billion to help keep the bank afloat. This included the €900 million the Central Bank had given the previous night to tide it over until the Tuesday morning. The money would be provided on an asset-swap basis: Anglo would give some of its loans to the Central Bank in return for funding.

The bankers left Government Buildings after 2 a.m. Neary began calling the chairmen and chief executives of the banks who had not been present at the meeting to tell them that the government had agreed to guarantee the liabilities of their institutions.

Lenihan meanwhile phoned the other government ministers, waking them up to seek their approval for the guarantee. John Gormley, the Minister for the Environment, could not be reached as the battery on his mobile phone had run out of power. A Garda was sent to Gormley's house to wake him up with the message that he had to call Lenihan immediately. 'Are we going for the David McWilliams option?' asked Gormley when he phoned the Minister for Finance. 'Yes,' said Lenihan.

Lenihan called the French finance minister Christine Lagarde, who was then chairing the EU group of finance ministers, and Jean-Claude Trichet, the president of the European Central Bank, telling them in fluent French that he was guaranteeing Ireland's banks. Lagarde expressed surprise at Ireland's decision to act alone to protect its own banking system at a time of great stress for the global financial system.

The government's guarantee of the Irish banks was the biggest financial decision taken in the history of the state. It made the state guarantor of deposits, bonds and loans worth €440 billion at the six domestic lenders: AIB, Bank of Ireland, Anglo, Irish Life & Permanent, EBS and Irish Nationale. This amounted to more than twice the economic output of the country and over ten times the national debt. No other country in the world had taken such a step in response to the 2008 financial crisis.

It was a huge gamble. It tied the country to the fate of its banks and to their massive exposure to the property market. The government was not guaranteeing to cover losses on bad loans, but this would become largely academic: if losses on loans escalated to a level where the banks would be unable to meet their liabilities as they fell due, then the guarantee could be triggered. The government was ultimately on the hook for all the rubbish on the banks' balance sheets.

On 30 September 2008, the day the legislation enacting the guarantee was debated, Brian Lenihan told the Dáil that the value of the assets – mostly loans – of the six Irish banks exceeded their guaranteed liabilities by about €80 billion. 'By any measure there is, therefore, a very significant buffer before there is any question of the guarantee being called upon,' he said. This was intended to be reassuring, but it was based on what would soon be shown to be a greatly inflated estimation of the value of the banks' assets.

Drumm woke on the morning of Tuesday, 30 September and turned on his phone to find two voice messages left overnight by Pat Neary. Drumm passed the news on to FitzPatrick, who had got a call from a contact at the Central Bank at 5.30 a.m. to tell him the news. FitzPatrick was elated.

When Drumm spoke to Neary, he had the impression that the state's top banking regulator had been rattled by the previous night's events. Drumm thought the Department of Finance must have been asking Neary how the banks could have got to this point, how problems had been allowed to go so far.

FitzPatrick discussed the guarantee with Drumm and the board later that day. 'We spoke during the day about the relief of all that,' FitzPatrick told Tom Lyons in an interview for *The FitzPatrick Tapes*. 'It wasn't that the guarantee was a relief. It was that the government had stepped in behind the banks . . . Everyone was happy that that was going to be it. Suddenly we got up the next day and it was a brand-new day.'

As a gambit to halt the run on the Irish banks, the announcement of the guarantee worked brilliantly. The deposit outflows stopped. Treasury executives in large companies, banks and financial institutions stopped asking for their corporate and inter-bank deposits back as they matured, and executives at Anglo and other Irish banks worked the phones, ringing company treasurers across Europe to see what deposits they could get back into the banks.

'It was like drugs coming back onto the street,' says a former senior banker. 'We were like junkies rushing to get a fix.'

★

The UK Chancellor, Alistair Darling, was surprised and angry when he heard about the guarantee. In an interview in February 2010 he told me that one of his officials had 'picked it up at about half-past six' on a radio news bulletin. He called Lenihan, seeking to have the guarantee reversed and warning that the government's decision would draw deposits out of the British banks to the benefit of the Irish banks.

Darling was right to worry. Ulster Bank, owned by Royal Bank of Scotland (RBS), estimated that it lost about €5 billion in deposits to the Irish banks over the following two weeks. Anglo touted for business on the back of the guarantee, telling their own developer customers who had current accounts at Ulster Bank to move their cash to a guaranteed bank like Anglo. (Anglo knew where its customers had their current accounts because loan repayments were made from accounts at other banks.) Anglo's approaches to customers were reported to senior management at Ulster Bank, who made a complaint to the Financial Regulator about Anglo's behaviour, but no action was taken.

The Financial Regulator later fined Irish Nationwide €50,000 after Michael Fingleton Jr, the son of the building society's chief executive and the head of its London office, circulated an email to his contacts in the days after the guarantee touting for deposits. Incredibly, it was the first time an Irish bank or building society had been fined by the Financial Regulator in the five years since it had been established as a distinct entity from the Central Bank.

Although no bank was singled out in the statement read out by Lenihan announcing the guarantee, government officials were briefing journalists in private that the most pressing reason for the guarantee was to protect Anglo. The *Financial Times* published a report in the newspaper on Wednesday 1 October saying that the government agreed the emergency move 'amid concerns about a run on Anglo Irish Bank'.

The Dublin correspondent of the *Financial Times*, John Murray Brown, who was one of three journalists who contributed to the report, received a phone call from Matt Moran, the bank's chief financial officer. Moran gave him an earful, threatening legal action against the *FT* if it didn't retract the article. Moran said that Anglo had been in no more difficulty than any other Irish bank.

At 5.59 p.m. that evening Murray Brown received an email out of the blue from Neil Whoriskey, the press officer at the Central Bank. Whoriskey then telephoned Murray Brown to make sure he had received the email, which contained quotes from Pat Neary that would be broadcast on the six and nine o'clock news bulletins on RTE television that evening. 'This was not a problem confined to any individual bank,' said Neary in the second of four quotes in the email. 'The problem was one for the system and caused entirely by the international market turmoil.'

This was just not true – Anglo's difficulties were the catalyst for the guarantee – and Murray Brown felt the bank and the Regulator were working in tandem to spin the story that the guarantee was not provoked by any one institution.

On the same day the *Financial Times* story was published, Billy Murphy at Drury Communications, which handled Anglo's public relations, received a call from the Marian Finucane radio programme asking if Sean Fitz-Patrick would take part in their Sunday programme as a panellist to review that day's newspapers. Murphy contacted FitzPatrick, who asked him to come in to the bank to discuss it.

FitzPatrick wanted to appear on the programme. He believed that some-one from one of the banks had to speak publicly about the guarantee. He felt that most other bankers would hide away and that it was important for someone to come out and express gratitude for the government's actions. Murphy was asked to prepare FitzPatrick and to go through all the inter-national events that took place following the collapse of Lehman Brothers to show how the guarantee had come about. FitzPatrick later presented his appearance on the show as something that Drumm pushed him to do, but sources close to the bank say that FitzPatrick made up his mind on that himself. The researcher from the programme contacted FitzPatrick dir-ectly on Wednesday with an alternative proposal. He agreed to be the main interviewee on the Saturday programme as opposed to a panellist on the Sunday show.

In the interview FitzPatrick characterized the events of the previous Monday as arising from a liquidity crisis that faced all the Irish banks fol-lowing the collapse of Lehman Brothers. He told Finucane that Anglo had been in touch with AIB and Bank of Ireland, though he didn't disclose the fact that Anglo had gone to them with the begging bowl.

'This was not caused by one bank,' he said. 'It was not caused by any one issue with any one bank. This was caused by the global crisis, and we as banks were going to fall eventually if we didn't get money and therefore the government was the only place we could turn to.'

FitzPatrick said that liquidity had dried up for his bank and the other banks, but that Anglo didn't have a problem with bad property loans. 'Anglo Irish Bank has made mistakes,' he said. 'It had made mistakes in the past because we're in the business of risk and we have made mistakes and I'll admit that. Have we been reckless? No, we haven't. We cover all our loans in a belt-and-braces way. Ask any of our customers about that. So we don't believe we've been reckless.'

The guarantee wasn't a bailout of the banks, said FitzPatrick; it was a bailout of the economy and bankers must be grateful for that. Finucane put it to him that very few bankers had said thank you. 'Well I'm saying thank you unashamedly because we owe our lives to the government and what they did,' he replied.

Asked would he 'go the whole hog and say sorry to the Irish people', FitzPatrick said: 'Well, Marian, you know it would be very easy for me to answer a call like that and say sorry. What I've got to say is this, is that the cause of our problems was global, not directed, nothing. So I can't say sorry with any type of sincerity and decency. But I do say a very genuine thank you because that was, that is right.'

A news reporter approached FitzPatrick as he was leaving the RTE radio building. He asked FitzPatrick if he was going to resign. FitzPatrick said no.

He later told Tom Lyons that he left thinking he had done 'a good interview', that Drumm was 'thrilled' with how the interview went, and that he received calls of support from Pat Molloy, the former chief executive of Bank of Ireland, and Mick Bailey, one of Anglo's long-standing developer clients. 'There was an almost evangelical rejuvenation afterwards,' says a source who saw FitzPatrick after the interview. However, FitzPatrick's refusal to apologize created a wave of controversy as excerpts from his interview were replayed in news bulletins and reproduced in the newspapers.

He compounded the damage by speaking at a business event in the Charlesland Golf Club near his home in Greystones, Co. Wicklow later on the day of the Finucane interview. Speaking about the forthcoming budget that Brian Lenihan was preparing, FitzPatrick said that the government should tackle the 'sacred cows' and abolish universal state pensions and child benefit, and medical cards for the over-seventies. The budget needed to be 'brave', he said. Having riled the public with his refusal to apologize for the government being forced to introduce the guarantee to save Anglo, this was like pouring petrol on a fire.

FitzPatrick didn't know that *Irish Times* reporter Tim O'Brien was in the room covering the event for the newspaper. His comments caused uproar when they were published the following Monday. One letter writer to the newspaper captured the mood of anger against FitzPatrick: 'One would think that humble pie would be on this fellow's menu, but, realistically, it probably features more of the champagne and caviar to which he and his ilk, and indeed some of the rest of us, have become far too accustomed.'

Later in the weekend FitzPatrick received a call from Bank of Ireland chairman Richard Burrows. He was upset that in his radio interview FitzPatrick had portrayed the crisis over the previous days as something that had affected all Irish banks equally. He told him that AIB and Bank of Ireland had been asked by the government to lend €10 billion to Anglo to keep the bank afloat and went to great efforts to find it. FitzPatrick said he knew nothing about this.

A few days later FitzPatrick received a rocket of a letter sent to Anglo's offices by courier from Dermot Gleeson, AIB's chairman. He said pretty much the same thing as Burrows but in an angrier tone. He told FitzPatrick that he had conveyed on the programme that all the banks were in the same boat when in fact Anglo could not have opened on the Tuesday.

'The truth is that on Monday night AIB was asked by the governor of the Central Bank of Ireland (in the presence of the Taoiseach and others) to provide emergency funding to solve Anglo's liquidity problem, not just on Tuesday, but for every succeeding day until the end of the week,' said Gleeson.

'AIB acceded to the request and arranged to provide Anglo with €5 billion in liquidity until the weekend. The reason AIB was able to do this, was because it had liquidity in excess of its own requirements available on Monday, not just for Monday night but for the rest of the week and beyond; Anglo was not going to be able to balance its books without assistance.'

Gleeson said that it was 'frankly outrageous' to indicate that AIB's liquidity was good for only a matter of days and 'entirely inaccurate' to say that no one bank caused the crisis when the truth was that Anglo alone had to be saved on Monday.

'The reason I am writing to you now rather than speaking to you is that I am not any longer prepared to risk you sharing confidential telephone conversations with a chat show in which AIB's position on critical issues is significantly misrepresented,' he said.

He signed off the letter saying he reserved the right 'to put the record straight on each of the foregoing issues at a time and manner of my choosing and at any time from today onwards'.

FitzPatrick's interview with Marian Finucane had made him an outcast among bankers and the general public.

15.   Cooking the Books

October 2008 – Anglo's value: €3 billion

On Wednesday, 1 October – the day after the announcement of the bank guarantee, and the day after Anglo's accounting year ended – Ciaran McArdle, who worked in Anglo's treasury department, spoke to Claire Taylor, a junior official at the Financial Regulator's office, over the phone. Another member of staff at Anglo, Steven Hiles, listened in on the call. It went like this:

> Claire Taylor: I just want to ask about one of the figures on the funding template – the corporate figure, the 8 billion, is that still a net figure there?
>
> Ciaran McArdle: Yes, that's still a net figure . . . that's correct . . . [pause]. That is correct. Do you want me to continue? It's trying to manipulate our balance sheet for our financial year-end last night.
>
> CT: Yes.
>
> CMcA: And what we have done is we have boosted our customer funding number which we didn't include in our liquidity number, but we boosted our customer funding number so when our snapshot is produced at the beginning of December, it looks as good as possible, it is not a real number. If you looked at the other side of the balance sheet you will see an inter-bank placement of 8 billion, OK, so I wouldn't read too much into it. It just happens to fall on the last working day of the month, the last working day of the template, etc., etc., so you know it's something that we did.
>
> CT: Is it in the ratios?
>
> CMcA: It won't appear in the ratios, no, it's excluded from the ratios, it's going back out today and sort of over the next three or four days.
>
> CT: OK, that's grand, right, I think that's everything.

Taylor and McArdle were referring to figures on Anglo's balance sheet relating to a series of deposits between Anglo Irish Bank and Irish Life & Permanent over the last few days of Anglo's financial year. The money had followed the same route as it had in March, when back-to-back deposits between the two institutions had swelled Anglo's corporate deposits figure by €750 million before their half-year snapshot: Anglo placed the money as an inter-bank deposit at IL&P, and it came back to Anglo as a corporate deposit from Irish Life Assurance. The 'corporate figure' cited by Claire Taylor was, as Ciaran McArdle pointed out, balanced by the 'inter-bank placement'.

Anglo treasury executive Matt Cullen later told special investigator John Purcell, who examined the transaction for the Chartered Accountants Regulatory Board, that, on the instructions of David Drumm, he had approached IL&P in mid-August to propose a September transaction larger in size than the €3.33 billion deposit Anglo had made to IL&P before the latter's year-end in June. According to Cullen, IL&P 'came back to say, look, we'll do it on the basis that you will do a similar size, six or seven [billion], for us in December' – the end of IL&P's accounting year.

According to IL&P records, on 15 September – the day that Lehman Brothers collapsed – David Gantly sent Denis Casey an email to report that Anglo had sought about €5 billion in funding and that IL&P had agreed that the funds would – as in the March transaction – be supplied through Irish Life Assurance and be used by Anglo to 'bolster' its corporate deposits. The email made reference to the meeting between Casey and Drumm earlier that day in the Westin to discuss Anglo's proposal for a merger with IL&P.

Amazingly, considering that by the end of September Anglo was hours from being unable to continue trading, IL&P's funding situation was, at certain points in the latter half of the month, even worse than Anglo's. And so, even as the two banks were planning an enormous back-to-back funding transaction intended to make Anglo's balance sheet look better at its year-end, Anglo provided two emergency loans to IL&P: €800 million on 22 September and another €300 million the following day. These were normal inter-bank deposits and no collateral was provided by IL&P to support them.

As the end of the month approached, IL&P made preparations for what was at that stage intended to be a €5 billion circular deposit transaction with Anglo. In normal times IL&P had a risk limit of €500 million for any deposit given to Anglo where it wasn't providing any collateral; Irish Life Assurance had its own limit of €100 million for Anglo. But the risk limit would not apply here because IL&P's deposit with Anglo was backed by cash coming in from Anglo. Still, Peter Fitzpatrick wanted to make sure all IL&P's bases were covered. 'If this goes wrong, I would need to head to Siberia . . . never to return,' he told IL&P's head of risk, Hilary Flood.

The cash started flowing in from Anglo on 26 September. Three sterling amounts were received from Anglo's subsidiary in the Isle of Man – £250 million, £253 million and £475 million – making a total of £978 million (€1.2 billion). Like the March transaction, the money came in to IL&P's treasury department and was then sent back to Anglo as a corporate deposit through Irish Life Assurance.

Two further tranches of €1 billion arrived from Anglo on the morning of 29 September, and were in turn deposited back with Anglo, bringing the total to €3.2 billion of the total €5 billion approved by IL&P. At some point on 29 September, Anglo ran out of cash: for the moment, the transaction could go no further. Peter Fitzpatrick was getting nervous. He emailed David Gantly at 1.29 p.m. to make sure he was happy there was no risk to IL&P with the Anglo transactions: 'Dave, we need to be ultra sensitive that this is really nailed down.' Fitzpatrick told Gantly that if he needed any help, including advice from IL&P's chief legal officer Cathal McCarthy, he should 'just shout'.

That same afternoon Gantly received a phone call from Anglo. Would IL&P provide another €500 million in funding? The request was relayed to Casey and Fitzpatrick. Casey asked if Anglo would be providing collateral and was told there was no collateral available this time. Casey, Gantly and Fitzpatrick agreed that a cash deposit of that size without collateral was too great a risk. Tell Anglo no, Casey said.

Around 3.45 p.m. a treasury executive at IL&P, Paul Kane, received another call from Anglo requesting a lower amount, €250 million. The request was relayed to Gantly, who spoke to Casey. Again Casey asked if Anglo was providing any collateral; again Gantly said no; and again Casey said there could be no deal. A short time later Anglo requested €100 million unsupported by any collateral, and once more IL&P said no.

'Each of these requests was declined by IL&P on my direction,' Casey later said in his affidavit, 'as Anglo Irish Bank was not in a position to provide collateral for the proposed additional support.'

The next morning, 30 September, the situation had changed dramatically: the state bank guarantee had been introduced. Anglo, having been out of money the previous afternoon, now had €4 billion in cash to support another back-to-back deposit with IL&P. If the two banks did another circular transaction to the tune of €4 billion, it would bring the total value of the back-to-backs to more than €7 billion. Anglo asked IL&P would it increase the original limit from €5 billion to this higher amount. On the basis that there was collateral available and it would be a back-to-back transaction, Casey agreed.

The additional cash was transferred in four €1 billion tranches, starting around noon on 30 September and ending at 4.10 p.m. (Garda investigators later examined whether this was the same €1 billion being recycled four times, but it wasn't – the transaction was broken up this way because €1 billion was the maximum sum that the money transmission system could handle at any one time.) The transactions breached Anglo's internal 'limit excess', but this deviation from the rule was signed off formally by Willie McAteer as the bank's chief risk officer and Mike Nurse, the head of risk in the treasury department, according to a report carried out for the bank in January 2009 by Matheson Ormsby Prentice.

An email, which was later passed on to Garda investigators, was sent to a small number of staff within the treasury department requesting that the IL&P transaction not be included in the daily credit reports, which showed where the bank had placed deposits that day. Because the transaction had breached the bank's excess limit with IL&P by a whopping €6.7 billion, it should have been included. Excluding the transaction meant that it was hidden that day from as many as forty people who would normally see credit reports on a daily basis.

All told, the various transactions helped to boost Anglo's corporate deposit figure by €7.2 billion on the day of the bank's annual results snapshot – the vast bulk of the €8 billion corporate deposits figure referred to by Claire Taylor of the Regulator and Ciaran McArdle of Anglo in their telephone conversation on 1 October. The last €4 billion that Irish Life Assurance gave Anglo was repaid the next day; the £978 million in sterling provided on 26 September was repaid on 2 October; and the €2 billion provided on 29 September was repaid on 3 October. No cash changed hands in these repayments, which were effected by 'netting off': the matching amounts were simply cancelled in the books of IL&P and Anglo by way of accounting entries.

Short-term deposits between banks for the purpose of making half-year or year-end figures look better are known colloquially as 'bed-and-breakfast arrangements' or as 'balance-sheet management', and they are not uncommon. A 2009 internal investigation by Anglo found that the bank had had arrangements with Lloyds TSB, Credit Suisse, Rabobank, Royal Bank of Scotland and HBOS similar to the IL&P arrangement: Anglo would make deposits to banks within these groups and take deposits of the same size from their non-bank entities.

The report also said that requests for 'balance-sheet management trans-actions' came from Merrill Lynch, Lehman Brothers, ABN AMRO and two German banks, West LB and Hypovereins Bank, over an eighteen-month period to January 2009; it did not disclose whether Anglo agreed to participate in these transactions.

Because the purpose of 'balance-sheet management' was to deceive the markets, banks did their best to keep these arrangements under wraps. One example of this was on 20 May 2008 when Anglo issued a three-year bond, borrowing €200 million. German bank Hypo Real Estate agreed to lend the money. In return Anglo agreed to buy a €200 million bond from Hypo. A manager in Anglo's capital markets division told more than a dozen of his colleagues in an email that the nature of the transactions was to be kept secret. 'Do not mention the back-to-back nature of this trans-action,' he wrote, 'this was purely a reverse inquiry private placement deal as far as the market is concerned.' (A reverse inquiry is where one bank approaches another to see if they have any bonds they are willing to issue and a private placement is where a bond is issued specifically to one institu-tion rather than sold openly in the market.) The Anglo–Hypo bond transactions were not 'back-to-back' in exactly the same sense as the Anglo–IL&P transactions of March and September 2008: the bonds had different start and end dates and were priced differently, so they did not cancel each other out. The manager pointed out that the transactions helped Anglo show the market that it could raise money at a time of severe financial instability.

The Anglo–IL&P transactions in September 2008 were remarkable, and have been seen as scandalous, for two reasons. Firstly, their scale: trans-actions in excess of €7 billion were unheard of for banks the size of Anglo and IL&P. Secondly, the back-to-back nature of the transactions – whereby the liquidity positions of the two banks did not change at all – meant that the deception involved was of a different kind from the more conventional sort of year-end window-dressing whereby one bank gives another a short-term deposit. However artificial such a transaction might be, it is a real deposit, involving at least notional risk for the institution placing the money. But the back-to-back depositing between Anglo and IL&P involved no net cash changing hands and no risk to either institution. Its purpose, for Anglo, was purely to distort its balance sheet in a way the bank thought would be advantageous; its purpose for IL&P was as *quid pro quo* in what had been, and might continue to be, a mutually beneficial funding relationship.

Were the transactions illegal? EU market-abuse rules forbidding intentional falsification of accounts provided for penalties of ten years in prison and a fine of up to €10 million, but these rules have never been tested in an Irish court. Kevin Prendergast, corporate compliance manager at the Office of the Director of Corporate Enforcement, told a conference on white-collar crime in July 2010 that he did not really know what the crime of 'market abuse' meant in practice. 'Only when we take a case will we know how the courts will interpret the law on it,' he said.

The Regling-Watson report into the banking crisis, published in June 2010, referred to the transactions between Anglo and IL&P as 'window-dressing of balance sheets beyond acceptable levels', implying that a certain degree of window-dressing was tolerable. (At an Anglo board meeting on 13 January 2009, when the full details of the IL&P transaction were disclosed to all the directors for the first time, Noël Harwerth said that during her time at Citibank they had invented a product to carry out 'balance-sheet management', but never on the scale of the Anglo–IL&P transaction.)

The September window-dressing amounted to about 7 per cent of Anglo's balance sheet and almost a quarter of IL&P's loan book. One member of Anglo's treasury team, Matt Cullen, said it was the largest transaction he ever handled during his time at the bank.

The 9 p.m. news bulletin had just started on the television at the far end of the green room in RTE's studios in Donnybrook. Pat Neary, the chief executive of the Financial Regulator, was pacing the room. He was to be interviewed by journalist Mark Little on *Prime Time* following the news bulletin.

It was Thursday, 2 October – two days after the introduction of the bank guarantee – and I had been asked to sit on a panel with the minister for state at the Department of Finance Martin Mansergh and economist Colm McCarthy to discuss, after Neary's interview, what would happen next with the banks. Now we were waiting for the fun to begin.

I greeted Neary and shook his hand. He looked nervous. He had just been to make-up – a must before any television appearance – and his bald head and sergeant-major moustache exuded a strange orange glow in the green room. We exchanged some pleasantries and general comments about how it must be such a busy time for both of us, given what was happening with the banks. 'You must be up the walls,' I said. He didn't seem very interested in small talk. We sat down to watch the news, waiting until *Prime Time* started broadcasting.

There was a report about business in the pub trade being down and one
of the vintner organizations warning about job losses. To ease the tense
atmosphere, I joked that there appeared to be another liquidity crisis brewing. Neary didn't laugh.

We were escorted to the studio. Mansergh, McCarthy and I, as panellists
for the follow-up discussion, took our seats at one end of the studio with
the other *Prime Time* presenter, Miriam O'Callaghan. We had the perfect
vantage point to see Little dissect Neary with his questions at the other end
of the studio. Just before Little put his first question, O'Callaghan whis-
pered to me under her breath, 'Pat Neary doesn't know what he's in for.'

Little started off by asking Neary about how, just two weeks earlier, he
had said the banks had 'good shock-absorption ability' to deal with the
financial crisis. Neary seemed to be working from a script he had rehearsed
carefully. He answered questions that weren't put to him. He refused to be
drawn on the scale of the bad debts at the banks: 'By any estimate, the Irish
banks are so well capitalized compared to any banks anywhere across Europe that I am confident that they can absorb any [bad] loans or any
impairments that emerge in the ordinary course of business over the foreseeable future,' he said.

Colm McCarthy, who had a front-row view of Neary's performance
sitting next to me and Martin Mansergh on the panel, summed up the general reaction brilliantly in a comment to Michael Lewis for Lewis's article
on Ireland in the March 2011 edition of *Vanity Fair* magazine: 'What happened was that everyone in Ireland had the idea that somewhere in Ireland
there was a little wise old man who was in charge of the money, and this
was the first time they'd ever seen this little man,' said McCarthy. 'And
then they saw him and said, "Who the fuck was that??? Is that the fucking
guy who is in charge of the money???" That's when everyone panicked.'

The interview put Neary and the office of the Regulator under huge pressure. He was accused of being asleep at the wheel while the banks lent
heavily into property, and of downplaying the Irish crisis, misleadingly
portraying it as a by-product of a global problem.

Four days after his disastrous performance on *Prime Time*, Neary was
invited to appear before an Oireachtas committee to explain how the banks
had been allowed to get so close to collapse as to require the guarantee.
When he gave evidence on 14 October Neary said that the six domestic
financial institutions guaranteed by the state had €42 billion of capital to
cover estimated bad debts of just €2.1 billion. Speculative lending on Irish

construction and property development amounted to €39 billion, he said. However, some €15 billion of this was secured on the properties themselves and €24 billion on 'additional collateral or alternative sources of cash flow and realizable security'. It was just like listening to an Anglo banker – yes, we lent lots on property, but our loans are backed by cash flow and other assets.

Matt Moran and others at Anglo meanwhile began briefing journalists about the bank's exposure to land and development. They circulated a list of the top ten land deals over each of the three peak years of the property boom, from 2005 to 2007, and the banks that financed them, hoping to show that it was not as badly exposed as the other banks.

The value of the thirty deals totalled €3.4 billion and Anglo – on its own or with another bank – financed five of them, with a total value of €652 million, all in Dublin. They were the purchase of the Central Park site in Sandyford by developer John Lally (€50 million); the purchase of the Aldi site, also in Sandyford, by John Fleming (€85 million); a site in Stillorgan bought by Treasury Holdings (€65 million); the Irish Glass Bottle site, jointly financed with AIB (€412 million); and the purchase of the Mont- rose Hotel by Bernard McNamara (€40 million).

AIB was linked to an estimated €1 billion of the €3.4 billion overall value of the thirty deals; Bank of Scotland (Ireland) was the second most prolific lender, followed by Anglo, Ulster Bank and Irish Nationwide.

The list was potentially misleading in a few different ways. It only gave the value of the deals; Anglo provided no insight into just how much equity each developer put into the deals, even on its own deals, so it was not clear how much actual exposure each bank had. The list obviously didn't take into account the smaller development loans that Anglo and the other banks had provided – and during the period in question the number and value of such deals was enormous. The list also tended to understate Anglo's property exposure because it covered a period when Anglo had pulled back somewhat on Irish lending while dramatically increasing its foreign lending.

The circulation of the list was all part of Anglo's strategy to convince the world, in the weeks following the guarantee, that it was not the rotten- est Irish bank. Matt Moran set up a meeting with the two top opposition politicians, Fine Gael leader Enda Kenny and his finance spokesman Rich- ard Bruton. The meeting was arranged, strangely enough, with help from a Fianna Fáil TD Beverly Flynn, whom Moran knew from their shared home county of Mayo. Kenny and Bruton met Moran, finance director Willie McAteer and David Drumm in the bank's St Stephen's Green offices.

'It was very much a PR sort of thing,' Bruton told me. 'There was a charm offensive to say that everything was perfect, they had the best of customers and the best of loans. The Establishment was trying to say that the banks were facing a liquidity problem, not a solvency problem. But there was nothing particularly newsworthy in what Anglo were saying.'

It was widely perceived that Anglo had strong political connections, but by Irish standards this was not really the case. 'Just because Fianna Fáil was up the ass of developers didn't mean that Anglo was up there too, close to Fianna Fáil,' says a former Anglo executive.

Anglo management did not really know how to work the government channels or politicians to put their case forward. 'They didn't have sophisticated public affairs,' says a source close to the bank. 'They didn't invest time with politicians and public servants. I don't think there was any cause or effect from that dinner with Brian Cowen [and the Anglo board in April 2008]. Dealing with politicians was a waste of time for them.'

Now, facing dire liquidity and solvency problems and beholden to the government for the guarantee, Anglo had to change its attitude.

All hell broke loose at the Financial Regulator on 24 October when Pat Neary got a call from Kevin Cardiff, the second secretary at the Department of Finance in charge of banking. Cardiff had just received a call from the National Treasury Management Agency. They had spotted an unusual transaction in the report the government had commissioned on Anglo by PricewaterhouseCoopers. Neary asked Mary Burke, the head of banking supervision at the Regulator, to get to the bottom of the transaction. She rang Willie McAteer, Anglo's finance director. He got on to Colin Golden, Anglo's head of finance, and asked him to call Burke.

The matter had arisen separately within Anglo the day before. The bank had a meeting with Vincent Bergin, the partner at their auditors Ernst & Young. Golden's note of the meeting said that they discussed the €7.2 billion back-to-back IL&P deposits. He gave Bergin the context, saying that it had been a tough environment for funding and that Anglo had a strong relationship with IL&P.

Bergin later recalled the 23 October meeting in an interview with special investigator John Purcell. Golden told Bergin that the Regulator was aware of the transaction, according to Golden's account of the meeting detailed in an internal Anglo note of the conversation. Bergin shrugged his shoulders and said he believed that the transaction was 'technically sound', according to Golden's account.

'The transaction itself I was comfortable with,' Bergin later told Purcell. 'I did not think any of the accounting aspects of it were particularly difficult or challenging in any way, and overall it was a transaction that I was comfortable with, did not have massive concerns over. While it was in my head for a period of time, by the time we were coming to the end of the audit I had concluded on it and put it away in my head as a significant issue.'

Mary Burke subsequently spoke to Golden about the transaction on the phone. According to Golden's account, he told Burke that Ernst & Young's initial view was that the transaction was 'technically sound'. He said that he had been led to believe that the Regulator had approved the transaction. At this, Golden recalled in the internal note, Burke sniggered, adding that she didn't know if this was the case.

Burke called Peter Fitzpatrick, the finance director at IL&P, on the evening of 24 October. She asked whether IL&P had provided a significant amount of support to Anglo on 30 September 2008. It had, he replied. He added that the actual amount provided was higher than originally intended. Fitzpatrick said that IL&P had acted in accordance with its understanding of what it had been encouraged to do at a number of meetings with the Central Bank and the Financial Regulator: support the Irish banking system. IL&P saw this transaction as one Irish bank supporting another at a very difficult time of unprecedented turmoil in the financial markets, he said.

He did not pick up any hint of concern in Burke's voice. The tone of the conversation was relaxed. He asked whether the Regulator had any difficulties or worries about the level of support IL&P had given Anglo. She replied that the matter had only recently been brought to her attention by her staff and that she was ringing simply to confirm that it had taken place.

After speaking with Fitzpatrick, Burke emailed Neary and Horan. She told them that Fitzpatrick had 'positioned this transaction as a response to the governor's suggestions that the Irish banks should help each other out', and also that 'Anglo advised that they understood that the Financial Regulator was aware of the transaction, referring to yourselves'. She signed off with a blunt direction that it was up to them to decide who should talk to Cardiff about this the following Tuesday (after the Bank Holiday Monday, when the office would be closed). 'As discussed with Pat if Kevin Cardiff returns my call I will advise that someone will ring him back on Tuesday. You can decide among yourselves who it should be.'

★

Within weeks of the Irish bank guarantee, the focus of the financial crisis in Europe had turned from liquidity to solvency. Investors wanted to see how banks were increasing their 'core capital ratios' and 'core tier-one capital ratios' – closely watched metrics of how much rainy-day money they had to protect themselves from the collapsing value of assets backing their loans. In Ireland, an overwhelming proportion of these assets were property.

By mid-October the UK government had unveiled plans to pump £37 billion into its beleaguered banks Royal Bank of Scotland, which owned Ulster Bank in Ireland, and Halifax Bank of Scotland (HBOS), which owned Bank of Scotland (Ireland), taking the banks into either partial or majority state ownership. Germany and France pledged to inject fresh capital of up to €140 billion in their banks on top of a combined €720 billion in guarantees.

In Ireland, Minister for Finance Brian Lenihan appeared to have no similar intentions of pumping billions of taxpayers' cash into the banks. In a speech to the Leinster Society of Chartered Accountants on 24 October he described the state's bank guarantee as 'the cheapest bailout in the world so far' compared with other countries where 'billions and billions of taxpayers' money are being poured into financial institutions'. His comments would come back to haunt him.

PricewaterhouseCoopers had been infected by the same optimism. The accountants reported back to the government that the six financial institutions guaranteed by the state had capital levels in excess of the minimum allowed by the Regulator on the day the guarantee was introduced. They went further, estimating from their examination of the loan books, in particular the borrowings of property developers, that the banks would still be above their regulatory capital thresholds in 2011. The accountancy firm indicated in its November 2008 report on Anglo that the bank had the management capacity to deal with problems in its loan book, saying that most of the senior lenders at the bank had more than fifteen to twenty years' experience in the property market and had worked through previous economic downturns. (PricewaterhouseCoopers earned €5.4 million from the state for their work from September 2008 to January 2009.)

Few in the markets believed PwC's analysis. Eyeing possible bargains, international private equity firms such as Apax, Texas Pacific Group, Blackstone and Kohlberg Kravis Roberts started to come to Dublin in October and November, some arriving in their private jets and staying in some of the city's top hotels, including the five-star Merrion across the road from the Department of Finance and Government Buildings. These firms saw an opportunity to inject capital in negotiated deals where the government would provide a backstop guarantee against losses in return for a private equity company or market investors taking a bank off their hands.

Most bargain hunters circled Bank of Ireland, which had less exposure to the property market than the other big Irish banks. One group called Mallabraca, led by Nick Corcoran and Nigel McDermott of Dublin-based Cardinal Capital Group, and ex-Anglo banker Bryan Turley of Sorrento Asset Management, told the government in November that it had a fund of €5 billion ready to invest. The group of investors said that it would be willing to take a stake in Bank of Ireland but only if it was merged with Irish Life & Permanent and potentially Anglo. The deal was conditional on the government sharing the losses at the banks with the consortium.

Mallabraca had lined up some heavyweight investors in US buyout firm JC Flowers, New York investment bank Sandler O'Neill and private equity group Carlyle, with Olivier Sarkozy, the half-brother of French president Nicolas Sarkozy, playing a lead role in talks with the government as head of Carlyle's European banking team. The consortium also claimed that it had secured the funding from an unnamed sovereign wealth fund from one of the cash-rich Middle Eastern states. During November, the subject of mergers between Irish banks had been broached with FitzPatrick by economist David McWilliams at a dinner for the UCD Foundation. As the function was drawing to a close, FitzPatrick and McWilliams chatted privately at an empty table about the talk circulating at the time that Anglo would be taken over by Bank of Ireland or AIB. McWilliams recalled in *Follow the Money* that a takeover by Bank of Ireland, an 'Establishment bank, almost the Ascendancy bank', was anathema to FitzPatrick.

McWilliams described the scene: '[FitzPatrick] came closer, squeezed my arm and practically hissed between clenched teeth: "No fucking Protestant is coming near us. Those establishment fuckers and Bank of Ireland have been running our country before we came along, and those fuckers are not going to bring me down. None of them are ever going to look down on us again. We are the outsiders, and this is our moment. Those fuckers don't own us any more."'

Anglo hired Morgan Stanley again to see if they could find any new capital for the bank. The bank believed that it required just €1 billion to €2 billion to cover itself. Property values really didn't start their steep dive until the final months of 2008, and Anglo still clearly did not share the view of many economists, who were warning that the property bubble would burst and that it would be prudent to plan for a more severe downturn.

Anglo was working with the Financial Regulator on the bank's plan to raise capital, but the going was very tough. The bank's share price dropped below the €1 mark for the first time on 17 November 2008. In a meeting with the Regulator, Drumm and FitzPatrick discussed the dwindling prospects of securing €1–2 billion when the bank was valued by the market at less than €800 million. Drumm told Neary that the bank was struggling to find private investment and that it might have to turn to the government to invest. Neary pointed out that given the current share price this could lead to the nationalization of the bank. Drumm agreed: he was concerned that the bank could not stand on its own. At that, FitzPatrick kicked Drumm under the table.

'He kicked me after something I said,' said Drumm in an article in the *Irish Daily Mail* in January 2011 based on the November 2010 conference call with Garrett Kelleher. 'It was just about the survival of the bank. I got a lash under the table because all Sean could think about was his shares.' At this stage, FitzPatrick's shareholding in Anglo was worth less than €4.9 million, down from a high of almost €80 million. Nationalization would wipe out his stake entirely. Neary noticed FitzPatrick kicking Drumm, and afterwards he asked Drumm not to bring FitzPatrick to meetings again. 'He is a problem down here,' said Neary, according to Drumm's report back to colleagues.

Tensions between Drumm and FitzPatrick had reached boiling point. On one occasion during a meeting between the men around this time, FitzPatrick accused Drumm of being 'too fucking accountant' and how he needed to 'widen his lens' as he vented his frustration that Drumm had failed to see the importance of a particular strategy he was suggesting. During another blow-up, Drumm told FitzPatrick, 'I never want anything to do with you again in the future. You are an impossible person to deal with.' FitzPatrick would carry on as if nothing had been said – he had a hard-shell ego and was impervious to Drumm's growing ire.

Sean Quinn asked to meet Drumm on 19 November. It would be their final meeting.

It took place in one of the basement meeting rooms at Buswell's. Pat Whelan accompanied Drumm, while Quinn brought Liam McCaffrey. At this stage, the bank's share price had collapsed to just 92 cents – a fall of

93 per cent from the average price Quinn had invested at. The meeting began with talk about the dramatic events in the marketplace and the state's bank guarantee.

Quinn no longer took an aggressive tone with the bank. His mood was more reflective and apologetic. This was hardly surprising, given that the share price had fallen from €4.36 since the Maple Ten transaction. It had softened Quinn's position.

He told Drumm and Whelan how good the bank had been and said that in his experience no other bank was as good at what it did. He said that he regretted going against the advice of his family and investing so heavily in Anglo. His bull-headedness had landed him in the stew, he said, and he apologized for the difficulties he had caused Anglo and Drumm personally.

Then, inevitably, the conversation turned to the cash needs of the Quinn Group. The bankers saw this coming. 'Sean Quinn never left anyone owed money,' said Ireland's former richest man, referring to himself in the third person. 'If Sean Quinn says he will repay someone, Sean Quinn will repay them. My word is my bond.'

This had become a mantra for Quinn. The bankers had also got used to him telling them how his group made €500 million a year in 'Ebitda', which stands for 'earnings before interest, taxes, depreciation and amortization'. Ebitda is a crude measure for the amount of cash generated by a business.

'Quinn constantly went on about his Ebitda, Ebitda, Ebitda . . . Yabba Dabba,' says a former Anglo executive, mimicking Quinn's Fermanagh accent. 'We had to hear this every time we met him.'

Drumm stressed that Anglo could not lend Quinn one cent more unless the Regulator said so. Things were out of Anglo's hands now: since the guarantee the bank had to be extremely conscious of its new stakeholder, the state. They discussed packaging up some of Quinn's prime assets and selling them on to an outside investment fund to reduce Anglo's loans. Drumm asked Quinn straight if he would be willing to cooperate, because if he wasn't going to, the bank wouldn't be able to help him. Quinn was conciliatory. The bank felt he had come to terms with his losses and that he wanted to move on.

As Drumm was leaving the meeting, Quinn called him back. He shook his hand and, holding on, said he wanted to apologize to him personally for what had happened.

On 18 November, the day before the last meeting between Drumm and Quinn, Anglo board member Donal O'Connor was in Australia at a global

meeting of PricewaterhouseCoopers. O'Connor had been managing part-
ner of the firm until the previous year and still had close ties to it. It was
early in the morning in Australia when he rang in to a meeting of Anglo's
audit committee, which was preparing the bank's results for the year to 30
September. The other board members on the committee were Gary
McGann, as chairman, and Michael Jacob. Anglo's finance director Willie
McAteer, chief financial officer Matt Moran, Colin Golden and Kevin
Kelly, another senior executive from Anglo's finance department, also
attended the meeting and walked the non-executive directors through
various issues. The meeting was focused primarily on how much the bank
was writing off to cover bad loans – the number that investors would be
most interested in when the accounts were published.

Golden and Kelly specifically raised the IL&P transaction, the details of
which were highlighted in the report to the audit committee. O'Connor
butted in on the line from Australia. 'That sounds like window-dressing,'
he said. McAteer responded immediately. 'Lookit, this is normal balance-
sheet activity,' he said. The non-executive directors were told that the
Regulator and the auditors, Ernst & Young, were aware of the IL&P transaction and had no issue with it.

McAteer's intervention effectively killed the item off as an issue. The
committee moved on through the agenda. There was no mention of the
IL&P transaction when the committee met again on 24 November.

The next morning, 25 November, Drumm met Kevin Cardiff to walk
him through the annual results that the bank would be releasing the following week. There was no mention of the IL&P transaction by either
Drumm or Cardiff, despite the fact that the transaction had been flagged by
the NTMA to Cardiff as a concern one month earlier. Cardiff later told an
Oireachtas committee that he assumed that the Regulator had taken care
of the matter after he had flagged it with them and left it at that.

The audit committee's report to the board on 25 November made no
reference to the IL&P transaction. The report cited feedback from Ernst &
Young that Anglo had 'a strong internal control environment' and that 'a
strong risk management function and culture is deeply embedded in the
bank'.

On 3 December Anglo reported its financial results for the year ended 30
September. They showed that customer deposits had fallen to €51.5 billion
from €54 billion the previous March, but were up from €49.6 billion from
a year earlier. This was a remarkable performance, given the turmoil of
September. (The night before, Drumm had given an upbeat assessment of

the bank's performance at the annual results presentation for staff in the Shelbourne hotel – an event which left the bank with a bill of €55,000 for staff entertainment.)

Speaking to the media about the results, Drumm said that the bank had lost €4 billion in deposits over the end of September, but it had gained deposits after the guarantee. What he didn't say was that the books had been flattered by the €7.2 billion 'corporate deposit' from IL&P. Without that transaction, Anglo's figures would have looked a hell of a lot worse. It would be another two months before the curtain was fully pulled back to reveal the scale of Anglo's window-dressing.

IL&P chief executive Denis Casey said in his June 2010 affidavit to the Anglo investigations that the Department of Finance, Financial Regulator and Central Bank were aware of the €7.2 billion transaction before Anglo published its annual results on 3 December, yet they did not intervene to 'scrutinize or influence' the way Anglo would report the transaction.

But there was another more pressing issue that the bank was grappling with. At the bottom of the five-page report submitted by the audit committee to the Anglo board on 26 November were 'two issues of "sensitivity"': the note on directors' pay, and 'the directors' loan note'.

16.   Seanie's Secret

November 2008 – Anglo's value: €680 million

On the evening of Thursday, 20 November David Drumm met Brian
Lenihan for the first time. The Minister for Finance had summoned
Drumm and FitzPatrick, along with all the other chief executives and
chairmen of the six Irish banks, to the state-owned residence at Farmleigh,
formerly a home of the Guinness brewing family, in the north-west corner
of the Phoenix Park.

Heading to Farmleigh, FitzPatrick was nervous. The last time he had
met Lenihan the minister had dismissed his proposal for an Anglo/Irish
Nationwide takeover. That meeting had gone particularly badly. Since
then, FitzPatrick had made his ill-fated appearance on Marian Finucane's
show, a public display that had got everyone's backs up, including the
government's.

Drumm advised FitzPatrick that it would be a bad idea to drive up to
Farmleigh in his Mercedes. There was a strong likelihood that press photographers would be lying in wait and it would look terrible if the two
bankers showed up in a Merc. The last thing Drumm and FitzPatrick
wanted was to confirm the stereotype of fat-cat bankers arriving in style to
meet their political masters.

They decided to take a taxi. On their arrival they asked the driver to wait
outside while the meeting went on. Lenihan kept them waiting in an ante-
room for three hours as he met the chairmen and chief executives of Allied
Irish Banks and Bank of Ireland. No one on the government side spoke to
the Anglo bosses during that time. It was a long three hours for two bankers
who were barely on speaking terms. Drumm later recounted the story to
colleagues at the bank, joking that it would make a good stage play.

To ease the awkwardness of the situation, FitzPatrick started telling
stories about growing up in Greystones and asking Drumm what it was
like growing up in Skerries. FitzPatrick had no problem telling stories. He
was highly entertaining company. From time to time FitzPatrick would
jump up out of his seat, pace around the room and then sit back down
again. Drumm talked about his father, who had died around the time he
joined Anglo in 1993.

As the time passed, Drumm noticed that his companion was becoming increasingly restless. FitzPatrick, a diabetic, needed to eat before injecting insulin. (Colleagues remember FitzPatrick often having small spots of blood on the front of his shirt from injection pricks.) Drumm was concerned. He had seen FitzPatrick's eyes roll in his head when his blood sugar levels dropped. The last thing he wanted was for FitzPatrick to collapse ahead of their crunch meeting with Lenihan.

Drumm found one of the attendants at Farmleigh and asked if he could bring FitzPatrick something to eat. A short time later a woman arrived with a slice of chocolate cake. FitzPatrick tucked in and then took his insulin.

The two bankers were finally shown into the meeting room some time after 9 p.m. Lenihan shook Drumm's hand, saying he believed that Drumm was one of his constituents in Dublin West. Drumm thought he was mixing him up with Denis Casey, the chief executive of IL&P, who lived in Castleknock, but let it pass, not wanting to embarrass the minister at the start of their first meeting by pointing out a mistake.

Lenihan sat flanked by John Hurley and Pat Neary, as well as Pádraig Ó Riordáin, the managing partner at Arthur Cox, the law firm hired by the government to advise on legal matters relating to the banks. The minister started at the beginning. 'Now you are the Anglo Irish Bank,' he said, speaking slowly in his usual barristerial tones, looking down at a file in front of him. 'And you have approximately €100 billion of a balance sheet at today's date, is that correct?' Drumm said that was correct. Given this opening, the two bankers thought they might be there all night.

Lenihan asked if Anglo was the most exposed bank to construction-related loans. (This was the minister's term; the banks called them development loans.) Drumm said that Anglo was not the most exposed – AIB had €25 billion of development loans, while Anglo had €16.8 billion – but this statement was misleading: Anglo had a greater share of construction loans than AIB as a proportion of its overall balance sheet.

The meeting didn't go smoothly. Drumm challenged Lenihan's assumptions more than once and this irked the minister. At one point Lenihan asked Drumm, 'Have you got a bit of a persecution complex?' Drumm said he hadn't – he was just trying to explain what was going on in the bank.

FitzPatrick tried to speak a few times but Drumm kept interrupting him. Drumm had been advised through a political contact close to Fianna Fáil not to let FitzPatrick speak because the chairman was *persona non grata* following his Marian Finucane interview.

Drumm felt as though they were being cross-examined and lectured by Lenihan, who had been a senior counsel and law lecturer before becoming a politician. At one stage the bankers were asked to step out of the room. When they were called back in they were told that the government needed to look at Anglo's future capital requirements and potential bad loans.

Lenihan raised the prospect of mergers to strengthen the weakest banks. The previous day Lenihan had fuelled merger speculation by confirming publicly that private equity consortiums had made 'informal approaches' to the government about investing in the banks. Now, the minister asked the Anglo bankers their thoughts on possible mergers. Beggars can't be choosers, said Drumm – he accepted that Anglo might have to be merged with another financial institution. Merging Anglo with AIB wouldn't work, he said, because the two banks were both so heavily exposed to the property sector. Drumm raised the possibility of a tie-up with IL&P to create a more universal bank as a possible 'third force' to rival AIB and Bank of Ireland. Lenihan quickly discounted Drumm's idea. As the meeting ended, Lenihan asked to see the bankers again on the 28th, at the Department of Finance.

The waiting taxi dropped Drumm at his car in the city centre and then headed on to Greystones, where FitzPatrick was landed with a fare of €300.

Eight days later, on Friday, 28 November, FitzPatrick and Drumm went to see Lenihan again as requested. The Anglo men were the last of the six banks' representatives to meet the minister that day. It was a case of leaving the worst till the end, it seemed. Lenihan met the bankers in the meeting room on the ground floor, where photographs of every finance minister since the foundation of the state line the walls.

'It was the same shit, more specifics,' Drumm reported back to his colleagues. Lenihan told the bankers that he thought Anglo's banking model was broken, but there was no clear discussion of what might be done about it. FitzPatrick was even more nervy than he had been at Farmleigh. 'He was out of his comfort zone,' Drumm reported back. He was right to be nervous. There was a major problem coming down the track towards him.

As one of Ireland's best-paid bankers, FitzPatrick had been approached in the mid-1990s to invest in property deals through partnerships that allowed him to reduce his tax bill. Property-based tax reliefs had become hugely popular in Ireland at the time. Cash-rich investors could enjoy a double benefit: make money from the rising value of property and at the same time pay less tax. The government's decision to maintain tax reliefs for property through the boom years was later cited by the reports into the banking crisis as one of the factors that inflated the bubble.

Anglo provided many of the loans to these partnerships, and because FitzPatrick was a member of the partnerships and a director of the bank he was required, under stock market rules, to declare his loans in the bank's annual report every year. He didn't. The reason, FitzPatrick told Tom Lyons for *The FitzPatrick Tapes*, was that the partnerships were structured in such a way that every member of the partnership was jointly liable for the entire value of the loans, which meant FitzPatrick's declaration in the annual report would have to refer to the entire cumulative value of the loans against his partnership investments, and not just his own proportional share of them. He claimed that this would 'give an exaggerated figure of my indebtedness', though this is not quite correct: directors' loans were given as a single cumulative figure in the annual report, and so the level of FitzPatrick's personal indebtedness – exaggerated or otherwise – would not have been revealed.

In any case, FitzPatrick decided to conceal the loans. In the days before Anglo's financial year-end, he would draw a fresh loan from Irish Nationwide Building Society and repay the money he owed Anglo; thus his borrowings from Anglo would not appear in the year-end accounts. When the year-end date had passed, he would draw down the same loans again from Anglo and use them to repay Irish Nationwide. The practice was known as 'warehousing', as the loans would be put into storage, so to speak, when the auditors checked the books. FitzPatrick would later describe it somewhat misleadingly as 'refinancing'.

A file note at Irish Nationwide written by the building society's secretary Stan Purcell, second-in-command to chief executive Michael Fingleton, shows that FitzPatrick's warehousing arrangement was established following a meeting in 1996 between Purcell and senior Anglo executive Kieran Duggan, who was close to FitzPatrick. (Duggan told me that he could not recollect any meeting with Purcell about the loans, while Purcell declined to comment.) In subsequent years the loans were dealt with by lower-ranking staff at Anglo and Irish Nationwide.

Avoiding the disclosure of property loans relating to investment syndicates may have been the initial motive for warehousing his loans with Irish Nationwide, but by 2001 FitzPatrick had started hiding loans unconnected with syndicates. By 2003 the scale of FitzPatrick's investments – and, by extension, his rate of borrowing – had moved to another level after he made €27 million selling shares in Anglo. He started investing heavily in projects outside Ireland – a Hungarian golf resort, a hospital operator in the US, a casino in Macau and buildings in Munich, among others. An internal Anglo document shows that his loans from the bank quadrupled to €122 million between 2005 and 2007. The bank's internal record showed that his borrowings increased as follows:

1999: €4.2 million
2000: €4.2 million
2001: €5 million
2002: €4.4 million
2003: €14.9 million
2004: €23.9 million
2005: €27.2 million
2006: €48 million
2007: €122 million

These figures were not reflected in Anglo's annual reports because of the movement of the loans to Irish Nationwide for a few days over the bank's year-end. Anglo's 2006 annual report said that twelve directors had loans totalling €31 million; that would have been €79 million if FitzPatrick's loans had been included. The following year's report said that thirteen directors had loans totalling just €41 million; a true accounting would have given a figure four times that size.

Every year in early September a document was prepared showing a full list of FitzPatrick's loans from Anglo. This was discussed with FitzPatrick. The document was then sent to Irish Nationwide, and loan letters were issued to be signed by FitzPatrick. Anglo then issued a letter to Irish Nationwide undertaking to hold the security supporting FitzPatrick's security for Irish Nationwide; these were mostly properties and his shares in Anglo.

FitzPatrick usually drew the loans down around 25 September every year, and Anglo would issue new loans to repay Irish Nationwide around 3 or 4 October. Internal Anglo records show that at least twelve senior lenders and managers were on the lending teams that dealt with FitzPatrick's loans. They would have had knowledge of the annual warehousing.

Internal Irish Nationwide records show that in 2007 the building society used FitzPatrick's 4.5 million shares in Anglo, then valued at €55 million, and various properties as security for his loans. The previous year the building society said it had received an undertaking from Anglo to hold the shares in trust to cover the loans. It was a cosy relationship between the two financial institutions to hide FitzPatrick's loans from Anglo's shareholders and the general public. Irish Nationwide chairman Danny Kitchen later said that they agreed to do it on the basis that Anglo might throw Irish Nationwide a little business from time to time and include the building society in some of Anglo's lending deals.

In the summer of 2007 FitzPatrick started looking to move his borrowings out of Anglo permanently. The private banking division of Bank of Ireland agreed to offer him a loan of €70 million, but before it was drawn down the bank changed the terms and FitzPatrick decided to use Irish Nationwide again as a temporary hideaway.

In early 2008, during a routine site visit at Irish Nationwide, staff of the Financial Regulator discovered the warehoused loans. The Regulator contacted Willie McAteer, asking him to explain the loans, whether Anglo had a reciprocal arrangement for Irish Nationwide, whether they were legal, and what the bank intended to do about them.

Anglo obtained advice from Matheson Ormsby Prentice that characterized the transfers as legal. McAteer passed the advice to the Regulator, and also said that the issue would be resolved. The Regulator left the matter at that. Through 2008 McAteer and FitzPatrick continued to speak regularly about refinancing the loans permanently so that the Irish Nationwide subterfuge could be ended. At the same time Irish Nationwide's external auditors, KPMG, warned about the potentially significant damage to Irish Nationwide's reputation by providing the controversial week-long loans to FitzPatrick.

Two years earlier, Anglo's auditors Ernst & Young had changed tack when it came to signing off on the note regarding directors' loans in the bank's annual accounts. When a company is about to submit accounts, the directors usually sign what is known as a 'representation' or 'rep letter'. Nominally, this is a letter sent from management to the auditors, but it is typically written by the auditors. In the rep letter signing off on the September 2005 accounts, Ernst & Young wrote in relation to the note on directors' loans: 'Neither the group or the company had any arrangement, transaction or agreement to provide credit facilities (including loans, quasi-loans or credit transactions) for directors (or persons connected with them) or to guarantee or provide security for such matters, except as disclosed in note 46 [the note on directors' loans] to the financial statements.' The note in the following year's rep letter started differently: 'At no time during the year has the company had any arrangements, transaction or agreement to provide credit facilities . . . except as disclosed in note 53 to the financial statements.'

It is unclear why the auditors changed the phrasing of this in the rep letter. Regardless, the letter to the September 2006 accounts was signed by David Drumm on 5 December 2006 but the note was not accurate. At various points in the year, Anglo had provided well in excess of the loans disclosed in the annual accounts to Sean FitzPatrick. The bank should have known this and amended the rep letter accordingly.

The loans didn't become an issue at Anglo until the bank started preparing the annual report for the year ending 30 September in late November 2008. FitzPatrick had failed to refinance or warehouse the bulk of the loans, so the directors' loans figure in the annual accounts would jump from €41 million to about €137 million. The bank would have to provide an explanation in the 2008 accounts for the enormous surge in lending to directors.

In late November 2008 David Drumm and Willie McAteer told Drury Communications executive Billy Murphy, the bank's public relations man, about the bed-and-breakfasting arrangement for FitzPatrick's loans but not the amounts involved. They said the bank would have to disclose the full extent of FitzPatrick's loans in the upcoming annual report and that he would have to help them draft a note to explain them. Murphy blanched.

A short time later Drumm informed FitzPatrick that the bank would have to explain the loan transfers in the report. FitzPatrick played it down, saying that the issue was less significant than a cash payment of €1.6 million made to Drumm in lieu of a contribution to his pension. This payment, which arose from a deal Anglo had agreed with Drumm in 2006 after the state changed the way it taxed pensions, was a very generous deal for Drumm. It had been agreed by the remuneration committee, which was chaired by Ned Sullivan and of which FitzPatrick and two other non-executive directors, Anne Heraty and Gary McGann, were members. In the radically altered climate of late 2008, FitzPatrick thought (or affected to think) that this payment would be seen as more significant than his own loans, but he was wrong.

On 2 December, the day before announcing its annual results, Anglo raised €1.5 billion by selling its first state-guaranteed bond into the market. It is highly unusual for a bank to sell a bond before a major results announcement, but Anglo needed the funding and the Financial Regulator had agreed a coordinated sequence of guaranteed bond sales by the banks in early November. Anglo was supposed to come after IL&P in the sequence but was pushed ahead of it in the queue – much to IL&P's anger – as its funding position was more critical.

On Wednesday, 3 December Anglo announced its financial results for the year to 30 September. The bank's reporting date meant that it was the first bank in Ireland or the UK to report annual results since the collapse of Lehman Brothers. All eyes were on Anglo.

The bank reported profits of €784 million after writing off €724 million to cover bad loans. Willie McAteer described this as 'a demonstration of prudence'. He said that under a worst-case scenario Anglo could lose up to €2.76 billion cumulatively over the following three years and still make profits of €784 million each year.

The bank was trying its best to reassure the markets, but another disclosure spooked investors. The previous March, Anglo had said that 15 per cent of the bank's loan book, or just under €11 billion, was development lending. At the December announcement Anglo said that the correct figure was €16.9 billion, or slightly over 23 per cent of the bank's €73 billion loan book. Anglo said that most of this arose from a 'reclassification' of loans previously booked under property investment. Matt Moran, the bank's chief financial officer, explained the reclassification in a complicated and meandering answer to a question at Anglo's results presentation to banking analysts from Dublin and London. (The bank also revealed that a whopping 28 per cent of the €5 billion loan growth over the second half of the financial year related to development and the completion of existing projects. The bank was still lending heavily on speculative business into a property market that had turned sharply.)

For the first time, the full extent of Anglo's exposure to speculative property deals had been revealed. This was an implicit acknowledgement that the bank had been pulling the wool over the eyes of investors for years by not showing the true extent of its development lending.

Anglo had no choice but to come clean at this stage. The bank's loan book was being pored over by external consultants PricewaterhouseCoopers, working on behalf of the government. The bank was also opening its books to other outsiders in the hope of attracting investors to raise capital in the face of market concerns about its capacity to absorb bad debts.

Investors were stunned by the development-lending figures. Anglo's share price fell to 67 cents, the lowest level in eleven years, valuing the bank at just €509 million. At this price, there was little or no chance of the bank raising external capital. The state was the only place to turn.

On Friday, 12 December FitzPatrick, Drumm, McAteer and Jacob met Kevin Cardiff at the Department of Finance and Pádraig Ó Riordáin of the government's legal advisers Arthur Cox. Drumm said that the board of

Anglo had decided the previous day that the bank couldn't survive on its own and that it would need the state's help to raise €2.5 billion in capital. (The Central Bank believed the bank would need €3 billion.)

To secure this investment, Anglo would have to disclose everything to the officials of the state.

Despite requiring billions to stay in business, Anglo didn't skimp on the Christmas party it threw for staff at the Mansion House later that evening. Security was tight at the party and employees were given wristbands in advance to prevent the media from infiltrating. Partygoers arriving at the Mansion House were met by a reporter from the *Sunday Tribune*, but refused to say which company was throwing the bash.

The party cost the bank €175,000. Anglo also spent €53,000 on hampers and wine for clients that Christmas, and €24,000 on tickets for the Gaiety Theatre Christmas panto in Dublin for big customers of the bank and their children.

On Saturday, 13 December Billy Murphy was at a club rugby match when he received a call from FitzPatrick. He went to a quiet part of the ground to speak to him. FitzPatrick, who had been having difficulty getting through to Drumm, asked Murphy if Drumm had been in touch about his loans. He wanted to know from Murphy how the loans issue was going to be handled.

FitzPatrick told Murphy for the first time about the scale of the loans. He said that there was nothing legally wrong with bed-and-breakfasting loans with another financial institution and added that the loans were insignificant in relation to the size of Anglo's loan book. Murphy thought FitzPatrick seemed almost flippant about the loans, but he knew it was a huge problem for the bank.

FitzPatrick later told Tom Lyons that on the same day he asked his three closest friends who were or had been on the board of Anglo – Gary McGann, Donal O'Connor and Fintan Drury – to meet him in the offices of Smurfit Kappa in Clonskeagh. He said he told them that he was going to resign as chairman of Anglo over the moving of his loans.

That same weekend the government announced that it was going to inject €10 billion into the banks and that the recapitalizations would be based on the 'systemic importance' of the institutions. This didn't fill Anglo with confidence, as the bank always knew that the government believed AIB and Bank of Ireland to be more important.

At this stage the government had, under the terms of the guarantee, appointed 'public interest' directors to the boards of the banks. Anglo's new directors were Alan Dukes, the former Fine Gael leader, and Frank Daly, the former head of the Revenue Commissioners. Dukes had some familiarity with banking crises, having been Minister for Finance in 1985 when the government had to rescue AIB over its disastrous investment in the Insurance Corporation of Ireland. Daly had been in charge of the Revenue when it targeted customers who had hidden undeclared money in bogus offshore accounts across the Irish banking sector.

At 5.15 p.m. on Tuesday, 16 December FitzPatrick asked to see Daly and Dukes with Ned Sullivan, Anglo's senior independent director and chairman of the bank's remuneration committee. The meeting was part of their induction onto the board, and FitzPatrick walked Daly and Dukes through part of the bank's draft annual report. He said that because they were the public-interest directors he wanted to tell them about his loans. He showed them the note on directors' loans. Dukes noticed the dramatic increase in the figure from the previous year. FitzPatrick produced a handwritten note listing the borrowings of each of the directors by name.

Both Dukes and Daly were taken aback at the scale of the loans. They asked about Tom Browne's borrowings of €14 million and Gary McGann's €11 million. But it was the increase in FitzPatrick's borrowings from €7 million to €87 million that really caught their eye. Dukes asked FitzPatrick what was the reason for the substantial increase in his borrowings.

FitzPatrick told them that it had been his practice every year to 'refinance' his loans with another financial institution. The reason for the increase at September 2008, he said, was that he was unable to secure the 'refinancing' that month because of the credit crunch. Dukes suggested to FitzPatrick that it appeared this refinancing was a manoeuvre designed to move the loans off Anglo's books 'at a material time' – in other words, on the day the bank took the snapshot that would be reported in its results. FitzPatrick became visibly agitated and said that the loans were perfectly respectable and the refinancing was done on a commercial basis and at arm's length, and that this was all carried out on his behalf by officials within the bank. Dukes responded by asking FitzPatrick: 'Who is going to say no to the chairman of the bank?'

FitzPatrick told Daly and Dukes that he would inform the Department of Finance about the loans.

That evening Daly received a phone call at home from FitzPatrick requesting that they meet. Daly agreed.

FitzPatrick was distracted at the annual Christmas dinner for Anglo pensioners in Heritage House later that night. He was on his mobile so often throughout the dinner that he had the phone recharging near him. During the meal and in conversation with the pensioners afterwards Fitz-Patrick was in a nostalgic mood, but the difficulties at the bank were not far from his mind.

'He gave the impression that while things were tough, the cavalry were at hand,' says one Anglo pensioner who was in attendance. He gave no indication that he was about to resign, says the pensioner.

The following morning, on Wednesday, 17 December, Dukes and Daly had a quiet coffee together to reflect on the previous day's seismic meeting with FitzPatrick. They couldn't believe what they had heard. They joked, wondering what they had gotten themselves into. 'No one will touch us with a forty-foot bargepole after this,' Dukes told Daly in an exchange he recounted to colleagues.

Daly then met FitzPatrick at about 11 a.m. in Heritage House. Fitz-Patrick told Daly that he had seen how shocked he and Dukes had been when he told them about the loans.

'Am I finished?' FitzPatrick asked Daly, according to an account of the meeting relayed afterwards.

'If I was on the board and I found out this, either you would go or I would resign and say why I was resigning,' said Daly.

Early that Wednesday FitzPatrick called Billy Murphy and told him that he had decided to step down as a result of the transfers of his loans to Irish Nationwide. He asked Murphy to meet him at the bank to help him draft his resignation statement.

Murphy spent most of the day with an emotional FitzPatrick in his office in St Stephen's Green as he called each of the bank's non-executive directors to tell them he was resigning. FitzPatrick then called the company secretaries of Smurfit Kappa, food company Greencore, Aer Lingus and investment company Gartmore to tell them that he would be resigning from their boards. Murphy then returned to his office to work on the bank's press statement, while FitzPatrick went home to draft a separate personal statement that he planned to issue.

At 7 p.m. Drumm phoned Murphy and said that he thought the contro-versy surrounding FitzPatrick's loans would be huge and cause major damage to the bank. This was in stark contrast to the view of FitzPatrick, who believed that by resigning he would defuse the issue.

Drumm was travelling on business in Edinburgh that day, with Declan Quilligan, when he received a call from Ned Sullivan to tell him FitzPatrick was resigning. FitzPatrick called Drumm afterwards saying that he was going to step down because he thought that the Department of Finance was going to release details of his loans to the media.

A board meeting was called for 10 p.m. Drumm and Quilligan rang in from Drumm's hotel room in Edinburgh. FitzPatrick told his fellow board members that he was very ashamed of what he had done with his loans and how he had brought shame on the bank. He apologized and confirmed that he was going to resign. It was then decided that Donal O'Connor should be appointed chairman to succeed FitzPatrick. O'Connor's appointment made sense, as he was the newest board member – relatively untainted by Anglo's past – and had good relations with the government. (Minister for Finance Brian Lenihan later consulted his cousin, Fergal O'Rourke (son of Fianna Fáil TD Mary O'Rourke), who knew O'Connor well as they were both partners at PricewaterhouseCoopers, to ask about his credentials before agreeing to his appointment as chairman.)

The directors discussed whether FitzPatrick had been legally obliged to disclose his loans at the bank. One of the biggest problems for the bank was that they couldn't get a handle on the exact scale of his loans. The numbers kept moving around because the records and systems within the bank weren't great. The directors wanted to release a definite final number on the size of the loans, but they struggled to distinguish between FitzPatrick's personal loans and loans to the various syndicates with which he was connected. (They managed to agree on a figure, but it had to be changed in the weeks following the release of the press statement.)

The next morning, Thursday, 18 December, FitzPatrick, Sullivan and O'Connor met senior Department of Finance officials Kevin Cardiff and Ann Nolan, who were accompanied by Pádraig Ó Riordáin of Arthur Cox. Cardiff and Nolan expressed their disappointment over the loan issue. They said that further questions remained to be answered. They asked whether the loan transfers broke any of the Financial Regulator's rules and they sought reassurances that there were no other such issues lurking within Anglo. They also asked whether FitzPatrick would be able to repay his loans.

There was a general discussion about how the cash payment that was given to Drumm in lieu of a pension payment would be disclosed in the accounts. (In the end, when the cash payment was publicly disclosed in the accounts in February 2009 it didn't cause much of a stir as there were far more scandalous issues emerging at the bank.)

Another matter relating to Drumm's compensation had already caused

deep suspicions within the department towards Anglo. In a previous discussion about directors' pay at Anglo, the bank had reassured the department
that Drumm would be taking a cut in his basic salary for the year to 30 September 2008. But by the time this had come up for discussion, Drumm's
entire salary, with no reduction, had been paid. Senior department officials
became aware of this, and it created a breakdown in trust between the
department and the bank.

At 12.30 p.m. on 18 December the board of Anglo met in Heritage
House. FitzPatrick read out his resignation statement and O'Connor was
approved as chairman. Drumm tendered his resignation as well. He felt
that the bank would not be able to raise cash from investors, which was
central to the bank's survival, if he remained on as chief executive.

O'Connor told the meeting that it was important 'to draw a line in the
sand' on the directors' loans and to send out a public statement saying that
no other directors of the bank were involved. Lar Bradshaw, who attended
the board meeting by conference call, realized that he might have a problem. He and FitzPatrick had taken out a joint loan of $38 million (about €28
million) from Anglo to invest in Movido Exploration and Production, a
firm based in Lagos, Nigeria. Movido believed that a field to which it had
rights in the Niger Delta could be worth about $500 million (€370 million)
if it was put into full production to tap an estimated 20 million barrels of
oil. What if their joint loan was one of those that FitzPatrick had moved off
the books?

After the meeting, Bradshaw called FitzPatrick. 'Sean, please tell me
that our loan is not one of these loans,' he said. 'I have to come back to you
on that,' said FitzPatrick. Bradshaw was at home with his wife, nervously
waiting by the phone. FitzPatrick rang back five minutes later. 'That is one
of the loans,' he said. Bradshaw was devastated. He knew he would have to
resign too. He immediately called O'Connor.

The warehousing of FitzPatrick's loans and FitzPatrick's resignation
were announced to the world in two statements – one from the bank, one
from the resigning chairman – at 8.44 p.m. that evening. FitzPatrick's statement was predictably contrite, though it asserted that nothing he had done
was illegal. He admitted that the transfer of his loans was done on his own
initiative. FitzPatrick said that Bradshaw had no knowledge of the transfer
of their joint loan. Half an hour later the Financial Regulator issued a
statement saying that it had become aware of the loans earlier in 2008 and
that the matter remained under investigation.

Despite the ructions at Anglo that day, the bank was relieved when

Brian Lenihan issued a statement saying that the government was still committed to underwriting the capital requirements of Anglo to ensure its viability 'as a bank of systemic importance in Ireland'. This was the backing that the bank required.

In the aftermath of the FitzPatrick revelations, there was surprise that Drumm had not recognized the warehousing of the loans as a serious reputational issue for the bank. The recent recruits to the board were also shocked to learn that so many people in the bank were aware of the loans. But people who knew Anglo more intimately than the new directors were less surprised.

'There was a great sense in Anglo that they could deal with anything that came their way – that was part of their culture,' says a source close to the bank. 'They had a great sense of confidence. That was why, notwithstanding the gravity of the events of 2008, they didn't realize the extent of the problems with FitzPatrick until the end of the year. Issues didn't faze them. They'd deal with problems as they cropped up.'

Drumm later privately claimed that he was first told about the transfer of FitzPatrick's loans in January 2008 by Willie McAteer when the Financial Regulator contacted the bank about them. However, Drumm was subsequently asked about an email that was sent to him on 11 September 2006 from Mark Redmond, a manager at Anglo who had responsibility within the bank for looking after FitzPatrick's financial affairs. (Over the years various lending teams, amounting to at least a dozen people, would have worked on – and been aware of – FitzPatrick's loans at the bank.) Redmond mentioned the refinancing of FitzPatrick's loans in the email and asked whether Drumm would like his own loans refinanced too. 'Thanks Mark – I will talk to Sean in the morning,' said Drumm in response. As it happened, Drumm did nothing on the back of the email, which makes it clear that he was aware of the issue long before January 2008.

In its news bulletins reporting FitzPatrick's resignation, RTE replayed clips from a lengthy television interview he had given a year earlier in which he said that Ireland didn't have major financial scandals like other countries and that regulation needed to be measured. 'You need regulation,' he said, 'but you don't need over-regulation. What we need is appropriate regulation.' A speech he gave the same year – in which he said regulation had gone too far and seemed to treat entrepreneurs like criminals – was also resurrected. 'This is corporate McCarthyism and we shouldn't tolerate it,' he said in the June 2007 speech.

The day after he resigned, the Office of the Director of Corporate

Enforcement said that it would start an investigation into the loans. The government expressed concerns that the Financial Regulator had known about the loans for so long and had not pursued the matter as a major concern.

Drumm announced his resignation shortly after noon on 19 December, having been asked by the board to wait a day to consider his decision. He said he had to go as the bank would never be able to get the government to agree to support it if he stayed on. Noël Harwerth, a non-executive board member, responded that investors would never come on board if he left. O'Connor and Ned Sullivan, a non-executive director, asked him not to resign immediately after FitzPatrick, believing that the last thing the bank needed at a critical time when it was trying to raise external investment was to be destabilized further with the resignation of its chief executive as well as its chairman. According to one director of the bank, the board felt that FitzPatrick's loans were more of an issue for FitzPatrick than for Drumm, and it was actually impressed with how Drumm handled the resolution of the Quinn unwinding. But Drumm knew that the Department of Finance wanted him to go – it would just be at a time of their choosing. He also felt that, following FitzPatrick's resignation, the spotlight would now move to him. Outside the bank, questions would be asked about his role in the affair. If he had known about FitzPatrick's loans, then why hadn't he done anything about them, and if, as chief executive, he didn't know, then why not?

On the day of FitzPatrick's resignation, AIB and Bank of Ireland agreed to provide Anglo with loans of €4 billion, which subsequently rose to €6 billion, to prevent the bank from having to access emergency lending from the Central Bank – a move that could have been even more damaging to the wider Irish banking system.

Ironically, almost three months after being asked to provide emergency loans to Anglo on the night of the guarantee, AIB and Bank of Ireland were finally coming to the rescue of their rival. But the money wouldn't be enough.

January 2009 – Anglo's value: nil

Four days before Christmas, with the country still reeling from the Anglo scandal and the resignations of Drumm and FitzPatrick, Brian Lenihan announced that the government would inject €1.5 billion into the bank and take 75 per cent ownership. The minister said that the move was needed because Anglo's prospects of raising money from private investors were 'poor'. An extraordinary general meeting of Anglo shareholders was arranged for Friday, 16 January to approve the injection of capital.

Speaking the next day, Lenihan said that the state was resisting taking full public ownership of the bank. 'Were we to go the nationalization route, we would be affirming that we have no confidence in the bank as a bank to survive,' he said. It didn't matter; institutional investors were rapidly losing confidence, and dumping the stock. US group Invesco, the largest shareholder in the bank after the Quinn family, sold 16.1 million shares, reducing its stake to 4.7 per cent from 6.9 per cent over the following two weeks.

On Sunday, 21 December Anglo executives met Vincent Bergin of Ernst & Young to discuss what to include in the circular to shareholders telling them about the January extraordinary meeting. Bergin said that only information in the public domain should be included. Colin Golden queried whether it should contain details of the IL&P transaction, given the media attention on FitzPatrick's loans. Bergin said he had thought about this too. The IL&P transaction had the potential to attract as much controversy as FitzPatrick's loans, but in the end it wasn't included in the circular.

The run-up to Christmas was a frenetic time. The board was meeting for up to four hours at a time, sometimes twice a day, as the bank tried to figure out how it would fund itself over the Christmas period. It was hard work for the board members. Donal O'Connor, the bank's newly appointed chairman, was working seventeen-hour days and through weekends. For one evening meeting of the Anglo board two days before Christmas, Frank Daly had to telephone in from his car. He had stopped in the car park of a garden centre on his way back home to Waterford for the holidays. For two and a half hours Daly listened in while the family dog waited patiently next to him.

Following the scandal over Sean FitzPatrick's loans, the bank revisited all its directors' loans to make sure they were arranged on acceptable commercial terms. The documentation on loans provided to directors to buy shares in January 2008 was in a mess. This was typical of Anglo, operating at a breakneck pace with the back-office administration struggling to keep up with management decisions. (Investigators from the Office of the Director of Corporate Enforcement later questioned Anglo executives on why the bank did not keep a register of loans to directors as it was legally required to do.) In September 2008 the bank had belatedly prepared paperwork for the January loans. Letters of offer were issued to the directors, backdated to January. (One detail in the letters of offer gave away the fact that they were backdated: on the Anglo letterhead Donal O'Connor is listed as a non-executive director. He only became a director in June 2008 and the letterhead was not printed until the autumn of 2008.) The letters stated that the only security held by the bank was the Anglo shares themselves. This meant, for example, that on David Drumm's loan of €7.7 million the bank had only Drumm's 886,000 Anglo shares as security if he could not repay the loan. The decision to draft such letters at a time when the bank's share price was collapsing was consistent with a pattern of lending at Anglo where borrower-friendly deals were cooked up for the bank's own senior staff and its most loyal customers. It put the directors at a distinct personal advantage and severely handicapped Anglo's ability to recover its money.

Early in 2009, freshly nationalized and keen to avoid further controversies over directors' loans, the bank received a legal opinion from a senior counsel to say that even though the September 2008 loan documents didn't say that they granted the bank recourse to the borrowers' assets, it was still possible to give the bank recourse with the consent of the borrowers.

Following his resignation Drumm had told O'Connor and Quilligan that he accepted that the share loans to directors were in fact made with full recourse to the borrowers' assets, despite this not being reflected in the documentation. It is not clear why Drumm accepted this without a fight, but the fact that the original non-recourse nature of the loan was based on a backdated letter probably weakened his hand. He maintained that the loan documentation should have said that the bank had recourse to the assets of the borrower, not just the shares. There was a big difference between the two positions – the former meant the bank could pursue the borrower; the latter meant it was stuck with only the shares to cover the loan.

Now the bank put pressure on Drumm to formally change the terms of his share loans to full recourse. Drumm, who wanted to make sure that he would not be asked to repay the €8.3 million he owed immediately, wrote Anglo a letter in which he said that it was his understanding that the bank did not intend to pursue any legal action against him or seek to take possession of his family home to recover the loans. He later claimed in Anglo's legal action against him that he reached an agreement with Declan Quilligan, who was effectively filling the role of chief executive, and Donal O'Connor that when the loan matured in December 2009 the bank would sit down with him and agree a workable repayment plan. He assumed that the letter and his conversations with Quilligan and O'Connor protected him, but such a view was naive at best.

Likewise, finance director Willie McAteer also agreed to change his loans to full recourse after he resigned on 7 January 2009 over FitzPatrick's hidden loans. The following month McAteer signed a new loan agreement relating to the €8.25 million he had borrowed from Anglo the previous September to repay Bank of Ireland. It had originally been granted as a non-recourse loan: the bank's only security was the shares. The bank had used a standard non-recourse template for the loan. Under the new deal, the bank gained full personal recourse, though the agreement stipulated that Anglo wouldn't seize McAteer's family home or pension. Seeking some protection on the terms of the new loan, McAteer argued that he could have cleared his loans with Bank of Ireland in full by selling his shares in the bank in September 2008 but under pressure from Drumm he had decided not to, fearing the reaction in the market.

Two days after McAteer's departure, Pat Neary resigned as chief executive of the Financial Regulator over his handling of the investigation into FitzPatrick's loans. An internal investigation had found there had been a breakdown in communications within the Regulator's office that meant the issue was not dealt with after being discovered in January 2008. When it emerged that Neary, who had started his career at the Central Bank in 1971, received a severance payment of €630,000 on top of the annual pension of €142,670 he was entitled to, there was public uproar. Here was a public servant who had failed to do his job getting a massive golden parachute payment.

During preparations for the extraordinary general meeting of shareholders scheduled for 16 January, Anglo's treasury division informed Donal

O'Connor that a credit-rating agency had been asking questions about the €7.2 billion transaction with IL&P. O'Connor asked for more details. By the time Anglo held a board meeting on 13 January, the structure of the September 2008 back-to-back deposits with IL&P was clear and the board was briefed. The board received legal advice from Matheson Ormsby Prentice that there had been 'no right of set-off' on the transactions – in other words, if one party did not repay its deposit, that did not mean the other party could default on the matching deposit – and that it had been right to report the deposits as distinct transactions, even though there was no net transfer of cash. The law firm also said that the transactions involved separate legal contracts and that the nature of the transactions 'did not force/compel either party to act in any particular manner'. In other words, Anglo's decision to place deposits with IL&P 'did not legally compel ILA to place deposits with AIBC [Anglo]'. Furthermore, 'Transactions of this kind are not unusual at reporting period ends, in particular in the context of the environment at the time they were entered into.'

While the Anglo board was receiving this somewhat optimistic interpretation, the transactions were causing growing alarm outside the bank – at the Financial Regulator and in government. On Wednesday, 14 January Brian Lenihan told his Cabinet colleagues about the IL&P transaction. This news changed everything. The gist of the discussion at Cabinet was that this latest revelation confirmed that the government really didn't know the extent of the rot at Anglo; they had no idea what might come next. Anglo was a can of worms and there was no way that the government could stand behind the bank and offer a €1.5 billion guarantee to investors buying new shares.

Nationalization was a dirty word for Lenihan and Cowen. They had resisted it since enacting the guarantee the previous September, but now it was clear that they had no alternative: Anglo – haemorrhaging both cash and scandals, and unable to fund itself – had no future as a stand-alone private bank. The state would have to take it over.

On the afternoon of Thursday, 15 January Donal O'Connor was called to a meeting at the Department of Finance. He attended with Alan Dukes, Frank Daly and the bank's senior independent director, Ned Sullivan. Kevin Cardiff, the second secretary at the department who was in charge of banking, told them that the government had decided to withdraw its offer of a €1.5 billion capital injection. He asked the Anglo board to consider two options – liquidation or nationalization. A stunned O'Connor called an immediate board meeting.

The board was gobsmacked. It didn't consider the liquidation option for very long, assuming that the government didn't want this but only presented it as an option to force the board to accept nationalization.

The state had no legal mechanism to take control of failed banks. In the US, the authorities had the nationalization of banks down to a fine art – they could take control of a bank over a weekend, protect depositors, carve up the good bits of the bank and park them in other banks, and resolve the bad, burning bondholders and other creditors as required – but no such legal or administrative capacity existed in Ireland. This was one of the reasons why the financial crisis caused such headaches for the Irish government in 2008 and thereafter. It just didn't have the tools to repair the banks or dismantle the bad ones.

The Anglo board decided quickly that they had no option but to accept nationalization. The bank could not survive without state support and no cogent arguments could really be made against it. As soon as the transfers of FitzPatrick's loans emerged, most of the board members had seen the writing on the wall. In addition, the government-appointed directors couldn't be sure that there were no more skeletons lurking within the bank, and they weren't willing to take any more chances. Also, the bank's liquidity was still under pressure. O'Connor was receiving reports on the flow of deposits in and out of the bank five times a day.

Anglo had meanwhile been trying to replace Drumm as chief executive. The board had asked Drumm to participate in the recruitment of his successor. He had attended a meeting of a sub-committee of the board on 23 December at which he helped prepare a job description and profile, and identified topics that candidates should be asked to present on. Drumm was also appointed to a panel that prospective participants could call to discuss the recruitment process. Interviews had been conducted with a number of candidates, including director Declan Quilligan, Tony Campbell, the head of Anglo's US operations, and Mark Duffy, who was about to announce his resignation as chief executive of Bank of Scotland (Ireland).

Duffy met the board of Anglo for his interview at the offices of PricewaterhouseCoopers on the north quays in the Docklands. He was surprised to be told by a receptionist when he arrived that Sean Fitzpatrick would be with him shortly, but then realized that Anglo's head of human resources and the bank's former chairman were almost identically named. There was an awkward moment at the start of the interview where Duffy chose not to sit in the seat reserved for the interview candidates in front of the directors, fearing he might be disadvantaged by the light from the window behind him. He chose instead to sit at one end of the table in a seat normally reserved for a chairman, much to the bemusement of the Anglo directors on the interview panel. He told the panel that the best way to deal with Anglo was to split it into a good bank and a bad bank, the latter of which would be wound down over time.

Such a split was a tried-and-tested way of nursing critically ill banks back to full health. The 'bad bank' would not be a licensed bank at all but an asset-recovery company, which meant it wouldn't have to adhere to the capital regulations that applied to banks. Meanwhile the 'good bank', purged of its toxic assets and freed of the need to maintain capital reserves against them, could start funding itself once more.

Duffy told the board that he believed Anglo's losses would be greater than €20 billion. This was a shocking figure, about seven times more than the worst-case losses cited by Drumm and McAteer the previous month in the annual results presentation and way beyond any other internal estimates at that time. But Duffy, having spent several years running Bank of Scotland (Ireland) and emulating Anglo's aggressive development lending, had good insight into the situation faced by the big developers and, by extension, into what Anglo's losses might be.

Duffy did not in any case win the favour of the directors, and at its meeting on 13 January the Anglo board decided to appoint Quilligan as Drumm's successor. News of the appointment was leaked by the bank, but Anglo had not yet secured the approval of the Regulator. The bank waited and waited for the approval, but it never came. This was presumably the Regulator's way of telling Anglo that it didn't want an insider taking over the top job, given what was emerging at the bank. Quilligan instead later took over the role of chief operating officer. In the end, no chief executive was appointed – Donal O'Connor carried out the responsibilities of the role, receiving the beefed-up title of executive chairman on 19 February.

Anglo's board signed off on nationalization around tea-time on Thursday, 15 January. There was consternation within the bank: many employees who had taken share options in the bank instead of cash as part of their bonus arrangements now found their Anglo shares completely worthless. A large number of employees had also borrowed from Anglo and other banks on the strength of the value of their shares during the boom times. One former Anglo executive remembers a number of staff tapping at calculators on the Thursday evening, trying to work out the disintegration of the value of the shares on their personal finances.

There was stony silence in Anglo's third-floor boardroom as senior executives watched news of the bank's nationalization break on RTE's nine o'clock bulletin. At a hastily arranged press conference that evening Lenihan had insisted that there had been no run on Anglo and that the bank was not insolvent, but it was 'in a fragile position'. He blamed the FitzPatrick loans for causing 'serious reputational damage to the bank when overall market sentiment towards it was negative'.

The previous week Lenihan had told me in an interview that if the government nationalized the bank, the taxpayer would be 'taking an awful lot of risk with no return'. Now his comments were repeated back to him several times in various media interviews. News reports about the bank's nationalization over the following days replayed FitzPatrick's extended interview with RTE broadcaster Áine Lawlor from December 2007 in which he spoke about how other banks through the years had written Anglo off. 'Will they last? They're a fine bank but will they last? That was said about us in the seventies, the eighties, the nineties and indeed even in recent years. But we have arrived, and we ain't going anywhere.'

The Anglo board now faced the tricky question of how to deal with the extraordinary general meeting that had been called for the following day to approve the government's plan to inject €1.5 billion – a plan that was now a dead letter. The board considered cancelling the meeting, but legally it couldn't do so. They could open the meeting and then close it immediately – that would fulfil the legal obligation – but the board felt this was impossible, given the fury of the public, its shareholders and the government.

The directors knew they had to face the music. They agreed that every director would sit at the top table on the podium for all the shareholders to see them. A number of the non-executive directors argued strongly that they preferred to sit in the front row with the shareholders, where non-execs normally sat. The podium was usually left to the chairman, the chief executive and the company secretary. Not this time. Matt Moran, who was not a board member, was shocked to find that there was a place for him on the podium when he arrived at the meeting. He argued that he should not have to sit up there, but given that he was doing the job previously held by Willie McAteer, the finance director and a board member, it was felt that Moran had to be on the podium.

Eight hundred angry Anglo shareholders, facing the final disappearance of the prospect that they might recover any value from their shares, showed up at the Mansion House. Donal O'Connor opened the meeting by apologizing to shareholders. He said that FitzPatrick's 'temporary refinancing of his loans was unacceptable and wrong' and that there had been a weakness in the bank's systems relating to the loans that was being investigated.

The shareholders were having none of it. FitzPatrick's loans were raised again and again in the questions to the bank. 'It was a cosy cartel at the top, with no supervision, and nobody to keep an eye on each other,' said one shareholder. 'Anglo Irish is a cowboy bank and, until the cowboys are gone, we won't have the solution.' Another shareholder said, 'The patient is dead. The Minister for Finance administered the last rites last night. This is the wake today and we won't know what we get until the will is read.' One pensioner stood up and said that she had lost her husband the previous year and now had lost her life savings in Anglo shares. She said that O'Connor could have no idea how she felt.

One person in attendance at the meeting was broadcaster Gay Byrne, whose son-in-law, Ronan O'Byrne, worked for the bank in London. Byrne told reporters afterwards that FitzPatrick would have been hung 'upside down from a lamp stand in Dawson Street' if he had shown up at the meeting. 'A great number of grey-haired old crinklies like myself obviously have lost a great deal of money in their pension funds and their shares and they wanted somebody to be held responsible and they got very little consolation from anybody at the meeting.'

The following Monday the five remaining non-executive directors at Anglo who shared the podium with O'Connor in the Mansion House – Gary McGann, Ned Sullivan, Noël Harwerth, Anne Heraty and Anglo's longest-serving board member, Michael Jacob – resigned with immediate effect.

The purge of the bank's non-executive directors was complete. It would take some time before the senior executive directors were also cleared out.

On 15 January, the day the government announced the decision to nationalize Anglo, staff of the Financial Regulator met Vincent Bergin and another partner from Ernst & Young to discuss the €7.2 billion Anglo–IL&P transaction. The Regulator's note of the meeting said that the accountancy firm had signed off on the bank's accounts on 2 December and was aware that the transaction had occurred. Bergin said that he had been informed by Anglo that the Regulator had been made aware of the transaction. He said that Anglo had told him that the bank had got legal advice to say there wasn't an issue but he had not seen the letter.

'VB indicated that he wanted to emphasize that he was not happy now with the transaction and that no licensed bank should be engaging in transactions of this nature,' said the note. 'He would not comment on his happiness when he first became aware of the transaction.'

The Regulator said that it had asked Anglo on 11 December for the legal advice it had received on the transaction regarding whether the bank had broken market-abuse or transparency rules but that the bank had not responded.

Ernst & Young reported back to Anglo that they found the Regulator's stance on the transaction 'aggressive, nearly disturbing'.

The following Wednesday, 21 January, IL&P chief executive Denis Casey, finance director Peter Fitzpatrick and chief financial officer David McCarthy met Mary O'Dea, the acting chief executive of the Regulator following Neary's departure, along with Central Bank governor John Hurley and director Tony Grimes. As the meeting drew to a close, O'Dea rounded on the IL&P bankers, asking them why they had agreed to the €7.2 billion transaction with Anglo. Casey replied that Anglo had asked for support during September 2008 and 'we had helped them out'. The bankers also said they had been asked by Hurley and Neary to put on the 'green jersey'. Casey reminded Hurley that he had raised IL&P's support of Anglo with the governor at a meeting which was also attended by Neary and Brian Halpin of the Central Bank on 30 October 2008.

O'Dea accused IL&P of entering into a transaction for no reason other than to enable Anglo artificially to boost the corporate deposits figure on its balance sheet. Casey replied that IL&P was not privy to how Anglo had accounted for the transaction. (That may have been true strictly speaking, but it is hard to imagine what IL&P thought Anglo wanted from the March and September transactions other than a bigger corporate deposits figure on the balance sheet.) Grimes replied that the point of the 'green jersey agenda' was that banks would support each other by offering regular loans to the other banks to help them with funding problems; the kind of trans-actions that Anglo and IL&P had engaged in did not fit this description. O'Dea warned the two IL&P executives that the matter would be followed up. (She later appointed two regulators to IL&P to investigate the transaction further.)

Shaken by the regulators' aggressive questioning, Denis Casey and Peter Fitzpatrick raised the matter with Kevin Cardiff, the second secretary at the Department of Finance, at a meeting the following day, explaining the nature of the transaction and why they had done it. According to IL&P's

note of the meeting Cardiff, who was well-briefed on the transaction, said that the issue was how Anglo accounted for it. He added that Anglo's accounts for the year to September 2008 had not been finalized and that the issue was still under review. Cardiff also said, according to the IL&P note, that the support afforded to Anglo by IL&P had been 'enormously helpful'.

Peter Fitzpatrick asked IL&P's head of risk, Hilary Flood, to check the cash flows relating to the transaction with Anglo to make sure Anglo had provided cash as collateral to IL&P before IL&P placed any money with Anglo. The cash flow records would confirm that IL&P took on zero risk in the transactions: every penny deposited with Anglo had already been covered by a matching deposit from Anglo. Fitzpatrick had one scare – paperwork showing instructions settling the transactions produced by the company's in-house system had been binned. It later turned out that this didn't matter – proper procedures had been followed – but it still had Fitzpatrick worried enough to tell David Gantly in an email, 'This has us firmly in the manure business.'

Soon after the nationalization of Anglo, Donal O'Connor decided to meet Sean Quinn to see where the bank stood with its biggest borrower. Once again the setting for the meeting was Buswell's Hotel. O'Connor was accompanied by Quilligan and Whelan; Quinn as usual brought along the chief executive of the Quinn Group, Liam McCaffrey. The meeting was cordial, but as it was drawing to a close Quinn warned O'Connor that he could be a difficult customer if he was forced to repay his borrowings. He used the analogy of how a rat would react if it was backed into a corner. It was a veiled threat to the bank. The bank believed that Quinn was laying down a marker following the change in the bank's management and ownership.

The next Anglo scandal to become public was not the IL&P affair – which was still known only to bankers and state officials – but the Maple Ten transaction, details of which were revealed on 25 January in the *Sunday Times*. The newspaper reported that Anglo had assembled a 'golden circle' of investors to buy 10 per cent of the bank's shares the previous summer. The article only referred to 'a group of business people', many of them long-standing customers of Anglo; it didn't identify any of the investors.

At this stage the bank was looking at heavy losses from both Quinn's loans and the €451 million it had lent the previous summer to the Maple Ten to buy Quinn's shares. Quinn's borrowings had spiralled to €2.75 billion at the end of 2008 due to the accumulation of interest. The value of his shares in the bank – worth €400 million in September 2008 – had been wiped out by its nationalization.

The Maple Ten deal, too, had blown up on the bank. The outstanding loans to the ten investors varied in size at this stage, as some of them had sold shares and repaid part of their loans, but they totalled €360 million at the time of nationalization. Under the deal agreed with the Ten, Anglo only had recourse against the borrowers personally for 25 per cent of whatever balance was outstanding on the loans, i.e. about €90 million, leaving the bank facing a loss of about €270 million on the remaining 75 per cent.

There had also been problems around the loan paperwork on the deal. In the autumn of 2008 some of the Maple Ten started to get nervous about the prospect of Anglo being taken over by another bank or being nationalized. They were worried about a scenario in which the value of the shares fell so far that a new owner would seek the 25 per cent recourse on the loans. The bank assured them that the loans advanced to buy the Quinn shares wouldn't be called in, but everyone knew that if a new owner took over, all bets were off.

Drumm, feeling it was necessary to reassure the Ten, asked that letters be added to the loan files so that the investors would be protected in the event that the bank was taken over. Such changes should have gone before credit committee, but Drumm wanted the letters put on file as soon as possible in case there was a quick takeover. The new letters eliminated the recourse provision, limiting the bank's security to the shares themselves. This meant that if the shares became worthless – as they would in a nationalization scenario – then the borrower could walk away without owing a penny.

Anglo held a management meeting on 5 February to decide what to say in the annual report for the year to September 2008, which was scheduled to be published on 20 February. The meeting was attended by O'Connor and the three government-appointed directors, Frank Daly, Alan Dukes and Maurice Keane, a former chief executive of Bank of Ireland who was appointed to the board by Lenihan on 21 January. (Apart from O'Connor and Declan Quilligan, the only other directors on the board at this time were appointees of the Minister for Finance.) About a dozen senior executives also attended, including Quilligan, Whelan, Moran and Golden.

Handwritten minutes of the meeting reveal the pressure the bank was under to disclose various controversial transactions, including the IL&P

deal. Daly told the meeting that the wording of how the bank would describe the IL&P transactions was with Ernst & Young and had also been given to the Financial Regulator. O'Connor said that the Department of Finance had not gone through it yet and had not made a formal reply to the bank regarding the transaction.

There was a discussion about how the bank would deal with 'reputational risk' in the 2008 report, given the controversies that had emerged over the previous weeks. Dukes said that the bank needed to make a break from the past and to be careful to reflect in the report that 'what we're doing now conveys [what] we weren't [doing] before' but it was also important that they 'don't add to reputational risk'.

There was also a discussion around a golden-parachute payment of €3.75 million to Tom Browne, the former head of the bank's Irish division who had retired from the bank in November 2007. The bank had believed that the figure was actually €2.6 million, and Moran said that the higher figure had only become known two days earlier. Incredibly, the bank had very little documentation on file concerning the payment.

The uncertainty related to deferred bonus payments. When Anglo awarded bonuses in respect of performance in a given year, it usually spread their payment over three years to minimize the likelihood of an exodus of staff after a particularly successful year. The minutes of the meeting record that Browne had waived his right to deferred bonus payments over subsequent years after leaving the bank and taken a lump sum payment instead, hence the discrepancy in the figures. Daly said that such payments were 'pretty rare'. He asked whether the bank could say in the accounts that the payment related to Browne's deferred bonuses and whether this would be a problem for Browne. Dukes asked whether it was the bank's policy to make such payments in lieu of deferred bonuses; O'Connor said that John Rowan and Tiarnan O'Mahoney had received similar payments when they left the bank.

Another concern at the management meeting was Anglo's huge exposure – about €4 billion – to customers to whose assets the bank had little or no recourse. Non-recourse lending had been widespread among the bank's biggest developer customers, but it had also been made available to Anglo management. At the 5 February management meeting there was considerable discussion of the €8 million loan given to McAteer the previous September to repay Bank of Ireland. The loan was initially provided on the basis that it was secured only against McAteer's Anglo shares. At the meeting the government-appointed directors asked whether the loan had been written off or whether McAteer was personally liable to repay it. O'Connor said that the bank might have to pursue this further with McAteer.

One executive asked was it necessary to mention the nationalization of the bank three times in the draft annual report. Dukes, Daly, Moran and another executive, Kevin Kelly, head of finance reporting, said that it was.

On 8 February the *Sunday Business Post* reported that the Financial Regulator was examining whether Anglo had 'artificially boosted its deposits around its year-end to inflate its financial strength'. A report on RTE on Tuesday, 10 February linked the Anglo deposits to IL&P. The *Irish Times* and the *Irish Independent* reported the next day that the figure involved was around €7 billion. IL&P issued a short statement saying that it had provided 'exceptional support' to Anglo during September 2008 and particularly following the bank guarantee on 30 September.

Following the issuing of the statement, O'Connor met IL&P chair Gillian Bowler in a hotel in Dublin. O'Connor wanted the two banks to reach some agreement around how they were treating the transaction in their respective accounts. According to an IL&P report of the meeting, O'Connor told Bowler that no agreement existed to prove that there was any right of set-off on the deposits. In other words, Anglo proposed to show that the cash it lodged with IL&P had nothing whatsoever to do with the deposits of identical size placed by Irish Life Assurance with Anglo. IL&P, by contrast, accounted for the transaction as having a right of set-off: in other words, it was not a coincidence that Anglo lodged sums with IL&P that matched the sums Irish Life placed with Anglo, and in case of default by one party the other party was entitled to set off an equivalent sum.

When Bowler reported Anglo's position back to Casey and Fitzpatrick, they were furious: they felt that because she was not an accountant she did not have the expertise to challenge O'Connor, an experienced accountant, on this complex issue. Bowler showed the two IL&P executives a draft press release prepared by Anglo which O'Connor had given her. O'Connor had told her that it had been agreed with the Department of Finance. She had taken notes on the one-page draft statement in her discussion with O'Connor. In her own handwriting she noted O'Connor's comments that there was a 'clear understanding [that] no right of set off [existed]', according to a copy of the document seen by the author.

On Thursday, 12 February Casey and Bowler were called to a meeting with Lenihan and Cardiff at the Department of Finance in the early after-noon. Lenihan wasn't happy about IL&P's involvement with Anglo in the September deposits. Bowler reported back that the minister wanted the resignations of IL&P's 'chairman, chief executive, head of finance [Peter Fitzpatrick] and head of investments', which she said was David Gantly (although his title was head of treasury), according to Peter Fitzpatrick's recollection of events as recounted to Garda investigators.

IL&P held a lengthy board meeting that evening which lasted until after 3 a.m., at which Fitzpatrick and Gantly agreed to resign. Casey had offered his resignation but it was declined by the board at the marathon meeting. During the meeting Bowler received several telephone calls from O'Connor. She stepped out into a private room next to the boardroom to take one of the calls. O'Connor wanted to know what IL&P was going to say about the transactions with Anglo in a press release that it was prepar-ing to issue. Bowler told him that she was willing to cooperate as best she could but that it had to be within the boundaries of what she saw as the truth.

Around 9 p.m. she stepped out of the board meeting to take another call, this time from Kevin Cardiff. Anxious about the pressure that she felt she was being brought under, she asked a senior partner from IL&P's law firm A&L Goodbody – who was advising the board at their meeting – to listen in on the call. Cardiff asked Bowler whether IL&P and Anglo could come up with a formula of words to describe the transaction that both banks could agree on. She repeated the point she made to O'Connor: only if it was within the boundaries of the truth. At that, the conversation became frosty.

In the end, IL&P went ahead and issued its own press release the follow-ing morning without consulting O'Connor. In the statement, the company announced the resignations of Peter Fitzpatrick and David Gantly. Bowler said that while it was clear that their only motivation in agreeing the €7.2 billion transaction with Anglo had been to support 'the policy objective of the Financial Regulator and the Central Bank', the manner in which the financial support had been provided was wrong. She said that mistakes had been made for which she and the board apologized unreservedly. IL&P fired a rocket at Anglo in the statement. The transaction had been 'properly accounted for' in the IL&P's books and records, and had been fully dis-closed in reports to the Financial Regulator, the company said.

Anglo quickly issued a statement in response, saying that there was no set-off arrangement and that Anglo's deposits with IL&P did not serve as cash collateral for deposits from Irish Life Assurance. (This line was not in the draft press release that O'Connor had given Bowler two days earlier.) Anglo also said that the transactions were 'appropriately recorded in its books and records and financial statements and its daily, weekly and monthly regulatory returns'. This created the highly unusual situation of two public companies describing the same transaction in their respective books and returns to the Regulator in different ways.

The Financial Regulator responded with a statement of its own, saying that it 'utterly rejects' any suggestion that it would have encouraged circular transactions of the type engaged in by Anglo and IL&P. Such transactions did not help the liquidity of banks, it said.

All hell broke loose after the statements were issued, and Lenihan called another meeting with Bowler to find out what was going on. In the meantime, Casey agreed to resign.

Shortly after the resignations of Fitzpatrick, Gantly and Casey, David McCarthy, IL&P chief financial officer, who had been promoted the previous day to replace Fitzpatrick, received a phone call from Matt Moran, his counterpart at Anglo. Using typically colourful language, Moran asked McCarthy if IL&P was going to withdraw its press release following the departure of its three senior executives and issue a new one, clarifying that Anglo had not placed any cash with IL&P to support its deposits with Anglo. McCarthy refused point blank to change IL&P's position or how the company had described it. Moran was furious.

McCarthy soon afterwards received a phone call from Donal O'Connor, who repeated the request made by Moran even more forcefully. Was IL&P going to change its position on the transaction to match that of Anglo? McCarthy again refused. Anglo's accounting policies were for Anglo to consider and IL&P's accounting policies were none of his business, he told O'Connor.

McCarthy then received a third phone call – this time from Kevin Cardiff at the Department of Finance. McCarthy was left with the distinct impression that O'Connor had 'turned' the department on to him. McCarthy defended IL&P's position on the transaction and the decision to issue its own press release. Cardiff told McCarthy that this was 'an accounting spat' between Anglo and IL&P, and urged him to 'sort it out between you'.

When Anglo published its 2008 annual report on 20 February, its view on the IL&P transactions remained the same as in the press release. The €7.2 billion from Irish Life Assurance was treated as corporate deposits, just as it had been in the bank's annual results presentation (which made no reference to the IL&P cash), despite the Financial Regulator's clear statement that the IL&P transaction had not improved Anglo's liquidity.

On the same day, the government published Project Atlas, the PricewaterhouseCoopers report into Anglo. For the first time publicly it showed the scale of the run on Anglo the previous September, when the bank had been pushed to the brink of collapse before being saved by the government guarantee.

The bank lost €10 billion in customer deposits over the course of the month, including more than €5 billion in the last week of September leading up to the guarantee. But Anglo's own accounts did not reflect this – the bank used its own money, channelled through IL&P and back again, to mask the true scale of lost deposits and to massage its books, making them look much healthier than they actually were at 30 September 2008.

Shortly after the nationalization of Anglo, Brian Lenihan met Nigel McDermott and Nick Corcoran, two of the Dublin businessmen who led the Mallabraca private equity consortium which had considered investing in the bank the previous November. The meeting took place in the Merrion Hotel, across the road from the Department of Finance. Over coffee, Lenihan asked McDermott and Corcoran whether they were interested in investing in Anglo. They were, they said, but would do a deal only if the government was willing to share the risk and cover a proportion of potential losses.

McDermott and Corcoran later met Anglo's O'Connor and Moran to discuss a possible investment. The meeting didn't go well. The private-equity executives felt that O'Connor and Moran were too closely linked to the bank's old management team and refused to work with them on a deal directly; they said they would work only with the National Treasury Management Agency on behalf of Anglo and the government. On 23 January they met David Doyle, the secretary general of the Department of Finance. That meeting didn't go well either. 'So are you the guys shorting the Irish banks?' asked Doyle, who could be prickly at the best of times. McDermott and Corcoran had not gone short on the banks, but this didn't matter: in their view there was nothing wrong with shorting a stock. 'So what if we are?' Corcoran said in reply to Doyle.

Corcoran wrote to Doyle three days later to complain about what he saw as the 'dismissive attitude' of the government and its officials: 'The abject hostility, perceived or otherwise, of a secretary general of any government department in the face of inward investment of €5 billion to the

Irish state is wholly unacceptable,' he said. He told Doyle that Mallabraca had prepared a plan to restructure Anglo and 'to mitigate and minimize prospective losses'. He offered to meet Doyle for an informal one-to-one meeting to talk about Mallabraca's objectives, but, unsurprisingly, there were no further meetings between them.

Still undaunted, Corcoran wrote to Lenihan on 2 February proposing an investment of up to €5 billion into Anglo and offering a guarantee that the consortium would source at least €15 billion in international deposits to help the bank's funding. Mallabraca also restated its requirement for a risk-sharing deal with the state. He asked that the consortium be allowed to carry out a detailed examination of Anglo's books for a twenty-day period starting on 4 February. He also wanted the government to agree to exclusivity on talks on a proposed deal, ruling out any other potential investors in the bank.

On 9 February Lenihan wrote to Michael Somers, the chief executive of the NTMA, asking the agency to work with Mallabraca on their proposed investment and to deal with the consortium's demands for exclusive negotiation rights until 23 February. Following rounds of letters between Mallabraca, the NTMA and Anglo, the bank refused to sign a non-disclosure agreement or to divulge confidential and sensitive bank information to the consortium until it gave more detail on its investment proposal. Anglo told the NTMA in a separate letter on 23 February that the bank had been approached by the UK private equity company Carlton Partners representing a Middle Eastern investment consortium that was interested in investing in the bank.

The following day, Tuesday, 24 February, about twenty detectives from the Garda Bureau of Fraud Investigation and the Office of the Director of Corporate Enforcement raided Anglo's head office in St Stephen's Green. The detectives had secured three search warrants at the Dublin District Court the previous day. During the raid they examined paper and electronic documents and computers and took away boxes of files and other paperwork. Central Bank regulators were meanwhile carrying out their own investigation into the Maple Ten loans and had taken over a floor of Heritage House for the purpose. Anglo had two groups of investigators to deal with.

The raid was an attempt at a very public statement by the government that 'white-collar' crime would not be tolerated. 'We operate the rule of law,' Minister for Justice Dermot Ahern said about the raid. 'As far as I am concerned, that provides that, whether you have a balaclava, a sawn-off shotgun or a white collar and designer suit, the same rules apply.'

But Ireland had a miserable track record on investigating and punishing white-collar crime, particularly in banking, and the raid on Anglo was widely perceived as something of a joke: coming weeks after the revelations about FitzPatrick's loans and the circular transaction with IL&P, it left plenty of time for the alteration or destruction of records and documents, had anyone in the bank been so minded. Ahern's pronouncements were hard to take seriously.

Following the Garda raid, any chance of Mallabraca agreeing an investment was gone. The consortium told the NTMA that they felt compelled to place their interest in Anglo on hold pending the outcome of the investigation. The consortium was also uncomfortable with Donal O'Connor remaining as chairman of the bank, given that he had been appointed to the board by FitzPatrick and Drumm. Mallabraca saw him as part of the old guard and felt that they couldn't do a deal with him.

The Garda raid prompted the resignations of two former Anglo directors from the boards of other companies: Anne Heraty resigned from the boards of state companies Bord na Mona and Forfás, and Gary McGann resigned as chairman of the Dublin Airport Authority. McGann said in his resignation statement that he had 'acted with honesty and integrity' at all times at Anglo.

In March, O'Connor, Dukes and Daly began digging into the loan book to determine what sort of losses the bank was facing as a result of the collapsing property market. Property values had fallen particularly sharply in the last three months of 2008 and the early months of 2009. Up to the end of September 2008 Anglo had made a provision of just €724 million, or 1 per cent of the bank's loan book, to cover bad debts. This would obviously need to be increased, given how far property prices were falling.

Anglo hired two former senior Bank of Ireland executives, Michael Connolly and Kevin Holden, to carry out an independent review of the loan book and put a figure on the losses faced by the bank. They were recommended by Maurice Keane, the new government-appointed board member at Anglo, who had worked with them during his time as chief executive of Bank of Ireland, and O'Connor knew Connolly well. Connolly and Holden looked at the top twenty borrowers and projected losses of about €4 billion. Anglo lenders reacted angrily to their analysis, believing it was too pessimistic.

In late March O'Connor, Dukes and Daly met Cardiff and his Department of Finance colleague Ann Nolan. They told the officials that the assessment of bad loans carried out by the bank was showing a black hole of €4 billion. The directors could see the disbelief on the faces of Cardiff and Nolan – the Anglo board members were left with the distinct impression that the department officials thought they were over-egging the losses in hope of convincing the state to overcapitalize the bank.

The department again asked their consultants of choice, PricewaterhouseCoopers, to assess the losses across the bank's loan book to corroborate Anglo's analysis. The accountancy firm compiled a report called Project Stephen, which went to the bank in May 2009. The report, which was marked 'strictly private and confidential', said that an impairment charge of €4 billion at the end of the bank's half-year at 31 March 2009 was 'not unreasonable' but warned that the firm's assessment was based on a 'limited review' of loans. There would also be an €800 million charge for incurred but not recognized (IBNR) losses, said PwC. This was accountancy-speak for loans that had gone bad but had not yet been recognized by the bank in its accounts.

A number of the bank's large borrowers were 'beginning to show signs of impairment', said PwC, and this was a reflection of what was going on in the economy, with recession biting, credit extremely tight and asset values plummeting. Rental agreements were being broken and tenants in commercial properties were going bust. House-builders who in the good times could sell a hundred new houses to first-time buyers over a weekend were lucky to secure any sales at all. First-time buyers were forgoing the deposits they'd put down on new properties rather than complete the purchases, given the collapse in property values and the rising cost of drawing down a mortgage. As a result, Anglo, like the other banks, was left with what became popularly known as 'ghost estates' – half-built and derelict housing projects that the bank or the developer could not afford to complete or that were not worth finishing because of the property crash.

PwC also warned in the Project Stephen report that Anglo would face additional funding costs, including the cost of drawing loans from the Central Bank's exceptional liquidity assistance facility. This, together with one-off costs in the second half of the bank's 2009 financial year, would 'absorb the majority of the bank's operating income before impairments'. The department's disbelief at Anglo's assessment of the state of its loan book gave way to acceptance when it saw the PwC figures. (What they didn't realize was that the true picture was in fact much, much worse than either Anglo or PwC had recognized.)

★

On 8 April Lenihan unveiled the government's plans to establish the National Asset Management Agency (NAMA), a state 'bad bank' that would acquire toxic property loans from the banks, including Anglo. Lenihan said that the government might have to part-nationalize the other banks if NAMA bought land and development loans at deep discounts reflecting the drop in property values, thereby crystallizing huge losses on the banks' balance sheets. The minister said the banks were denying and postponing the losses on their land and development loans and that this was damaging the economy. NAMA would stop this by making its own assessment of the value of the loans it was acquiring and force the banks to accept the losses they had been unwilling to face.

The government believed that putting all the toxic land and development loans into one agency was the best way of dealing with them. It would allow the state to see the total exposure of the banks to each borrower. Another purpose of NAMA was to help the banks' liquidity: the agency would issue state-backed bonds as payment for the loans that the banks could then exchange for cash at the European Central Bank to fund their operations. It would have been impossible otherwise for the banks to raise any amount of cash in respect of the toxic assets NAMA would be acquiring.

For several months the government tried to sell NAMA to a disbelieving public – which never liked the idea of the state acquiring tens of billions of euros' worth of toxic loans – as a means of increasing the flow of credit into the economy. This was never a realistic prospect. Internal Department of Finance records later showed that a senior official at the International Monetary Fund, Steven Seelig, told Lenihan in April 2009 during its annual review of Ireland's economy and public finances – soon after NAMA was announced – that it would not lead to a significant increase in bank lending. Seelig's comments were published in an article I wrote that appeared in the *Irish Times* in February 2010. The government spin about NAMA increasing lending was not heard again.

Critics of NAMA viewed the agency as another bailout for the banks: a political tool to recapitalize them by stealth by overpaying for assets that nobody else in the world would touch, and to deceive the public about the true cost. Whether or not this was the state's intention, in practice NAMA provided no such cushion.

The process of valuing toxic portfolios loan-by-loan was so protracted – it took about six months to value the loans of the ten biggest of the 850 borrowers moving to the agency – that by the time a clear picture of the mess at the banks emerged, the financial markets had lost confidence in both the banks and the country. As a result, the banks did not just have a capital problem from the heavy loan losses, but a fresh funding problem as deposits flooded out their doors as confidence ebbed away.

Various interested parties, including the IMF and the Labour Party, argued initially that nationalizing the entire banking system would be a better option, and they were proved correct. If the banks had been taken into state ownership, the somewhat adversarial wrangling over asset values that caused the NAMA process to move in slow motion – and thus fail in its purpose of drawing a line under the banking crisis – could have been avoided. In the end, the banks were largely nationalized anyway after an extremely protracted process.

The government believed that NAMA would be a mechanism to fix the banks; in the end, it merely presided over their slow death.

On 29 May O'Connor presented Anglo's half-year figures to the end of March 2009 to startled financial journalists. O'Connor disclosed that the bank would be receiving a cash injection of €4 billion from the state as a loss of €4.1 billion during the six-month period had wiped out the bank's cash reserves. The loss was a record for an Irish company. Together with the €7 billion being injected into AIB and Bank of Ireland, this brought the cost of the state bailout of the banks to €11 billion.

O'Connor felt that the black hole at Anglo had the potential to get even bigger. The latest review of the bank's loan book showed that the stress being experienced by borrowers was so great that losses could spiral to €11.5 billion, which included the bank's estimate of losses on NAMA and non-NAMA loans. The value of loans on which a borrower had missed at least one repayment had soared to €23.6 billion in March 2009 from €2.5 billion in September 2008. This showed an alarming trend and supported O'Connor's estimate on losses. The figures were shocking, showing the bank's real exposure to the collapsing property market.

The debate suddenly turned to whether shutting the bank down would be a cheaper option for the Irish state than rescuing it. Lenihan warned that the bank's €64 billion of deposits from customers and other banks could be withdrawn, collapsing the bank, if its future was called into question. But it was the right question to ask.

The other question that was raised was whether the old management team had lied about the extent of the bank's problems when it presented the 2008 results for the bank in December. The answer to this was not obvious. Although there was ample evidence at the time that the Irish property bubble had been inflated to a truly staggering degree and the country now faced an equally staggering crash, there is little evidence that anyone at Anglo (or the other Irish banks, or in government, the Department of Finance, the Central Bank or the Financial Regulator) recognized what was happening.

David Drumm later pointed to the decision of O'Connor's new management team to stick with the figures he had reported the previous December for the year to September 2008 when they published the bank's annual report for the same period in February 2009: 'The government has to decide which poison it wants to take,' he said in an interview with the *Sunday Independent* in October 2010. 'Did it agree with our accounts in 2008? I presume it did because it signed them. Or did they sign the accounts knowing that those accounts were misleading? You have to choose one.'

Accounting rules complicated matters – they prevented companies from booking losses on loans before they had actually gone bad. This meant that even if it had taken a properly pessimistic view of the market, Anglo had to treat a loan that was performing as of September as though it would continue to perform. Now, as the crash started to push big borrowers into default, Anglo suddenly had to post huge losses on its books.

The figures announced by O'Connor were shocking – but they were just a small foretaste of what was coming.

18.   Mopping Up

September 2009 – Anglo's cost to the State: €4 billion

With Declan Quilligan having failed to win the approval of the Financial Regulator as the board's choice to replace Drumm as chief executive, Anglo still needed a new boss.

Mike Soden, a former chief executive of Bank of Ireland, had become friendly with an Australian banker, Mike Aynsley, at National Australia Bank in Sydney and at Hoare Govett, the stockbroker owned by investment bank Security Pacific. Realizing that Anglo needed a chief executive, Soden contacted Donal O'Connor, who was serving as interim executive chairman. O'Connor asked his headhunters to get in touch with Aynsley, who was doing work for the Asian Development Bank at the time. During the summer of 2009 Aynsley travelled to Ireland and met O'Connor, Maurice Keane and Frank Daly. He later met Kevin Cardiff at the Department of Finance. Eventually Aynsley was offered the top job at Anglo, which had been vacant since David Drumm resigned the previous December.

By the time Aynsley joined Anglo on 7 September 2009 the bank had received a state bailout of €4 billion the previous June to cover the record half-year loss, negotiated a discounted pay-off with some subordinated bondholders making a gain of €1.8 billion, and carried out extensive checks on the size of the holes in its loan book. But Aynsley had no real understanding of the true extent of the losses the bank was facing.

At the first meeting between Aynsley and Lenihan, the minister said that the government would have to decide whether the bank would be closed. Aynsley was taken aback. He had been hired, he believed, with the brief of rescuing the bank, not shutting it down. Aynsley raised Lenihan's comment with Donal O'Connor, who was equally surprised.

A week after Aynsley's arrival at Anglo, Lenihan announced that NAMA would be buying in property loans with a book value of €77 billion from five financial institutions, including Anglo, at a cost of €54 billion. This amounted to an average discount or 'haircut' of 30 per cent. The losses would be borne by the banks, and if they couldn't raise the money to cover them, they would be nationalized like Anglo. The value and number of the loans it was acquiring made NAMA arguably the biggest property company in the world.

The government said that it would be acquiring €28 billion in loans from Anglo. This amounted to about 40 per cent of the bank's loan book.

One of the first tasks that Aynsley undertook was to pursue former Anglo directors for money they owed the bank. David Drumm was top of the list: he owed the bank €8.3 million. Most of this related to the loan of €7.7 million provided to buy Anglo shares in January 2008, when a number of directors had invested in the bank to demonstrate their confidence in it. Drumm had also borrowed €406,000 to invest in a fund managed by Anglo's wealth management division to invest in UK banks and drawn down a €9,200 loan to invest in a film company called Darkroom Productions, which was developing a movie for the Hollywood star Colin Farrell.

On 9 September, two days after he started at Anglo, Aynsley wrote to Drumm at his Cape Cod holiday home, where he and his family were now living, about his Irish home at Abington in Malahide, Co. Dublin, which he had put on the market. (Drumm later said in a court affidavit that O'Connor told him that he should consider moving to the US to avoid the 'blame culture' in Ireland and the UK.) The Drumms were looking for about €2 million for the Malahide property. Aynsley demanded an undertaking from Drumm that the money from the sale of the house be retained within the jurisdiction pending the resolution of the bank's claim for €8.3 million against him. In May Drumm had transferred the house from the joint ownership of himself and his wife, Lorraine, into Lorraine's sole name, a move the bank took as an attempt to put the house out of its reach.

On 28 September Aynsley wrote again to Drumm, this time demanding full repayment of the €8.3 million by twelve noon on Friday, 2 October, otherwise the bank would take legal action. Aynsley was unhappy that Drumm had failed to supply a statement of affairs to the bank showing his assets and liabilities, despite several requests from the bank, and that he was not making payments on one of his loans.

Lawyers for Drumm replied to Aynsley on 30 September, saying the family home in Malahide had been transferred to his wife for tax reasons following discussions with his US financial advisers and that he was unwilling to send the bank a statement of affairs as he feared it might end up in the public domain. Nine days earlier I had written a front-page news story in the *Irish Times* saying that eight senior managers at Anglo owed the bank amounts ranging from €835,000 to €7.1 million in 2008; Drumm wrote to Anglo two days later saying that he had a grave concern that 'confidential information is regularly and systemically being leaked to the media'. In the same letter he said that he resented the bank's reference to his 'leaving the jurisdiction'. He said that he left Ireland 'out of utter desperation and certainly not by choice'.

Drumm's lawyers said that he would be willing to meet Aynsley to provide a statement of affairs in person, and on 7 October Drumm travelled to Dublin to see him at Heritage House. As he arrived he was approached by *Irish Times* journalist Colm Keena and photographer Alan Betson. 'How did you know I would be here?' Drumm asked. 'I just got a call from the office to get down here,' Keena replied. Betson photographed an angry Drumm as he entered the building. His photograph appeared in the following day's newspaper next to a story saying that Drumm was in Dublin to discuss his loans with the bank's new chief executive.

Drumm emailed Aynsley the following day to complain about being doorstepped as he entered the meeting. 'It is entirely unacceptable that my rights to confidentiality are being so clearly breached,' he said. Aynsley replied that the recent media focus on directors' loans was 'probably the source of the conclusions they have drawn around why you were at the bank'. He told Drumm that it was likely he was spotted coming through the airport or on the street. Photographers and journalists were regularly seen waiting in a van across the road outside the bank to see who turns up, said Aynsley. Drumm emailed Aynsley back the following day, saying that it was very unlikely that a senior journalist and photographer from the *Irish Times* would be 'sitting in vans waiting for people to come out of the bank'.

The meeting between Drumm and Aynsley resolved nothing. Legal letters flew back and forth between Drumm's solicitors Eversheds O'Donnell Sweeney, his wife's solicitors Noel Smyth & Partners, and Anglo's solicitors McCann FitzGerald. Frustrated by the bank's unwillingness to give him more time to repay the loan, Drumm wrote to O'Connor on 16 November and copied in Aynsley and the rest of the board, which at this point comprised the three government-appointed directors, Dukes, Daly and Keane. (Declan Quilligan had stood down from the board when Aynsley was appointed.) Anglo, he wrote, had 'persisted in acting in a manner which seems to indicate that the bank's preference is to pursue litigation against me'. He complained that the bank had demanded repayment of his loans when they had not even matured, but this was an empty complaint: they were 'on demand' loans that could be called in at any time. To make matters worse, Drumm wrote, private information about him had been leaked to the media 'in an effort to harass and humiliate me' and there had been a stream of threatening legal letters from the bank's solicitors and 'a most upsetting phone conversation' with Anglo executive Tom Hunersen in which 'he also threatened me and my wife with litigation'.

Aynsley had hired Hunersen, an American consultant whom he had got to know at National Australia Bank, as Anglo's 'head of corporate development' and charged him with the tricky job of managing the loans to former Anglo directors as well as to Sean Quinn. Aynsley liked his no-nonsense approach. Staff at Anglo nicknamed him 'The Gunner'.

On 25 November Anglo issued legal proceedings against Drumm in the High Court seeking recovery of €8.3 million. The bank also sued Drumm and his wife Lorraine to reverse the transfer of the Malahide property back into their joint names so the bank could pursue its claim on it.

Drumm alleged in an affidavit that he understood from conversations with a number of former senior executives at the bank that Anglo had been instructed by the Department of Finance 'to litigate my loans regardless of the consequences'. 'My view is that the bank has been uncommercial, unnecessarily aggressive and vindictive in dealing with my loans,' he said.

Drumm counter-sued Anglo for €2.6 million, arguing that he had resigned as chief executive of the bank in December 2008 but not as an employee and therefore was entitled to compensation. He claimed that he was owed an annual salary of €1.2 million for his notice period because his employment had not been validly terminated, that he was owed a pension payment of €715,224 and benefits of €44,471, and that he was also entitled to a bonus payment of €661,000, which had been deferred to December 2009, in respect of the bank's profitable performance in 2006.

On 6 November, as Anglo was battling it out with Drumm in legal correspondence, the bank demanded repayment of loans due from Sean FitzPatrick and a number of his family members. FitzPatrick and his family owed the bank €110 million. On 18 December, following negotiations, the bank agreed to grant him an extension so that FitzPatrick and Lar Bradshaw could try to sell their Nigerian oilfield investment for which they had borrowed €20 million.

In January FitzPatrick's financial adviser Bernard Somers (a former AIB board member) had written to Anglo suggesting that the bank take full security over the oilfield and that any profits made from it could go towards reducing FitzPatrick's debt with the bank. The executives at Anglo were deeply sceptical about the prospects for the Movido field. Anglo's new management team used to joke that correspondence about the oilfield read like those widely circulated Nigerian emails that promised the recipient access to tens of millions of state money sitting in a random bank account if they just fulfilled a few simple tasks. Despite this, Anglo agreed to revised loan terms on 26 February 2009 which limited the bank's recourse to the FitzPatrick family but improved its overall security, particularly over the oilfield.

When FitzPatrick and Bradshaw had failed to sell their holding by 10 March 2010, the bank issued High Court proceedings against FitzPatrick for recovery of the loans. Fearing for his personal financial situation, Fitz-Patrick successfully applied to the court for protection under a rarely used measure in the 1988 Bankruptcy Act which blocked creditors from taking action against a debtor who was attempting to agree a deal to repay the debts over time. It was a gamble. If he failed to secure the support of his creditors, he would be declared bankrupt. Anglo held all the cards. Fitz-Patrick needed the support of three-fifths of his creditors – in terms of both number and value. Given that Anglo accounted for more than three-fifths of the value of FitzPatrick's borrowings, this plan was doomed to fail.

FitzPatrick argued that the bank was not acting in its best commercial interests to recover the most amount of money on his loans but was instead acting with political motivation to create the 'public perception that for-mer executive officers of the bank should not somehow be "let off the hook"'. The bank rejected this. 'There has been no discrimination on the basis of his former position, but equally there is no favouritism being afforded to him,' said Hunersen in an affidavit.

The pursuit of Drumm's and FitzPatrick's debts was a high-profile but, in the scheme of things, relatively minor drama for Anglo. Considerably more significant was the restructuring plan the bank was required to file, under EU Commission rules governing state aid. Following the state's €4 billion capital injection in May, the bank was required to show that it either had a viable future and that it could repay the money, or else outline plans to shut itself down.

The new management team at Anglo believed that the bank had a future as a going concern and that following the transfer of an estimated €28 bil-lion in property loans to NAMA, a good bank could be carved out of Anglo. While NAMA would be handling its troubled property loans, Anglo would still be left with poorly performing loans in other areas, and the bank planned to move these to a new internal 'bad bank' to be run down over time.

Anglo hired a large number of external consultants to see what it would cost to put this 'good bank/bad bank' plan in place. The alternatives were to close the bank as soon as possible, which would take about a year, or to show how they would close the bank over ten years.

Accountancy firm KPMG in the Netherlands, which had helped a number of troubled financial institutions in Europe to repair their operations, looked at how large banks had been shut down in other countries. Aynsley asked them to identify a bank about the size of Anglo that accounted for a comparably large portion of a country's banking sector and that had been closed down. KPMG couldn't find one. Anglo's balance sheet had grown to €100 billion, accounting for about a fifth of the Irish banking system. No other bank in the world representing such a large part of a country's banking sector had ever failed before. Even the mighty Wall Street bank Lehman Brothers, whose collapse brought the global financial system to its knees, didn't have such a 'systemic' role in US banking. Lehman's balance sheet was the equivalent of 7 per cent of the economic output (GDP) of the United States; Anglo's amounted to about 60 per cent of Ireland's.

To help him devise a plan to clean up this gargantuan mess, Aynsley turned to a Dutch banker, Maarten van Eden, asking him to become his chief financial officer. Van Eden joined Anglo in January 2010. As head of capital management at ING, van Eden had managed a balance sheet of €1.4 trillion, trading billions in the money markets on any one day. He had also worked for US bank JP Morgan, UK bank HSBC and a subsidiary of Royal Bank of Canada after stints in the Dutch military and the Dutch finance ministry.

The brief at Anglo was a tricky one, but van Eden was not new to financial or political hot spots. While visiting his brother-in-law, a diplomat, on the Jordanian border with Iraq shortly after the US invasion in March 2003, and inspecting 2,000 Dutch marines, he had been shot in the chest by a sniper hiding in the surrounding dunes and knocked unconscious. Fortunately, he had been wearing a bulletproof vest, but the incident left van Eden with a permanent circular burn mark. Colleagues at Anglo nicknamed him 'Scaramanga' after the James Bond villain in *The Man With The Golden Gun* who was notable for possessing a third nipple.

Van Eden had a way with words – much to the amusement of the new management team at Anglo. He enjoyed using idioms, sometimes directly translated from Dutch, to make his point. In a discussion about one struggling borrower who could not repay a loan, van Eden said emphatically:

'You can't pluck a naked chicken.' There would be a lot of that kind of talk during his time at Anglo.

Acting on advice from KPMG, JP Morgan and consultants Bain & Co, Aynsley and van Eden determined that the best and least expensive option for the state would be to split Anglo into a 'good bank', dubbed 'New Bank', and a 'bad bank' which would be run down over time called 'Old Anglo'. The €36 billion in loans remaining on the bank's books following the transfer of €36 billion in loans to NAMA would be divided between the two operations, depending on how they were performing. Aynsley's team submitted a voluminous plan to the EU Commission in Brussels at the end of November 2009 setting out the good bank/bad bank proposal.

The new Anglo team believed in their proposal and thought it merited serious consideration. They later included plans to address the shortage of credit to small and medium-sized businesses, which were clamouring for more lending from the troubled Irish institutions as the banking crisis worsened, and lending on environmental projects as a means to carve out a new niche for itself. But the state authorities were sceptical about the plan, seeing the proposed new areas of lending as 'bells and whistles', in the words of one senior official.

Officials simply believed that the losses at Anglo were so great and the problems within the bank so deep that no part of it could be salvaged as a good bank, that the markets would not see a good bank/bad bank plan as being credible, and that there was no choice but to close the whole operation down over time.

While awaiting a response to the plan from the Commission, Aynsley set out to complete the purge of the old guard at Anglo. Pat Whelan, the head of the bank's Irish division, and Matt Moran, Drumm's chief financial officer and later head of finance following the bank's nationalization, resigned in December 2009. Declan Quilligan, the former head of the UK division, left in March 2010, while Tony Campbell, Anglo's US boss, resigned the following month. A further thirty senior managers left the bank between December and April.

The departures coincided with a redundancy plan launched in November 2009. The bank wanted 460 redundancies over two years. Morale in the bank was at a very low ebb, and demand among staff to leave was very high, even though severance terms were well below average for banks. In an interview with the *Irish Times*, one Anglo employee spoke anonymously about the mood at the bank in October 2009: 'Employees here have stopped wearing their Anglo jackets and I've also noticed that most employees would prefer to get wet in the rain to using the Anglo umbrellas. Previously, when employees were asked where they worked, they would say Anglo Irish Bank. Now they say financial services, or insurance or some even lie about it completely. If there is no need to bring it up, it is just not volunteered.'

Many senior Anglo managers who had worked closely with Drumm knew their number was up as soon as the bank was nationalized but bided their time until the bank introduced the redundancy plan. 'It was very unsettling – the whole period. You felt a little isolated. You were like one of those managers of a football team who knew you were going to get the sack,' says one former executive.

Anglo managers left what they thought were cordial meetings with O'Connor and would realize only when they got back to their offices that they had just been forced out. 'Donal would sit in front of you and he would gut you,' one former manager says. 'You would leave the room and only realize afterwards that your guts were hanging out.'

On Friday, 19 February 2010 – shortly after his six-month anniversary in the job – Aynsley met Sean Quinn. The Quinn family's debts to the bank stood at €2.8 billion and interest was mounting at a rate of almost €3 million a week.

At the meeting Aynsley suggested that Quinn Insurance – the most profitable part of the Quinn Group – be restructured so that the bank could recoup some of its money. Anglo believed it had a better chance of recovering what it was owed if it had control over Quinn's businesses.

Despite being fined €200,000 by the Financial Regulator and forced to leave the board of Quinn Insurance, Quinn was still playing an active role in the insurance business in early 2010. The Financial Regulator knew this and Anglo knew it too. The bank pushed the point with Quinn that he would have to 'restructure himself out of the business'. According to one account of the meeting, Quinn warned Aynsley that if he or another member of his family was not involved in the management of the insurance business, it would fail.

'You always felt that you were being warned,' says one former Anglo executive. Quinn always wanted the bank to know exactly who it was dealing with and of the influence that he believed he had in government circles, given that he had built one of the largest businesses in the country and employed 6,000 people, mostly in the economic black spot that is the border region of the country.

Despite Quinn's dark warning, the meeting ended cordially, and Quinn and Aynsley exchanged correspondence in subsequent days to thank each other. But the bank still had a major problem on its hands and no clear strategy for solving it.

At 6.30 a.m. on Thursday, 18 March, three days after FitzPatrick sought bankruptcy protection from Anglo, the former Anglo chairman was arrested in Greystones during a surprise Garda search of his home. He was taken into custody under the Criminal Justice (Theft and Fraud Offences) Act, which is used to deal with white-collar crimes such as false accounting. He was brought to Bray Garda station, where he was detained for thirty-one hours by detectives investigating Anglo.

He later told journalist Tom Lyons, as quoted in *The FitzPatrick Tapes*, that he would remember being in the Garda station for the rest of his life. 'Meeting the member in charge. Taking off my tie and watch. There was no shoelaces because I was wearing slip-ons. They put me in a cell and referred to me formally as "the prisoner".'

The following Wednesday, 24 March, Anglo's former finance director Willie McAteer was arrested, also at 6.30 a.m. He was brought from his home in the south Dublin suburb of Rathgar to Irishtown Garda station and detained for more than thirty hours. The questioning of both Fitz-Patrick and McAteer was focused largely on the September 2008 deposits between Anglo and IL&P. Both men were released without charge.

On the day of McAteer's arrest I interviewed Mike Aynsley for the *Irish Times*. The Anglo chief executive said that the bank would require another €9 billion in state recapitalization to keep afloat and to reinvent the bank as a lender to businesses under its good bank/bad bank plan. This would increase the total capital cost to the government of supporting the bank to €13 billion. Liquidating or winding down Anglo over time would lead to 'an incineration of taxpayers' money in horrendous terms', Aynsley said. Closing the bank would cost the state between €27 billion and €35 billion, while running the bank down over ten years would cost between €18 billion and €22 billion. 'I don't think the right thing to do is to shoot the organization – it just makes the hole bigger for the country and the problem bigger for the country,' he said. (Van Eden's own characteristically colourful take on this, to Anglo colleagues, was that shutting down a bank quickly in such circumstances is 'like pissing down your leg – it feels good for just a few seconds'.)

The European Commission, which had been analysing Anglo's restructuring plan since November, had serious doubts about it. EU competition commissioner Joaquin Almunia wrote to the government in March saying that Anglo's proposed 'good bank' or 'New Bank' could potentially be taking on too much risk and would remain very exposed to the property market. Privately, the Commission felt that nothing was changing at Anglo – it would still be engaging in the same type of business as before and, given the scale of the losses, a good bank/bad bank plan with no radical change in the business was impossible.

On the morning of Tuesday, 30 March Anglo was expecting news from NAMA on how much the agency would be paying for the first land, development and associated property loans it was acquiring from the five participating institutions. That Tuesday marked the government's third bank recapitalization announcement, but the first to assess the depth of the losses that would be crystallized by NAMA's purchases of their first property loans.

With regard to Anglo, the state agency was taking over loans linked to the bank's ten most heavily indebted borrowers: Liam Carroll, Bernard McNamara, Sean Mulryan, Treasury Holdings, Michael O'Flynn, Joe O'Reilly, Gerry Gannon, Gerry Barrett, the Cosgrave brothers and Derek Quinlan. After Sean Quinn, O'Reilly was Anglo's biggest borrower with debts of €1.8 billion, followed by McNamara and Mulryan with €1.4 billion each, Treasury with €1.2 billion and Gannon and O'Flynn with about €1 billion each.

NAMA contacted Anglo that morning to say that the average discount on loans it was acquiring linked to the top ten borrowers was coming in at around 50 per cent. In some cases, NAMA paid just 10 per cent of the value of the loan, applying a horrendous 90 per cent haircut on land outside Dublin which had been purchased for speculative development. NAMA also applied an 87 per cent discount on the bank's €173 million loan on the Irish Glass Bottle site. The co-owners of the site, the Dublin Docklands Development Authority, meanwhile wrote down the value of the site, once €412 million, to €50 million.

Underlying its status as the biggest basket case in a comprehensively broken banking system, Anglo accounted for €9.25 billion of the first €16 billion in loans acquired by NAMA; and the average discount taken on its loans was second only to Irish Nationwide, which took a 58 per cent hair-cut. Speaking in the Dáil later that day, Lenihan announced that the state would be pumping a further €8.3 billion into the bank, bringing the capital cost of Anglo to the state to €12.3 billion, and that this would not be the end of it: capital 'of the order of a further €10 billion' would be needed to cover future losses.

It was an astonishing disclosure, and it caused widespread confusion and disbelief. Did Lenihan really say another €10 billion on top of the €12.3 billion? Later that day, speaking on Newstalk radio, Alan Dukes, who was due to take over as the bank's new chairman from Donal O'Connor, said that he couldn't say with confidence that the cost would not rise further. The figures were mind-boggling.

The government was also hampered by the fact that it couldn't afford the upfront cost of bailing out Anglo. The €8.3 billion earmarked for Anglo was being made available in the form of promissory notes, a type of state IOU against which the bank would draw down a certain amount every year.

At a press conference, Lenihan said the detailed information that had emerged from the banks as NAMA valued the loans over the previous months was 'truly shocking': 'At every hand's turn our worst fears have been surpassed.'

Anglo too was stunned at the scale of the discounts that NAMA was applying to its loans. It believed that somewhere during the valuation process the agency had started applying a more severe mark-to-market valuation – the price that could be realized in the event of a liquidation – as there was no functioning market. NAMA had said it would apply its 'long-term economic value' approach to valuing loans and the tangible assets underlying them, but the banks felt NAMA was applying fire-sale values.

AIB complained that this was nationalization by stealth: the bigger the NAMA discount, the bigger the capital hole in the bank, hence a bigger state recapitalization, hence a higher level of state ownership. But such a response was to be expected, and in truth no one could say with any real confidence what the banks' distressed assets were worth: only time and the market would tell. And the banks had not helped themselves in their lax approach to security and their poor loan documentation, which made it harder to pursue the borrowers for the debts.

As if there wasn't enough happening that Tuesday, the Financial Regulator successfully applied to the High Court to put Quinn Insurance into administration, having expressed 'very serious' concerns about the company's ability to meet its liabilities to policyholders. The Regulator had discovered the previous week that guarantees had been given by the Quinn Group on the assets of subsidiary companies of Quinn Insurance which reduced the solvency of the insurer by €450 million.

Sean Quinn, furious, wrote to every member of the Cabinet and to the leaders of Fine Gael and Labour, demanding that the move be reversed. He described the Regulator's action as 'highly aggressive and unnecessary' and later as the worst decision in Irish corporate history. He warned that the administration would make the repayment of the group's debts 'extremely difficult' and endanger 6,000 jobs.

Privately, Anglo hated the move too, believing that informal pressure and a more gentle approach to a restructuring may have been the better option. This could have helped retain some value in the business, which was necessary if Anglo was to have any chance of recovering the €2.8 billion it was owed by Sean Quinn. But Anglo's requirements were not at the forefront of the Regulator's considerations. The Regulator was acting primarily to minimize the danger of an insurance company failing, which would jeopardize the insurance cover of more than a million policyholders.

The new bankers at Anglo had bigger problems. They would be reporting the bank's results the following day and NAMA had pulled the rug from under them.

On the day after the government's banking announcement, the front page of the *Star* newspaper carried photographs of Sean FitzPatrick and Michael Fingleton with the screaming headline: 'They deserve to be shot.' The subheading read: 'These two bastards have cost us €25 billion.'

Public anger and political tensions were running high. Labour Party leader Eamon Gilmore accused Taoiseach Brian Cowen of 'economic treason' over the further €8.3 billion bailout of Anglo and for supporting the bank on the night of the bank guarantee in September 2008.

That morning Mike Aynsley and Maarten van Eden published Anglo's results to a shocked public. The bank made a loss of €12.7 billion for the fifteen months to the end of 2009 after writing off €15.1 billion on bad loans and investments, including €10 billion on the €35.6 billion of loans that were heading to NAMA. (This amounted to a haircut of just 28 per cent – the figure Anglo expected NAMA to apply to loans – leaving the bank with further heavy losses to take.) This was the biggest loss ever recorded by an Irish company and amounted to roughly the sum generated in income tax in the state in any one year. In July 2010 *The Banker*, the international magazine for the industry, said that based on the absolute figure Anglo's 2009 losses were the worst reported by any bank in the world.

Anglo said that of the €155 million in loans owing by former directors of the bank, it expected that €109 million would remain unpaid. Van Eden said that Anglo would try to recoup every single cent owed but that the bank was 'not in the vengeance business'. Some of the amounts owed – by Sean FitzPatrick (€85 million), David Drumm (€8.3 million), Willie McAteer (€8.3 million), Lar Bradshaw (€27.3 million), Gary McGann (€10.6 million), Pat Whelan (€5.8 million) and Declan Quilligan (€3.8 million) – were enormous.

Incredibly, the accounts showed that Sean FitzPatrick and four former executive directors received €2 million in fees and pay. FitzPatrick received €131,000 for his last three months at the bank, Drumm €654,000 and Willie McAteer €240,000. The other executive directors, Declan Quilligan and Pat Whelan, received €752,000 and €277,000, respectively. Four executives, including David Drumm, were paid another €2 million in bonuses which had been deferred from previous years. Aynsley said that he was 'personally offended' by the large sums paid to former directors but that the bank was legally obliged to make the payments.

One quote from the day captured well how Drumm's management team had run the bank, lending heavily into a property market which they thought would never decline. 'If you get lucky for a long period of time, you start to think the rules don't apply to you,' van Eden told the *Irish Independent*. 'These guys thought they could walk on water. They weren't smart, they were lucky.'

As the losses at Anglo and the cost to the state increased, so too did the public anger and the demands to shut the bank down. Anglo's €22 billion bill was now around the same level as the new management team's estimate of the cost of gradually closing the bank down. Staff felt the public anger first hand as customers made their feelings known. In one shocking incident, a priest walked into the public deposit-taking offices of the customer branch in the St Stephen's Green headquarters and told a cashier that if he had a gun he would blow her brains out.

19. Bailout

May 2010 – Anglo's cost to the State: €22 billion

In March 2010 Anglo's chief financial officer Maarten van Eden started warning the Department of Finance that all the Irish banks – not just Anglo – faced a major problem. He pointed out that the state's two-year guarantee of liabilities was due to expire on 29 September and that the Irish banks would have to repay about €31 billion to bondholders over the course of that month on borrowings they had drawn on the strength of the guarantee. Anglo, for its part, had about €8 billion falling due. Van Eden was told by the department that he should only be concerned with Anglo's problems, not those of the wider banking system – this was none of his business.

The banks had also been raising longer-term funding using the Eligible Liabilities Guarantee scheme, an outgrowth of the original guarantee, which was introduced by the state in December 2009. Anglo managed to borrow €2.25 billion as late as April 2010 on a guaranteed bond even after announcing record losses and a further capital support from the state. But everything changed in early May. Following months of pressure, rising borrowing costs and speculative betting against its debt in the financial markets, Greece succumbed to pressure and agreed to take a €110 billion bailout from the European Commission and the International Monetary Fund. The deal was as much about preventing the country's debt crisis from spreading to other highly indebted countries such as Ireland and Portugal as about solving Greece's own financial woes.

The Greek bailout pushed the interest rate Ireland had to pay to borrow money to nearly 6 per cent, from below 5 per cent over the previous months. Matters were complicated by fears that the cost of bailing out the Irish banks would rise above the €32 billion recapitalization bill announced on 30 March following the first loan transfers to NAMA. The new governor of the Central Bank, Patrick Honohan, believed that a line had been drawn under the banking crisis with the March announcement, but he worried that the Greek situation would create a problem for Ireland down the track. He wanted Lenihan to announce the closure and winding down of the country's worst bank, Anglo. The lack of a final solution for Anglo was not helping the country as there was no certainty around the scale of the losses at the bank. Honohan also had concerns that Lenihan's budgets had not gone far enough, given the deteriorating economic outlook. However, there was little political incentive to move any faster, because the European Commission and the ECB were holding up Ireland, which had introduced budgetary austerity, as an example of how an EU member state should behave in a debt crisis.

At the end of May Anglo received another €2 billion in promissory notes from the state to cover its losses on the first €9.25 billion of loans transferred to NAMA. This brought the bank's cost to the state to €14.3 billion. Bank of Ireland, in which the state still had only a minority shareholding, managed to raise more than €3.5 billion during the Greek debt crisis, but no other bank was able to raise any significant funding in the public debt markets after April 2010. Almost two years on from the September 2008 liquidity crisis, Irish banks were being shut out of the money markets again.

On 31 May the Anglo management team completed a second, more detailed restructuring plan for the European Commission. Like the first, this plan pushed for the splitting of Anglo into a good bank and a bad bank, but this time it said that at least 80 per cent of the bank's loans would be wound down. Supporting the plan, the Department of Finance sought urgent approval by the Commission, fearing that prolonged uncertainty could affect the funding of Anglo and the wider Irish banking system. But Irish government borrowing costs dropped again over the remaining weeks of May and early June as concerns that Ireland would follow Greece petered out. The Commission never approved Anglo's plan.

In June, Honohan's report on the causes of the banking crisis was published. The report was damning of the failure of the Central Bank and Financial Regulator to rein in property lending, allowing a situation to develop in which the Irish banks had followed Anglo along the path of unsustainable lending on property. Even before the failure of Lehman Brothers in September 2008, Anglo and Irish Nationwide were 'well on the road towards insolvency', given that heavy losses on property development loans had become inevitable by that stage, Honohan wrote. Staff at the Regulator viewed Anglo as ' "slick and buccaneering" but not as presenting a large or imminent risk', he said. It was clear to top decision-makers at the Regulator, Honohan found, that senior Anglo figures were 'well-liked in political circles' and that this conceivably played a part in Anglo management being allowed to stay in their jobs for months after the September 2008 guarantee. But, he added, 'There was, until very late in the day, no perceived need to take regulatory action against them.'

Honohan took the view that a default by Anglo on its debts could have created contagion across the entire Irish banking system. For this reason, he said, the 'systemic importance' of Anglo 'cannot seriously be disputed'. In other words, it had to be saved. He concluded that the bank guarantee had been 'exceptionally broad', and that this had narrowed the options available to the state and increased the state's potential share of the losses in the banks.

A week after the report was published, Anglo's new management team explained the devastation caused by the bank to politicians from various parties sitting on an Oireachtas committee. Chief executive Mike Aynsley admitted that the 'lion's share' of the €22 billion being pumped into the state-owned bank would 'never be seen again'. Anglo had turned into a black hole for taxpayers' cash.

Shortly after 9 a.m. on Wednesday, 7 July Sean FitzPatrick stood up to speak in the offices of his solicitor, Willie O'Grady, on Percy Place beside the Grand Canal. To O'Grady's right was Bernard Somers, who was acting as FitzPatrick's financial adviser. 'Clearly today is a particularly sad day for me personally and also for members of my family,' FitzPatrick began. 'There have been seismic happenings in the global economy over the past two years, twenty-four months, but I accept full responsibility for my own ruin, personal and professional, which has left me now facing the real possibility of being made a bankrupt.'

In front of him were some of his many creditors. He expressed deep regret for any losses they would incur due to his inability to repay money he had borrowed. 'Throughout my business dealings, both personal and during my time in Anglo Irish Bank, I acted at all times in good faith and I always believed I was acting properly and prudently,' he said. 'I used my best judgment in my investment decisions and in taking on loan obligations. In consequence you can now understand that I feel an abiding obligation to do whatever I can to minimize losses to my creditors and to maximize the returns from the assets that have survived the collapse of my business ventures.'

O'Grady told the creditors that a major portion of FitzPatrick's assets were shares in Anglo, AIB, Bank of Ireland and other publicly quoted financial institutions, and that the substantial fall in the value of these shareholdings had left FitzPatrick in financial difficulty. His Anglo shares, valued at about €80 million at peak, were now worthless. Incredibly, the meeting was told that FitzPatrick had had credit lines available to him of up to €100 million from banks other than Anglo on the strength of the value of his shareholding in Anglo, AIB and Bank of Ireland.

The meeting was told that FitzPatrick's assets were now valued at €51.2 million, including €8.5 million in investments in property and €35.5 million in shares and financial investments, while his liabilities were €147.9 million. FitzPatrick was €96.7 million in the red – he was bust.

The creditors were asked to vote to make FitzPatrick what is known as 'an arranging debtor', where he would avoid being declared bankrupt in return for selling his assets under a deal agreed with his creditors. O'Grady said that if a deal was agreed FitzPatrick's assets could be sold and the proceeds distributed to creditors within three years. If he was declared bankrupt, it would take between four and seven years before they would receive a payment. Creditors were told that if they accepted a deal, they would receive more than twice what they would get if FitzPatrick was declared bankrupt.

Noel Wall, a senior official at the Revenue Commissioners, asked FitzPatrick what he would live on if creditors accepted his deal and he avoided bankruptcy. Speaking with some hesitation, he replied, 'I will have no source of income other than, you know . . . you will see that my wife will be looking for 50 per cent of the pension and that will be it, unless I can get some work . . . consultancy work.' Under the deal his wife would keep 50 per cent of their family home as well as half his €6.8 million pension.

Some creditors backed FitzPatrick's proposal, but Anglo refused to support it. The bank evidently believed that it would recover more money from FitzPatrick if it chose not to sign up to the deal, though FitzPatrick suspected that the bank refused to vote for it on the grounds that Anglo could not be seen to agree to terms sought by the man who had presided over its collapse. Anglo accounted for 85 per cent of FitzPatrick's unsecured debt of €70 million, which effectively gave it veto power.

The following Monday, 12 July, between the hospital-green walls of Court 11 in the Four Courts, FitzPatrick was declared bankrupt. The hearing took just twelve minutes. The court was told that Anglo was unwilling to accept any settlement proposed by FitzPatrick to avoid bankruptcy. Following the court hearing, the once multimillionaire chief executive and chairman of a bank worth €13 billion at its peak had under the law to disclose he was bankrupt if he wanted to borrow any amount greater than €650. As it stood, his debt to Anglo amounted to €110 million.

FitzPatrick's failed court application gave the outside world a glimpse at the astonishing array of his investments. Most – unsurprisingly, given Anglo's business – were in property, and many in deals led by customers of Anglo and in some cases financed by the bank. He was an investor in Jurys Inns with Derek Quinlan's property investment firm, in a commercial property deal in New York with the Dublin firm Warren Private Clients, and in an office block in London's West End with the Irish property company D2 Private. His other investments ranged from a chain of Irish pubs in the US to a shareholding in Barry O'Callaghan's publishing company EMPG to a chain of golf and country clubs in Britain. He, like the bank he had run for twenty-six years, had been a deal junkie.

On Tuesday, 10 August the European Commission gave the government approval to increase the state aid to Anglo to €24.3 billion. Brussels approved a capital injection of €8.58 billion to cover losses being crystallized by the second tranche of loans being moved to NAMA, at an average discount of 62 per cent. The Commission also approved a €1.4 billion buffer that was needed because of the way Anglo was valuing the bonds issued by NAMA as payment for the loans.

The other Irish banks valued them at 98.5 per cent of their face value. This was the amount they would get from the European Central Bank if they used them as collateral to borrow from the Frankfurt bank's regular lending facility for EU banks. But van Eden believed that the bonds should be valued as the market would value them if they were being traded – he reckoned this was around 85 per cent of their face value.

Anglo's valuation of the NAMA bonds made the bank's balance sheet look even worse than it otherwise would, and caused consternation at the Department of Finance and the National Treasury Management Agency. There were heated exchanges between state officials and Anglo; at one meeting in April, a senior Department of Finance official had described van Eden as 'a rotten fish'. But van Eden and the bank refused to bow to pressure to change his accounting treatment and complained to the Central Bank about the pressure being exerted.

During the row over the valuation of the NAMA bonds, Anglo's chairman Alan Dukes told Lenihan that the bank had received advice from accountancy firm Deloitte about how similar state-backed bonds were valued internationally. The firm had approached its consultants in the UK and the US to seek out comparisons, he said. Lenihan reacted angrily, and arguably with an element of paranoia, saying he was not going to take account of the views of American and UK consultants whose only interest was making sure that the euro failed. Dukes was stunned that this was Lenihan's reason for not taking the advice seriously but didn't feel he was in a position to question the minister, who was in effect the bank's sole shareholder.

The rising cost of Anglo and the continuing uncertainty around the final bill pushed up the state's borrowing costs in the debt markets in the second half of August. On 25 August Standard and Poor's said that the cost of bailing out the Irish banks could reach €45–50 billion and that Anglo alone could account for up to €35 billion of this. Having fallen in the weeks after the Greek debt crisis in May, the interest rate paid by the state on its debt rose sharply again to 5.6 per cent, or about 3.5 percentage points above the equivalent German bonds. The latter figure was known as the 'spread' – a barometer for how risky Ireland was perceived in the markets compared to the country perceived to be the safest in the eurozone. The bigger the spread, the more trouble Ireland was in.

Any increase in the government's borrowing costs meant an increase in the borrowing costs of the banks: the two were inextricably linked as a result of the state's bank guarantee. This meant that the banks were in effect frozen out of the debt markets. There were only two places that they could turn to keep them in funds through the end of September: the European Central Bank or, in more desperate circumstances, the Irish Central Bank, which has the ability to provide emergency lending. While the Irish Central Bank loans were ultimately coming from the ECB and being signed off in Frankfurt, borrowing from the Central Bank in Dublin was viewed as a sign that a bank had exhausted the vast amount of eligible loans that the ECB would approve as collateral for its own loans.

Anglo's half-year results to the end of June 2010, announced on 31 August, showed that the bank had lost €5.5 billion in deposits in the first half of the year. Anglo also reported a record Irish corporate loss for a six-month period, having lost €8.2 billion in the first half of the year. It had broken its own record.

The results confirmed that Anglo was the country's running sore. Anglo had become 'systemically destructive of Ireland's capacity to recover and to restore its banking system', according to Labour Party finance spokeswoman Joan Burton, one of the most outspoken critics of Brian Lenihan's banking policy. 'Anglo Irish is not just the biggest bank failure in Irish economic history, either before or since Independence, it has also turned out to be one of the biggest corporate failures anywhere in the world,' she said.

Presenting the results, van Eden gave a plain-spoken account of how Anglo had come to rack up such large losses. 'There was no substance behind the borrowers,' he said. 'They had nothing but the collateral [property assets] they were providing. There was no equity in the system. They took all the equity out of deals and replenished it in new deals. It was one big leveraged play. It was one big Ponzi scheme.'

Aynsley again defended the bank's plan to split Anglo into a good bank and a bad bank, saying that this was the lowest-cost option. He said that the bank would be no more than 20 per cent of its original size and that it would eventually be sold off or merged with another bank. 'The bank is effectively being closed,' he said. But what Aynsley didn't know at the time was that the National Treasury Management Agency, assisted by the Central Bank, was working on an alternative plan for Anglo behind the scenes.

Around the end of August the NTMA privately drafted a brief proposal to split Anglo into an asset-recovery bank, which would wind down the remaining €36 billion in loans over a long period of time, and a funding bank aimed at preventing the withdrawal of about €54 billion in deposits and other funding such as bonds that would be lost if the bank was closed over time in a straightforward wind-down. If Anglo were to lose this funding, the government would have to step in, and with the country's public finances in disarray it could not afford to cover this all at once. Under the NTMA's plan, which it worked on with the Central Bank, there would be no good bank as the new management wanted. Privately, the NTMA and Central Bank had concerns that the new team at Anglo was approaching this problem bank in the wrong way, looking to carve out a new bank rather than running down an old one, and this was a factor behind the new plan. The European Commission had signalled that it would not be willing to approve further state aid for a bank that it believed had no viable future and whose proposals to create a new good bank were not plausible. There was also a (rather unfair) sense within the Commission that the same villains were still running the bank.

The first Anglo heard of this was on 7 September, when William Beausang, a senior official in the banking policy division at the Department of Finance, told Aynsley that the department had submitted the asset recovery/funding bank plan to the Commission the previous day as an alternative to the bank's own good bank/bad bank proposal. Aynsley and his colleague were furious. 'We can't let the camel's nose into the tent,' van Eden told colleagues, citing the old Arab proverb made famous by US senator Barry Goldwater; this was his way of saying that the bank should dismiss the idea immediately before it took hold. But it was too late. Lenihan announced the plan the following day. The minister could not say at the announcement how much this new approach would cost or provide any detail as to how it would work.

Joan Burton described Lenihan's latest plan for Anglo as having been 'cobbled together' and said it failed to clarify matters. 'Having spent two years insisting that Anglo must continue in its present form, the government has finally abandoned their failed policy,' she said. 'Yet, even as they make a U-turn, the announcement has left a whole series of questions unanswered about the future of Anglo at a time when the markets urgently require clarity from the Irish government.'

Burton was right: the Anglo plan was cobbled together at the last minute in an attempt to reassure the markets that the government had a final and definitive plan for Anglo. The government believed that the markets just wanted to know that it had a solution for Anglo; but the markets were not satisfied.

'Our timing was poor on the Anglo announcement,' said a senior source closely involved in devising the plan. 'There was a half-announcement at the start of September . . . Sometimes when you have just managed to get the majority decision, you are afraid that if you don't announce it quickly it will unwind. We should have taken more time on it. We had a general agreement but we didn't have our ducks in a row.'

The absence of any costings in the government's new plan for Anglo ensured that it failed to reassure the markets. The following week Ireland's borrowing costs soared past the 6 per cent mark. This was disastrous for the banks, which couldn't raise funding to repay the bonds falling due at the end of September. The NTMA came up with a novel approach, suggesting to Anglo that the bank issue bonds to itself and then go to the European Central Bank to exchange them for cash. Anglo had run out of eligible collateral that it could use to borrow from the ECB and was borrowing heavily from the exceptional liquidity assistance (ELA) facility at the Irish Central Bank. Under the ECB's lending rules, state-guaranteed bonds were eligible as collateral for loans so it had to provide the loans if the banks offered the bonds as security. Privately the ECB was uncomfortable with the idea of banks that had no obvious future issuing bonds to themselves to serve as collateral for borrowing: Irish Nationwide had raised €4 billion in this manner in September 2008.

Anglo inquired in the marketplace whether 'own-use' bonds were common. They weren't, the bank was told, according to a source with first-hand knowledge of how the international debt markets operate. 'It was a symptom of everything coming to an end,' this source says. 'It was dangerous for the ECB to allow it because you are pretending that you have a lot of collateral when you don't.' In the end Anglo decided against the self-issued bonds gambit.

At this stage, in terms of GDP Ireland accounted for just 2 per cent of the eurozone economy, yet the country's banks were drawing close to 25 per cent of ECB funding available to banks in the currency bloc. Central Bank governor Patrick Honohan later described this to the author in an interview for the *Irish Times* as 'a huge, almost unprecedented level of support to the financial system of a single country'.

But the borrowing didn't stop there. Irish banks drew on emergency loans under the ELA facility at the Irish Central Bank, which accepted certain forms of collateral, such as commercial property loans, that the ECB didn't accept. ELA borrowing by the banks surged from €14 billion to €21 billion.

ELA was, as its name suggested, for exceptional use only and borrowing from it had to be signed off by the ECB. It was backed by what were believed to be good loans and valuable property assets that the Central Bank claimed were worth well in excess of the loans that it had provided. So it felt it was covered. Ultimately, if it wasn't, there was a guarantee from the government – however weak that might be – that the Central Bank would be repaid.

Anglo drew heavily on ELA loans as it had less collateral eligible for ECB loans than the other banks. The loans helped Anglo repay almost €8 billion to senior bondholders, who received 100 per cent of their money despite the disintegration of the bank they had lent to.

The government was now at odds with the ECB over what to do with Anglo. Ireland couldn't afford the upfront cost of shutting Anglo, Lenihan told the *Irish Times* economics editor Dan O'Brien in an extended interview conducted in March 2011 for a BBC radio documentary aired the following month, so the government's policy was to spread the loss over as long a future period as possible. 'This has always been the big difficulty with Anglo,' said Lenihan, 'that this particular meteorite grew so large that it became a threat to the sovereign and to the banking system in Ireland.' Lenihan's interview with O'Brien was his last major public statement before he died on 10 June after losing an eighteen-month battle with pancreatic cancer.

While liquidity was a growing concern through September, the solvency of the banks once again became an issue as the NAMA valuations on the second and third tranche of loans started emerging in August and September. They revealed the full extent of the massive losses on the land and development loans and the speculative property mania that had gripped Ireland. The discount on Anglo's loans had jumped from 55 per cent in the first tranche to 62 per cent in the second tranche. The valuations of loans in the third tranche were not much better.

The devastating analysis by NAMA meant that the capital bill set by the Central Bank's stress test of the banks in March 2010 was proving woefully inadequate. The €32 billion for the banks – and €22 billion for Anglo – would not be enough. The government would have to try to draw yet another line under the banking crisis.

Before sunrise on Thursday, 30 September, Dublin City Council's road-sweepers were still cleaning the cobbled streets around Temple Bar below the imposing Central Bank building on Dame Street when a small group of financial reporters were shown through the back entrance of the Central Bank and up to a boardroom on the seventh floor. On the table lay the final estimate of how much Anglo Irish Bank would cost the Irish people.

The new head of financial regulation at the Central Bank, Matthew Elderfield, and his team had assessed the capital requirements for all the Irish banks. (The government had tried to correct the mistakes of the banking crisis and the woeful supervision of the banks by rehousing the Financial Regulator within the Central Bank.) Elderfield estimated that, based on the discounts NAMA was applying to Anglo's loans, the government would have to pump €29.3 billion into the bank, and that this could rise to €34.3 billion if the commercial property market failed to recover for ten years. Previous estimates on the upfront cost of the bank had put the figure at €1.5 billion in December 2008, €4 billion in May 2009 and €22 billion in March 2010. None of the figures was nearly big enough. This was confirmation that Anglo required the biggest bailout in the world relative to the size of the bank – 30 per cent of the size of its balance sheet. (The next biggest was the German government's bailout of Hypo Real Estate, which amounted to 15 per cent of its balance sheet.)

Central Bank governor Patrick Honohan described the sums involved in propping up Anglo as 'colossal', saying that the €29.3 billion being pumped into Anglo was 'essentially lost money'. The aim of the announcement, the fourth official announcement of a recapitalization of the banks, was to put a final cost on Anglo and the other banks. The media dubbed the day 'Black Thursday'. The overall capital bill facing the banks was €46 billion and possibly as high as €51 billion.

The higher cost of the banks put even more pressure on the government to show that it could put the country's financial house in order. But the markets were not optimistic about this. Over the two years to August 2010 the state had taken €14.5 billion out of the economy by way of tax increases and spending cuts, and it hoped to save a further €7.5 billion over four years of further harsh budgets. But its projections were based on the international economy recovering more quickly and robustly than was generally expected. The government's forecasts were seen as too optimistic.

Honohan realized this, and during August he wrote to Lenihan warning him that the government would need to consider far more severe measures to get the public finances back on track. 'Your numbers are wrong,' Lenihan told Honohan, according to the governor's account of their exchange during a discussion on *Tonight with Vincent Browne* on 10 June 2011 to mark the death of the politician. Honohan hinted at his concerns about the need for further budgetary measures publicly in a speech on 20 September, when he said that the government's multi-year plan to get the public deficit back to 3 per cent of GDP – the limit set by the European Union – by 2014 needed 'explicit reprogramming'.

The ECB also wanted the government to act faster and go further in fixing the state finances. A senior member of the ECB's executive board, Lorenzo Bini Smaghi, told the *Irish Times* in January 2011 that the bank's president Jean-Claude Trichet had told Cowen and Lenihan several times privately during September and October 2010 that they needed to bring forward the next budget from the scheduled date in December as market confidence was draining from Ireland, but that they had refused.

The cost of Anglo was pushing Ireland's deficit to a staggering 32 per cent of GDP for 2010, more than ten times the EU limit. Honohan and the government kept pointing out that this included the one-off cost of Anglo and asserting that the banking bailouts were 'manageable'. But the ECB was 'becoming hostile', as Lenihan later put it, to the growing borrowing by the Irish banks from Frankfurt.

In September the NTMA cancelled the monthly state bond auctions due to Ireland's high cost of borrowing: Ireland would not be borrowing any money that month. Lenihan said that the state was funded up to the

middle of 2011, but officials knew that they would have to return to the
bond markets – or find some other source of borrowings – sooner than
that.

On 24 September David Drumm's lawyers in Dublin, Eversheds O'Donnell
Sweeney, wrote to Anglo's lawyers, McCann FitzGerald. The bank's case
against Drumm to recover €8.5 million in loans was due to begin on 26
October. Drumm's solicitors made one final offer on his behalf to try to get
Anglo to call off its action: Drumm would hand over all his assets, excluding personal items such as clothes and jewellery, but including his €1
million half-share in the house in Malahide, the property in Cape Cod and
a further €200,000 to cover a half-share in his Boston home bought with his
wife's money in January 2010. He also offered the bank his €5.4 million
pension, from which he would be entitled to draw €271,000 a year from the
age of fifty-five, some eleven years hence. Drumm also offered to drop his
counter-claim of €2.6 million. His lawyers said that the offer would be on
the table for just fourteen days. The ball was in Anglo's court.

The bank had reservations about the offer. Rules on accessing pensions
were tight and the bank felt that it would not be able to access the full €5.4
million as there would be a tax charge if the pension fund was raided before
Drumm's retirement. Overall, Anglo felt that the settlement would leave
the bank with a €4 million shortfall on the €8.5 million that Drumm owed
the bank. The bank also wanted Drumm to agree to cooperate with the
inquiries into the bank as part of the settlement and agree a deal to pay any
outstanding debts following the sale of assets from any future income that
he made. Drumm's side believed that the bank was pursuing him for political reasons rather than on commercial grounds of getting the best deal for
the state.

At 10 a.m. on Thursday, 14 October, with no deal in prospect, Drumm
filed a voluntary petition to declare himself bankrupt in a Boston court. He
could not afford the legal fees involved in fighting a prolonged court action
with his former bank in the High Court in Dublin, and bankruptcy in the
US was a far less punishing process than in Ireland. While it was likely to
take at least seven years for Sean FitzPatrick to emerge from bankruptcy in
Ireland, it would be highly unusual for Drumm's bankruptcy to last any
longer than five years in the US.

Records filed in the Massachusetts bankruptcy court showed that
Drumm had assets of $13.9 million (€9.9 million) and liabilities of $14.2
million (€10.1 million), including the €8.5 million owing to Anglo. He was

earning about $9,400 a month and spending about $10,600. Later filings would show that he had earned €12 million in the years from 2004 to 2009. Such sums made him a figure of public hate: he had earned and spent millions at a time when Anglo was making decisions that would eventually kill the bank and cost the country a fortune. Drumm's refusal to return to Ireland to assist in the Garda and Director of Corporate Enforcement investigations into Anglo made him even more of a villain in the eyes of the public.

The court records showed that as well as a property in the upmarket resort town of Chatham on Cape Cod, valued at $5.9 million, and the Malahide house, valued at $2.9 million, Drumm also owned a house near his childhood home in Skerries, which was rented out to his sister, Susan. He had surrendered a 2011 SUV valued at $64,000 and a 2010 Mercedes Sedan worth $47,000 just days after being declared bankrupt. The requirements of the bankruptcy filing were so thorough that Drumm even had to list among his personal property the Drumm family dog, which he valued at $1. He also included books, CDs and iPods worth $500, his watch, clothing, racing bike and a set of golf clubs. On top of his €8.5 million debts at Anglo, Drumm had loans with four other banks, three in the US, totalling €1.6 million, and owed €46,000 on various credit cards.

On Tuesday, 16 November Drumm walked up the street to the John W. McCormack Post Office and Court House in downtown Boston for the first meeting of his creditors since he filed for bankruptcy. It was also his first public appearance since 3 December 2008, when he had presented the bank's annual results at Heritage House. A scrum of Irish and US journalists, photographers and cameramen had gathered to greet the man who had run the world's rottenest bank. 'I am not going to comment to the media at all today,' he said, entering the building.

The hearing lasted just fifteen minutes and was dominated by a row between lawyers for the trustee appointed to oversee Drumm's bankruptcy, and Anglo's lawyers. The bank wanted to put in its own trustee to manage the bankruptcy. The appointed trustee, Kathleen Dwyer, refused to step down, and even filed a lawsuit against the bank claiming that it had acted fraudulently in changing Drumm's €7.65 million loan for share-buying from being secured only on the shares to giving the bank full recourse against him personally. The spat came to nothing, and Anglo eventually accepted Dwyer's appointment.

Following the hearing, Drumm left, entering one of the lifts to make his way out. A group of journalists made a dash for it. A confined space like that was the perfect place to put a few questions to him and ten floors would give them time. As the last few reporters crammed into the packed lift, Drumm joked: 'There are only so many journalists you can fit in an elevator.'

There was only time for a few questions. He just shook his head at each of them.

By the start of October Ireland was at the centre of the eurozone debt crisis. The soaring cost of the bank bailouts announced on 30 September was to blame. The euro was coming under pressure and the price that investors demanded to lend to Ireland continued rising.

On 18 October the German chancellor Angela Merkel and the French president Nicolas Sarkozy announced at a meeting in the French seaside resort of Deauville that from 2013 any future rescues of euro countries should involve losses being passed on to bondholders – investors who had lent money to the sovereign states. The German and French leaders were playing to their electorates at home, stressing that countries could not expect to be bailed out by Europe without lenders to those countries taking some of the pain.

The statement deepened the crisis, increasing borrowing costs for Ireland and other heavily indebted EU countries. It extinguished any possible chance of Ireland entering the debt markets again to borrow before its cash started running out through the first half of 2011.

'Deauville was the final kick in the bollocks,' says a senior government official. 'It was a perfectly rational thing to say at absolutely the wrong time.'

Discussions among government and Central Bank officials started turning from national solutions that could fix the deteriorating financial situation to possible international options such as an external bailout. By the end of October alarm bells were ringing at the ECB. Not only had Irish bank borrowings from Frankfurt soared to €130 billion – an increase of €45 billion in just two months – but the banks were also borrowing heavily from the exceptional liquidity assistance facility at the Irish Central Bank, which had now advanced €34 billion, an increase of €20 billion in just two months. Anglo was responsible for most of this increase, but the two big banks were also suffering greater levels of lost deposits and funding as customers and bondholders withdrew their money.

On Wednesday, 3 November the government announced that it would hold the long-delayed Donegal by-election later that month, which had the potential to whittle down even further the government's slender three-seat majority. Political instability fed financial volatility. Government borrowing costs soared to 7.45 per cent for ten-year loans as the risk premium that investors demanded to hold Irish debt over the benchmark German bonds soared past 5 per cent. Passing this level triggered automatic sell-offs of Irish government and bank debt by many investors.

The following day, acknowledging that there would be slower economic growth over the medium to long term, the government announced more severe budgetary cuts and tax increases. The savings targeted under a revised four-year economic plan were doubled to €15 billion, with €6 billion of that in the first year, double the €3 billion previously planned. But this still wouldn't be enough to convince the international markets that Ireland could survive without outside loans. The cost of the banks was causing a massive strain on the government's position.

On 8 November Morgan Kelly published an article in the *Irish Times* flagging up the likelihood of further massive losses at the Irish banks relating to mortgages. He also predicted that the government would have to take an external bailout. 'During September, the Irish Republic quietly ceased to exist as an autonomous fiscal entity, and became a ward of the European Central Bank,' he wrote. He put the eventual cost of the bank bailouts at €70 billion. (Again, he would be proven right: at the time of writing the figure stood at exactly that.)

Ireland had faced a painful choice of either imposing a resolution on banks that were too big to save and forcing losses on bondholders or becoming insolvent, Kelly said, and the government had chosen the latter. 'Sovereign nations get to make policy choices, and we are no longer a sovereign nation in any meaningful sense of that term,' wrote Kelly. 'From here on, for better or worse, we can only rely on the kindness of strangers.'

Honohan believes that Kelly's article added one percentage point to the Irish spread over German debt as it presented to international readers a scenario wherein they might not be repaid – a striking claim about the influence of a single newspaper article, though of course unprovable. All forces were, in any case, pushing in the same direction. On 10 November the interest rate for Irish government ten-year loans reached 8.9 per cent, pushing the spread over German debt to 6.5 percentage points.

European leaders met on the fringes of the G20 meeting of the biggest industrial countries in Seoul on 11 and 12 November to discuss the growing EU debt crisis and whether Ireland would have to be bailed out. Irish government borrowing costs soared over 9 per cent on Thursday, 11 November, pushing them to their highest levels since Ireland joined the euro. The leaders meeting in Seoul expressed fears that the failure to deal with the Irish banking crisis could topple other countries and ultimately the currency.

'It was made very clear to the Irish finance minister that it is not just about Ireland,' Germany's deputy finance minister Jörg Asmussen later told *Irish Times* economics editor Dan O'Brien in an interview for his April 2011 documentary for the BBC. 'It was made very clear that his decision has an influence on the economic well-being of other parts of the euro-zone. The functioning of the currency union was at stake.'

On Friday, 12 November the Reuters news wire reported in a story written by one of its correspondents in Brussels that Ireland was in talks to receive emergency funding from the European Union. ECB officials in Frankfurt were also briefing that Ireland should seek outside help to rescue its banks and contain a debt crisis. That day, ECB president Jean-Claude Trichet wrote to Lenihan to express his concern at the high level of borrowing by the Irish banks from Frankfurt and asked whether Ireland would be seeking a bailout – the first top-level acknowledgement that this was a very real possibility.

Cowen rejected the wire reports that the government would be applying for a bailout from the EU, but in the background Irish officials were having technical discussions about how the government would go about applying for one.

On the same day Bank of Ireland said it had lost €10 billion in deposits over August and September. The following week, AIB reported that it had lost €13 billion since the start of the year, €12 billion since June. Anglo had also suffered deposit withdrawals of about €12 billion since the start of the year. This slow-motion run on the Irish banks was turning out to be almost as dramatic as the September 2008 crisis. The big difference this time was that the banks had the benefit of a state guarantee that could at least let them borrow readily from the ECB.

Over the weekend of 13 and 14 November, various factions within the ECB started a behind-the-scenes lobbying campaign to force Ireland into accepting a bailout. Journalists were briefed around Europe by senior figures at the ECB that Ireland would need a bailout to restore confidence in the Irish banking system. Lenihan would later accuse members of the ECB executive of 'betrayal' and criticize Central Bank governors who sat on the ECB governing council for the 'damaging' manner in which they briefed some sections of the media about Ireland's problems. The Irish Central Bank took a similarly dim view of the ECB briefings.

On Sunday, 14 November two government ministers, Dermot Ahern and Noel Dempsey, came out publicly to describe reports about Ireland being in talks for a bailout as 'fiction'. The government was sticking with its four-year budgetary plan, they said. Ahern said that he had been briefed by the Taoiseach and the Minister for Finance that talk of a bailout was unfounded. The disclosure in the following weeks that there were discussions on a possible bailout already going on in the background left the two senior Fianna Fáil politicians deeply embarrassed.

The following Monday ECB vice-president Vitor Constâncio startled reporters when he gave an unexpected briefing in which he said that the European Financial Stability Facility, the €440 billion fund created by the EU to bail out distressed countries, could be used by Ireland to prop up its banks. 'The Irish state is financed until part of next year, but it is also a problem of the banks that are at the centre of problems in Ireland and considerations have to be pondered,' he said. Asked would the ECB support an application by the Irish government to borrow from the facility, Constâncio replied, 'Yes, of course.'

On the Tuesday, Lenihan attended a meeting of EU finance ministers in Brussels. He was put under pressure by the ECB and the German government to say publicly that Ireland was applying for a bailout but he declined, saying he had no mandate from the government to make an application. Privately, government ministers were concerned that Ireland's corporation tax rate of 12.5 per cent could be at risk in negotiations, so Lenihan held out until it was taken off the table.

EU finance ministers agreed that a team from the IMF, the EU Commission and the ECB should be sent to Dublin for a short and intensive fact-finding mission to assess Ireland's fiscal problems, gauge the depth of the black hole in the banks and lay the groundwork for a bailout.

The catalyst for the bailout was the massive and growing funding crisis that the Irish banks were facing. Ajai Chopra, the leader of the IMF delegation, would tell Dan O'Brien: 'What we were trying to do was avoid a situation where you had a fully fledged bank run. The banks were already in cardiac arrest. We had a common purpose of making sure that what was already a difficult situation did not become totally chaotic. We were prepared for pretty much any eventuality at that point.'

But the IMF was not the driving force behind the bailout; the ECB was, according to Lenihan in his March 2011 interview with O'Brien. Lenihan later reflected that the key point was that 'people sitting in Frankfurt simply didn't trust the Irish government to implement a bank restructuring that was proportionate to the scale of the crisis'. Lenihan also said that he did not feel he had to make public his back-room discussions with Trichet on a bailout. 'We were simply having exploratory official discussions and I don't think that would be an appropriate time to alert the public generally as to the fact we were having such discussions. I'd have weakened our diplomatic hand in that regard,' he told O'Brien. The day after Lenihan's trip to Brussels, government ministers and officials were still briefing that a bailout was not inevitable.

Late on the night of Wednesday, 17 November Patrick Honohan was in his room at the Steigenberger Frankfurter Hof Hotel, not far from the ECB's headquarters in Frankfurt. He received a text from a friend asking whether he had seen the editorial in the following day's *Financial Times* which had just been published on the newspaper's website. He accessed the *FT*'s website on his iPhone. The editorial said that the EU Commission should start preparing for a series of bank runs across Europe. Honohan was uneasy with the impression given by the article that nothing was being done to address the Irish situation and this was having a damaging effect on Ireland and the Irish banks.

Honohan knew that there had been preliminary discussions with the IMF on a possible bailout and he felt that the public needed to be told that a bailout was likely, particularly with a large team from the 'troika' of the EU, IMF and ECB arriving at the Central Bank the following morning. He slept on it, and woke feeling that he had to do something. 'I thought, here's a situation where there seems to be considerable public anxiety,' he told Dan O'Brien. 'I know what's happening, I'd better get that out there.'

Early that Thursday morning the Central Bank governor called RTE and said that he wanted to go on *Morning Ireland*, the most listened-to radio programme in Ireland. During his interview with Rachel English, he told listeners that he expected talks with the EU, IMF and ECB to result in the government accepting a 'very substantial' loan running to 'tens of billions': 'The IMF and the European Union Commission and the ECB would not send a large team if they didn't believe, first of all, that they could agree to a package, that there is a [loans] programme that is fully acceptable to them,' he said.

The government was furious that Honohan had dismissed Lenihan and his ministerial colleagues outright. Later that day, the Taoiseach told the Dáil that he did not share Honohan's views on the figure or that there would be a bailout, saying his comments were premature ahead of the negotiations. 'The governor gave his view,' he said, curtly. 'He is entitled to give his view.'

The public and media overwhelmingly welcomed Honohan's intervention and attacked the government for its refusal to come clean about the bailout negotiations, but in a controversial and influential May 2011 article Morgan Kelly gave a dissenting analysis. 'Rarely has a finance minister been so deftly sliced off at the ankles by his central bank governor,' Kelly wrote of the events of 18 November, taking the view that until Honohan went on the radio Ireland was in a stronger negotiating position than has been generally accepted – and that the bailout eventually agreed was ruinous to Ireland.

On Sunday, 21 November the government formally applied for a financial aid package.

The government's policy of continuously deferring the banking problem had failed. The state simply didn't have the cash to pay for the banking bailouts. Anglo accounted for two-thirds of the latest €51 billion bill. On 1 September 2010 a reporter for the *New York Times* asked in an article about Anglo: 'Can one bank bring down a country?' He got his answer three months later.

The details of the bailout were announced on Sunday, 28 November. It involved a loan package of €85 billion, of which €35 billion was earmarked specifically for the banks. Some €17.5 billion would come from the National Pension Reserve Fund, which had already been raided to recapitalize Bank of Ireland and AIB in 2009. The IMF would provide €22.5 billion and the European Financial Stability Mechanism (an EU fund) €22.5 billion. The remaining €22.5 billion would come from the European Financial Stability Fund, which was set up by eurozone countries after the Greek bailout of May 2010, and bilateral loans from the UK, Denmark and Sweden. The UK's contribution was about €3.8 billion.

The bailout addressed one of the three problems at the banks – the need for more capital to reassure markets. But it contained no detail about how the Irish banks would shed excess loans and other assets of €72 billion to make them self-sufficient again or a long-term funding facility to soothe investor concerns that the ECB would not pull its loans.

Even among observers who broadly supported the idea of a bank guarantee in 2008 as a means of keeping the Irish banking system from running out of liquidity, the blanket nature of the guarantee – covering not just ordinary customer deposits but also dated subordinated bonds held by large financial institutions that carried a risk premium – was controversial. Even within financial markets, the Irish government's view that investors should not lose a penny on their Irish bank bonds frequently came in for criticism.

In the pecking order of who should take losses first in the event of a bank failure, shareholders come first, followed by undated subordinated bondholders, dated subordinated bondholders, and then senior bondholders and depositors. The view in the markets and within official circles across the eurozone was that no losses could under any circumstances be inflicted on senior bondholders and depositors – they were regarded as untouchable because of the dangerous domino effect it might have across Europe if these kinds of investors and bank customers were not going to be protected in full. Merrill Lynch had advised the government in the days leading up to the bank guarantee in September 2008 that dated subordinated bondholders had to be protected as there were cross defaults between these bonds and the senior bonds at the banks. This meant that if a bank didn't pay out on a dated subordinated bond, then a senior bondholder could claim that there had been a default by the bank and demand immediate repayment in full. But it was hard for many observers to understand why financial institutions that had taken the risk of lending money to Irish banks should be so thoroughly protected against losses.

By September 2010 the two-year guarantee had lapsed and dated subordinated bondholders were no longer protected. Given that these lenders were paid a premium for their loans, it was accepted that the government could force losses on these investors as they had taken a risk in lending to the Irish banks. But that was the extent of the so-called burden-sharing with bank bondholders that was considered possible.

There was plenty of senior debt in the banks that was unsecured – meaning that it was not supported by bank loans as collateral as 'covered bonds' would be – and fell outside the government guarantee. By November 2010 there was about €16 billion of this kind of senior bank debt, including almost €4 billion at Anglo.

The government had continuously argued in public that senior bonds could not be touched, either by forcing losses on these lenders or by seeking voluntary deals to buy back their debt at a discount. Lenihan had argued that this would ruin the government's ability to borrow in the future – there was no way the state could expect these lenders to take losses one day and then ask them for new loans the next.

But when it became clear in mid-November 2010 that Ireland would be taking a bailout and would not be borrowing in the debt markets for some time, Lenihan argued in his private discussions with Trichet and the IMF that senior bondholders in Anglo and Irish Nationwide should face substantial haircuts. This would save the state some of the costs of bailing out these two institutions. The IMF appeared to be for the idea, but the ECB was strongly against it.

Morgan Kelly's May 2011 *Irish Times* article, citing 'a source who was there', gave an account of the reaction to the proposal among the central players when the idea was floated. Kelly asserted that the IMF, which believes that 'lenders should pay for their stupidity before it has to reach into its pocket', presented the Irish government with a plan to haircut €30 billion of unguaranteed bonds by two-thirds on average. Lenihan was 'overjoyed', according to Kelly's account, telling the IMF: 'You are Ireland's salvation.'

According to Kelly's account, the proposal was torpedoed by US treasury secretary Timothy Geithner, who 'believes bankers take priority over taxpayers'. Kelly wrote that the only one to speak up for the Irish plan was UK chancellor George Osborne, but Geithner got his way.

A senior US government official denied Kelly's account, but there is no doubt that senior European figures were strongly opposed to burning senior bondholders who had lent money to the Irish banks. 'It was coming back from the highest levels that no we couldn't do this – we could not put this question mark around the European bond markets,' says a senior Irish government source. Opponents warned that doing so would lead to a European banking crisis far worse than what happened after the failure of Lehman Brothers. 'If you burn senior bondholders, the whole market will seize up,' says one senior European banker. 'It is like throwing sand into the engine . . . If you do that, then it will be the ECB that needs to be recapitalized.'

We'll never know what would have happened if Ireland had ever seriously attempted to compel senior bondholders to take losses on their investments in Irish banks. What is clear is that every key event from the guarantee in September 2008 to the EU–IMF bailout in November 2010 was structured in such a way as to make Irish taxpayers responsible for the massive private losses of the banks and for protecting the vast majority of the institutions and investors that lent to them.

The conditions of the bailout involved a real loss of sovereignty for Ireland. This spelt the end of the government. Tensions between Cowen and the Green Party leader, John Gormley, ran high over the onerous terms of the EU–IMF bailout and the interest rate of 5.8 per cent being charged. 'This is the Versailles Treaty and what we need is the Marshall Plan,' Gormley told Cowen in private on the night the EU–IMF deal was agreed. 'Don't be using language like that,' Cowen responded angrily. The following day, Monday, 22 November, the junior coalition party announced that it wanted an election in the second half of January. Cowen acquiesced, saying that there would be an election in the New Year once the 7 December budget changes had been passed into law.

20.   Endgames

April 2011 – Anglo's cost to the State: €29.3 billion to €34.3 billion

Under the terms of the bailout, the government would be forced to put a bullet in Anglo once and for all.

Aynsley's management team set about drafting a new plan, to be submitted jointly with Irish Nationwide, to run down the two institutions over time. Even after transferring €36 billion in land, development and associated property loans to NAMA, Anglo would still have 11,000 loans and 6,100 loan accounts of less than €5 million to work out over a ten-year wind-down. This included 7,000 accounts in Ireland, 2,500 accounts in the UK and 1,500 accounts in the US. Behind each of those loans was an asset, in most cases either a property or a business, which had to be managed carefully to get the best return for the taxpayer. This was why Aynsley and his team at Anglo believed that it would take many years to close the bank down and why they had felt that the best way to do this was through a good bank/bad bank split.

But the scale of the business left behind didn't matter. The desire among government authorities to shut Anglo down overrode all other considerations.

At the end of 2010 Lenihan published a far-reaching piece of legislation. The Credit Institutions (Stabilisation) Bill empowered the government to break up, merge and close banks; sack managers, stop bonuses and overrule shareholders; and jail bankers or anyone else for up to three years or fine them €100,000 if they disclosed anything that the minister planned to do under the law. The government would use this far-reaching new law to issue the last rites to Anglo.

For the bank's chief financial officer Maarten van Eden, it was the final straw. Among the first acts sanctioned using the law was the sale of Anglo's deposits and the start of the merger and wind-down of Anglo and Irish Nationwide, the country's most toxic banks. Even though van Eden disagreed with the government's plan to close Anglo, this wasn't what bothered him about the act. It was the powers it gave the Minister for Finance over bankers and the Irish banking industry.

Van Eden decided he had had enough – he sat down and penned a letter of resignation to the bank's chairman Alan Dukes and chief executive Mike Aynsley. After noting that he opposed the closing of Anglo and referring to the row over the NAMA bond valuations, he wrote: 'I have great concerns regarding the concentration of power that the new law for the financial sector will put into the hands of the government and I do not think I will want to make myself subservient to it. I have no confidence whatsoever in the ability of the government to do the right thing for the financial sector.'

Van Eden told Aynsley and Dukes that he felt bad about letting the team down. 'But I am convinced it is the right thing to do to accept personal responsibility if the advice one gives is not acted upon,' he said.

The national agenda for the first weeks of 2011 was dominated by the publication of *The FitzPatrick Tapes* by *Sunday Times* business journalists Tom Lyons and Brian Carey. The book, based on seventeen tape-recorded interviews of Sean FitzPatrick conducted by Lyons between January and November 2010, contained the revelation that Brian Cowen had – while Minister for Finance in March 2008 – taken a phone call from Sean Fitz-Patrick about the collapse in Anglo's share price and that he had played golf with FitzPatrick in July 2008 at Druid's Heath, part of the Druid's Glen complex, in Co. Wicklow.

FitzPatrick said that even though he was replaced as chief executive in 2005 by David Drumm, he couldn't abdicate responsibility because he became chairman. 'In a way I was still in a pivotal position to stop it. Cries from me that I wasn't really responsible diminish when you take that stance. I accept that,' he said. He acknowledged that hiding his loans by moving them to Irish Nationwide was 'wrong in hindsight' and a 'mistake' but that 'it does not deserve the odour or the punishment that has been inflicted on me over the last two years'. He claimed that he wasn't aware of 'the funding mountains' facing the bank and that it 'wasn't belted home to the board' until August 2008.

The day after the publication of the book, I contacted David Drumm in Boston to see if he would like to comment on FitzPatrick's views. He agreed to an interview. He took issue with FitzPatrick's characterization of his position as Anglo chairman in 2008 as some kind of back-seat role, leaving the management of the bank to Drumm. This was 'bullshit', said Drumm. He claimed that FitzPatrick began 'interfering' in his management of the bank from late 2007 after problems developed over Sean Quinn's investment in Anglo shares.

Drumm dismissed FitzPatrick's claim that he was not told the names of the Maple Ten clients assembled by the bank to take 10 per cent of the shares held by Quinn at the time of the transaction. 'He absolutely and utterly was told the names – he knew who they were,' Drumm told me, saying that FitzPatrick was given the names as the transaction was being executed in July 2008.

On Friday, 14 January 2011 the *Irish Daily Mail* ran a story on its front page under the headline 'Now Drumm Knifes Cowen'. The story was based on the conference call the previous November involving developer Garrett Kelleher, journalists Bruce Arnold and Jason O'Toole, and Drumm. The newspaper ran Drumm's claim that Cowen asked the NTMA to invest in Anglo and that FitzPatrick was a regular at Cowen's 'kitchen cabinet' – allegations that were subsequently denied by Cowen.

The political fallout from *The FitzPatrick Tapes* was huge. It precipitated the downfall of Brian Cowen, the collapse of the Fianna Fáil–Green coalition and a change of government.

The fall of the government was inevitable following the EU–IMF bailout, but the revelations in *The FitzPatrick Tapes* sparked a series of events – including an unsuccessful challenge to Cowen's leadership of Fianna Fáil, followed by a botched Cabinet reshuffle – that made it impossible for Cowen to hold on any longer.

On Thursday, 20 January Cowen called a general election for 25 February. Two days later he said that he would stand down as leader of Fianna Fáil but remain on as Taoiseach until a new government took power. The Greens pulled out of government the following day.

Micheál Martin subsequently won the leadership battle, but it didn't matter – Fianna Fáil suffered the worst election defeat in the party's history, losing fifty-seven seats as the party's support slumped to just 17 per cent, down from almost 42 per cent at the 2007 general election.

On Tuesday, 8 February the government went to the High Court using the Credit Institutions (Stabilisation) Act to kick-start the transfer of Anglo's deposits to another financial institution, starting the process of winding down the bank. The following day Anglo set another record when it published its unaudited financial results for 2010. The bank announced losses of €17.6 billion for 2010, beating its previous record set a year earlier for the worst losses ever recorded by an Irish company. Customers had withdrawn €16 billion in deposits over the twelve months, including €12 billion in the second half of the year.

Anglo's borrowing from the Irish and European Central Banks had shot up from €23.7 billion to €45 billion over the course of the year to make up the shortfall in the deposits. More worryingly for Ireland's public finances was that €28 billion of the €45 billion had been borrowed under 'special liquidity facilities' – i.e. the ELA facility at the Central Bank.

By February Irish bank borrowings from central banks stood at €187 billion – some €117 billion from the ECB and a further €70 billion from the Irish Central Bank. In May 2011 at the ECB's monthly press conference its president Jean-Claude Trichet said: 'The level of commitment of the euro system to Ireland has absolutely no precedent.'

Anglo by 2010 was a zombie bank, doing no new lending and seeing its loans and deposits moved off its balance sheet, and yet the bank's overheads for the year totalled €354 million, compared with €328 million for Anglo's financial year to September 2008. Included in the 2010 expenses were €27 million paid to staff in redundancy costs. There was another €62 million of one-off costs to outside consultants hired to advise on the bank's multitude of restructuring plans (three of which were rejected or shelved, despite the final one having the support of the Department of Finance), the transfer of loans to NAMA, and 'legacy matters' such as dealing with legal cases involving the bank's murky past and pursuing former directors and irate borrowers over unpaid loans. Millions also had to be spent on updating the bank's haphazard computer systems.

Figures released to the Public Accounts Committee by the government showed that Anglo paid out a total of €98 million to consultants between October 2008 and September 2010. The demise of the bank meant bonanza fees for lawyers, who were paid €41 million, investment bankers (€10 million), accountants (€15 million) and other professionals (€32 million) hired to assist in the restructuring plan and to carry out valuations of properties and loans for the transfers to NAMA. The beneficiaries were the big accountancy firms – KPMG, Ernst & Young, Pricewaterhouse-Coopers and Deloitte; the big Irish law firms – McCann FitzGerald, A&L Goodbody, Arthur Cox and Matheson Ormsby Prentice; and the big investment banks – JP Morgan, Deutsche Bank, Barclays Capital and RBS.

For investment banks, consultants, accountants and lawyers, it was like winning the lottery, with the jackpot paid for by the Irish taxpayer.

On Thursday, 10 February – two days after Anglo issued its unaudited figures – the bank announced the resignation of Maarten van Eden. He had alienated the authorities – at one of the last meetings Dukes had with Lenihan the minister said: 'You have to get rid of that Dutch guy' – but the decision to go was his. Shortly before van Eden's resignation was announced to staff at the bank, he emailed Dukes and Aynsley with further concerns that he had about what was happening at Anglo. In the email, van Eden went further than in his resignation letter the previous December and criticized the state's treatment of the new management team at Anglo and the wider approach to dealing with the banks.

In a wide-ranging attack on the state's handling of Anglo and the banking sector generally, van Eden slammed the authorities for pushing the Irish banks into issuing government-guaranteed bonds to themselves to draw cash from the ECB, saying that this 'increases the essentially unsecured exposure of the ECB to Ireland'. He said that he found it 'shocking' that the government had tapped the National Pension Reserve Fund – the state's nest egg which was originally set up to pay for the pension entitlements of public servants and social welfare payments after 2025 – to bail out Bank of Ireland and AIB and 'shore up the financial sector'.

'Ireland is now in a situation where possibly the entire financial sector will be owned and controlled by government,' said van Eden. 'The government does not have the expertise to run the financial sector. Mind you, nor did the bankers themselves previously.' He also said that the NTMA had 'its fingers in a lot of pies, is conflicted and is a power within the state with insufficient checks' and that the Central Bank should be 'the guardian of the integrity of the financial system but instead is the government's chief provider of cheap funding'.

Two weeks after Anglo announced its results, some €8.6 billion of deposits held by 150,000 customers were transferred out of Anglo to Allied Irish Banks. This marked the beginning of the end of the bank. Some thirty-three years after Sean FitzPatrick took control of Anglo its deposit book – the traditional lifeblood of any bank – was gone.

In a demonstration of just how little banks knew about their customers' dealings with their other banks, AIB found that some of their own indebted customers who had claimed to have no further cash to repay loans had deposits at Anglo.

On Friday, 25 March David Drumm received a letter from Anglo's head of compliance, Michael Deeny. Deeny told Drumm that there had been 'a possible loss of personal data' as a result of a robbery at the private home of a senior Anglo executive on 16 November 2010. The executive, unnamed in the letter, was Mike Aynsley. A laptop, a digital camera and other items had been stolen from the south Dublin house he was renting.

'The laptop in question had password and fingerprint security measures in place to protect against unauthorized third party access but was not fully encrypted,' wrote Deeny. He told Drumm that the laptop contained copies of about seventy emails or attachments and that the computer may have contained 'personal data relating to you'. The material related to the bank's legal action against Drumm.

On 1 April Drumm faced his final meeting of creditors at the Boston court where he had filed for bankruptcy the previous October. The focus of much of the bank's questioning was on his management of Anglo in the run-up to the government guarantee in September 2008 and the bank's nationalization in January 2009.

The bank had escalated its legal battle against Drumm within the bankruptcy proceedings on 14 February, issuing a claim for breach of fiduciary duty against its former chief executive arising from alleged misconduct and deception related to Sean FitzPatrick's hidden loans and the loans to the Maple Ten. The bank said in its lawsuit that it would be seeking damages from Drumm arising from loans to other directors, including the September 2008 loan to former finance director Willie McAteer that was secured on Anglo shares.

For much of the final creditors' hearing on 1 April Drumm was grilled by Anglo's lawyer Kenneth Leonetti. The lawyer alleged that money the former bank boss claimed to have borrowed from his wife was in fact salary and bonuses from Anglo totalling €13 million between 2004 and 2009. Starting in September 2008 – the month of the bank's collapse – Drumm had begun transferring his earnings and property held jointly with his wife Lorraine into her name alone. The transfers totalled $1.6 million, said Anglo's lawyer.

'Mrs Drumm set up her own account for the first time on 24 September 2008 with €150,000 which you transferred,' Leonetti said. 'What was going on in the world?'

'The world was falling apart,' replied Drumm.

'Isn't the real reason you transferred all this money because you wanted to keep it safe from creditors?' Leonetti asked.

'No,' said Drumm. 'It dawned on [me] she didn't know where the money was, so she took a lot of money over.'

The largest transfer was €372,561 from a shared account in AIB in the names of Drumm and his wife to an account at the same bank belonging to his wife on 15 December 2008 – four days before Drumm resigned from Anglo.

The creditors' hearing didn't mark the end of Drumm's trials. After the 1 April hearing, Anglo attempted to stop him being discharged as a bankrupt to fight its lawsuit against him on his stewardship of the bank.

While Drumm was being pursued through the bankruptcy courts in the US, the regulatory body set up by Chartered Accountants Ireland, the body that represented the profession, was also looking at his involvement in Anglo.

The institute's Chartered Accountants Regulatory Board (CARB) had appointed the former Comptroller and Auditor General John Purcell to investigate the roles of Drumm, Sean FitzPatrick, Willie McAteer and Irish Life & Permanent finance director Peter Fitzpatrick in the events preceding the collapse of Anglo. The board wanted to know whether they had broken any of the profession's by-laws. Purcell ruled in December 2010 that the four accountants had a *prima facie* case to answer over what had happened at Anglo.

On 21 March – two weeks before FitzPatrick was to appear before the board at a disciplinary hearing – the matter was adjourned after the Director of Public Prosecutions told CARB that its hearing could prejudice future criminal proceedings if such actions were ever to be taken. The hearings against Drumm, McAteer and Peter Fitzpatrick were also adjourned on 24 March.

Anglo's auditors Ernst & Young, who were also investigated by Purcell, tried to halt the inquiry in the High Court on 15 April 2011, but Ms Justice Mary Irvine ruled against the firm on 13 May. The judge said that the accountancy firm had shown no arguable grounds entitling it to bring proceedings to 'effectively torpedo and thus fatally terminate' Purcell's two-year investigation into the bank.

The investigations into Anglo by the Garda Bureau of Fraud Investigation and Office of the Director of Corporate Enforcement (ODCE) continued to drag on into the first months of 2011, despite the high-profile raid on Anglo's offices in February 2009 and the arrests of Sean FitzPatrick and Willie McAteer in March 2010. (In the autumn of 2010 the Garda added a new strand to its investigation. The new management team had discovered that two unnamed former senior figures at Anglo had allegedly lodged money in the bank's subsidiary in the Isle of Man around 2005 before withdrawing it and then trying to delete all record of the accounts. Information technology and forensic accountancy experts managed to recover the deleted electronic records and examine them. The two former executives were contacted by Garda fraud squad detectives who investigated whether the money had been declared for tax purposes.)

The slow pace of the investigations bothered many, not least the leading judge in the Commercial Court, Mr Justice Peter Kelly. On 10 May 2011 the judge refused to grant a six-month extension to the ODCE's investigation, expressing frustration at the progress of the inquiry. The ODCE sought orders to allow it to retain and deal with material seized in February 2009. It was the sixth time the ODCE had sought these orders. The judge would allow only a two-month extension to hold on to the records.

'An apparent failure to investigate thoroughly yet efficiently and expeditiously possible criminal wrongdoing in the commercial/corporate sectors does nothing to instil confidence in the criminal justice system,' said a frustrated Kelly.

The judge had been told in March 2011 that the investigation into directors' loans at Anglo and Sean FitzPatrick's transferring of loans to Irish Nationwide was 'substantially complete', yet in May 2011 he was told that fifty people still had to be interviewed. Among those was Drumm – the key figure in the Anglo saga – who refused to return to Ireland to be questioned or to assist in the investigations. (The ODCE later said that there were ten witnesses in the Anglo investigation who could be described as 'reluctant'.)

In refusing the extension, Kelly summarized the damage caused by Anglo. Typically, he didn't pull any punches. The collapse of the bank 'had profound and serious consequences for the economic well-being of this state and its citizens', he said. It had 'caused hardship to many small shareholders who invested in it in good faith' and played 'no small part in seriously damaging Ireland's business reputation throughout the world'.

Another legal action that brought Anglo into the court's spotlight was the bank's lawsuit against former board member Tom Browne, who ran the bank's Irish division until his departure from the bank in November 2007. The bank had issued legal proceedings against Browne on 15 October 2010, seeking the recovery of €50 million in loans advanced for property deals in the UK after he left the bank.

Browne's defence was novel. He claimed that 'entirely wrongful and probably unlawful actions' by Anglo and some of its executives ultimately led to the nationalization of the bank in January 2009 which wiped out a large part of his net worth – his shares in Anglo. He cited the concealment of Sean Quinn's shareholding in the bank, the Maple Ten transaction, the Irish Life & Permanent deposits and Anglo's loans to directors. In his affidavit, Browne said that he held 2.4 million shares in Anglo in November 2007 which were worth more than €28 million. He sold about 1 million shares in three tranches between November 2007 and September 2008. The conduct of senior officials at Anglo had 'ultimately proved to be the single largest contributor to the financial difficulties which now afflict this country', he said.

Browne claimed that he had been instrumental in introducing 'a more conservative lending policy' with the bank's Irish division after he took charge of it in 2005 and ran it until late 2007. (During that time he received €8.2 million in salary and benefits from Anglo.) He argued that his conservative approach to banking was 'a source of rancour' within Anglo and that there was a perception the bank was losing market share. He added that he had had a difficult relationship with David Drumm.

In a replying affidavit, Anglo banker Ciaran McAreavey argued that Browne had to take responsibility for the losses on loans agreed under his watch. McAreavey pointed out that the bank's Irish lending grew by 284 per cent from €13 billion to almost €38 billion in the years between September 2004 and September 2007, for most of which time Browne was directly responsible for Irish lending, and that it was on loans advanced during this period that Anglo incurred the heaviest losses.

In legal papers filed in the case, his lawyers claimed that Browne was advised by David Drumm and Pat Whelan at a series of meetings and telephone calls that he should hold his shares and not sell them. He was told that the share price would recover.

Had he been aware of Anglo's 'wrongful, fraudulent and probably unlawful activities' from late 2007 to early 2009 he would not have exercised his share options and he would not have retained his very substantial shareholding, he said in his defence.

Browne's arguments appeared plausible enough to warrant the court granting him wide-ranging discovery over documents at Anglo. On 14 April 2011 Mr Justice Peter Kelly directed the bank to provide sworn information on the loans to Sean Quinn and his family and the Maple Ten deal as well as details concerning the €7.2 billion in deposits moving between Anglo and Irish Life & Permanent in autumn 2008.

★

The fifth attempt at drawing a line under the banking crisis – and the third by the new team at the Central Bank led by governor Patrick Honohan and head of financial regulation Matthew Elderfield – came on 31 March 2011.

The previous recapitalizations of the banks had pushed the running total to €46 billion in September 2010 (and up to €51 billion when a worst-case scenario for Anglo was included), based on the estimated cost of the final loan transfers to NAMA. Honohan and Elderfield now said that the banks would require a further €24 billion, bringing the cost of socializing the private losses of Ireland's financial institutions to a staggering €70 billion. This was almost half the country's economic output in a year and more than double the amount raised in taxes per year.

The recapitalization would push the banks' capital ratios to the highest levels of any banks in the world – a condition of the EU–IMF bailout. The money wouldn't just cover potential losses for highly unlikely future scenarios. It would also be enough to allow the banks to offload €72 billion of loans and other assets to bring them back in line with deposits so they wouldn't be as reliant on outside funding. This was a way of reducing the ECB's exposure to Ireland – one of the reasons for the €85 billion EU–IMF bailout loans. (For the first time in the succession of bank bailouts, Anglo didn't require further capital.)

Announcing the latest bank recapitalization, Minister for Finance Michael Noonan had a pop at the decision of the previous government to tie the state to the banks. 'Tuesday, 30 September, 2008 will go down as the blackest day in Ireland since the Civil War broke out,' he said, referring to the date of the bank guarantee.

On Thursday, 14 April Sean Quinn arrived at Anglo's new head office at Connaught House on Burlington Road in leafy Dublin 4 for a crunch meeting with the bank's management team. Accompanying him were Kevin Lunney and Dara O'Reilly, two of his most trusted managers, both directors of Quinn Group.

They went up the steps to the entrance of the building and walked past the towering statue of Queen Medbh of Connaught who, in Irish mythology, invaded Ulster to capture the great Brown Bull of Cooley. The statue portrays a naked Medbh in a warrior-like pose holding the severed head of the bull. Quinn, an Ulsterman, would learn at his meeting with Anglo that the bank would be cutting off the head of the Quinn Group, removing him from the businesses he set up and built over thirty-eight years.

The bank's top management had moved from the bank's former head office on St Stephen's Green to break from the old regime. They chose the home of Anglo's wealth management division, Connaught House – owned by one of Anglo's biggest customers, Treasury Holdings – as its headquarters.

Quinn and his two managers went up to the fifth floor and were shown into the office of the bank's chief executive Mike Aynsley. Also present were the bank's chairman Alan Dukes and banker Richard Woodhouse, a corporate restructuring expert who managed some of Anglo's biggest and most problematic clients. Woodhouse had been working for months trying to devise a plan that would guarantee the recovery of as much of the €2.88 billion owing by the Quinn family as possible. Realistically, the bank believed that it would recover less than half of this.

Aside from the family's massive debts to Anglo, the Quinn Group owed almost €1.3 billion to banks and bondholders. Sean Quinn had proposed a plan whereby he would repay Anglo in full over seven years if Quinn Insurance remained within the Quinn Group and the ownership of the family. The bank had refused to support it, for three reasons: the Quinn family would remain the owners of the business (a state of affairs the Central Bank would not accept); there would be no interest payments on the €2.88 billion of debt; and the bank would be required to make a cash injection of €650 million. It wasn't a runner.

Quinn had already lost control of the insurance company – traditionally the most profitable part of his business – and was not going to get it back. The joint administrators, who were appointed the previous March after the Central Bank raised concerns about the company's solvency, had put the company on the market. Now Quinn was about to lose control of Quinn Group too.

Prior to the meeting the bank's management had agreed that it would be best if Quinn heard the bad news from an Irishman rather than from Aynsley, an Australian, or Woodhouse, a well-spoken Englishman who wore a pocket handkerchief (and whose father had been commander of the British nuclear submarine fleet), so Dukes was chosen to do all the talking. He told Quinn that the bank would be appointing a share receiver, Kieran Wallace of accountancy firm KPMG, over the Quinn family's ownership in the flagship company, Quinn Group (ROI), that morning. They would also appoint a receiver to the group of companies which held the Quinn family's vast international property portfolio, stretching to Turkey, Ukraine,

Russia and India. It would be business as usual at Quinn's companies but the bank would now be in control rather than Quinn.

Anglo was taking a 75 per cent share of the Quinn Group and the banks and bondholders were taking the other 25 per cent. Quinn was also told that it would be announced later that day that Anglo and US insurance giant Liberty Mutual would be named preferred bidders to take over Quinn Insurance from the administrators.

Quinn was being shut out of the ownership and management of his business empire. Anglo was able to take such a wide-ranging step on the back of legal charges taken against the Quinn children's ownership of the group during the first half of 2008, when the bank lent hundreds of millions of euros to Quinn to help him meet his losses on Anglo shares.

The bankers gave Quinn a proposal document and asked him to take it away to examine it before coming back to the bank to discuss it. It set out a plan to try to reduce his debts.

Quinn, as usual, spoke quietly but defiantly, referring to himself in the third person, as was his habit. He acknowledged again that he had lost €3 billion, mostly on Anglo shares, but he said that no other man in Ireland had created as many jobs in the country as Sean Quinn. He said that his manufacturing and property businesses should not be touched as they were profitable. The international properties were his children's inheritance, he said, and he warned that there would be a hard-fought battle if the bank attempted to take them. He threatened that he would seek legal advice on the bank's appointment of a receiver.

The meeting lasted half an hour. It was obvious to the Anglo management that Quinn wasn't prepared for the events of the day ahead.

Just over an hour later, in the first of a series of statements, Anglo announced that it had taken control of the family's shares in the group. This was followed by statements from the Quinn Group announcing the restructuring and by the Minister for Finance in the newly formed Fine Gael/Labour government, Fine Gael's Michael Noonan, supporting the bank's actions.

The moves against Quinn had kicked off earlier that morning, before his meeting with the bank. At 5.30 a.m. Anglo had dispatched eighty-seven people, including legal and financial representatives, security staff and drivers, to Quinn's offices in Cavan and Fermanagh to issue demand notices for the repayment of some of the family's €2.88 billion loans to the bank and to take control of Quinn's business.

The following Monday Quinn issued a statement saying that the appointment of a receiver to his group was the 'greatest upset' of his business career. He said that mistakes in business should not result in a life sentence – a reference to the whopping personal debts accrued by his family and to the possibility that he might have to endure Ireland's crippling bankruptcy process. He blamed the fact that he had followed the consensus view on the stability of the Irish banks.

'Our mistake was to place an over-reliance on the Irish banking system and the many predictions for continued sustained growth in the Irish economy from some of the country's leading financial services experts,' said Quinn. This statement is at odds with Quinn's own long-held personal conviction that Anglo was under-valued as its share price declined from June 2007 before being wiped out with the nationalization of the bank in January 2009.

On the day of Quinn's statement a large dumper truck was driven into the bollards at the entrance to the group's head office in Derrylin, Co. Fermanagh. A fibre-optic cable running between the head office and the nearby cement plant was severed. Threats were made to a member of staff who repaired the cable, who was advised to mind his personal security as a 'traitor'. A second cable was later cut. One major customer withdrew a large order from Quinn's building materials business, saying that he would reverse his decision if Anglo agreed a humane deal with Quinn in relation to his family home and his children's employment and a cash settlement was paid.

The sabotage attempts continued over subsequent weeks. In early May electricity poles were cut down, collapsing power cables running to the businesses in Derrylin. The weighbridge at the group's cement plant was also damaged. The new Anglo-installed chief executive of Quinn Group, Paul O'Brien, appealed for calm. On 6 May he held a two-hour meeting with a local community action group who had issued a series of statements supporting the Quinn family.

On Monday, 16 May Sean Quinn's wife Patricia and five children – Sean Jr, Ciara, Colette, Brenda and Aoife, shareholders of the Quinn Group – issued a lawsuit against Anglo claiming negligence, breach of duty, and intentional and negligent infliction of economic damage over the loss of the family's control of the group. They contested some €2.34 billion of the debt owing to Anglo (corresponding to the cumulative sum provided by Anglo to cover Quinn's CFD margin calls), sought an undefined sum of money in damages and sought to regain ownership of the group. The figures confirmed Quinn's losses on Anglo at about €3 billion.

In later court submissions the Quinns claimed that Anglo had provided €500 million of the €2.34 billion in loans in December 2007 under the 'false guise' that the loans related to property when they were in fact to cover losses on Anglo shares. They said that these loans had been agreed following conversations between Sean Quinn and David Drumm during that month. The family also charted the heavy levels of borrowing by the family following the St Patrick's Day Massacre of March 2008 to show that the bank knew that it was covering losses on the bank's shares.

On Monday, 30 May the Quinn family had the case listed in the Commercial Court, the division of the High Court that deals with big business disputes. The court said that it was likely that the trial of the action would not be heard until early 2012. Aoife Quinn – the only member of the family to swear an affidavit in the action – said that in October 2008 her mother, Patricia, and her siblings received loans of almost €500 million through six companies registered in Cyprus to buy shares in Anglo. While the family acquired a direct stake of almost 15 per cent in the bank in July 2008, the loans to fund the transaction were not completed until October. Anglo advanced each of the Quinn children €77 million and €102 million to Patricia Quinn through the six Cypriot companies.

Aoife Quinn claimed that at the time the loans were advanced personal guarantees in the names of the family were executed without their knowledge and that this was done by the bank without the Quinns being told that the bank was in a 'precarious' financial position. No legal or financial advice was ever given to the family members. She said that the bank's loans to the family were 'unenforceable' as they were provided for 'an illegal objective' of manipulating the stock market to support the bank's share price during 2008. Anglo's lending was 'tainted with illegality' and 'intended to support an illegal purpose' in breach of EU market-abuse rules.

It was the largest claim ever to come before the Commercial Court and would be the start of a complex legal battle as they attempted to regain control of their businesses. Within weeks the battle was extended to courts in Sweden, Russia and Cyprus – all home to Quinn companies – as the family moved to protect their international properties from Anglo.

On 19 April Minister for Finance Michael Noonan published the third report into the causes of the banking crisis. This report, by former Finnish civil servant Peter Nyberg, a one-time official at the IMF, blamed 'herding' and 'groupthink' among the Irish banks as they followed Anglo heavily into property lending and tried to match the bank's profitability. He described the external auditors to the banks as 'silent observers' and the public authorities – including the Central Bank and the Financial Regulator – as the 'enablers'.

According to sources close to him, Nyberg was startled at the high regard in which Anglo had been held by Irish investors, market analysts, the media, credit ratings agencies and foreign banks which lent to it right up until the start of the financial crisis in September 2008. He thought the bank's model was odd, the sources say – it had few customers, made rapid decisions on very large sums of money and had a huge concentration in property. And yet, while all this appeared obvious and was unconcealed, only a few questioned Anglo's business model or saw anything wrong with this one-trick pony leading an unregulated race.

On Wednesday, 20 April Mike Aynsley launched his 'Baghdad strategy'. At 2 p.m., in a coordinated operation, workmen removed the Anglo Irish Bank signs and logos from the bank's branches in Dublin, Cork, Limerick and Galway. The Baghdad reference was a nod to the way the US soldiers pulled down the statue of Saddam Hussein after the fall of the Iraqi capital in April 2003. Aynsley said the removal of all the bank's signs would 'give people an incredibly strong sense of finality in terms of the fate of this institution that has cost Ireland so dearly'.

Passers-by beeped horns and workers returning from their lunch cheered as workmen took the signs down from the bank's flagship office on St Stephen's Green.

In a matter of hours, the Anglo Irish Bank name was erased from Irish streetscapes, though not from the Irish consciousness. On 1 July the union of the country's two worst banks was sealed by an order at the High Court on an application by the Minister for Finance, Michael Noonan; Anglo took over Irish Nationwide under a plan to wind down their failed operations over ten years. The bank's new name was Irish Bank Resolution Corporation.

An internal Anglo document dating back several years – obtained by the author on the day the bank's signs were removed – described the rationale behind the bank's arrowhead logo as 'a true merger of past and future, of security and progression'. 'The current brand is in it for the long haul,' the document said.

That proved not to be the case. But it would be a long haul for the country to recover from Anglo Irish Bank's shattering losses, which had pushed Ireland to the edge of ruin.

Acknowledgements

I would like to thank Michael McLoughlin, managing director of Penguin Ireland, for approaching me with the idea of writing a book about Anglo Irish Bank, and Brendan Barrington for his long hours toiling over the manuscript during his edit. Many thanks also to Conor Devally and Trevor Horwood for their important contributions, and to Cliona Lewis, Patricia McVeigh and Nicola Evans at Penguin.

Special thanks go to my wife, Vanessa Carswell, for her support and assistance. Without her this book could not have been written. John Downes, Philip Berman and Nick McGinley offered helpful suggestions and I am very grateful to them for reading chapters and for their advice. My sister-in-law, Hannah Carswell, gave much valuable help with her research and sourced nuggets of information from the past. Many thanks also to my fantastic family, the Carswells and the Bermans, and all my friends.

I owe a debt of gratitude to John McManus, the business editor at the *Irish Times*, not just for his support and generosity in allowing me to take time away from a busy day job but also for his encouragement and guidance in my work covering the Irish banking crisis day-to-day over the past three years. I am also indebted to Geraldine Kennedy and Kevin O'Sullivan for their support, and to Dominic Coyle for his helpful advice.

I would like to thank all my other colleagues at the *Irish Times*, especially the Business and Finance team for tolerating my absences – Laura Slattery, Barry O'Halloran, John Collins, Ciaran Hancock, Una McCaffrey, Colm Keena, Suzanne Lynch, Caroline Madden, Dan O'Brien and Ciara O'Brien. Thanks also to Arthur Beesley, who left our section to move to Brussels, where he has chronicled the chaos in the wider eurozone superbly. I also have to mention Mary Carolan in particular for her indefatigable work covering the Commercial Court, which puts the banking crisis under a unique microscope. Frank Miller, David Sleator and Shay Kenny on the picture desk were brilliant to take time out of their busy schedules to source the photographs that appear in this book – I am really appreciative of their help. Thanks also to Carolyn Fisher in RTE's press office and John Glendon at RTE Libraries and Archives.

I would also like to thank fellow journalists Tom Lyons, John Murray Brown, Joe Brennan, Dara Doyle, David Clerkin, Pat Leahy and Ian Kehoe for letting me pick their considerable brains. I would also like to acknowledge the sterling work of Brian Carey, David Murphy, Cliff Taylor, Richard Curran, Emmet Oliver and Laura Noonan on the banking crisis.

To write this book, I have drawn on a wide range of documentary evidence and interviews with key sources who have connections with Anglo Irish Bank. Most chose to speak only on the basis that they would remain anonymous. I would like to thank these sources for being so generous with their time and trust. Their contributions have been so important; I hope they understand how important.

Photo Credits

All photos copyright the *Irish Times* and reproduced with kind permission. Individual photographer credits follow.

Alan Betson: p. 6 top and bottom right

Cyril Byrne: p. 6 second from top

Brenda Fitzsimons: p. 2 top

Matt Kavanagh: p. 2 second from top, p. 2 bottom, p. 3 top, p. 4 top and bottom, p. 5 middle, p. 7 top, p.8 bottom

Pat Langan: p. 1 top

Eric Luke: p. 2 third from top

Dara Mac Donaill: p. 3 middle

Jack McManus: p. 3 bottom

Frank Miller: p. 7 bottom

Bryan O'Brien: p. 5 top

David Sleator: p. 6 bottom left

Joe St Leger: p. 1 bottom

Index

Page references in *italic* indicate Tables.